AQA
A-level History

USA 1865–1975
The Making of a Superpower

Steve Waugh
Peter Clements

Approval message from AQA

This textbook has been approved by AQA for use with our qualification. This means that we have checked that it broadly covers the specification and we are satisfied with the overall quality. Full details of our approval process can be found on our website.

We approve textbooks because we know how important it is for teachers and students to have the right resources to support their teaching and learning. However, the publisher is ultimately responsible for the editorial control and quality of this book.

Please note that when teaching the **AQA A-level History** course, you must refer to AQA's specification as your definitive source of information. While this book has been written to match the specification, it cannot provide complete coverage of every aspect of the course. Please also note that the practice questions in this title are written to reflect the question styles of the AS and A-level papers. They are designed to help students become familiar with question types and practise exam skills. AQA has published specimen papers and mark schemes online and these should be consulted for definitive examples.

A wide range of other useful resources can be found on the relevant subject pages of our website: www.aqa.org.uk.

HODDER
EDUCATION
AN HACHETTE UK COMPANY

Photo credits

p.v *l* © CORBIS, *r* © Bettmann/Corbis; **p.vi** © Glasshouse Images/Alamy; **p.vii** © Stocktrek Images, Inc./Alamy; **p.viii** ©2005 TopFoto/AP; **p.1** Library of Congress Prints and Photographs Division Washington, D.C. [LC-USZ62-128619]; **p.14** Library of Congress Prints and Photographs Division Washington, D.C. [LC-USZ62-128619]; **p.21** © Bettmann/Corbis; **p.23** © CORBIS; **p.30** © HIP/TopFoto; **p.36** © ClassicStock/Alamy; **p.43** © ClassicStock/Alamy; **p.50** Library of Congress Prints and Photographs Division Washington, D.C. [LC-USZC4-954]; **p.61** © Everett Collection Historical/Alamy; **p.72** Library of Congress Prints and Photographs Division Washington, D.C. [LC-USZC4-435]; **p.79** Library of Congress Prints and Photographs Division Washington, D.C. [LC-USZC4-435]; **p.93** © Glasshouse Images/Alamy; **p.106** © Hulton-Deutsch Collection/CORBIS; **p.119** © Hulton-Deutsch Collection/CORBIS; **p.136** © The Builder (colour litho), Beneker, Gerrit Albertus (1882–1934)/Private Collection/Peter Newark American Pictures/Bridgeman Images; **p.144** © The Builder (colour litho), Beneker, Gerrit Albertus (1882–1934)/Private Collection/Peter Newark American Pictures/Bridgeman Images; **p.165** © World History Archive/Alamy; **p.173** © The Granger Collection/TopFoto; **p.185** © The Granger Collection/TopFoto; **p.200** © Stocktrek Images, Inc./Alamy; **p.208** © Pictorial Press Ltd/Alamy; **p.224** © Pictorial Press Ltd/Alamy; **p.231** © Corbis; **p.236** © 2005 TopFoto/AP; **p.241** © Black Star/Alamy; **p.248** © Wally McNamee/CORBIS; **p.258** © 2002 Credit: Topham/AP; **p.259** © John Olson/The LIFE Images Collection/Getty Images; **p.261** © Black Star/Alamy.

Text acknowledgements

p.15 *C* Foner, Eric, Professor of History at Columbia University, 'Civil War and Reconstruction' (2014), accessed at http://www.gilderlehrman.org/history-by-era/essays/civil-war-and-reconstruction-1861–1877 from the Gilder-Lehrman Institute of American History; **p.16** *E* Stampp, Kenneth (2014), The Tragic Legend of Reconstruction. Reprinted from Commentary, January 1965, by permission; copyright © 1965 by Commentary Inc.; **p.42** *A* Grover Cleveland, Veto Message, February 16, 1887, *B* 'Public Life and Conduct of Politics' by L. L. Gould in *The Gilded Age Perspectives on the Origins of Modern America* C. W. Calhoun, ed. Rowman and Littlefield 2007; **p.47** *D* Invitation to attend the meeting in Haymarket Square, sent out by the Black International Movement; **p.56** *F* Speech by Chief Joseph in 1877 in Washington D.C.; **p.64** *I* 'The Turner Thesis: A Historian's Controversy' in *The Wisconsin Magazine of History, Vol. 31, No. 1*, pp70–83. Reproduced with permission of the Wisconsin Historical Society; **p.70** *B* Adapted from *The Gilded Age: Perspectives of the Origins of America* C. W. Calhoun, ed., Rowman and Littlefield 2007; **p.74** *A* People's Party Platform, Omaha Morning World – Herald, 5 July 1892; **p.80** *C* An Assessment of Theodore Roosevelt's Presidency (1909), *Independent Magazine*; **p.85** *E* From an eye-witness account of the Bowery district of New York City, written in 1898; **p.121** *D* W. E. B. Du Bois Returning Soldiers', in *The Crisis*, XVIII, May, 1919, p13; **p.123** *E The Strangest Friendship in History: Woodrow Wilson and Colonel House* by George Sylvester Viereck. Copyright 1932, by George Sylvester Viereck. Copyright © renewed 1959 by George Sylvester Viereck. Used by permission of Liveright Publishing Corporation; **p.129** *A* Adapted from 'Protectionist Empire: Trade, Tariffs, and United States Foreign Policy' Benjamin O. Fordham *North American Review* 1911; **p.130** *B* Adapted from 'Phases of Empire: Late Nineteenth Century US Foreign Relations' by J. A. Fry in *The Gilded Age* C. W. Calhoun Ed. Rowman and Littlefield 2007, *C* S. D. Cashman (1993) *America in the Gilded Age*, New York University Press; **p.147** *D Only Yesterday: An Informal History of the Nineteen Twenties*, by an American journalist, Frederick Lewis Allen, 1931; **p.158** *F* Walter F. White (1921). Reviving the Ku Klux Klan. Forum; **p.237** Source: Montgomery Bus Boycott by Martin Luther King Jr., Reprinted by arrangement with The Heirs to the Estate of Martin Luther King Jr., c/o Writers House as agent for the proprietor New York, NY. Copyright: © 1995 Dr. Martin Luther King, Jr., © renewed 1983 Coretta Scott King; **p.245** *A* Dallek, Robert (2002), 'How Do Historians Evaluate the Administration of Lyndon Johnson?' History News Network, accessed at George Mason History News Network HNN http://hnn.us/article/439; **p.253** From *The Memoirs of Richard Nixon* by Richard M. Nixon. Copyright © 1978 by Richard Nixon. Used by permission of Grand Central Publishing.

AQA material is reproduced by permission of AQA.

Every effort has been made to trace or contact all copyright holders, but if any have been inadvertently overlooked the Publishers will be pleased to make the necessary arrangements at the first opportunity.

Although every effort has been made to ensure that website addresses are correct at time of going to press, Hodder Education cannot be held responsible for the content of any website mentioned in this book. It is sometimes possible to find a relocated web page by typing in the address of the home page for a website in the URL window of your browser.

Hachette UK's policy is to use papers that are natural, renewable and recyclable products and made from wood grown in sustainable forests. The logging and manufacturing processes are expected to conform to the environmental regulations of the country of origin.

Orders: please contact Bookpoint Ltd, 130 Milton Park, Abingdon, Oxon OX14 4SB. Telephone: +44 (0)1235 827720.
Fax: +44 (0)1235 400454. Lines are open 9.00a.m.– 5.00p.m., Monday to Saturday, with a 24-hour message answering service. Visit our website at www.hoddereducation.co.uk

© Steve Waugh, Peter Clements 2015

First published in 2015 by
Hodder Education
An Hachette UK Company
Carmelite House
50 Victoria Embankment
London EC4Y 0DZ

Impression number 10 9 8 7 6 5 4 3 2

Year 2019 2018 2017 2016

Cover photo © Bettmann/Corbis

Illustrations by Integra Software Services

Typeset in 10.5/12.5pt ITC Berkely Oldstyle Std Book by Integra Software Services Pvt. Ltd., Pondicherry, India

Printed in Dubai

A catalogue record for this title is available from the British Library

ISBN 9781471837609

Contents

Part 2: Crises and the Rise to World Power, 1920–75

Section 1: Crisis of Identity 1920–45

Section 2: The Superpower 1945–75

Introduction

This book on the history of the USA from 1865 to 1975 is written to support the USA option of AQA's A-level History Breadth Study specification. This is a fascinating period in the history of the USA, which includes the assassination of four presidents, such as Abraham Lincoln and John F. Kennedy, the most far-reaching political scandal in American history, the Watergate scandal, as well as the achievements of two of the most iconic figures of twentieth-century history, Martin Luther King Jr. and John F. Kennedy. This was also a period of massive change as the USA emerged from isolation to become the leading world economic and political power and became involved in a Cold War with the Soviet Union, as well as a controversial war in Vietnam. Moreover, there were significant divisions within the USA due to the unfair treatment of African Americans and Native Americans throughout the period and, in later years, the differences over Communism and US involvement in Vietnam.

▲ A painting of 1872 entitled 'Manifest Destiny'.

v

The key content

'The Making of a Superpower: USA, 1865–1975' is one of the breadth studies offered by AQA, and as such covers over 100 years. The content is divided into two parts:

- Part One (1865–1920) is studied by those taking the AS examination.
- Parts One and Two (1920–75) are studied by those taking the full A-level examination.

Each part is subdivided into two sections.

PART ONE: FROM CIVIL WAR TO WORLD WAR, 1865–1920

This covers developments in the USA from the end of the Civil War to the end of American involvement in the First World War and the return to isolation. It includes very significant political and economic changes as well as social changes, including mass immigration, the plight of African Americans after emancipation, and the impact of Western expansion on Native Americans.

The Era of Reconstruction and the Gilded Age, 1865–90

This period, which begins with the assassination of Abraham Lincoln, focuses on the aftermath of the Civil War, particularly the period of Reconstruction which has had profound long-term effects on the position of African Americans especially in the Southern states. This is also a period characterised by massive economic change, particularly in industry, as well as political corruption which brought widespread disillusionment with government at national and state level.

Progressivism and Imperialism, 1890–1920 and Emergence on the World Stage, 1912–20

This period saw further profound changes. It began with the announcement of the end of westward expansion and ended with the USA becoming the leading world economic power. The USA also emerged from a long period of isolation in international affairs, to greater interest and involvement in imperialism as well as participating in two wars, the Spanish–American War of 1898 as well as the First World War. Politically, the corruption which characterised the Gilded Age gave way to new ideas such as Populism and Progressivism, which profoundly extended the role of the presidency and federal government and encouraged a series of political, economic and social reforms. This, in turn, led to a conflict of ideas over the role of federal government.

PART TWO: CRISES AND THE RISE TO WORLD POWER, 1920–75

Part Two covers further profound changes in US society, including significant fluctuations in the economy, developments in the role of the USA in international affairs and the influence of key individuals such as F. D. Roosevelt, Martin Luther King and John F. Kennedy. Again, the focus is not just on the personalities but also on issues of breadth as highlighted in the key questions.

Crisis of identity, 1920–45

Economically, there was a boom in the 1920s which ended with the Wall Street Crash of 1929 and was followed by depression and massive unemployment. Recovery was encouraged by the New Deal policies of F. D. Roosevelt but, more importantly, the impact of the Second World War. Economic developments also facilitated political change, especially a greater role for the presidency which, in turn, brought further conflict about the role of federal government.

Socially, many Americans experienced the benefits of prosperity in the so-called 'Jazz Age' with a higher standard of living. However, there were continued divisions in US society as most African Americans were still very much second-class citizens who did not benefit from this prosperity. In international affairs the USA moved from a policy of isolationism in the 1920s and 1930s, which included Roosevelt's 'Good Neighbor' policy, to direct involvement, in 1941, in the Second World War.

The superpower, 1945–75

The USA emerged from the Second World War as a political, economic and military superpower and with an even greater role in international affairs, particularly due to the Cold War and rivalry with the Soviet Union. American society became even more divided due to the threat of Communism, US involvement in the war in Vietnam, the campaign for civil rights for African Americans and the student movement of the 1960s. Many Americans, especially in the 1960s, were inspired by key personalities such as Martin Luther King and John F. Kennedy, both of whom were assassinated. However, this gave way to political disillusionment with the presidency of Richard Nixon and his involvement in the unbelievable Watergate scandal of the early 1970s.

These are the stories you will encounter, and the events you will analyse.

Key concepts

But the study of history does not just include narrative – interesting though the stories often are! There are four concepts that steer our thinking and our understanding of the past. These are important in your study, and questions are likely to involve assessing these concepts.

- Change and continuity: To what extent did things change? What are the similarities and differences over time?
- Cause and consequence: What were the factors that led to change? How did the changes affect individuals and groups within society, as well as the country as a whole?

In relation to these concepts, the essay questions you will face will be asking you to assess, for example:

- the extent you agree with a statement
- the validity of a statement
- the importance of a particular factor relating to a key question
- how much something changed or to what extent something was achieved.

In addition, you will be learning about different interpretations: how and why events have been portrayed in different ways over time by historians. In the first section of both the AS and A-level examination you will be tested on this skill with a selection of contrasting extracts.

The key questions

The specification lists six key questions around which the study is based. These are wide-ranging in scope and can be considered across the whole period. They reflect the broadly-based questions (usually covering 20–25 years or more) that will be set in the examination.

1 How did government, political authority and political parties change and develop?
You will learn how the two main political parties, the Republicans and Democrats, came to dominate the political scene and how there was conflict over the increased role of the presidency and federal government.

2 In what ways did the economy and society of the USA change and develop?
You will discover how the US economy experienced periods of boom and bust including sustained growth in the 60 years after the Civil War, followed by the Great Depression of the 1930s and a further period of prosperity in the years after the Second World War.

3 How did the role of the USA in world affairs change?
You will examine how the role of the USA in world affairs changed significantly during this period from the isolationism that characterised the first 50 years to fighting in two world wars. Indeed, US policy after the Second World War was dominated by the fear of Communism, which precipitated the Cold War as well as involvement in the war in Vietnam.

4 How significant a role was played by key individuals?
You will discover that key developments were profoundly influenced by key individuals. Progress for African Americans was due to the work not only of Martin Luther King but other important individuals such as Marcus Garvey, Booker T. Washington and Malcolm X. John F. Kennedy was one of the most popular presidents but others such as Woodrow Wilson and F. D. Roosevelt greatly changed US society. However, groups such as the Ku Klux Klan, the student and women's movements also had a key role in developments.

5 How important were ideas and ideology in change and continuity?
Ideals and ideology were to underpin and challenge many of the changes that took place in these years. Indeed, the period began with a clash of ideas about the role of Reconstruction. New ideas of Populism and Progressivism were to seriously challenge the dominance of the two leading political parties at the turn of the century as well as the role of federal government. Ideology, and particularly the belief in capitalism and the fear of Communism, was to dominate the role of US policy in world affairs after 1945 as well as encourage the Red Scare and McCarthyism of the later 1940s and 1950s.

6 How united were the states during this period?
You will find out that the United States was anything but united during this period. The Civil War and Reconstruction accentuated divisions between the North and South and these divisions were exacerbated by the mass immigration of the later nineteenth and early twentieth centuries and the prejudice these immigrants faced. These divisions were to reach a climax in the 1960s with the emergence of the student and women's movements as well as the opposition to US involvement in the war in Vietnam.

How this book is designed to help your studies

1 With the facts, concepts and key questions of the specification

At the beginning of each chapter, the book flags up the elements of the specification and the key questions that are being covered.

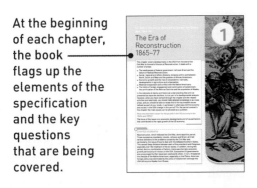

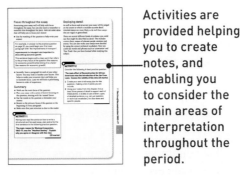

Activities are provided helping you to create notes, and enabling you to consider the main areas of interpretation throughout the period.

The Look Again feature encourages you to look back and compare your learning with previous periods in the book, to make comparisons across time.

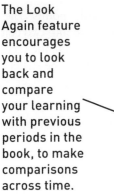

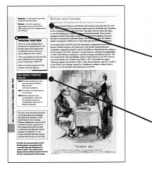

Key words and phrases are defined at the first relevant point in the text, and there is a full glossary on pp. 289–91.

Key dates are listed throughout.

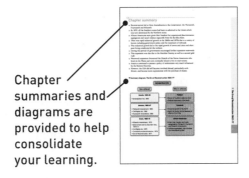

Chapter summaries and diagrams are provided to help consolidate your learning.

2 With the skills needed to answer examination questions

The book provides guidance in answering different types of examination questions in the form of a separate 'skills' section at the end of each chapter.

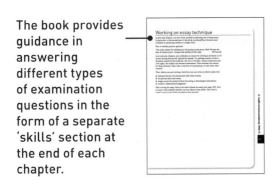

Interpretation skills are developed through the analysis of extended pieces of writing by leading academics.

3 With the skills in reading, understanding and making notes from the book

Note-making

Good note-making is really important. Your notes are an essential revision resource. What is more, the process of making notes will help you understand and remember what you are reading.

How to make notes

Most note-making styles reflect the distinction between key points and supporting evidence. Below is advice on a variety of different note-making styles. Throughout each section in the book are note-making activities for you to carry out.

The important thing is that you understand your notes. Therefore, you don't have to write *everything* down, and you don't have to write in full sentences.

While making notes you can use abbreviations:

Full text	Abbreviation
Twentieth century	C20
President	Pr
F. D. Roosevelt	FDR
Development	Devt

You can develop your own abbreviations. Usually it is only yourself who has to understand them!

You can use arrows instead of words:

Full text	Arrow
Increased	↑
Decreased	↓

You can use mathematical notation:

Equals	=
plus, and	+
Because	∵
Therefore	∴

Note-making styles

There are a large number of note-making styles. However you prefer to make notes, by hand or on a laptop or tablet, the principles are the same. You can find examples of four popular styles below. All of them have their strengths, so it is a good idea to try them all and work out which style suits you.

Style 1: Bullet points

Bullet points can be a useful method of making notes because:

- They encourage you to write in note form, rather than in full sentences.
- They help you to organise your ideas in a systematic fashion.
- They are easy to skim-read later.
- You can show relative importance visually by indenting less important, or supporting points.

Usually it is easier to write notes with bullet points after you have skim-read a section or a paragraph first in order to get the overall sense in your head.

Style 2: The 1–2 method

The 1–2 method is a variation on bullet points. The method is based on dividing your page into two columns: the first for the main point (side headings), the second for supporting detail. This allows you to see the structure of the information clearly. To do this, you can create a table to complete, as follows:

Main point	Supporting detail

Style 3: Spider diagrams or mind maps

Spider diagrams or mind maps can be a useful method of making notes because:

- They will help you to categorise factors: each of the main branches coming from the centre should be a new category.
- They can help you see what is most important: often the most important factors will be close to the centre of the diagram.
- They can help you see connections between different aspects of what you are studying. It is useful to draw lines between different parts of your diagram to show links.
- They can also help you with essay planning: you can use them to quickly get down the main points and develop a clear structure in response to an essay question.
- You can set out the spider diagram in any way that seems appropriate for the task, but usually, as with a spider's web, you would start with the title or central issue in the middle with connecting lines radiating outwards.

The Era of Reconstruction 1865–77

This chapter covers developments in the USA from the end of the Civil War to the end of the era of Reconstruction. It deals with a number of areas:

- The weaknesses of federal government: Johnson Grant and the failure of Radical Reconstruction.
- Social, regional and ethnic divisions: divisions within and between North, South and West and the position of African Americans.
- Economic growth and the rise of corporations: railroads, developments in agriculture and urbanisation.
- Westward expansion and conflict with the Native Americans.
- The limits of foreign engagement and continuation of isolationism: the continuation of the Monroe Doctrine and the acquisition of Alaska.

In the interests of clarity and historical understanding they are not presented as separate sections, but as part of a developmental analysis. However, when you have worked through the chapter and the related activities and exercises, you should have detailed knowledge of all those areas, and you should be able to relate this to the key breadth issues defined as part of your study, in particular in what ways did the economy and society in the USA change in this period? For the period covered in this chapter the main issues can be phrased as a question:

What was the main reason for the growth in the US economy in the 1860s and 1870s?

The focus of the issue is on economic developments and of causal factors that contributed to the rapid growth of the US economy.

CHAPTER OVERVIEW

Reconstruction, which followed the Civil War, dominated this period. Three successive presidents, Lincoln, Johnson and Grant, all tried various solutions to the problems caused by the Civil War and, particularly, the issue of how to deal with the defeated Southern States. This caused deep divisions between each of the presidents and Congress, especially over the treatment of the ex-slaves. In addition, during this period, due to a combination of factors, there was dramatic economic growth particularly of industry in the USA. Successive US governments also encouraged further expansion westwards which, in turn, threatened the lifestyle of the Native Americans, especially on the Plains. American foreign policy was dominated by the policy of isolationism although the USA did acquire Alaska from Russia.

1 Background: The USA in 1865

The USA experienced a Civil War in the years 1861–65 which had far-reaching political, economic and social effects. This first section is background information. You will not be examined on this as the specification begins in 1865. However, it will help you to understand developments after 1865.

NOTE-MAKING

Your notes for this section should focus on two main aspects – the political and the economic situation in the USA.

Constitution – A document containing the rules by which a country is to be governed. The American Constitution originally had seven articles, the first of which described the role of Congress and the second that of president.

The US political and economic situation

How democratic was the American political system?

The USA was formed as a result of the original thirteen colonies, all located on what is now the east coast of the USA, defeating their British rulers in a war which was fought in the years 1776–83. The USA was the first nation with a constitution which established how the country was to be governed. Moreover, in the first half of the nineteenth century, there was considerable expansion particularly westwards, so that by 1850 the USA included 30 states and extended from the Atlantic to the Pacific. However, there were several differences between the Northern and Southern states which intensified after 1850, including cultural and industrial differences, the ownership of slaves and the powers of the presidency and the federal government compared to those of the state governments. These differences were to culminate in the outbreak of civil war in 1861.

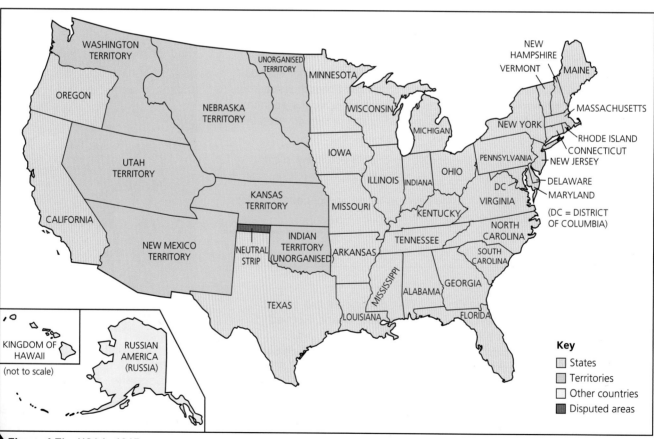

Figure 1 The USA in 1865.

Political system

The USA had a federal system of government. This means that there is both a federal, or central, government situated in Washington DC and a series of state governments. By the 1820s the USA was much more democratic than Britain with almost all white males having the right to vote.

The US federal system of government is summarised in Figure 2 below.

Federal system of government
– There is a central system of government and state governments. Each state has its own powers that are not subject to interference from central government.

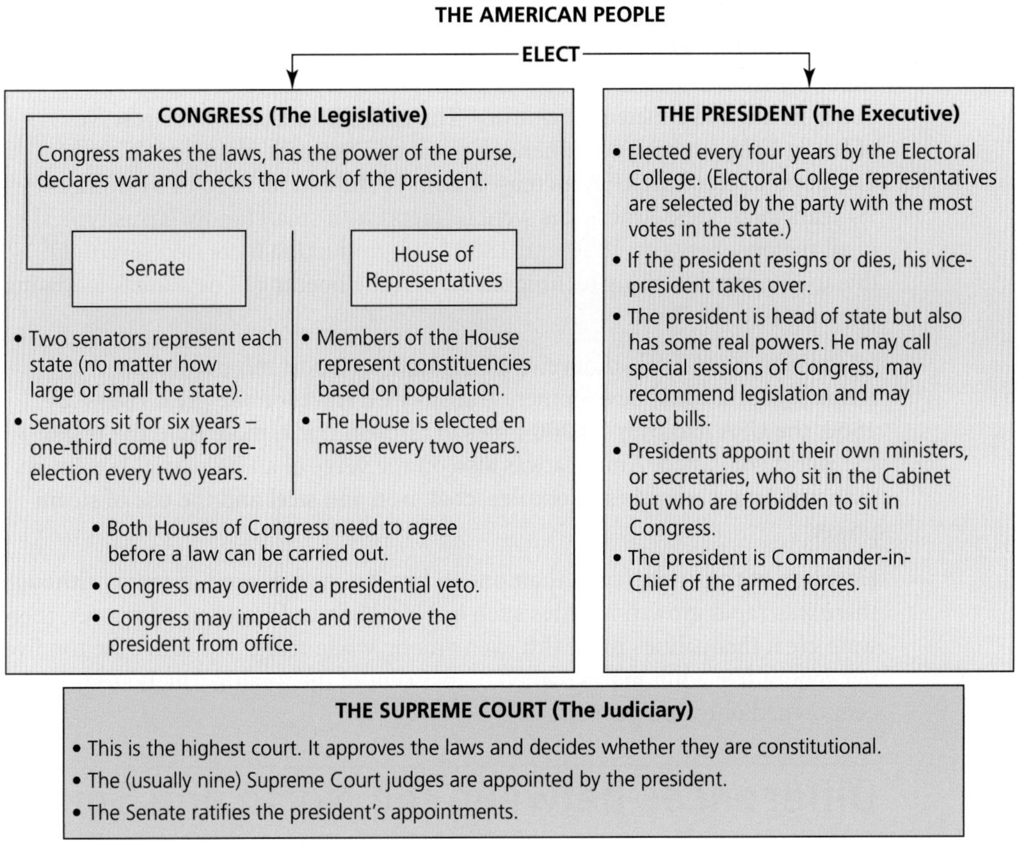

THE AMERICAN PEOPLE

ELECT

CONGRESS (The Legislative)

Congress makes the laws, has the power of the purse, declares war and checks the work of the president.

Senate

House of Representatives

- Two senators represent each state (no matter how large or small the state).
- Senators sit for six years – one-third come up for re-election every two years.

- Members of the House represent constituencies based on population.
- The House is elected en masse every two years.

- Both Houses of Congress need to agree before a law can be carried out.
- Congress may override a presidential veto.
- Congress may impeach and remove the president from office.

THE PRESIDENT (The Executive)

- Elected every four years by the Electoral College. (Electoral College representatives are selected by the party with the most votes in the state.)
- If the president resigns or dies, his vice-president takes over.
- The president is head of state but also has some real powers. He may call special sessions of Congress, may recommend legislation and may veto bills.
- Presidents appoint their own ministers, or secretaries, who sit in the Cabinet but who are forbidden to sit in Congress.
- The president is Commander-in-Chief of the armed forces.

THE SUPREME COURT (The Judiciary)

- This is the highest court. It approves the laws and decides whether they are constitutional.
- The (usually nine) Supreme Court judges are appointed by the president.
- The Senate ratifies the president's appointments.

▲ **Figure 2** The US federal system of government.

State governments tended to replicate the federal government with each state having its own government, its own legislative body and its own Supreme Court.

By the end of the Civil War, the USA had two main political parties, Republicans and Democrats. The Republicans tended to favour wealth, business and a reduced government role. The Democrats, on the other hand, tended to have a wider base of support and were in favour of more government involvement, especially in social issues.

Weaknesses of federal government

Although there was much interest in politics, with political campaigns often generating real excitement and high voter turnouts, government, especially at federal level, had a limited impact on the lives of most Americans. The Constitution's system of 'checks and balances' meant that it was very difficult for one party to control the presidency, the Senate, the House of Representatives and the Supreme Court at the same time. Therefore, it was very difficult for federal government to do very much.

The role of the federal government and the presidency was further limited by the belief by many, especially the Democrats, that the normal work of government should be carried out at state rather than central level. Issues such as education and public health were seen as the responsibility of state governments. The federal government only had a few departments which were the State, Treasury, Interior, Navy and the Post Office. The latter employed 30,000 of the over 36,000 people employed by the federal government in 1860.

Presidents were often figureheads rather than policy-makers and Congress, which was not often in session, passed few laws. Indeed, American citizens rarely came across federal officials.

The economy

Americans were described as a 'People of Plenty' by the historian David Potter in the mid-nineteenth century. The country had enormous reserves of fertile land, timber and minerals as well as a network of navigable rivers. The population of the USA increased from 17 million in 1840 to 31 million 20 years later. Most Americans were farmers, with small family farms typical of all regions. Between 1840 and 1860 food production increased sevenfold, due to improved farming techniques as well the opening of new areas following expansion to the West.

In addition, the USA had developed a sound transport infrastructure. Steamboat and canal development transformed travel on the great rivers. By 1860, the USA had over 30,000 miles of railroad track, more than the rest of the world combined. America was also on the verge of an industrial revolution with important advances in textiles, coal, iron and steel and the use of steam power.

However, at this time, fewer than one in five Americans lived in towns although there was rapid growth in cities such as New York and Chicago. Moreover, there were great inequalities in wealth even among white males. By 1860, the top five per cent of free adult males owned 53 per cent of the wealth. The bottom 50 per cent owned only one per cent.

NOTE-MAKING

Using a spider diagram (see page x), make notes on the main differences between the North and South.

Differences between the North and South

Why were there significant differences between the North and South of the USA?

There were significant economic and social differences between the North and South, some of which brought about the Civil War of 1861–65.

Economic differences

Economic differences between the North and the South became very apparent especially after the Northern states abolished slavery in the early nineteenth century. Population growth was one major difference. By 1860, the original thirteen states of the USA had grown to eighteen free states and fifteen slave states. The North's population was 18.65 million to the 10.5 million of the South. Unlike the South, the North had a growing number of immigrants. In the years 1830–60, most of the 5 million immigrants to the USA settled in the North which meant that 1 in 30 of its population was foreign born. In the North, a quarter of the population lived in towns. In the South, it was only one in fourteen and there were only twenty towns with 2,000 or more people.

Another major difference was the growth of industry in the North. Increasing internal and foreign trade and improvements in transport by canal, river and road, led to the growth of a range of industries such as engineering and textiles.

Indeed, the South, despite having 35 per cent of the population, produced only ten per cent of the nation's manufactured goods in 1860. The North had twice as much railroad track. The South did not welcome industrialisation and largely retained its agrarian, farming-based economy. In 1860, only eight per cent of US factories were located in the South. A large part of the Southern workforce was involved in the production of cotton, with some tobacco and rice. Slaves were essential to the harvesting of certain crops.

Foreign competition had brought down cotton prices on the world market with many of the larger farmers and slave owners falling into debt. In addition, the South also felt that it was exploited by the North. The Southern states were dependent on Northern credit to finance their sugar, cotton and tobacco plantations as well as to transport and market their goods, and resented the profits made by their rivals in the North. There was a growing feeling in the South that its economic interests were being sacrificed in order to increase the profits of Northern industrialists.

There were also differences over trade. By the 1850s, more than half the US exports consisted of raw cotton which was mainly sold to Britain. The South supported free trade in order to encourage greater trade with Britain. The North, on the other hand, favoured tariffs to protect the new industries from competition from industries in Europe, especially Britain. Some historians suggest that these economic differences were more important than slavery in causing the Civil War.

> **Free trade** – This refers to international trade that is left to run its course according to market forces and is not subject to duties or taxes.
>
> **Tariffs** – These are taxes paid on certain imported goods.

Cultural differences

The North and South were also divided culturally. For example the 'code of honour' was still of importance in the South. If your honour was questioned you still had to defend it, if necessary to the death. However, it was assuming far less importance in the North where states began passing laws that suppressed duelling. To a certain extent, an independent Southern nationalism had developed based on slavery, honour and a strong Christian faith. On the other hand, the North's identity was more based on free labour, liberty and more puritanical Christianity.

These cultural differences were accentuated by education. Northerners were generally better educated than Southerners and more willing to accept new ideas and reform. Southerners tended to resent change. Northerners saw Southerners as backward and out of touch with new ideas. Southerners viewed Northerners as ill-mannered and aggressive.

Political differences

The two regions were also split on the powers of the president and Congress. Many Southern states and Democrats from the South were anxious to prevent a president or Congress introducing legislation which might affect their interests, particularly with reference to slavery. They wanted to ensure that states kept the power to legislate for themselves rather than be dictated to by the federal government in Washington DC.

On the other hand, Northern politicians were less hostile to the growth in power of the president and Congress and less supportive of the rights of individual states.

Slavery

This caused major divisions between the North and South. The Southern states strongly supported the institution of slavery for economic, social and political reasons. The economy of the South relied on cotton and tobacco, both labour-intensive in their cultivation. As capital was tied up in slave ownership, slaves became a measure of wealth, and a sign of status. The large plantation owners, with 500 or more slaves, were the social and political elite of the South. They were convinced that the economy, and particularly plantations, would collapse without the use of cheap slave labour and resented interference from the North.

In addition, slavery was an institution of social control. It kept African-Americans in their place and ensured white supremacy. Southerners feared that an end to slavery would not just result in economic collapse but would lead to social disintegration and race war.

From 1777 to 1858, nineteen Northern states banned slavery and became 'free' states. Moreover, most of the North agreed with the abolitionists who wanted to abolish slavery, although they were not necessarily tolerant of racial issues. They were convinced that slavery went against the Declaration of Independence and that many slaves were badly treated in the South.

Declaration of Independence – This is the name of the statement made on 4 July 1776 which announced that the original thirteen American colonies, then at war with Britain, regarded themselves as thirteen newly independent colonies, no longer a part of the British Empire.

African Americans and slavery

To what extent was slavery a system of ruthless exploitation?

In 1860, there were nearly 4 million slaves in the Southern states and one in four Southern families owned slaves. Fifty per cent of slave owners owned no more than five slaves. However, more than 50 per cent of slaves lived on plantations with over twenty slaves. Most slaves were held by about 10,000 families. About half of these slaves worked in cotton production, with about ten per cent in tobacco, sugar, rice and hemp. In addition, in 1860 there were 250,000 free African-Americans in the South. Some 250,000 African Americans lived in the North where they suffered from discrimination. About ten per cent of slaves lived in towns or worked in a variety of industries.

Conditions for slaves

There has been much debate about the conditions for slaves before the Civil War. For example, in the early twentieth century Ulrich Phillips, a Southern historian, argued that most slaves were content with their conditions and that there was a reasonable relationship between owners and slaves. Those who support this view suggest that slaves did not work harder than most free Americans. They suggest that floggings were rare, there were few brutal owners and relatively little sexual exploitation.

In addition, they argue that given the standards of the day, slaves were quite well fed, clothed and housed and that slaves were usually able to choose their own partners. Furthermore, some slaves were granted or made enough money to be able to buy their freedom. There was no major slave revolt before 1830 and only a few hundred slaves a year attempted to escape to freedom in the North or Canada.

However, in the 1950s Kenneth Stampp claimed that slavery was harsh and that slaves were often not treated well by owners. Those who support this view suggest that slaves could be sold, punished by branding or flogging, sexually exploited and even killed by their owners. Slaves generally worked longer hours than free Americans and possibly a quarter of slave marriages were broken by forced separation. The evidence suggests that most slaves hated slavery and did not attempt to escape because it was too difficult to organise and, if caught, would lead to severe punishment.

Source A From an article in the *New York Tribune*, in 1859. The editor of the newspaper, Horace Greeley, was an abolitionist and staunchly opposed to slavery. He sent a reporter to cover the auction, in Savannah, Georgia.

The slaves remained at the race-course, some of them for more than a week and all of them for four days before the sale. They were brought in thus early that buyers who desired to inspect them might enjoy that privilege, although none of them were sold at private sale. For these preliminary days their shed was constantly visited by speculators. The negroes were examined with as little consideration as if they had been brutes indeed; the buyers pulling their mouths open to see their teeth, pinching their limbs to find how muscular they were, walking them up and down to detect any signs of lameness, making them stoop and bend in different ways that they might be certain there was no concealed rupture or wound; and in addition to all this treatment, asking them scores of questions relative to their qualifications and accomplishments. All these humiliations were submitted to without a murmur and in some instances with good-natured cheerfulness – where the slave liked the appearance of the proposed buyer, and fancied that he might prove a kind 'mas'r.

1 What can you learn from Source A about slavery in the South?

2 To what extent do you think it gives a reliable view?

Civil War, 1861–65

What effects did the Civil War have on the USA?

The Civil War was the culmination of many years of increasing divisions between the North and South and led to the deaths of over 600,000 Americans in the ensuing conflict.

Causes

The American Civil War, 1861–65, resulted from long-standing sectional differences and questions not fully resolved when the United States Constitution was ratified in 1789, as well as differences over the issue of slavery. There were uncompromising differences between the free and slave states over the power of the national government to prohibit slavery in the territories that had not yet become states.

Sectional – Political, economic and social differences between the North and South.

Secede – To withdraw from an organisation.

When Republican Abraham Lincoln won the presidential election of 1860 on a platform pledging to keep slavery out of the territories, seven slave states in the deep South seceded and formed a new nation, the Confederate States of America, which eventually grew to include eleven states. The states that did not join the Confederacy were known as the 'Union'. The incoming Lincoln administration and most of the Northern people refused to recognise the legitimacy of secession. They feared that it would discredit democracy and create a fatal precedent that would eventually fragment the no-longer United States into several small, squabbling countries.

Effects of the war

After four years of bloody conflict the Confederacy collapsed and the Union was preserved.

- The most striking immediate consequence of the Civil War was destruction and loss of life on a scale the country had never before imagined. Union war dead totalled 360,000; Confederate, 258,000. The combined total of 618,000 was significantly greater than the United States was to lose in the Second World War, its next bloodiest conflict.
- The economic expense of the war was also substantial. The Union spent some $2.3 billion on its war effort to the $1 billion of the Confederacy. The

North continued to experience prosperity during the war, with its total wealth increasing by 50 per cent during the decade of the 1860s. In stark contrast, the South was impoverished by the war. On top of its military spending, it suffered another $1.1 billion in war damage, or about 40 per cent of its pre-war wealth, including 40 per cent of its livestock and 50 per cent of its farm machinery. In addition to all of this, most of the South's invested capital – some $1.6 billion – was wiped out by the freeing of the slaves. The South took more than half a century to recover from the effects of the war.

- Politically, although the war had preserved the Union there were still very deep divisions between the North and the South and the problem of what to do with the defeated states.
- The other immediate consequence of the Civil War was the emancipation of 3.5 million slaves. Many of them were initially declared free by Abraham Lincoln in his January 1863 Emancipation Proclamation, which was aimed only at slaves in areas then still in rebellion against the United States.

2 Johnson, Grant and the failure of Radical Reconstruction

Reconstruction was the term applied to the process of reintegrating the Southern states into the USA and building new social structures in the South to replace the old slavery-based ones. This process began during the Civil War under Abraham Lincoln and continued during the presidencies of Johnson and Grant. Reconstruction included the treatment of the Southern states and their reintegration into the Union as well as the emancipation of the slaves. Moreover, it came to embrace two different formats – presidential Reconstruction driven by presidents Lincoln, Johnson and Grant and radical Reconstruction which was controlled by the Republican-dominated Congress.

Reconstruction under Lincoln

What had Lincoln achieved in Reconstruction by 1865?

Lincoln faced several problems in dealing with Reconstruction during and immediately after the end of the Civil War. These included:

- How to treat the Southern states. More radical Republicans wanted to impose a much harsher settlement on the South than Lincoln.
- What to do with the thousands of ex-slaves. Radical Republicans wanted them to have the same rights as white Americans and, especially, the vote. This may have been for selfish reasons to gain the support of African Americans in the South. Lincoln had supported the idea of colonising these ex-slaves but this proved impractical as most refused to participate.
- Who would decide the policy of Reconstruction policy, Congress or the president? Lincoln felt it was his role but this led to conflict with Congress.

In April 1864, Lincoln introduced the Ten Percent Plan. The rebel states would be admitted if ten per cent of their electorate agreed to an oath of future allegiance to the USA, they supported all existing acts of Congress regarding slavery and they allowed African Americans to vote. Louisiana met the Ten Percent rule and was admitted to the Union.

Radical Republicans were, however, dissatisfied with this Plan and two radical Senators, Henry Winter Davis and Benjamin Wade, introduced the Wade–Davis

NOTE-MAKING

The following section covers the achievements of three presidents in connection with Reconstruction. You could use the following questions as a template for your note-making for each president:
- What were their aims in connection with Reconstruction?
- What policies did they introduce?
- How successful were these policies?

Bill in June 1865. This required 50 per cent of the electorate to take a much tougher oath of allegiance of past and future loyalty to the Union, stating that they had never given any voluntary help to the Confederacy. It also excluded all those involved in the Confederacy from any role in future government and demanded that the state constitution be changed to abolish slavery. Lincoln vetoed the bill, which led to a further deterioration in relations between Congress and President.

The Thirteenth Amendment

This was introduced by Lincoln in November 1864 and approved by Congress in January of the following year. By the end of 1865 enough states had approved the Amendment for it to become law. This formally freed all slaves in the USA.

The Freedmen's Bureau

In March 1865, Lincoln and Congress also introduced the Freedmen's Bureau, a US agency set up for just one year to help former slaves in a variety of ways. It provided advice on education and employment for former slaves and helped in establishing schools for African Americans.

In 1865, Lincoln's position on Reconstruction was still not very clear. However, he does not appear to have wished to punish the South and seemed to be moving towards accepting that African-Americans should have equality before the law and even giving some the vote. On 14 April Lincoln was assassinated by the actor John Wilkes Booth who had wanted to strike a blow for the Southern cause.

Reconstruction under Johnson (1865–68)

To what extent was Johnson's Reconstruction policy a failure?

Vice-president Andrew Johnson now became president and was keen to push ahead with Reconstruction. Johnson has generally been given a poor press by historians who criticise him for sharing the racial views of most white Southerners and appearing to be unconcerned about the plight of ex-slaves. However, some recent biographers have been more sympathetic, suggesting that Johnson introduced the right Reconstruction policies but lacked the ability to carry them out.

Johnson wanted to restore the Southern states as quickly as possible, realising that Congress was due to reconvene in December 1865 and he would soon face strong opposition from Radical Republicans. He favoured leniency and had no wish to promote the position of ex-slaves. He accepted the Wade–Davis Bill for the oath of loyalty, but agreed that when each former Confederate state held a convention to revise its own constitution, those attending the convention would be elected by the 1860 white electorate.

Andrew Johnson (1808–75)	
1808	Johnson was born in extreme poverty in North Carolina. Throughout his political career Johnson stressed his working-class origins and claimed an affinity with ordinary Americans.
1826	Moved to Tennessee.
1853	Elected Governor of Tennessee.
1857	Became a Senator and remained loyal to the Union on the outbreak of the Civil War.
1862	Appointed military governor of Tennessee.
1864	Nominated as Lincoln's vice-president.
1865	Became president.
1868	Faced and survived an impeachment trial.
1875	Died.

The Black Codes (1865–66)

The new state legislatures in the South passed a series of laws known as the Black Codes. These included:

- African Americans deemed to be unemployed could be forced into working for white employers.
- The children of African Americans could be forced into working on plantations as apprentices.
- African Americans could be prevented from receiving an education.

Impeachment – This is a formal process in which an official is accused of unlawful activity.

Opposition to Johnson

By the time that Congress met in December 1865, many Congressmen, including moderate Republicans, had serious doubts about Johnson's leniency towards the South. This was partly due to developments in the South, particularly the Black Codes.

The Civil Rights Bill, 1866

Instead of working with the moderate Republicans, Johnson sided with the Democrats. When Congress passed a bill strengthening the powers of the Freedmen's Bureau, Johnson vetoed the bill because he knew it would anger the South and make Reconstruction more difficult. Moderate Republicans now joined forces with radicals to introduce a Civil Rights Bill which gave minimum rights to blacks. Johnson vetoed the bill. However, for the first time in history, Congress overturned the presidential veto, which required a two-thirds majority in both Houses and ensured the passage of the 1866 Civil Rights Bill.

The Fourteenth Amendment

To ensure that the Civil Rights Bill could not be changed in the future Congress introduced the Fourteenth Amendment which stated that people who were born in the USA or who were naturalised were US citizens, and all citizens were guaranteed equality before the law. It also gave the federal authorities the right to intervene if states contravened its rules.

The Amendment was rejected by all the ex-Confederate states except Tennessee and failed to get the approval of 75 per cent of the states necessary for it to become law.

Radical reconstruction

In order to ensure the passage of the Amendment, Congress put real pressure on the South with a series of plans known as 'Radical Reconstruction'. These included:

- The Military Reconstruction Bill, 1867, which imposed military rule on the South with the exception of Tennessee. The ten remaining states were grouped into five military districts, each placed under a federal commander. To get back in the Union, Southern states had to elect national conventions which would accept black suffrage and accept the Fourteenth Amendment.
- The Command of the Army Act which reduced Johnson's military powers.
- The Tenure of Office Act which prevented Johnson from removing a host of office-holders. This was to try to protect the Secretary of State, Edwin M. Stanton, who was a fierce critic of Johnson, and a staunch Radical Republican, who as long as he remained in office would comply with congressional Reconstruction policies.

Johnson impeached

Johnson, however, ignored the Tenure of Office Act and dismissed Stanton. The Republicans now decided to impeach Johnson, with the impeachment proceedings taking place in the Senate in 1868. Congress issued eleven articles of impeachment against Johnson which included the removal of Johnson and replacing him with Thomas without the permission of the Senate, as well as making three speeches with intent to show disrespect for Congress among the citizens of the United States. After a two-month trial, 35 Senators voted against Johnson and 19 for him. This was one short of the two-thirds majority needed to impeach him. He remained president, but both his credibility and effectiveness were destroyed.

The presidency of Grant

To what extent was Reconstruction a success during the presidency of Grant?

In 1868, the Republicans chose General Ulysses S. Grant as presidential candidate. His Democrat opponent was Horatio Seymour who was opposed to Reconstruction and equality for African-Americans. Grant won 52 per cent of the popular vote, partly as a result of Southern African-American support.

Reconstruction under Grant

Grant was in favour of the firm treatment of the South in the Reconstruction process. New state governments had been established in the South which was now under military rule, although there were never more than 20,000 troops in the whole of the South. These new governments were often corrupt and inefficient. The majority of new officials were Northerners who were nicknamed 'carpetbaggers' after the type of suitcase they carried, and they were helped by a few renegade Southern whites who were called 'scalawags' with the term derived from a nickname for low quality farm animals. These were Southern whites who formed a Republican coalition with black freedmen and Northern newcomers to take control of their state and local governments. Real power lay with the carpetbaggers supported by the US army. Most Southern whites detested the Republican newcomers who, they believed, were determined to destroy the Southern way of life.

The Fifteenth Amendment

In 1869, the Fifteenth Amendment was introduced which stated that 'The right to vote should not be denied on account of race, colour or previous conditions of servitude'. This Amendment ensured that citizens of any colour or race could vote, wherever they lived.

Scandals

In 1872, Grant easily defeated Horace Greeley, in a second presidential election, winning over 55 per cent of the popular vote. Unfortunately, both of Grant's terms in office were dominated by a number of serious political scandals which involved some of his close associates.

- During his first term, a group of **speculators** attempted to influence the government and manipulate the gold market. The failed plot resulted in a financial panic on 24 September 1869, known as Black Friday. Even though Grant was not directly involved in the scheme, his reputation suffered because he had become personally associated with two of the speculators, James Fisk and Jay Gould, prior to the scandal.
- The Whiskey Ring scandal of 1875 involved a network of distillers, distributors and public officials who conspired to defraud the federal government of millions in liquor tax revenue. Grant's private secretary, Orville Babcock, was indicted in the scandal but, with the help of the President, was later acquitted.

The end of Reconstruction, 1876–77

The presidential election of 1876 and subsequent compromise of 1877 is often regarded as the end of the period of Reconstruction. In 1876, the Republican candidate was Rutherford Hayes, while the Democrats chose Samuel Tilden. Tilden won the popular vote by 4,284,020 to 4,036,572 to Hayes. However, Hayes won the crucial electoral college vote (see p. 3) by 184 to 165. The voting returns for Oregon, South Carolina, Louisiana and Florida were contested and

Ulysses S. Grant (1822–85)

Hiram Ulysses Grant was born in 1822 in Point Pleasant, Ohio. A year after his birth his family moved to Georgetown, Ohio. His father arranged for him to enter the United States Military Academy at West Point in 1839. Ulysses Grant was stuck with the name Ulysses S. Grant due to a mistake on his application form to West Point. The middle initial 'S' doesn't stand for anything and not wanting to be rejected by the school, he changed his name on the spot.

He graduated from West Point in 1843 and ten years later was promoted to captain and transferred to Fort Humboldt on the Northern California coast. In 1854, Grant resigned from the Army amid allegations of heavy drinking and warnings of disciplinary action.

With the outbreak of the Civil War he rejoined the army in 1861 and was promoted to major-general. Grant took control of Kentucky and most of Tennessee, and led Union forces to victory in the Battle of Shiloh, earning a reputation as an aggressive commander.

After the Civil War, between 1865 and 1868, Grant was Commanding General under President Johnson and led the US Army's supervision of Reconstruction in the former Confederate states.

Grant was elected President in 1868 and served two terms. He died after battling throat cancer, in 1885.

Speculators – Risk-taking investors with expertise in the market(s) in which they are trading.

these four states had 20 electoral college votes. If these went to Hayes, he would have won the election. This resulted in a long, complex and controversial process to try to resolve the problem with a special commission, set up to allocate the electoral college votes from the disputed states, allocating these to Hayes.

This ended the crisis. It was a secret deal between the largely Northern-based Republicans and the emerging Democratic Party of the South. The Democrats would accept Hayes as president. He, in return, agreed to withdraw all troops from the South and the departure of the 'carpetbaggers'. Hayes did withdraw troops from the South and this brought an end to Republican attempts to modernise the politics, government and racial attitudes of the South.

Interpretations of Reconstruction

To what extent have interpretations of Reconstruction changed?

There has been much debate about the effects of Reconstruction, with some historians very critical of its achievements and effects.

Political effects

In many respects, the North was not harsh on the South during Reconstruction. Only one man was executed and there was no major confiscation of property. For decades the Democratic Party, which ensured white supremacy, controlled the South. Carpetbagger influence has been exaggerated. In no state did Northerners constitute even two per cent of the population and they were not trying to economically exploit the South. Some were corrupt and accepted bribes but this was commonplace throughout the USA, not just the South, especially from the railroad companies. Moreover, in many Southern states Radical Reconstruction was over before it began. Tennessee was under

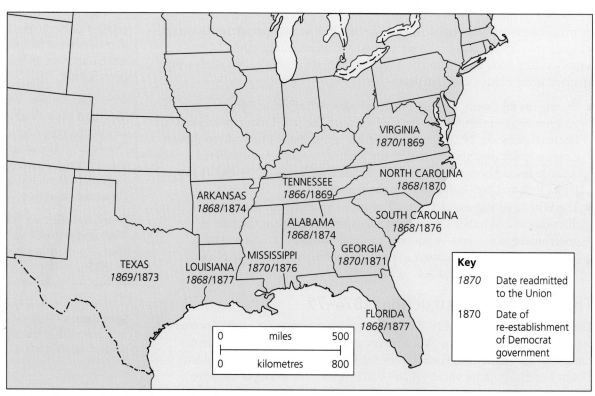

▲ **Figure 3** A map showing when the Southern states were readmitted into the Union.

Democrat control as early as 1869; Virginia, North Carolina, Georgia, Texas, Arkansas, Alabama and Mississippi by 1876. By 1876 only Louisiana, Florida and South Carolina were still under Republican control although this was changed by the compromise of 1877.

Nevertheless, Reconstruction did have some adverse effects on white Southerners. They did, temporarily, lose control of their Southern states. Moreover, after 1865 there was a major fall in the political influence of the South in the USA as a whole. Between 1788 and 1860 Southerners had held the presidency for 50 years and dominated the Supreme Court. In the 50 years from 1864 to 1914 there was just one elected Southern president and only seven of the 31 Supreme Court judges were from the South. Many state governments in the South felt even more distant culturally and politically from the government in Washington DC.

Economic effects

Reconstruction had a positive effect on the economy of the USA, which developed into a true industrial power (see pages 18–20). Moreover, from 1867 to 1873 the South benefited from general US prosperity and from high cotton prices. Railroads were rebuilt and textile manufacturing expanded.

However, this expansion did not keep pace with the North, and the South remained an economically depressed region with considerable poverty. By 1870 the average white Southerner's income had fallen to two-fifths that of a Northerner's income. The South remained a predominantly agricultural area heavily dependent on the cotton plantations. A glut of cotton in the early 1870s led to a sharp fall in prices and even harder times for the workers on the plantations.

African Americans and Reconstruction

The Civil War had led to the emancipation of around 4 million slaves. Lincoln's Emancipation Proclamation, and the subsequent Constitutional Amendments, showed how important African Americans were in the new society. In reality, there remained a massive gulf between the theory and reality of equality before the law.

The vote

Initially African Americans wielded some political power in the South. In South Carolina and Mississippi they were a majority of the electorate. As a result, two black Senators and 20 black Representatives were elected to Congress and large numbers of African Americans were elected to state legislatures.

Nevertheless, African Americans wielded very little influence in Southern states during and after Reconstruction. African Americans were a minority in many states and, assured of African American support, the Republican Party often put forward white candidates for office hoping to attract more white voters.

Employment

A major criticism of Reconstruction is that little or no land was given to the ex-slaves. Indeed, in the summer of 1865, Johnson had ordered that all land that had been confiscated by the Union must be returned to those Southerners who had been 'pardoned'. However, major land redistribution was never a realistic option as property in the USA was sacrosanct. Any confiscation and redistribution of land could well have permanently alienated white Southerners.

Colfax Massacre, 1873

The massacre took place at Colfax, Louisiana, against the backdrop of racial tensions following the hotly contested Louisiana governor's race of 1872, which was narrowly won by the Republicans. Democrats, angry over the defeat, called for armed supporters to help them take the Colfax Parish Courthouse from the black and white officeholders. The Republicans responded by urging their mostly black supporters to defend them. At Colfax, white men, including members of white supremacist organisations such as the Knights of the White Camellia and the Ku Klux Klan, armed with rifles and a cannon, opened fire on a crowd of black and white Americans, killing between 60 and 100 men, the vast majority of whom were African Americans. The leaders of the massacre were arrested and charged, but were later released as the Supreme Court ruled that the law they had broken was unconstitutional.

Sharecroppers – tenant farmers. A landlord allows a tenant to use an area of land in return for a portion of the crop produced on the land.

African Americans did have more control over their lives than under slavery. During the 1870s most became sharecroppers – white landowners provided the land, seeds and tools and black tenants provided the labour. It did give African-American farmers the freedom from day-to-day supervision. However, the fall in cotton prices of the early 1870s resulted in economic hardship for many sharecroppers.

Social position

Reconstruction also failed to guarantee African Americans civil rights. African Americans were treated as second-class citizens by most white Americans in the South. In the late nineteenth century every state introduced segregation including the 'Jim Crow' laws. Black and white Americans had separate schools, drinking fountains and public toilets, were allocated different areas of restaurants and public transport vehicles. In theory this meant 'separate but equal'. In reality the laws discriminated against African Americans whose facilities, schools, etc., were invariably inferior to those of their white counterparts.

However, there was some progress. The fact that there were black institutions, similar to those of the white Americans, meant that there were opportunities for African Americans to lead and manage. A small but increasing number of African American men became doctors, lawyers and teachers. Separate schools were inferior but they were better than no schools at all. Moreover, a number of African Americans favoured segregation. They had no wish to mix socially with whites.

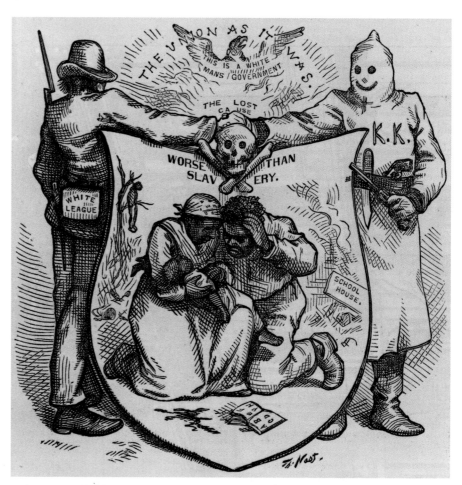

▲ A cartoon of 1874 by Thomas Nast with the title 'Worse than Slavery'.

The Ku Klux Klan

Many African Americans faced intimidation and violence from white racists in the South, especially the Ku Klux Klan (KKK). The Klan was set up in 1866 and became active in several states, intimidating African Americans into not voting through beatings and lynchings. Its terrorist activities reached a peak in the years 1869–71. Blacks who held public office, black schools and churches were particular targets. Even when Klan suspects were arrested, witnesses were frightened to testify against them and, if there was a Klansman on the jury, it proved impossible to convict them.

The White League, another white supremacist organisation, was set up in 1873 after the Colfax Massacre (see p. 13).

Source B From a newspaper report on Ku Klux Klan activities in central Alabama in 1868. It is from the website 'The Ku Klux Klan during Reconstruction'.

A reliable correspondent writes as follows to a friend in Memphis from Florence, Alabama:

About a week ago Saturday night the Ku Klux Klan came into town to regulate matters. They were here from eleven p.m. to three o'clock a.m. – five hundred in all. They shot one very bad negro, putting six balls through his head. Many heard the noise, but did not know what was going on. They also hung three or four negroes nearly dead, and whipped others severely in order to make them tell them about their nightly meetings, and what their object was in holding the same; also, as to who their leaders were. They made a clean breast of the whole matter, telling everything. The strongest thing about these Ku Klux was that they did not hesitate to unmask themselves when asked to do so; and out of the whole party none were identified.

> What can you learn from Source B about the activities of the KKK?

Different interpretations

There has been much debate about Reconstruction beginning with the traditional view put forward by Professor Dunning in the early twentieth century. He saw Reconstruction as 'The Tragic Era' and described the period of Republican rule as 'Black Reconstruction'. Dunning believed that this was a terrible time for Southerners who had to suffer from military occupation as well as corrupt governments which included 'carpetbaggers' and 'scalawags'. Dunning saw Johnson as a hero who tried to continue the work of Lincoln in the face of the opposition of the radical Republicans, the villains of Reconstruction.

Source C From an essay 'Civil War and Reconstruction', 2014, by Eric Foner, Professor of History at Columbia University and author of numerous books on the Civil War and Reconstruction.

For much of the twentieth century, both scholarly and popular writing presented Reconstruction as the lowest point in the saga of American history. Supposedly, Radical Republicans in Congress vindictively fastened black supremacy upon the defeated Confederacy and an orgy of corruption and misgovernment followed, presided over by unscrupulous 'carpetbaggers' (northerners who ventured south to reap the spoils of office), 'scalawags' (white southerners who cooperated with the Republican Party for personal gain), and ignorant and childlike freed people. More recently, in the wake of the civil rights revolution of the 1960s, scholars have taken a far more sympathetic approach to Reconstruction, viewing it as an effort, noble if flawed, to create interracial democracy in the South. The tragedy was not that it was attempted, but that it failed.

Source D From 'The Undoing of Reconstruction' by Professor Dunning, in the *Atlanta Monthly*, 1901.

The completion of Reconstruction showed the following situation: (1) The negroes were in enjoyment of equal political rights with the whites; (2) the Republican party was in vigorous life in all the Southern states, and in firm control of many of them; (3) the negroes exercised an influence in political affairs out of all relation to their intelligence and property. At the present day, in the same states, the negroes enjoy practically no political rights; the Republican party is but a shadow of a name; and the influence of negroes in political affairs is nil. Before the last state was restored to the Union, the process was well under way through which the resumption of control by the whites was to be effected.

However, this view was challenged in the 1950s and 1960s by historians such as Kenneth Stampp and John Hope Franklin. Stampp, especially, argued that the South got off lightly and that the real villains of the period were Johnson and the Ku Klux Klan. He believes that the radical Republicans were the real heroes because they fought for the rights of the African Americans, who, in turn, were the real losers of Reconstruction.

Source E From 'The Tragic Legend of Reconstruction', an article by Kenneth Stampp, 2014.

What, then, constituted the alleged brutality that white Southerners endured? First, the freeing of their slaves; second, the brief incarceration of a few Confederate leaders; third, a political disability imposed for a few years on most Confederate leaders; fourth, a relatively weak military occupation terminated in 1877; and, last, an attempt to extend the rights and privileges of Citizenship to Southern Negroes. Mistakes there were in the implementation of these measures – some of them serious – but brutality almost none. In fact, it can be said that rarely in history have the participants in an unsuccessful rebellion endured penalties as mild as those Congress imposed upon the people of the South, and particularly upon their leaders. After four years of bitter struggle costing hundreds of thousands of lives, the generosity of the federal government's terms was quite remarkable.

KEY DATES: RECONSTRUCTION

1865 Assassination of Lincoln. Johnson becomes president.

1868 Johnson impeached by Congress. Grant becomes president.

1876 Contested presidential election.

1877 Hayes becomes president. The end of Reconstruction.

ACTIVITY

1 What different views of Reconstruction are suggested by Source C (page 15)?
2 What evidence is presented by Stampp (Source E) against the traditional view of Reconstruction?
3 What differences are there between Sources D and E in their views of Reconstruction?
4 Make a note of the achievements and shortcomings of Reconstruction on a copy of the scales on the right.
5 Using this evidence, which do you think is the more valid interpretation? Give reasons for your answer.

Achievements Shortcomings

3 Economic growth

The USA experienced rapid industrial expansion in the 1860s and 1870s due to the interaction of a variety of factors. This, in turn, had important economic and social effects on the USA.

Reasons for industrial growth

Why did the USA experience rapid industrial growth in the years after the Civil War?

Many factors played a part in the USA's rapid industrial expansion including the Civil War, population growth, transport developments and technological and business innovation. The country was growing through Westward expansion and massive immigration. High tariffs kept out foreign goods and there was a dynamism within the period which encouraged risk and adventure. There is much debate about the most important factor. Was it the impact of the Civil War, the influence of the rapid growth of railroads or the influence of individuals such as Andrew Carnegie?

The impact of the Civil War

The Civil War provided the initial impetus for great expansion in US industry. This was partly because it stimulated the demand for manufactured goods, as the army needed guns and clothing as well as transport. Mass production and methods of distribution had to be developed.

Moreover, the war provided the necessary financial infrastructure to stimulate economic growth. The government had to raise money to pay for the war and this led to the development of a sophisticated capital-raising system based on Wall Street in New York. Moreover, during the war the government introduced paper currency which was known as the United States Note. This, in turn, meant that a banking system had to evolve to cope with the growing amount of money in circulation as well as the government's need to finance the war.

In addition, the introduction of tariffs, partly to provide income for the government, ensured the necessary protection for US-manufactured goods and greatly reduced competition from already industrialised nations such as Britain.

Availability of land

The USA greatly expanded especially with increased westward settlement during this period. This stimulated economic growth as it created a market for manufactured goods as well as encouraging further railroad development. Much of this land was very fertile and led to the mass production of wheat which, in turn, ensured that farming expanded and there was plenty of food for the population, especially the growing industrial cities.

Greater demand for food, both at home and for a rapidly expanding export market, also encouraged greater mechanisation in agriculture which, in turn, led to increased demand for manufactured goods.

Population growth

There was rapid growth in the population of the USA in the 1860s and 1870s which then provided an ample source of cheap labour for economic expansion. In 1860, the population of the USA was 31.5 million but this had increased to 50 million by 1880.

NOTE-MAKING

Using the 1–2 method (see page x) make notes on this section. For example on the left-hand side write reasons for economic growth and, on the right-hand side, a bulleted point list of the reasons.

- This was partly due to increased incomes which meant better food and housing as well as progress in public health and medical knowledge, which resulted in lower death rates.
- The other reason was immigration, with 2.8 million moving to the USA during the 1870s. People came from all over Europe and Asia in search of a better standard of living in the USA. The majority, particularly those from eastern and southern parts of Europe, headed for the cities and provided the cheap labour force that the industrial revolution needed. In addition, as consumers, they stimulated further demand for coal, clothes and food.

Transport

The USA also experienced a revolution in transport, especially the railroads, which not only provided a fast and efficient means of transporting raw materials such as coal from the West Virginia coalfields to the factories of New England, but also distributing the finished goods as well as cattle from Texas to the Chicago meatpacking plants. In 1869, the First Transcontinental Railroad opened up the far-west mining and ranching regions. Travel from New York to San Francisco now took six days instead of six months. Railroad track mileage tripled between 1860 and 1880. Between 1868 and 1873, 53,000 km of new track was laid across the country.

Railroads also stimulated economic growth for other reasons:

- They employed thousands of workers (1 million by 1900) all of whom were consumers.
- They encouraged demand as railroads required a lot of steel which, in turn, needed much coal. Manufacturers were encouraged to produce engines and railroad vehicles and used the building industry to provide railroad stations.
- This encouraged competition which pushed down prices and led to technological improvements to improve quality.
- Moreover, the rail centres needed roads in order to be able to distribute to outlying areas and this stimulated further growth.

The availability of capital

The availability of capital was essential as entrepreneurs would often need to borrow money in order to develop their businesses. The huge profits generated by the Civil War had encouraged the emergence of a highly developed stock market in which these profits were invested. By 1865, the annual turnover of the New York Stock Exchange was over $6 billion and, by 1890, it had become the second largest money market in the world. Businessmen were able to raise the necessary finance from this stock exchange.

The role of government

There was a long tradition of minimal government interference in the economy. Indeed, the Constitution gave the federal government virtually no role in managing the economy. As a result, businessmen had substantial freedom in running their enterprises. For example, there were no laws restricting hours of labour and there were no taxes on profits. Indeed, there were no rules on how businesses should be run.

Moreover, as Congress and State governments were dominated by business interests, very little national or local legislation was passed which interfered with business and industry. In addition, the commercial policy of the federal government also helped expansion. Congress was happy to impose protective tariffs to ensure that foreign-manufactured goods were more expensive than home-produced goods. These duties could be as high as 50 per cent of the cost

Entrepreneur – A person who sets up a business or businesses, taking on financial risks in the hope of making profits.

of the imported goods. Overall, tariffs ensured that US-manufactured goods were cheaper than those from abroad.

Businesses also did not have to deal with trade unions and were generally free to manage their workforce any way that they wanted. There was no tradition of trade unions and those that existed were generally weak and divided. Also, in the event of industrial disputes, employers were often supported by state and federal authorities who would even use troops to deal with workers' demands for better pay or shorter working hours.

Corporations and trusts

Economic growth was also encouraged by new business methods including the corporation and trust, each of which emerged due to the lack of government control and regulation. One such example was the corporation, which proved to be the perfect model for the growth of big industries in the USA. This is because it could own a number of businesses and could hire the management it wanted to run the corporation. Moreover, it could buy, sell and own property and take over even more companies.

The other favoured model for massive expansion was the trust. These emerged because in some states there were laws that stopped people from owning shares in more than one state or more than one company. Henry Flagler found a way of avoiding these laws. He was the secretary for Standard Oil, and he appointed himself as 'trustee' for stocks and property that the company was not allowed to own. Eventually, three employees of Standard Oil were told by the owner, John D. Rockefeller, who had set up the Standard Oil Company in 1870, to act as trustees for all property and assets of the company outside the state. Rockefeller created the Standard Oil Company and dominated the oil industry in USA and became the first American billionaire. Other companies soon followed the Rockefeller example and set up trusts, which were a perfectly legal method of avoiding the state laws.

Source F From a report on Standard Oil written in 1880 by the Hepburn Judicial Committee, which was investigating the company. From *The Growth of the American Republic* by S. E. Morison, H. Commager and W. Leuchtenburg, (OUP), 1969, p.68.

Standard Oil owns and controls the pipe lines of the producing regions that connect with the railroads. It controls both ends of these roads. It ships 95 percent of all the oil. It dictates terms and rebates to the railroads. It has bought out and frozen out refiners all over the country. By means of the superior facilities for transportation which it thus possessed, it could overbid in the producing regions and undersell in the markets of the world. Thus it has absorbed and monopolised the great traffic.

Technological innovation

The rapid growth in industry was also due to important changes in technology and business methods brought about by key individuals such as Andrew Carnegie.

Carnegie, who was born in 1835, began his working life as a messenger boy but grew to dominate the US steel industry (see page 44 for more on Carnegie). Steel had been costly to produce but in Britain a new process, the Bessemer Converter, made the process much cheaper. Carnegie brought the process to the USA and used it in his steel mills and his business rapidly expanded. Carnegie kept prices as low as possible and constantly re-invested in new manufacturing plants and equipment. He was totally ruthless and refused to allow any unions to be set up in his factories, using his own armed guards to deal with any union activities.

What can you learn from this report (Source F) about Standard Oil, the first trust?

WORKING TOGETHER

1 Put together a mind map which summarises the reasons for the rapid growth of industry in the USA in the 1860s and 1870s. Place these reasons in rank order, beginning with the most important at 12 o'clock on your mind map, moving clockwise to the least important.

2 Now compare your order with a partner. Explain to each other your reasons for your decisions.

NOTE-MAKING

Using bullet points (see page x) make notes on the impact of industrial growth. Use this method to summarise the depression of 1873, urbanisation, living conditions and agriculture.

The impact of industrial growth

To what extent did rapid industrial growth lead to economic and social problems?

Rapid industrial growth did come at a cost – a depression in 1873 as well as poor living conditions.

The Depression of 1873

The Depression of 1873 was partly due to a major economic reversal in Europe as well as the poor state of the American banking system. Anyone could set up a bank and operate it independently. Local banks generally kept their deposits in larger privately owned banks, especially in New York banks. The New York banks would invest these deposits, often unwisely, such as Jay Cooke and Company, a railroad speculator that went bankrupt. It was the principal investor of the Northern Pacific Railroad and its failure led to the collapse of hundreds of other companies and banks.

The New York Stock Exchange was closed for ten days and credit dried up. Factories closed their doors and thousands were laid off. One in four labourers in New York were out of work in the winter of 1873–74 and nationally a million became unemployed. Many of the major railroads failed and construction of new railroad lines declined drastically from 7,500 miles in 1872 to 1,600 miles two years later.

Urbanisation

Industrial development also brought massive changes to towns and cities. Before 1860, there were only sixteen cities in the USA with a population of 50,000 or more. This was to change rapidly. Chicago, which had 30,000 inhabitants in 1850, had over a million by 1890. It had been a railroad centre that served the upper-Midwest as a shipping hub for lumber, meat and grain; by 1870 it had taken the lead in steel production as well as meatpacking.

Previously, cities had served as commercial centres for rural hinterlands and were frequently located on rivers, lakes or oceans. Manufacturing occurred outside their limits – usually near power sources, such as streams, or natural resources, such as coal. As industry grew, cities changed. Post-Civil War Atlanta, another railroad hub and commercial centre, also developed a diverse manufacturing sector. Cities quickly became identified with what they produced – Troy, New York, made shirt collars; Birmingham, Alabama, manufactured steel; Minneapolis, Minnesota, produced lumber; Paterson, New Jersey, wove silk; Toledo, Ohio, made glass; Tulsa, Oklahoma, favoured the oil industry; and Houston, Texas, produced railroad cars.

Living conditions

However, two problems emerged due to this rapid urban growth – the spread of slums and the corrupt systems of running these new cities. The rapid influx of workers often led to the hasty construction of poor quality housing, often overcrowded and polluted slums. Those with wealth soon moved away from these slum areas into the suburbs. Moreover, many of these industrial cities were run by what became known as the 'Boss' system with the 'Boss' being the local mayor. He was often corrupt and would sell the rights to the highest local bidder to provide housing, transport and other basic utilities with all city employees, including the police, owing their job to the Boss. He would provide jobs and employment for immigrants or African Americans from the South who, in turn, would vote for him in future elections.

◀ Living quarters in the cellar of a New York City tenement house, 1891.

Agriculture

Agriculture did not prosper in the same way as industry in the years after the Civil War. For most farmers it was a life of subsistence farming and debt. The Homestead Act of 1862 (see page 24) opened up huge areas of the West to settlement and farming. However, many farmers faced hardships for several reasons. They incurred debts due to borrowing for the purchase of land and mechanisation as well as being over-dependent on unreliable overseas markets. Many small farmers tried, unsuccessfully, to compete with big 'agribusinesses' and some, especially in the South, were too dependent on a single cash crop, such as cotton. In addition, as prices kept dropping in the years after the Civil War, so did profits which, in turn, affected the ability to repay loans. For example, the price of a bushel of wheat fell from $1.45 in 1866 to only 76 cents three years later.

Source G From a description by a visitor from the North of a typical Georgia mill village in the 1870s. From 'Clare to Graffenried', *The Century Magazine*, 1891.

Flung as if by chance beside a red clay road that winds between snake fences, a settlement appears. Rows of loosely built, weather-stained farm houses, all the same ugly pattern and supported by clumsy chimneys are set close to the highway. No porch, no door-step even to these barrack-like dwellings. There are paneless windows. Inside, a ramshackle bed, a few old 'split-bottom' chairs and a jumble of battered crockery. The bare floors are covered with the tread of animals and the muddy outline of the bared feet of people that cannot afford shoes or socks. There is no outhouse (toilet) for the whole community.

Agribusiness – The business of agricultural production. It includes breeding, crop production, distribution, farm machinery, processing, supply, marketing and retail sales.

WORKING TOGETHER

1 What can you learn from Source G about living conditions in the South?
2 Working with a partner, compare the notes you have made on this section. Add anything that you have missed and check anything that you have disagreed on.

KEY DATES: ECONOMIC GROWTH

1869 The First Transcontinental Railroad opened.

1870 The setting up of the Standard Oil Company.

1873 Depression leading to the failure of the New York Stock Exchange.

4 Conflict with Native Americans

The Westward expansion of many white settlers, which began in the 1840s and accelerated in the 1860s and 1870s due to the Homestead Act and the growth of railroads, brought conflict with the Native Americans, especially those living on the Great Plains. There has been much criticism of the treatment of the Native Americans by the US government during this period.

Reasons for Westward expansion

Why was there large-scale Westward expansion in the 1860s and 1870s?

As always with such a major issue, there is a serious debate among historians as to exactly what were the motives for Westward expansion.

- One school of thought has suggested that there was no overriding motive and that it just happened.
- Another suggests that it was the result of simple **demography**. Once the first settlers arrived, millions more immigrants followed and reproduced at a high rate.
- Other historians believe it was a deliberate policy by the federal government during and after the Civil War and was very much following the ruthless and aggressive imperialism practised by the Spanish, French and British in North America in earlier centuries.
- Others argue that Westward expansion was part of a special mission to bring the benefits of the American way of life as well as democracy and freedom.

There were numerous reasons for this Westward expansion.

Westward expansion before the Civil War

Many settlers had begun to move to the West in the 1840s. This was partly due with regard to the Mormons, to escape persecution in the East, as well as high taxes and over-population. Moreover, the West seemed to offer the possibility of starting a new and better life together with cheap and fertile land. The government encouraged settlers to move west, for the more Americans living in an area, the better the government's opportunity to take it over. Furthermore, the discovery of gold in California in 1848 brought some 300,000 people to the area.

The Manifest Destiny

Moreover, the move west was also influenced by the 'Manifest Destiny'. This was a belief held by many Americans that God had chosen them to populate the lands from the Atlantic seaboard to the Pacific Ocean. It was first used by a journalist, John L. O'Sullivan, who had long been a supporter of the expansion of the USA. He first used the phrase in 1845 in an essay entitled 'Annexation' in the *Democratic Review*. In this article he urged the US to annex the Republic of Texas, not only because Texas desired this, but because it was 'our manifest destiny to overspread the continent allotted by Providence for the free development of our yearly multiplying millions'. It seemed to give white Americans a divine right to populate the whole North American continent and to spread its Christian and republican values. Incorporation into the USA would bring liberty and freedom to other American territories. If the USA did not acquire these territories, they could well be seized by a rival colonial power. This article inspired the belief in the idea of the Manifest Destiny.

The Manifest Destiny was also clearly a racial doctrine of white supremacy that granted no Native American or non-white claims to any permanent possession of the lands on the North American continent and justified white American

NOTE-MAKING

This section focuses on the reasons for Westward expansion. Using a spider diagram (see page x) make notes on these reasons.

Demography – The study of the characteristics of population, such as size, growth, density, distribution and vital statistics.

The Mormons

The word 'Mormons' most often refers to members of The Church of Jesus Christ of Latter-day Saints (LDS Church) because of their belief in the 'Book of Mormon' and they were set up by Joseph Smith in 1830. By 1831 they had settled in Kirtland, Ohio, where they built their first temple. However, their beliefs were unacceptable to most Americans at the time and they experienced severe persecution. They moved in 1837 but each time they tried to settle somewhere they were hounded out by local people. Smith and his brother were murdered by a mob in Illinois in 1844 and their new leader, Brigham Young, decided that they would move in 1847 to a remote new site where they would be free from persecution. He eventually chose the Salt Lake City area as it was barren but had mountain streams nearby that could be used for irrigation.

▲ A painting of 1872 entitled, 'Manifest Destiny', by John Gast.

expropriation of Native American lands. It was also a key slogan used to justify the expansion of the USA in the 1840s and 1850s especially into Texas and California, as well as being deployed in the United States' imperial ventures in the 1890s and early years of the twentieth century that led to US possession or control of Hawaii and the Philippine Islands.

Source H From an article 'The Great Nation of Futurity' by John L. O'Sullivan, published in 1839.

Our national birth (and the Declaration of Independence) was the beginning of a new history, which separates us from the past and connects us only with the future.

We are the nation of progress, of individual freedom, of universal enfranchisement. Our future history will be to establish on earth the moral dignity and salvation of man – the undeniable truth and goodness of God. America has been chosen for this mission among all the nations of the world, which are shut out from the life-giving light of truth. Her high example shall put an end to the tyranny of kings, and carry the happy news of peace and good will to millions who now endure an existence hardly better than that of beasts of the field. Who, then, can doubt that our country is destined to be the great nation of the future?

How does O'Sullivan justify the expansion of the USA (Source H)?

Westward expansion, 1865–77

Further Westward expansion was encouraged by several developments.

Federal territories

During the Civil War the federal government was determined to secure control of the lands west of the Mississippi. This was done by the creation of federal territories governed by officials appointed by the federal government in Washington and by populating these vast open spaces with settlers. As territories they became subject to the laws of the USA. When the population reached 60,000 the inhabitants could apply to become a state, which gave them the right to some degree of self-determination. They had their own elected state assembly and were given authority to make their own laws.

The Homestead Act, 1862

To encourage settlement in these areas, the government introduced the Homestead Act of 1862. This released land in 160-acre plots, available to farmers for free on the basis that they would farm the land for five years. The first claim under the Homesteads Act was made by Daniel Freeman for a farm in Nebraska on 1 January 1863. Settlers from all walks of life including newly arrived immigrants, farmers without land of their own from the East, single women and former slaves came to meet the requirements. People interested in homesteading first had to file their intentions at the nearest Land Office and after a check for any ownership claims, the prospector paid a filing fee of $10 to claim the land temporarily, as well as a $2 commission to the land agent. By 1865, 20,000 homesteaders had settled on the Plains. However, this expansion was at the expense of the Native American tribes who lived on the Plains. The Homestead Act was followed by several others:

- The Timber and Culture Act of 1873 gave homesteaders an additional 160 acres provided 40 acres were planted with trees.
- The Desert and Land Act of 1877 offered a further 640 acres at $1.25 dollars an acre provided some of it was irrigated.

'Bonanza' farms – Very large farms in the United States performing large-scale operations, mostly growing and harvesting wheat.

These acts were successful and people flocked to the West. This led to the development of 'Bonanza' farms. By 1880 there were nearly 3,000 of these large farms of more than 1,000 acres.

People moved to the Plains due to both pull and push factors. Pull factors included the offer of free or very cheap land such as offered by the Homestead Act or railroad companies which were also very active in advertising the opportunities for settlement. It also offered the chance of a new start. Moreover, letters home from those who had already gone West, and who were successfully farming, encouraged people to move onto the Plains themselves. Migration was also due to push factors. Many people were looking to escape poverty and unemployment in the East and were looking for good farmland. Some moved to the Plains to escape religious persecution, such as the Mormons. Ex-soldiers from the US Civil War saw a lack of opportunity when they returned home, so looked to the West for a new start.

Railroads

The government was also keen to encourage railroad expansion to the West, realising this would lead to even more migration to the area. In 1862, Lincoln signed the Pacific Railroad Act authorising two companies to build a transcontinental railroad. Significantly, the Native Americans were not consulted even though the railroad would run through their lands. The Central Pacific was to build eastwards from Sacramento, California, while the Union Pacific would build westwards from Omaha, Nebraska. Eventually the two lines met at the newly arranged site of Promontory, Utah, in May 1869.

The railroad companies, allocated land by the government to cover the cost of the enterprise, lured settlers on to the Plains with 'buy now, pay later' schemes. For the Native Americans, the trains disturbed the buffalo herds and even brought more land-hungry settlers to the Plains. In its first full year, 1870, the railroad carried 15,000 passengers but this reached a million twelve years later.

The second gold rush

This began in the Black Hills of Dakota in the mid 1870s. There had been rumours about gold in this area since the Civil War and prospectors found gold near present-day Custer in South Dakota in 1874, but these deposits were small. However, the following year much larger deposits were found in Deadwood Gulch and thousands of gold-seekers flocked to the new town of Deadwood. The main problem was that the US government had recognised the Black Hills as belonging to the Native American tribe, the Sioux, by the Treaty of Laramie of 1868. Once again, these rights were ignored.

The impact on Native Americans

To what extent did the position of the Native American tribes on the Plains worsen in the 1860s and 1870s?

The largest population of Native Americans occupied the vast area of the USA known as the Great Plains. The tribes were almost entirely nomadic and roamed the Plains freely, following the huge herds of buffalo that provided them with everything they needed to survive. The buffalo determined their lifestyle, living conditions, laws, government and religious beliefs.

> **NOTE-MAKING**
>
> Using the 1–2 method (see page x) make notes on this topic. For example, write 'The impact of Westward expansion' on the left-hand side and a bullet-point list of the impact on the right-hand side.

> **Nomadic** – The Native Americans did not live in any one place permanently. They followed the buffalo herds, living in tepee villages that could be quickly assembled or demolished in response to the movement of the buffalos.

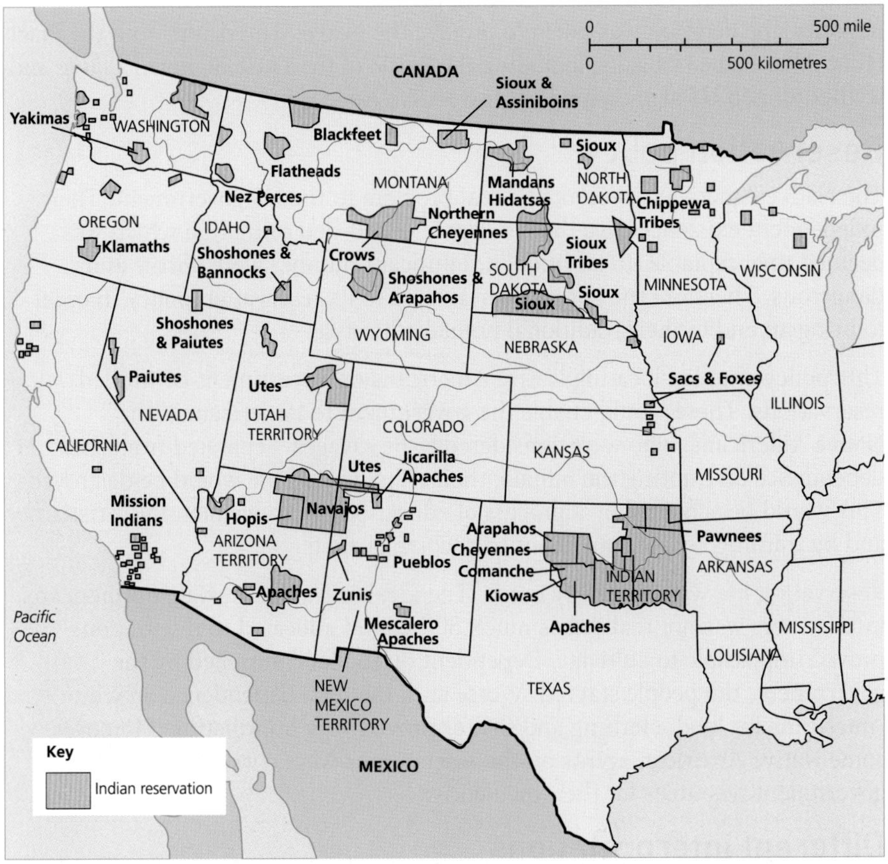

▲ **Figure 4** A map showing the Native American tribes of the Great Plains.

The impact of Westward expansion

Initially, the US government was content to leave the Native Americans to live freely on the areas of the country that white Americans did not want. Before the Civil War, this was the vast area in the centre of the USA known as the Great Plains. However, from the 1860s it became government policy to attract settlers to populate these vast open spaces in the West (see page 24). As white settlers pushed westwards beyond the natural frontier of the Appalachian Mountains, the Native Americans were gradually removed from their traditional lands.

By the early 1860s several tribes, but most notably the Sioux and Cheyenne, were hostile to the increasing encroachments of white settlers on the Plains and also the presence of the army on their lands. The army was stationed in the Plains to offer protection to wagon trains and settlers in areas where the Native Americans were known to be hostile.

The Great Sioux War, 1876

In 1876, the Great Sioux War broke out after the discovery of gold in the Black Hills of Dakota and gold prospectors and settlers poured into Native American territory. At first, the US government had tried to keep the prospectors out, but there were too many of them. The government then tried to do a deal with the Native Americans, offering $6 million, but this also failed. The government believed that the Native Americans were being unreasonable and hardened their attitude, demanding that all Native Americans should go to their reservations. Any who did not respond by 31 January 1876 would be treated as hostile. Many either did not hear about this threat or chose to ignore it.

Ultimately, due to popular and political pressure by the white American majority, the decision was taken to remove the Native Americans from the Black Hills. After some setbacks, including the Battle of the Little Bighorn, a large and well-equipped US army wiped out the Native Americans.

Reservation policy

The Native Americans presented a real problem to the US government. Their independent existence gave them a degree of self-determination which was deemed unacceptable. In addition, a significant number were hostile and dangerous. Therefore the government turned to its reservation policy in order to bring an end to their traditional nomadic lifestyle.

This policy entailed locating Native Americans on government-controlled reservations. These would enable the government to 'Americanise' the Native Americans, who were considered to be savages. Separated from their dependence on hunting the buffalo, their tribal way of life would be destroyed. This would be achieved by a process of education, by conversion to Christianity and by training Native Americans to become farmers.

Reservation life was extremely harsh. The ideal to transform Native Americans into farmers was not realised as much of the land allocated to reservations proved impossible to cultivate. Dependent on the food supplied by the government, the people starved. Worse still, the total dependence on white Americans for food, clothing and shelter proved very humiliating. Moreover, some Native American agents on the reservations were corrupt and used government resources for their own ends.

Different interpretations

In earlier American history books, the fate of the Native Americans on the Plains was often treated as a relatively minor part of the history of the United States and from the point of view of white Americans, some of whom reflected the traditional

The Sand Creek Massacre, 1864

As there was no fighting during the Civil War west of the Mississippi, regular soldiers were withdrawn from the Plains to fight in the East. They were replaced by volunteers who were untrained and ill-disciplined. This led to a number of brutal atrocities, the most notorious of which was at Sand Creek in 1864. A force of 700 troops of cavalry attacked an undefended camp of the Cheyenne tribe, killing and mutilating elderly men, women and children.

The Battle of the Little Bighorn, 25 June 1876

George Custer and his men were part of an expeditionary force sent to round up Sioux and Cheyenne tribes who had left the Great Sioux Reservation lands and were defying the authorities by refusing orders to return. Without waiting for the rest of the force to arrive, Custer divided his men into three units and attempted to encircle the encampment of the Native Americans. His unit of 200 came under attack and was quickly overwhelmed by superior numbers. All were killed.

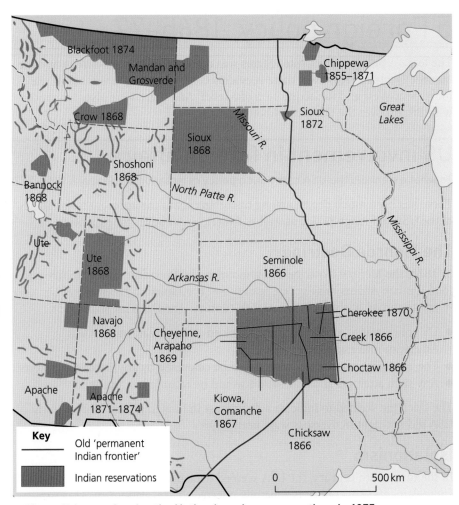

▲ **Figure 5** A map showing the Native American reservations in 1875.

view that expansion was justified by the need to bring 'civilisation' to the West. In the later twentieth century, younger historians began to take the point of view of the Native Americans, more especially after the publication in 1970 of Dee Brown's influential book *Bury My Heart at Wounded Knee* which tells how Native Americans lost their land, lives and liberty to white American settlers. This was followed in 1975 by Francis Jennings' *The Invasion of America: Indians, Colonialism and the Cant of Conquest* in which he challenged the original view of a civilising mission and instead sees Westward expansion as material interest and naked expansion.

Source I From a sermon on the Battle of the Little Bighorn, given by the Reverend D. J. Burrell in Chicago in August 1876.

Who shall be held responsible for this dark and sorrowful event? The history of our dealings with these Indian tribes from the very beginning is a record of fraud, and perjury and uninterrupted injustice. We have driven them each year further away from their original homes and hunting-grounds. We have treated them as having absolutely no rights at all. We have made beggars of them.

Source J From Crook's *Army and Navy Journal*, July 1878.

Buffalo is all gone, and an Indian can't catch enough rabbits to subsist himself and his family, and then there aren't enough rabbits to catch. What are they to do? Starvation is staring them in the face, and if they wait much longer, they will not be able to fight. All the tribes tell the same story. They are surrounded on all sides, the game is destroyed or driven away: they are left to starve, and there remains but one thing for them to do – fight while they can.

What can you learn from Sources I and J about the treatment of the Plains Indians?

27

KEY DATES: WESTWARD EXPANSION

1862 The Homestead Act.

1864 The Sand Creek Massacre.

1869 Completion of the Pacific Railroad.

1876 The Great Sioux War.

Isolationism – A policy by which the USA detached itself from foreign affairs. A policy of non-involvement and non-intervention in other governments' internal affairs and wars.

Secretary of State – US official responsible for the administration of foreign policy.

Colonisation – The forming of a settlement or colony by a group of people who seek to take control of territories or countries. It usually involves large-scale immigration of people to a 'new' location and the expansion of their civilisation and culture into this area.

5 Foreign policy, 1865–77

The foreign policy of the United States was dominated by isolationism and the Monroe Doctrine. However, there is evidence of expansion, most notably the movement West and the acquisition of Alaska. And there were also differences with Britain over the USA's neighbour, Canada.

US involvement in foreign affairs

To what extent did the USA carry out a policy of isolation in the years 1865–77?

There has been much debate among historians about the apparent isolationism of the USA in foreign policy as well as Americans' motives for expansion.

The Monroe Doctrine

In 1823, the Monroe Doctrine was announced by President James Monroe and John Quincy Adams, his Secretary of State. It established the scope of US interests abroad in the early nineteenth century. The Doctrine stated that:

- US policy was to avoid becoming involved in European wars unless American interests were involved.
- The 'American continents' were not to be colonised by any European powers.
- Any such attempts at colonisation would be regarded as 'unfriendly' acts.

The Doctrine seemed to indicate a disinterest in foreign affairs. Moreover, the USA did not fight in overseas wars until 1898.

Isolationism

In the nineteenth century, the USA seemed detached from foreign entanglements. This policy is generally referred to as isolationism. This isolationism was due to several reasons. Europe, the continent that was home to other major powers such as Britain, France and Germany, was thousands of miles away. Some historians have argued that the USA felt superior to those countries that took part in expansion and empire building. Moreover, the USA became populated by people often seeking to escape persecution and discrimination in their own lands. Therefore, the USA did not want to get involved in old regimes, which may have practised the very policies that it had rejected. The USA was different from other countries and would be guided by different, more morally-based principles than the older European states.

Such inward-looking attitudes were appropriate for a rural, agricultural nation. Moreover, when industrialisation began, America had sufficient raw materials available not to need imports. The Pacific and the Atlantic Oceans were also immense natural barriers and no state on America's borders (Canada, Mexico, Central and South America) was a major threat to their interests.

This policy was summed up by William Seward, the US Secretary of State from 1861–69 in 1863:

Our policy of non-intervention, straight, absolute, and peculiar as it may seem to other nations, has … become a traditional one, which could not be abandoned without the most urgent occasion, amounting to manifest necessity.

This was said at a time when Seward rejected an invitation to join with France, Britain and Austria in an attempt to persuade Tsar Alexander II to be more sympathetic to Poland.

However, the USA was never totally isolationist and was prepared to intervene when American interests were directly threatened. For example, in 1846 the USA went to war with Mexico to support a rebellion in California for independence from Mexican rule. Moreover, there was further involvement in Mexico in the 1860s when there was a direct threat to the Monroe Doctrine. France had taken advantage of the USA's preoccupation with the Civil War to establish a **puppet emperor**, Maximilian, supported by French troops. In 1866, Seward demanded that the French withdraw, and the USA moved 50,000 troops to the borders. The French backed down and abandoned Maximilian.

> **Puppet emperor** – A ruler controlled by others. In this case, Maximilian was controlled by France.

Expansionism

To what extent was US foreign policy expansionist in the years 1865–77?

The USA did also carry out a policy of expansion in the 1860s and 1870s, with the movement westward as well as the acquisition of Alaska. This sparked a debate, particularly over possible US involvement in the Dominican Republic.

The Far East and the Dominican Republic

In 1867, the USA acquired the uninhabited Midway Island in the West Pacific, originally to obtain supplies of guano to be used in the manufacture of fertiliser and gunpowder. In the following year, the Burlingame Treaty was signed to promote trade with China. This endorsed the free movement of people and free trade between the USA and China, in part to stimulate Chinese immigration to work on railroad building in the USA.

In 1869, the Dominican Republic actually offered itself for colonisation but Congress refused. In the following year an attempt by the federal government to annex the Republic stimulated a debate on imperial expansion in Congress. Those in favour argued that the USA would be able to exploit the wealth and resources of the Dominican Republic and sell its goods to a ready market there. However, those opposed to it argued that the USA would not deal with 'savages'. There was a fear that people regarded as inferior might one day have to be admitted into the Union or that former colonies might become states and reduce the influence of traditional, mainly white, American states. The Senate rejected the annexation of the Republic.

Alaska

There was no debate over Alaska, which was purchased from Russia in 1867 for $7.2 million although many people could not understand the motives of Seward in buying the area which was referred to as 'Seward's icebox' and 'Seward's folly'. Russia was keen to sell it because it had few settlers or resources. The USA was keen to acquire Alaska for a number of reasons:

- Seward felt that the development of Alaskan harbours might provide a gateway to northern Asia where US merchant ships could fuel and make provision for the long journey across the Pacific Ocean.
- It would expand the Pacific coastline of the USA, spread US rule and keep the British out.
- Moreover, it made sense to maintain good relations with such a powerful nation as Russia.

> **NOTE-MAKING**
>
> Make notes on key features of US foreign policy in this period using the side headings:
> - the Far East
> - the Dominican Republic
> - Alaska
> - Britain
> - Canada.

Dominion – A self-governing nation within the British Empire.

Fenians – An Irish republican organisation set up in the USA in 1858, fighting for Irish independence from Britain.

WORKING TOGETHER

There is much debate about the extent of isolationism in US foreign policy throughout the nineteenth century. Set up a class debate on the motion:

'This class believes that the USA was isolationist in its foreign policy in the years 1865–77',

with one group arguing for the motion, and one against.

KEY DATES: FOREIGN POLICY

1823 The Monroe Doctrine was announced by President Monroe and John Quincy Adams.

1867 The USA purchased Alaska from Russia.

1872 Britain agreed to pay compensation to the USA for damage caused by Confederate ships built in British shipyards.

The San Juan islands were part of the disputed area between the USA and Canada. In 1872 the British prime minister, William Gladstone, and the USA president, Grant, agreed that the dispute should be settled in Berlin by the German Kaiser (Emperor), Wilhelm II. The Kaiser decided that the islands should become part of the USA.

Mr Bull, the representative of the ▶ British people, is presented with a humble pie by Mr Gladstone in a waiter's outfit. This relates to the dispute between Britain and the US over the San Juan boundary with Canada.

Britain and Canada

To what extent did relations with Britain change in this period?

There were strained relations with Britain and Canada in the years after the Civil War. This was because of the apparent support given by the British and Canadians to the Confederacy during the Civil War. One aspect that the Union did object to was the building of Confederate ships in British dockyards. Thus manned, equipped and led, these ships wreaked havoc with Union shipping, forcing an increase in insurance for merchant ships. One Confederate ship, the *Alabama* (built in Liverpool in 1862) went to the Indies and took 40 US merchantmen.

At the end of the Civil War the USA demanded compensation from Britain. Senator Charles Sumner, the Chairman of the Senate Foreign Relations Committee, originally wanted to ask for $2 billion or alternatively the ceding of all of Canada to the USA. However, Canada became a self-governing **dominion** in 1867 while Britain continued to control its foreign and defence policies. The USA retaliated by allowing **Fenian** raids by Irish-American Civil War veterans across the border into Canada from 1866 to 1871. Eventually the Anglo–American dispute was settled in 1872, when Britain agreed to pay $15.5 million to the USA for the damage caused by Confederate commerce raiders built in Britain to the US merchant fleet during the Civil War.

"HUMBLE PIE."

MR. BULL. "HUMBLE PIE AGAIN, WILLIAM!—YOU GAVE ME THAT YESTERDAY?"
HEAD WAITER. "YES, SIR—NO, SIR—THAT WERE **GENEVA** HUMBLE PIE, SIR. THIS IS **BERLIN** HUMBLE PIE, SIR!!"

Chapter summary

- Reconstruction led to three Amendments to the Constitution, the Thirteenth, Fourteenth and Fifteenth.
- By 1870, all the Southern states had been re-admitted to the Union which was now dominated by the Northern states.
- African Americans were given their freedom but experienced discrimination, segregation and racial violence especially from the Ku Klux Klan.
- There was rapid industrial growth in the 1860s and 1870s due to a variety of factors including government policy and the expansion of railroads.
- This industrial growth led to the rapid growth of towns and cities and often poor living conditions for the workers.
- During this period US governments encouraged further expansion westwards.
- This expansion was also due to the Manifest Destiny as well as a second gold rush.
- Westward expansion threatened the lifestyle of the Native Americans who lived on the Plains and were eventually forced to live in reservations.
- America continued to pursue a policy of isolationism very much influenced by the Monroe Doctrine.
- However, the USA did still become involved abroad, particularly with Britain, and became more expansionist with the purchase of Alaska.

▼ **Summary diagram: The Era of Reconstruction 1865–77**

RECONSTRUCTION

How achieved

What it achieved

Lincoln, 1863–65
- Emancipation Act, 1863

Political
- Return of Southern states to Union
- Political dominance of the North

Johnson, 1865–67
- Thirteenth Amendment, 1865
- Civil Rights Act, 1866
- Fourteenth Amendment, 1866

Economic
- Industrial growth in the North
- South fell further behind because of effects of Civil War

Grant, 1868–76
- Fifteenth Amendment, 1870
- Enforcement and Ku Klux Klan Acts, 1870–71
- Civil Rights Act, 1875
- Contested presidential election, 1876
- End of Reconstruction, 1877

African-Americans
- Given their freedom and rights recognised by Thirteenth, Fourteenth and Fifteenth Amendments
- Suffered segregation, discrimination and intimidation by KKK

Working on essay technique: focus, structure and deploying detail

As well as learning the facts and understanding the history of the period you are studying, it is very important to develop skills in answering the types of question that will be set.

Essay focus

Whether you are taking the AS exam or the full A-level exam, Section B presents you with essay titles. Each question is marked out of 25.

AS examination	The full A-level examination
Section B – Answer ONE essay (from a choice of two)	Section B – Answer TWO essays (from a choice of three)

Several question stems are possible as alternatives, but they all have the same basic requirement. They all require you to analyse and reach a conclusion, based on the evidence you provide.

For example, 'Assess the validity (of a quotation)', 'To what extent …', 'How successful …', 'How far …', etc.

The AS titles always give a quotation and then: 'Explain why you agree or disagree with this view'. Almost inevitably, your answer will be a mixture of both. In essence, it is the same task as for the full A-level – just more basic wording.

Each question will reflect, directly or indirectly, one of the breadth issues in your study. The questions will have a fairly broad focus.

EXAMPLE

Look at the following AS-level practice question:

'The main reason for the growth in the US economy from 1865–77 was the improvements in transport.' Explain why you agree or disagree with this view.   (25 marks)

This type of question requires you to identify the reasons for the growth of the US economy in this period. You must discuss the improvements in transport as well as other reasons. So there are two parts to the question:

- The importance of the improvements in transport (your primary focus).
- Other reasons for the growth of the US economy (your secondary focus).

Structuring your answer

A clear structure makes for a much more effective essay. In order to structure the question in the example effectively you need several paragraphs. In each paragraph you will deal with one factor. One of these must be the factor in the question.

It is a good idea to cover the factor in the question first, so that you don't run out of time and forget to do it. After you have covered that factor, then cover the others in what you think is their order of importance.

Remember that you also need a short but clear introduction that briefly explains your argument in relation to the question and a conclusion that provides a summary.

Writing a focused introduction

It is vital that you maintain focus on the question from the beginning of your essay. One way to do this is to use the wording of the question to help write your argument. The first sentence in answer to the practice question, for example, could look like this:

> Improvements in transport certainly helped to stimulate the expansion of the US economy, but there were other important reasons for this growth.

That opening sentence provides a clear focus on the demands of the question, recognising that the task is to balance the part played by the improvements in transport against the importance of other reasons. It provides a spring-board for a clearly planned essay. Remember, you must learn how to apply this approach to other questions you may encounter. You are not just learning how to respond to this question.

Focus throughout the essay

Structuring your essay well will help with focus throughout the essay, but you also need to remember to maintain this throughout the piece. Here are some ideas that will help you to focus your answer.

- Use the wording of the question to help write your answer.

> For example, in answer to the practice question on page 32, you could begin your first main paragraph with 'the improvements in transport'.
>
> Improvements in transport were important in stimulating economic growth.
>
> This sentence begins with a clear point that refers to the primary focus of the question (the reasons for economic growth) while linking it to a factor (the reasons for economic growth).

- Secondly, have a paragraph for each of your other factors. You may wish to number your factors. This helps to make your structure clear and helps you to maintain focus. Later we will look at prioritising factors in order of importance.

Summary

- Work out the main focus of the question.
- Plan your essay with a series of factors focusing on the question, starting with the 'named' factor.
- Use the words in the question to formulate your answer.
- Return to the primary focus of the question at the beginning of every paragraph.
- Make sure that your structure is clear to the reader.

ACTIVITY 1

Having now read the advice on how to write a structured and focused essay, plan and write the first sentence to the following practice question:

'The main reason for Westward expansion, 1865–77, was the "Manifest Destiny".' Explain why you agree or disagree with this view.

(25 marks)

Deploying detail

As well as focus and structure your essay will be judged on the extent to which it includes accurate detail. Detailed essays are more likely to do well than essays that are vague or generalised.

There are several different kinds of evidence you could use that might be described as detail. This includes correct dates, names of relevant people, statistics and events. You can also make your essays more detailed by using the correct technical vocabulary. Here you could use words and phrases such as 'constitution' and 'Free Trade' that you have learned while studying this subject.

ACTIVITY 2

Consider the following A-level practice question:

'The main effect of Reconstruction for African Americans was the introduction of the Jim Crow Laws.' Assess the validity of this view. (25 marks)

1. Create your own brief essay plan for this question, making a list of points you will include.
2. Using your notes from this chapter, find at least three pieces of detail to support each of these points. It is best to use different types of detailed evidence, e.g. not just statistics or technical vocabulary, but also dates and specific people.

As well as studying the facts of an event in history, historians also use these facts in order to reach conclusions on, for example, why something happened. In other words, they have to interpret the facts in order to reach their conclusions. Often the evidence does not just point in one direction. There is scope for historians reaching different conclusions and producing different interpretations. Section A of the examination requires you to read and evaluate different interpretations – that is, looking at how historians do not always agree in the judgements they reach. In Chapters 2, 4, 5 and 7, there are contrasting interpretations for you to study and activities for you to practise your skills – that is, your skills in using evidence to see how far you agree with each interpretation.

In this chapter, as well as Chapters 3, 6 and 8, there is one, longer interpretation to read, followed by some questions that are designed to help you build up your skills as well as helping you to consolidate your knowledge of each chapter.

Working on interpretation skills: extended reading

To what extent did Reconstruction succeed?

Dr David Stefan Doddington considers what Reconstruction stood for, for various groups in society, and whether it can be deemed to have been a success.

After the devastation of the American Civil War (1861–65), the efforts to reconstruct a shattered nation mark one of the most controversial periods in the history of the United States. Frequently
5 bookmarked from the ending of the Civil War in 1865 until the 'corrupt bargain' of 1877, which led to the election of Rutherford B. Hayes as the Republican President and the withdrawal of federal troops from the South, the period
10 known as Reconstruction has elicited intense historiographical debate. Many historians have focused their attention on whether Reconstruction was a 'success' or 'failure', and it is to this debate that the following essay will speak to.

15 Working out the success of Reconstruction, however, is a complicated task; part of the difficulty in answering the above lies in the divergent aims, actions, and assessment of what Reconstruction stood for by different groups. It is known, for
20 example, that members of the Republican Party held different views on how best to 'reconstruct' the Union, and their views on the results could therefore differ accordingly. Indeed, in February 1866, President Andrew Johnson offered an impromptu
25 speech in Washington where he railed against the radicals in his party:

> I fought traitors and treason in the South … Now, when I turn round and at the other end of the line find men – I care not by what name you call them
30 – who stand opposed to the restoration of the Union of these States, I am free to say to you that I am still in the field.[1]

Johnson's sentiments about Reconstruction, and about members of his ostensibly unified party, paled in comparison to the divisions witnessed elsewhere 35 in the nation.

In this essay, however, it will be argued that Reconstruction offered freedom but ultimately failed to protect the newly freed black population of the South, who then faced the horrifying consequences 40 of this failure. As noted black intellectual W. E. Du Bois famously wrote, 'the slave went free; stood for a brief moment in the sun; then moved back toward slavery'.[2] The legislative changes of the period offered little protection to an impoverished and oppressed 45 population, and the 'redemption' of the South came with a brutal expansion of organised violence against black people (and white sympathisers) and the eventual replacement of formal slavery with the discrimination of the 'Jim Crow' laws. While the Republicans pushed 50 through the Enforcement Acts in 1870, with some success against groups like the Ku Klux Klan, violence and political intimidation quickly resumed; a variety of paramilitary organisations orchestrated the organised repression of the black population in the Southern 55 states throughout the 1870s, effectively preventing them from exercising their newly-won freedom.

The famous black activist Frederick Douglass noted in 1871 that 'until a man can express his opinion upon all possible subjects as freely and 60 as safely at the South as he does at the North … freedom is the merest farce, and reconstruction a failure.'[3] On these grounds, it is hard to argue for Reconstruction's success. As the 1870s drew on, black people found themselves overwhelmed, 65 outgunned, and forced back into second-class status by proponents of white supremacy, North and South. The violence integral to this was exemplified in the Colfax massacre of 1873, which saw approximately one hundred black people killed 70 by white Louisianans following a contested state election. Their killers were ultimately freed and the Supreme Court effectively removed federal protection from racist attacks in the related decision of *United States vs Cruickshank* (1876).[4] 75

This emphasis on violence and oppression should not downplay the significance of the Reconstruction Amendments. Nor should it deny the power of the short-lived but influential sight of African Americans participating in political and social life. However, it seems clear that radical aims to prevent extra-legal violence and successfully integrate the Southern black population into the political and public sphere ultimately failed in the face of organised resistance and widespread racist perceptions. This failure had very real consequences: thousands of black and white people were murdered for attempting to make good on the promise of emancipation.

To conclude, however, it should be noted many white contemporaries did not consider the declining fortune of the black population a failure of Reconstruction. Instead, this was evidence they simply did not belong in the rebuilt nation. In doing so, many white Americans – North and South – were able to forge a new narrative that stressed reunification. Indeed, *The Nation,* a New York magazine formed by Republicans in 1865, offered a stark epitaph for Reconstruction in April 1877:

> We believe the proposition to be almost self-evident, indeed, that heretoafter there is to be no South: none, that is, in a distinctively political sense. The negro will disappear from the field of national politics. Henceforth the nation, as a nation, will have nothing more to do with him.[5]

The fact that, despite the divisiveness of the Civil War, of military rule, and of deep economic, social, and cultural splits, the North and South were politically reunited and the Union prevailed, suggests that to some extent Reconstruction was a success. Nonetheless, it should not be forgotten that this success ultimately came at the expense of the black population of the South.

Dr David Stefan Doddington is Lecturer in North American History at Cardiff University.

[1] 'A Highly Important Speech by President Johnson', *The New York Times* (23 February 1866).

[2] W. E. B. Du Bois, *Black Reconstruction in America* (New York, 1992; first published, New York, 1935), 30.

[3] Frederick Douglass, 'Liberty of Speech South,' in *The Life and Writings of Frederick Douglass, Volume IV: Reconstruction and After*, ed. Philip S. Foner (New York, 1955), 245.

[4] For more information on this event, see: Steven Hahn, *A Nation Under our Feet: Black Political Struggles in the Rural South from Slavery to the Great Migration* (Cambridge, Mass., 2003), 292–295.

[5] 'The Political South Hereafter', *The Nation* (April 5, 1877), 202.

ACTIVITY

Having read the essay, answer the following questions.

Comprehension

1 What does the author mean by the following phrases?
   a) The 'Jim Crow' laws (line 43)
   b) 'Ku Klux Klan' (line 45)
   c) 'The Reconstruction Amendments' (line 68)

Evidence

2 Using paragraphs 3 and 4, list the ways in which the author suggests that Reconstruction failed to protect African Americans.

Interpretation

3 Using your knowledge from your study of Reconstruction list evidence to challenge the view that Reconstruction was to some extent a success.

Evaluation

4 The author suggests that Reconstruction failed to protect African Americans. To what extent can you support and challenge this view? Did African Americans benefit at all from Reconstruction?

5 The author also suggests that Reconstruction was a success because the North and South were reunited. To what extent can you support and challenge this view, economically, politically and socially?

2

The Gilded Age, c.1877–90

This chapter covers developments in the USA from the end of Reconstruction to the beginning of the Progressive era. It deals with a number of areas:

- The weaknesses of federal government: the presidencies of Garfield, Arthur and Cleveland.
- Economic growth and the rise of corporations: railroads, developments in agriculture and urbanisation.
- The growth and significance of immigration.
- Social, regional and ethnic divisions, particularly the position of African Americans.
- Conflict with the Native Americans and the end of Westward expansion.

When you have worked through the chapter and the related activities and exercises, you should have detailed knowledge of all those areas, and you should be able to relate this to the key breadth issues defined as part of your study, in particular: In what ways did the economy and society of the USA change and develop? The focus here is on political and economic developments in the Gilded Age. For the period covered in this chapter the main issues therefore, can be phrased as a question:

To what extent was this an age of political corruption and economic greed?

CHAPTER OVERVIEW

The period that followed Reconstruction is known as the Gilded Age. Politically, this was an age of limited political change and development, but of much political corruption. In addition, the economy continued to grow, particularly industry in the North and agriculture in the newly occupied areas of the West, but the economy was dominated more than ever by a few industrialists and businessmen. The period also saw the first major attempts to organise national labour unions as well as an ever growing influx of immigrants which, to some extent, challenged the US way of life. The segregation and discrimination against African Americans in the South was further reinforced during this period and the Native Americans of the Plains were more or less confined to the Reservations. The Gilded Age also included the announcement of the end of the frontier as well as the famous Turner essay on the significance of the frontier to the development of the USA.

1 Politics of the Gilded Age

The USA was ruled by four presidents in this period – Hayes, Garfield, Arthur and Cleveland. However, the political scene was dominated by accusations of corruption, especially in the civil service.

The 'Gilded Age'

What was meant by the 'Gilded Age'?

This is the name given to the period in American history which followed Reconstruction. The term 'Gilded Age' derives from the title of a novel published in 1873 by Mark Twain and Charles Dudley Warner. Responding to a dare from their wives, Twain and Warner wrote the book in four months with the aim, as Twain put it, of satirising 'speculativeness' and greed in business and 'shameful corruption' in politics. The novel came to symbolise US society and politics in the years 1878 to 1900.

Historians for decades tended to view Twain and Warner's extreme caricature as an accurate portrait of late nineteenth-century American society. However, more recently historians have undertaken a re-evaluation of the Gilded Age. While accepting that the benefits of industrialisation were not evenly distributed among the American people, and that many suffered, it was also true that economic development was crucial to the development of American society and would eventually deliver better goods, improved lifestyles, and higher wages for the vast majority of Americans.

Political stagnation

The last third of the nineteenth century is one of the most criticised periods in American political history. Throughout most of the twentieth century, historians portrayed this as a period of excessive corruption in political life with politicians only interested in furthering selfish, often economic, interests rather than the public good. Issues and principles counted for little in politics and there were few differences between Democrats and Republicans. It was described as an age of 'negation', 'cynicism' and 'excess'. One of the most influential critics was the Englishman James Bryce whose 1880s trip to the United States led to his two-volume study, *The American Commonwealth*, which was heavily critical of politics in this period. Bryce had come under the influence of Edwin L. Godkin, editor of the Mugwump journal *The Nation*, who showed great disdain for his contemporaries in politics. Twentieth-century historians such as Ray Ginger in *The Age of Excess, the United States from 1877 to 1914* and Richard Hofstadter in *The American Political Tradition and the Men Who Made It*, continued this cynical view of politics in the Gilded Age.

Traditional historians gave a stereotypical view of politicians in this period as small-minded and corrupt, using public office mostly to serve their own interests, and often for their own private gain, with little real concern for matters of policy or the public good. They were also critical of the spoils system in which federal patronage was dispensed by party bosses. Officeholders were selected on the basis of party loyalty rather than administrative competence. This was certainly the case in New York where a series of Senators, including Thurlow Weed and Roscoe Conkling, dominated politics by their control of the New York Custom House. New York was the main port, controlling commerce and collecting revenue from ports. Thus, its Custom House afforded unequal opportunities for extortion and was at the very centre of the spoils system. It employed 1,000 party workers.

NOTE-MAKING

Make notes on this section using the 1–2 method (see page x). For example, write 'The meaning of the Gilded Age' on the left and a bulleted point list on the right.

Mark Twain

Samuel Langhorne Clemens, better known by his pen name, Mark Twain, was born in 1835, in the tiny village of Florida, Missouri. In 1851, at the age of fifteen, he got a job as a printer and occasional writer at the Hannibal Western Union, a little newspaper owned by his brother, Orion. In July 1861, Twain climbed on board a stagecoach and headed for Nevada and California, where he would live for the next five years. At first, he prospected for silver and gold but with no success and by the middle of 1862 he was flat broke and in need of a regular job. He knew his way around a newspaper office, so that September he went to work as a reporter for the Virginia City Territorial Enterprise. He got a big break in 1865, when one of his tales about life in a mining camp, 'Jim Smiley and His Jumping Frog', was printed in newspapers and magazines around the country. Mark Twain went on to write the classic American novels *The Adventures of Tom Sawyer*, published in 1876, and its sequel, *The Adventures of Huckleberry Finn*.

Spoils system – The practice whereby a political party, after winning an election, gives government jobs to its voters as a reward for working towards victory, and as an incentive to keep working for the party – as opposed to a system of awarding offices on the basis of some measure of merit independent of political activity.

One example of corruption in the New York Custom House was to undervalue imports, then make an official discovery of the mistake. Under the law the entire value of an import that was falsely declared was forfeit. Half of the total then went to the head of the Custom House. Importers were often willing to settle out of court and bribe the officer in charge. For example, in 1874 the metal importers Phelps, Dodge and Company paid a bribe of $50,000 to Senator Roscoe Conkling, the leader of the New York Custom House.

A further criticism by traditional historians about the Gilded Age was that there was no real difference between the two main political parties which meant there was little real choice for the electorate. To a certain extent this was true. Republicans and Democrats did seek a broad consensus from the electorate and did not have the strong ideological differences that differentiated the British political parties of the later nineteenth century. Both contained conservative elements as well as reformers.

Revised view

From the 1960s revisionist historians such as Irwin Unger in *The Greenback Era* and H. Wayne in *From Hayes to McKinley: National Party Politics, 1877–96* have challenged this view, arguing that traditional historians have over-emphasised the negative political developments of the period and ignored more positive features such as political leaders who were hard-working public servants with positive achievements. They accept that some politicians took bribes and engaged in corrupt practices, but the percentage of those that took part was probably no higher than in other times in American history. Many leading politicians were not just in politics for personal and financial gain but did want to make a difference. Moreover, the presidents of the period did introduce a series of reforms to reduce corruption in the civil service and improve its efficiency. Furthermore, they stress that, for the most part, the presidents during this period did try to reduce corruption through reform of the civil service.

They have also suggested that there were significant differences between Republicans and Democrats. Republicans placed greater stress on government activism, especially at national level, to encourage further economic development. The protective tariff emerged as the centerpiece of the Republican's economic programme. They were more inclined to favour measures to hasten the assimilation of immigrants, such as requiring the use of English in local schools. Democrats on the other hand tended to cling to their party's traditional belief in very limited federal and state government intervention and opposed tariff reform and protectionism. One Democrat voting strength, for example, was solid support from white segregationists in the South. This reflected southern resentment of Republicans carried over from the Civil War and Reconstruction. Where African Americans had the vote, they were likely to vote Republican.

WORKING TOGETHER

Work with a partner.
- One of you should summarise the criticisms of the politics of this period from traditional historians.
- The other should summarise the views of revisionist historians.
- After you have finished, combine your findings.

Once you have read through this section, consider how accurate Twain's description of this period as the 'Gilded Age' is.

The presidents of the Gilded Age

To what extent were the presidents weak in this period?

During the period 1877–90 there were four presidents – Hayes, Garfield, Arthur and Cleveland – whose limited achievements provided further evidence for the critics of the Gilded Age. Contemporary historian Henry Adams said of politics in the Gilded Age, 'The period was poor in purpose and barren in results'. His verdict, 'One might search the whole list of Congress during this period and find little but damaged reputations', remains a popular one. The Gilded Age leaves an impression of political stagnation due to its procession of conservative presidents who thought of themselves as administrators rather than party leaders. However, there were some attempts at reform, particularly of the civil service. S. D. Cashman in *America in the Gilded Age,* first published in 1984, is especially critical of the presidents of this age and the previous period:

'Thus, in popular legend as well as in actuality there are the dud presidents: Grant, a president discredited; Hayes, a president defied; Arthur, a president dismissed; Cleveland, a president denied; and Harrison, a president derided.'

Hayes, 1877–81

Two major issues dominated the presidency of Hayes – civil service reform and the railroad strike of 1877.

Civil service reform

Hayes took office determined to reform the system of civil service appointments, which had been based on the spoils system since Andrew Jackson was president. Officeholders were selected on the basis of party loyalty and not administrative competence. By the 1870s the civil service was made up of incompetent and demoralised party hacks. Hayes was opposed by a faction of the Republican Party led by Senator Roscoe Conkling, who were given the nickname of the 'Stalwarts'.

Instead of giving federal jobs to political supporters, Hayes wished to award them by merit according to an examination that all applicants would take. Immediately, Hayes's call for reform brought him into conflict with those who favoured the spoils system, particularly New York Senator Roscoe Conkling, who fought Hayes's reform efforts at every turn.

To show his commitment to reform, Hayes appointed one of the best-known advocates of reform, Carl Schurz, to be Secretary of the Interior and asked Schurz and William M. Evarts, his Secretary of State, to lead a special cabinet committee charged with drawing up new rules for federal appointments.

Although he could not convince Congress to outlaw the spoils system, Hayes issued an executive order that forbade federal officeholders from being required to make campaign contributions or otherwise taking part in party politics. Chester A. Arthur, the Collector of the Port of New York, refused to obey the president's order. Hayes eventually sacked Arthur and replaced him with one of his own nominees. While reform legislation did not pass during Hayes's presidency, he had set the ball rolling for further civil service reform under his successors, particularly the Pendleton Act of 1883.

NOTE-MAKING

The following section covers the domestic policies of four presidents. Make notes on the achievements of each of the four – Hayes, Garfield, Arthur and Cleveland. After making your notes, assess each president's strengths and weaknesses. Then come to a conclusion about whether the presidents of the Gilded Age were weak.

Rutherford Hayes (1822–93)

Hayes was born in 1822 in Ohio and educated at Kenyon College and Harvard Law School. After five years of law practice in Lower Sandusky, he moved to Cincinnati, where he flourished as a young Whig lawyer. He fought in the Civil War, was wounded in action, and rose to the rank of major general. While he was still in the Army, Cincinnati Republicans ran him for the House of Representatives. He accepted the nomination, but would not campaign, explaining, 'an officer fit for duty who at this crisis would abandon his post to electioneer … ought to be scalped'. Elected by a heavy majority, Hayes entered Congress in December 1865 and between 1867 and 1876 he served three terms as Governor of Ohio. He declined to seek re-election in 1881 and retired from politics. He died twelve years later.

Railroad strike, 1877

In his first year in office, Hayes was faced with the United States' largest labour disturbance to date, the Great Railroad Strike of 1877. In order to make up for financial losses suffered since the panic of 1873, the major railroads cut their employees' wages several times in 1877, which led to a strike of railway workers. Hayes was prepared to send federal troops when requested to do so by several governors, such as those of New York and Baltimore, who feared possible riots. Business leaders praised the support of Hayes who seemed to establish the principle of federal government support for business and industry in the face of possible strike action.

Garfield, 1881

Garfield was a self-taught scholar who, nevertheless, found presidential duties beyond him. 'My God! What is this place that a man should ever want to get in it?', he exclaimed after a month in office. His presidency was to last only a matter of months.

Garfield also supported reform of the civil service, believing that the spoils system was damaging to the presidency. He strengthened federal authority over the New York Custom House, stronghold of Senator Roscoe Conkling, who was leader of the Stalwart Republicans and dispenser of patronage in New York. When Garfield submitted to the Senate a list of appointments, including many of Conkling's friends, he named Conkling's arch-rival William H. Robertson to run the Custom House. Conkling contested the nomination, tried to persuade the Senate to block it, and appealed to the Republican caucus to compel its withdrawal. Garfield would not submit. Conkling and his fellow Senator from New York resigned, confident that their legislature would vindicate their stand and re-elect them. Instead, the legislature elected two other men; and the Senate confirmed Robertson. Garfield's victory was complete.

Garfield also continued the work of his predecessor, Hayes, in reform of the Post Office. In April 1880, there had been a Congressional investigation into corruption in the Post Office Department, where profiteering rings allegedly stole millions of dollars, employing bogus mail contracts called 'star routes'. Hayes had stopped the implementation of any new 'star route' contracts in a reform effort. Garfield forced the resignation of one of the ringleaders of the 'star routes', Thomas J. Brady, who was indicted for conspiracy in 1883.

The assassination of Garfield

On 2 July 1881, less than four months after his inauguration, President Garfield arrived at the Washington railroad depot to catch a train for a summer's retreat on the New Jersey seashore. As Garfield made his way through the station, Charles Guiteau raced from the shadows and fired two shots point blank into the President. One grazed Garfield's arm; the other lodged in his abdomen. An unsuccessful lawyer and insurance salesman, Guiteau believed Garfield owed him a patronage position in the diplomatic corps, and that the President's political decisions threatened to destroy the Republican Party. He was convicted of murder and hanged on 30 June 1882.

Garfield did not die immediately. His life lay in the balance and he lingered for three months. The wound hardly bled and the doctors had great difficulty in locating the bullet, which had lodged in a muscle. Among those who tried unsuccessfully to do so was the inventor Alexander Graham Bell who used an electrical device. Ironically, it was not the bullet that killed the President but the efforts to save him. He died on 19 September 1881. His death greatly increased the demand for and support of further civil service reform.

James Garfield (1831–81)

Garfield was born in 1831, in Cuyahoga County, Ohio. He lost his father at the age of two and later drove canal boat teams, somehow earning enough money for an education. In 1856, he graduated from Williams College in Massachusetts, and he returned to the Western Reserve Eclectic Institute (later Hiram College) in Ohio as a classics professor.

In 1859, Garfield was elected to the Ohio Senate as a Republican. In 1862, when Union military victories had been few, he successfully led a brigade at Middle Creek, Kentucky, against Confederate troops. In the same year he was elected to Congress. Garfield repeatedly won re-election for eighteen years, and became the leading Republican in the House.

In 1880, at the Republican Convention, Garfield failed to win the presidential nomination for his friend, John Sherman, so finally, on the 36th ballot, Garfield himself became the 'dark horse' nominee. By a margin of only 10,000 popular votes, Garfield defeated the Democratic nominee, General Winfield Scott Hancock.

He was assassinated in 1881.

Arthur, 1881–84

Arthur continued the civil service reform of his predecessors, most notably with the Pendleton Act of 1883. Democratic Senator George Pendleton was the author of this Act, the first law specifically intended to begin the professional handling of the civil service. In standing up to Roscoe Conkling, he struck a strong blow against political corruption. President Arthur pushed for passage of the Act and signed it readily. The creation of the first Civil Service Commission was the beginning of the end of the spoils system. The Pendleton Act called for a merit system for promotions within the service and ensured continuity in federal employees from one administration to the next, even if the White House changed parties.

In another area Arthur signed the first federal immigration law that excluded paupers, criminals and the mentally ill. Congress also passed a Chinese Exclusion Act that would have made Chinese immigration illegal for twenty years and made Chinese immigrants permanent aliens by excluding them from US citizenship. Although Arthur vetoed the bill, he signed a revised bill that was not as harsh. Arthur also tried to lower tariff rates so the Government would not be embarrassed by annual surpluses of revenue. Congress raised about as many rates as it trimmed, but Arthur signed the Tariff Act of 1883, which only reduced tariffs by an average of 1.47 per cent.

Cleveland and the Mugwumps

The first Democrat elected after the Civil War, Grover Cleveland was the only president to leave the White House and return for a second term, four years later.

1884 presidential campaign

The 1884 election was one of the muddiest in American history. Cleveland's opponent, Republican candidate James G. Blaine, was scorned during the campaign as 'Blaine, Blaine, James G. Blaine, that continental liar from the State of Maine!' because of charges of corruption involving railroad interests. He was also suspected of an anti-Roman Catholic bias. His opponents used the fact that Grover Cleveland had allegedly fathered an illegitimate child.

Some Republicans united in a group known as the 'Mugwumps', reformers unhappy with the high level of corruption in government. They abandoned Blaine during the campaign and were then known as 'goo-goos'. The Mugwumps claimed they would support an honest Democrat such as Cleveland, the reform-minded Governor of New York. The election was very close; Cleveland's margin of victory was 25,000 votes out of 10 million cast and 37 electoral votes out of 401.

Cleveland's achievements

Cleveland continued to reform the civil service. Soon after taking office, he was faced with the task of filling all the government jobs for which the president had the power of appointment. These jobs were still typically filled under the spoils system, but Cleveland announced that he would not fire any Republican who was doing his job well, and would not appoint anyone solely on the basis of party service. He also used his appointment powers to reduce the number of federal employees, as many departments had become bloated with political time-servers. Later in his term, as his fellow Democrats chafed at being excluded from the spoils, Cleveland began to replace more of the partisan Republican officeholders with Democrats. While some of his decisions were influenced by party concerns, more of Cleveland's appointments were decided by merit alone than was the case in his predecessors' administrations.

> ## Chester Arthur (1829–85)
>
> Arthur was born in 1829 in Fairfield, Vermont, the son of a Baptist preacher who had emigrated from Northern Ireland. He graduated from Union College in 1848, was admitted to the bar, and practised law in New York City. Early in the Civil War he served as Quartermaster General of the State of New York.
>
> In 1871, President Grant appointed him Collector of the Port of New York. Arthur effectively marshalled the thousand Customs House employees under his supervision on behalf of Roscoe Conkling's Stalwart Republican machine. Honorable in his personal life and his public career, Arthur nevertheless was a firm believer in the spoils system when it was coming under vehement attack from reformers. He insisted upon honest administration of the Customs House, but staffed it with more employees than it needed, retaining them for their merit as party workers rather than as government officials.
>
> President Hayes, in 1878, attempting to reform the Customs House, removed Arthur, but two years later, at the Republican Convention Arthur was nominated for the Vice Presidency. In 1881, Arthur became president on the death of Garfield. He failed to be nominated three years later, and in 1885 he died.

Grover Cleveland (1837–1908)

Cleveland was born in New Jersey in 1837, one of nine children of a Presbyterian minister. He was brought up in upstate New York. He passed his law exams in 1858 and as a lawyer in Buffalo, he became notable for his single-minded concentration upon whatever task faced him. In 1881, running as a reformer, Cleveland was elected Mayor of Buffalo. A year later he was elected Governor of New York and in 1884 he became president. In 1886, Cleveland married 21-year-old Frances Folsom; he was the only president married in the White House.

Cleveland was defeated in the presidential election of 1888. Although he won a larger popular majority than the Republican candidate Benjamin Harrison, he received fewer electoral votes. In 1892 he was once again elected president for a second term, but four years later his party deserted him and nominated William Jennings Bryan.

He died in 1908 after suffering a heart attack.

1 What can you learn from this speech (Source A) about Cleveland's views on the role of the presidency?
2 What differences are there between Sources B and C in their views about politics in the Gilded Age?

Cleveland, however, believed in a very limited role for federal government. As a Democratic president, Cleveland faced a Republican-dominated Senate and often resorted to using his veto powers. He vetoed hundreds of private pension bills for American Civil War veterans, believing that if their requests had already been rejected by the Pension Bureau, Congress should not attempt to override that decision. When Congress passed a bill granting pensions for disabilities not caused by military service, Cleveland also vetoed that bill. In 1887, Cleveland issued his most well-known veto, that of the Texas Seed Bill. After a drought had ruined crops in several Texas counties, Congress appropriated $10,000 to purchase seed grain for farmers there. Cleveland vetoed the expenditure (see Source A).

Source A From a speech by President Cleveland in 1887 explaining his decision to veto the Texas Seed Bill. In *The Growth of the American Republic* by S. Morison, H. Commager and W. Leuchtenburg, (Oxford University Press), 1969, p.162.

I do not believe that the power and duty of the general government ought to be extended to the relief of individual suffering which is in no manner properly related to the public service or benefit. A prevalent tendency to disregard the limited mission of this power and duty should, I think, be steadfastly resisted, to the end that the lesson should be constantly enforced that, though the people support the government, the government should not support the people. The friendliness and charity of our countrymen can always be relied upon to relieve their fellow-citizens in misfortune. This has been repeatedly and quite lately demonstrated. Federal aid in such cases encourages the expectation of paternal care on the part of the government and weakens the sturdiness of our national character, while it prevents the [fulfilment] among our people of that kindly sentiment and conduct which strengthens the bonds of a common brotherhood.

Source B From 'Public Life and Conduct of Politics' by L. L. Gould in *The Gilded Age Perspectives on the Origins of Modern America* by C. Calhoun, ed., (Rowman and Littlefield), 2007.

The late nineteenth century witnessed profound changes in the United States. Scholars once treated political life as almost an embarrassment. Most historians now realise how inadequate that judgement was. In a rapidly evolving society, political leaders confronted problems of unprecedented intricacy and scope. They were hamstrung by the Democrats who believed that Americans wanted less government, not more. Even so, they were able to post some modest success in reaching solutions to the society's problems. In important ways they helped lay the groundwork for the USA of the twentieth century.

Source C From *The Growth of the American Republic* by S. Morison, H. Commager and W. Leuchtenburg, (Oxford University Press), 1969.

There is no drearier chapter in American political history than that which records the administrations of Hayes, Garfield, Arthur and Cleveland. Civil War issues were dead, though politicians continued to flay the corpses. National politics became little more than a contest for power between rival parties waged on no higher plane than a struggle for traffic between rival railroads.

KEY DATES: PRESIDENTS OF THE GILDED AGE

1877 Hayes begins presidency.
1881 Garfield becomes president. Assassination of Garfield.
1881 Arthur becomes president.
1883 The Pendleton Act.
1884 The 'Mugwumps' and the election of Cleveland.

2 Economic and social developments

American industry continued to expand rapidly in the years after 1877 which, in turn, encouraged further urban growth, more immigration and the emergence of a labour movement.

Further economic growth, 1870–90

How justified was the title of 'robber barons'?

Although in 1860 the USA was still a second-rate industrial power, by 1890 it led Germany, Britain and France. The value of its manufactured goods almost equalled the total of the others. By the 1880s, the American economy was growing at an annual rate of 3.8 per cent and the GDP almost doubled. American industry became dominated by a few individuals and corporations whose often ruthless and unscrupulous methods were criticised by contemporaries and historians of the period.

'Robber barons'

Big businessmen, not politicians, controlled the new industrialised America of the Gilded Age. These so-called 'captains of industry' were not regulated by the government and did whatever they could to make as much money as possible. These industrialists' business practices were sometimes so unscrupulous that they were given the name 'robber barons'. These men were able to gain direct political influence, especially within the Republican Party and over the emerging mass newspapers. They benefited from the prevailing belief in *laissez-faire*.

NOTE-MAKING

Make notes on this section using bullet points (see page x). For each of the key personalities, summarise his achievements and consider the question 'To what extent does he deserve the tile of "robber baron"?'

Laissez-faire – This is an economic and political doctrine which holds that economies function most efficiently when unencumbered by government regulation. *Laissez-faire* advocates favour individual self-interest and competition, and oppose the taxation and regulation of commerce. *Laissez-faire* reached its peak in the 1870s during the age of economic expansion as American industrialists operated with a free hand and very little government interference or intervention.

▼ A cartoon with the title 'Bosses of the Senate', published in 1889. It suggests that Big Business controls the government.

'Survival of the fittest'

This is the belief that individuals that are best equipped to survive and reproduce perpetuate the highest frequency of genes to descendant populations. This is the principle known popularly as 'survival of the fittest', where fitness denotes an individual's overall ability to pass copies of his or her genes on to successive generations. The theory of evolution by natural selection was proposed by Charles Darwin and Alfred Russel Wallace in 1858. They argued that species with useful adaptations to the environment are more likely to survive and produce progeny than are those with less useful adaptations, thereby increasing the frequency with which useful adaptations occur over the generations.

Vertical integration – When a company expands its business into areas that are at different points on the same production path, such as when a manufacturer owns its supplier and/or distributor.

Philanthropy – Showing a concern for human welfare and advancement, usually manifested by donations of money, property, or work to needy persons.

The methods used by these 'robber barons' seemed justified by a new philosophy, Social Darwinism. Remember that one of the key questions you have to consider is 'How important were ideas and ideology in change and continuity?' The leading exponent of Social Darwinism was an English journalist, Herbert Spencer. As early as 1850, nine years before Charles Darwin published his revolutionary theory of evolution, Spencer's *Social Statics* publicised *laissez-faire*. Spencer opposed state aid to the poor and disapproved of tariffs to aid agriculture or industry. 'Robber barons' were being told what they wanted to hear by Spencer who toured the USA in 1882 – how a political system that claimed all men were equal could also include economic inequality. There were a number of leading 'robber barons'. In time, many wealthy American businessmen, inspired by biologist Charles Darwin's new theories of natural selection, began to believe that they had become rich because they were literally superior human beings compared to the poorer classes. The wealthy applied Darwin's idea of 'survival of the fittest' to society.

Vanderbilt and the railroads

Cornelius Vanderbilt and his son, William, were perhaps the most famous railroad tycoons. Cornelius made his fortune through steamboat operations which were worth $11 million by 1862. He ploughed his profits into the great railroad boom and during the 1860s he bought out and consolidated many of the rail companies in the East, enabling them to cut operations costs. The Vanderbilts also established a standard track gauge and were among the first railroaders to replace iron rails with lighter, more durable steel. The Vanderbilt fortune swelled to more than $100 million during these boom years. When he died in 1877, at the age of 83, he was the richest man in America.

The bulk of his fortune went to his son, William, who, by ruthless manipulation of capital and labour alike, increased the family fortune so that when he died in 1885, he was the richest man in the world. His brutal handling of strikes made him one of the most unpopular men in America.

Andrew Carnegie and steel

Arriving in America as a poor Scottish immigrant, Carnegie started work in a railroad company and by the Civil War was selling iron, the profits from which he invested in an ironworks. He began to use the new, British-invented Bessemer Converters to make better and cheaper steel from iron. In addition, Carnegie brought all the processes of steel manufacturing together – smelting, refining, rolling – in his Homestead Steelworks in Pennsylvania. Initially, he mainly manufactured rails but, as the demand for these decreased, he changed production to provide for new markets in cities and industries such as bridges, machinery, wire, pipes and armour plating for the US navy. In 1900, he sold his empire to the banker J. P. Morgan for $480 million.

Carnegie rarely tried to buy out his competitors. He preferred to concentrate on production of good steel at a lower cost than others, selling at such prices as would give him the best advantages. He was able to monopolise steel production through vertical integration – in other words controlling all processes in production from extraction of iron ore to the making of finished products which, in turn, brought lower costs and greater profits.

In 1889, he published a collection of his writings, *The Gospel of Wealth*, in which he explained his philosophy of philanthropy. This is another new idea linked to the key question 'How important were ideas and ideology in change and continuity?' Carnegie was typical of many self-made millionaires prepared to help those who helped themselves. Carnegie made donations to universities, hospitals, free libraries, parks, swimming baths and churches. Moreover, he set up the Carnegie Endowment for International Peace for research and the advancement of knowledge. However, he did attract criticism for both extremes. On the one side, he was criticised by other businessmen for being a socialist because he gave money to help various people and societies. On the other hand, he was also criticised for making his fortune by exploiting his workforce through paying low wages and demanding long hours as well as being too ruthless in destroying rival businesses.

John D. Rockefeller and oil

John D. Rockefeller first visited the Venango oil fields in 1860, acting as a business agent for Cleveland investors. He was appalled by the disorganisation and confusion he found in the oil industry. He studied the industry carefully and realised that it could have the same universal scale as steel or copper. He realised that the best way to get control of the industry was not by producing oil but by refining and distributing it, as well as undercutting his rivals through cost-cutting measures such as securing cheap transport. His methods led to a public outcry and he was as much hated for his secrecy as his ruthlessness. For example, when he bought out his competitors in Cleveland, he kept it secret, so that companies associated with him pretended to be separate and competing.

Rockefeller bought his first oil refinery in 1862 and, eight years later, he set up the Standard Oil Company in Ohio. He ruthlessly eliminated competitors, used fixed prices, paid fierce attention to manufacturing processes and negotiated with immense skill. By the 1880s, he controlled 85 per cent of all American oil production and, by 1899, had a fortune of $200 million. He expanded into iron, copper, coal, shipping and banking. By 1913, he was the world's first billionaire. He also became a philanthropist, giving away an estimated $550 million to medicine, African-American educational institutions and the Baptist Church.

The defenders of Rockefeller suggest that the creation of a monopoly of the oil industry through the setting up of the Standard Oil Company rescued the industry from disaster. His critics claim that his secret arrangements with railroads and others prevented free and fair competition and brought ruin to those people not associated with Rockefeller.

J. P. Morgan and finance

J. P. Morgan was a skillful financier who inherited $12 million but increased his fortune through his skill as a financier. He was the major force behind the creation of large companies such as the US Steel Corporation, which was the first billion-dollar corporation in history. In 1871, Morgan began his own private banking company, which later became known as J. P. Morgan & Co., one of the leading financial firms in the country.

During his career, his wealth, power and influence attracted a lot of media and government scrutiny. He was criticised for creating monopolies by making it difficult for any business to compete against his. He was also criticised for his love of the high life and the way that he appeared to flaunt his wealth, often being seen in public in the company of actresses.

Technology

American technology made rapid progress in these years and did much to encourage further economic growth. A contemporary editor, Mark Sullivan, put this down to 'intellectual curiosity about the new, the instinct of the American mind to look into, examine, and experiment – a willingness to scrap not only old machinery but old formulas and ideas'. Two such inventors of the period were Thomas Edison, inventor of the light bulb and Alexander Bell, inventor of the telephone.

WORKING TOGETHER

'Robber barons'

Working in pairs, research and feed back to the whole class on one key businessman of the era, making a judgement as to whether he deserves the title of 'robber baron'. Pairs should research one of the following:
- Vanderbilt
- Carnegie
- Rockefeller
- Morgan

To what extent does the class believe that big businessmen such as Carnegie and Rockefeller deserve the title of the 'robber barons'?

RESEARCH

In pairs research the careers, achievements and importance of Alexander Graham Bell and Thomas Edison.
- One of you research Bell.
- The other research Edison.
- Share your findings.

KEY DATES: 'ROBBER BARONS'

1876 Bell patented the telephone.

1878 Edison Electric Company was set up.

1889 Carnegie published a collection of his writings, *The Gospel of Wealth*.

NOTE-MAKING

Using the 1–2 method (see page x), make notes on the key developments in organised labour during this period using the side headings:
- National railroad strike
- Knights of Labor
- Haymarket bomb outrage

Compare your notes with those of a partner and expand upon what each of you has written.

The rise of organised labour, 1877–90

How much progress was made by the labour movement during these years?

Trade unions emerged during this period due primarily to rapid industrialisation. However, much of the struggle for trade union and labour rights was focused on the right of trade unions to exist at all, to be recognised as representing their membership and to do so in negotiations with employers for improvements in pay and working conditions. They campaigned for appropriate structures to be put in place that obliged employers to bargain with the representatives of the workforce and that established systems for mediation, conciliation and arbitration as well as the right to strike.

Early unions

Before 1877, union organisation had been sporadic and largely local. Small craft unions organised local workers around local concerns. The great exception was the National Labor Union, formed in 1866. Seventy-seven delegates representing 60,000 workers gathered at Baltimore to launch this national organisation and adopt a platform focused on securing legislation protecting the eight-hour day. However, the union was short-lived. The economic depression of 1873 drove millions of workers into unemployment and out of their unions. By 1877, the nation's total union membership had fallen from a peak of 300,000 in 1872 to just 50,000.

The national railroad strike, 1877

In 1877, when the owners of the Baltimore and Ohio (B&O) Railroad announced a pay cut – the fourth in as many years – workers walked off the job and were joined by workers from rival railroads, and even workers from entirely different industries who abandoned their jobs in sympathy. Together, this growing mass of workers attacked railroad yards, burning trains and tearing up tracks. The violence was the worst in Pittsburgh, where a crowd of some 5,000 workers fought 650 federal troops in a pitched battle. The workers laid waste to the railroad yard, burning more than 500 cars, 104 locomotives and 39 buildings. The troops were brought in and 25 people were killed when they fired into the rioting crowd.

Military force eventually restored order along the nation's railroad lines, but not before strikers had destroyed more than $10 million worth of property and terrified middle-class observers of the events. The railroad strike of 1877 was therefore a terrifying shock to most Americans. For middle-class urbanites and small-town residents removed from many of the harsh realities of the new industrial order, the size, the rapid spread, the worker unity and the extreme violence of the strike raised a horrible possibility of social warfare just a decade after the end of the Civil War. However, the strike also convinced workers that they needed to organise. They had no chance to prevail in a power struggle against the combined forces of industrial owners and the US government unless they built stronger unions and advanced their course by political activity. Conversely, the business community resolved to suppress labour association by any means necessary. This attitude was summed up in a newspaper article in August 1877 (Source D).

The Knights of Labor

In the decade following the railroad strike, unions grew rapidly. The most ambitious of these was the Knights of Labor. Founded in 1869, the Knights sought to build a comprehensive organisation uniting workers of all races, genders, ethnicities and occupations. They lobbied government for the eight-hour day and child labour restrictions. They also campaigned for the initiative and referendum – electoral processes through which common citizens could draft and vote upon laws but most fundamentally, and most radically, they sought to build more cooperative labour–management relations. They aimed for industries governed by councils of workers and managers within genuinely democratic, and ultimately collectively-owned, enterprises.

Growth

During the 1880s, the Knights grew rapidly. By 1885, the organisation claimed 100,000 members and, in the same year, it experienced its greatest success. When the Wabash Railroad, one of the railroads within Jay Gould's Southwest System, tried to break a local union, the Knights walked out in sympathy. Within days, the entire Southwest System was paralysed and the Wabash was forced to negotiate with its workers. Flush with victory, the Knights drew in thousands of new members; within a year, 750,000 workers were united under the comprehensive umbrella of the Knights of Labor.

Decline

To a certain extent, the Knights' rapid success was also the cause of their downfall. In 1886, tens of thousands of newly-joined workers initiated labour actions – but only occasionally were the other members willing to walk out in support. Even more damaging, when an eight-hour-day rally in Chicago's Haymarket Square turned violent, all supporters of the eight-hour day were blamed. The Knights of Labor, because of their size and visibility, were condemned the most vehemently. Within a year of the Haymarket riot, the Knights' membership had been cut in half; within a decade, the Knights were all but extinct.

The Haymarket bomb outrage

A strike at the McCormick Harvester Works in Chicago in May 1886 precipitated a tragedy. On 3 May a pitched battle took place between strikers, strikebreakers and police protecting them in front of the plant. When police fired into the crowd several people were killed and many injured. In protest, anarchists of the Black International, a revolutionary organisation set up in Chicago in 1881, called a meeting in Haymarket Square, the centre of the lumber yards and packing houses.

The mayor attended the meeting, discovered it was peaceful and left. When it began to rain, the crowd dispersed. Someone then threw a bomb that killed a policeman and wounded more than 60, six of whom died later. The police retaliated, firing into the crowd, wounding more than a hundred, some fatally.

Public opinion was very hostile towards the anarchists, seven of whom were arrested, tried, found guilty and executed in 1887. The case was a public sensation at home and abroad.

Largely because of the Haymarket affair, the eight-hour movement of 1886 was a substantial failure. Of the many workers who took part in the movement, only 15,000 retained their gains at the end of the year. Once again, organised labour had failed.

Source D From the invitation to attend the meeting in Haymarket Square, sent out by the Black International Movement. In *America in the Gilded Age* by S. D. Cashman, (New York University Press), 1993, p.115.

The masters sent out their bloodhounds – the police. They killed six of your brothers at McCormick's this afternoon. They killed the poor wretches because they, like you, had the courage to disobey the supreme will of your bosses. To arms we call you, to arms!

What does the invitation (Source D) suggest about the aims of the meeting?

Samuel Gompers

Samuel Gompers was an English immigrant of Dutch-Jewish ancestry who had left London in 1863 at the age of thirteen. He spent his adolescence in the cigar-making shops of the Lower East Side of New York, absorbing the political discussions he heard among fellow workers and becoming interested in labour organisation. His prime concern was the status of skilled labour. Under his leadership the AFL attained greater stability than ever before.

KEY DATES: THE RISE OF ORGANISED LABOUR

1869 Setting up of the Knights of Labor.

1877 National railroad strike.

1885 Setting up of the AFL.

1886 Haymarket bomb outrage.

NOTE-MAKING

Using the 1–2 method (see page x) make notes on immigration. These notes should include the significance of push and pull factors in the reasons for immigration as well as reactions to immigration.

American Federation of Labor

The union that now played a central role in the labour movement was the American Federation of Labor (AFL) set up by Samuel Gompers in 1885.

Less a single union than a federation of semi-independent craft associations, the AFL admitted only skilled white men. Its objectives were also comparatively limited; the federation focused only on achieving higher wages and shorter workdays for its members, forsaking the larger social objectives that had motivated the Knights. But the AFL did grow – by 1892 it claimed more than a quarter of a million members.

The AFL acknowledged the discontent provoked by the Knights and determined to avoid its mistakes. It recognised the autonomy of each trade within it and the executive council could not interfere in the internal affairs of member unions. It levied a tax on member unions to create a strike fund and maintain a secretariat. To promote labour legislation in the cities and states, it formed central and state federations.

The policy of the AFL was to support unions in winning recognition and securing agreements from employers by collective bargaining, and to strike, and to strike hard, only when these failed. Gompers was elected as its first president in 1896 and served in that capacity until his death in 1924.

WORKING TOGETHER

Work with a partner.
- One of you should identify any evidence of achievements/progress for the labour movement.
- The other should note any failings/shortcomings.
- Overall, how far do you agree that the labour movement made progress in this period?

Immigration, 1877–90

Why was there so much immigration to the USA during these years?

Prior to the Gilded Age, the time commonly referred to as the old immigration saw the first real boom of new arrivals to the United States. During the Gilded Age, approximately 10 million immigrants came to the United States in what is known as the new immigration. Some of them were prosperous farmers who had the cash to buy land and tools in the Plains states especially. Many were poor peasants looking for the American Dream in unskilled manual labour in mills, mines and factories. Few immigrants went to the poverty-stricken South. Of the 10 million who crossed the Atlantic between 1860 and 1890, the majority came from Britain and Ireland, Germany and Scandinavia, Switzerland and Holland.

Reasons for immigration

Historians analyse the causes of immigration in terms of push factors (pushing people out of their homeland) and pull factors (pulling them to America). The push factors included economic dislocation, shortages of land, and anti-Semitism. Pull factors were the economic opportunity of good inexpensive farmland or jobs in factories, mills and mines, particularly the rapid growth of American industry during these years and the need for cheap labour.

Pull factors

Prospective immigrants saw advertisements in guidebooks, pamphlets and newspapers. For example, the guidebook *Where to Emigrate and Why* was published by 'Americus' in 1869. It described journeys by land and sea, calculated the cost, and reported on wages in the United States. It was one of a series of advertisements that described the advantages of life in America such as the economic opportunity as well as political equality and religious tolerance.

Steamship was the main form of travel across the Atlantic and steamship companies also did much to advertise and promote the benefits of immigration to the USA. However, states and railroads bore an even greater role for stimulating immigration. State bureaus concentrated their efforts on Britain, Germany and Scandinavia. Their pamphlets and newspaper advertisements emphasised future prospects. In *Minnesota, The Empire State of the North-West* published in 1878, Minnesota claimed it could support five million people.

Some historians suggest that railroads were the most significant promotional agencies. They had vast tracts of land to dispose of and were able to offer transport to reach it. The Kansas Pacific, Santa Fe and Wisconsin Central all distributed pamphlets. The Santa Fe even appointed a European agent, C. B. Schmidt who, in 1875, visited Russia to promote immigration. The railroads' lavish inducements to immigrants included reduced fares by sea and land, loans at low rates of interest, classes in farming and the building of churches and schools.

Push factors

It was political, economic and religious discontent in Europe that stirred immigrants to leave. Throughout the nineteenth century, industrial and agricultural revolutions transformed European society. The additional pressure of increasing population provided the impetus for emigration. Such changes began in Western Europe and, as the century progressed, they spread to the east. The causes and sources of American immigration moved with them. More German immigrants arrived than any other ethnic group in all but three years from 1854 to 1894. Agricultural depression as well as industrial depression were strong push factors for immigrants from Britain, Norway and Sweden. In Ireland, the root cause of unemployment and poverty was agricultural mismanagement by absentee landlords.

The impulse for migration from Russia was as much political and religious as it was economic. The greatest exodus was of Russian Jews fleeing new persecution. The assassination of Alexander II in 1881 set off anti-Semitic riots in the south and west. The number of Jewish immigrants to America rose from 5,000 in 1880 to 90,000 in 1900.

Source E An extract from *Laughing in the Jungle* published in 1932. It was written by Louis Adamic who emigrated to the USA from Slovenia. From *America 1870–1975 Modern Times Sourcebooks* by J. O'Keeffe, (Longman), 1984, p. 22.

My notion of the United States was that it was a grand, amazing, somewhat fantastic place – the Golden Country – huge beyond conception, untellably exciting. In America one could make pots of money in a short space of time, wear a white collar and have polish on one's boots – and eat white bread, soup and meat on week days as well as on Sundays, even if one was but an ordinary workman to begin with. In America even the common people were 'citizens' not 'subjects', as they were in the Austrian Empire and most of Europe.

In 1885, a Japanese exodus began after the emperor revoked a ban on emigration. Japan's population growth was greater than that of any Western country. In the 1880s and 1890s most immigrants went to Hawaii to work on American sugar plantations as contract labourers.

Years	Numbers of immigrants
1866–70	1,513,101
1871–80	2,812,191
1881–90	5,246,613
1891–1900	3,687,564

▲ **Figure 1** A table showing immigration to the USA 1866–1900.

Write a few sentences to summarise the trend in immigration during this period (shown in Figure 1).

Anti-Semitic – Hostility towards or discrimination against Jews as a religious group or race.

What can you learn from Source E about reasons for immigration to the USA?

Like Europeans, the primary motive of Chinese immigrants was economic. The Taiping Rebellion that began in 1848 devastated south-east China. The lure of high wages on the railroads enticed men from the province of Guangdong. The Chinese comprised an overwhelming majority of the labourers who laid the track of the Central Pacific through Sierra Nevada in the 1860s. In the 1870 census, there were 63,000 Chinese men (with a few women) in the entire US population. This number grew to 106,000 in the 1880s.

Reactions to immigration

Without massive immigration the USA would not have developed industrially at anything like the rate it did. In 1890, 56 per cent of the labour force in manufacturing and mechanical industries was of foreign birth or foreign parentage. Immigrants themselves chose as a symbol of welcome and promise the Statue of Liberty on Staten Island in New York harbour. The gigantic statue, unveiled before President Cleveland on 28 October 1886, was a gift from France.

However, economic fear bred ethnic intolerance. Immigrants came to be regarded not as a source of strength but as a drain on American resources. This was especially true in the East, where most immigrants arrived and where the social system was hard and fast. Labour unions, led by Samuel Gompers strongly opposed the presence of Chinese labour because of competition for jobs. Congress banned further Chinese immigration through the Chinese Exclusion Act in 1882; the Act prohibited Chinese labourers from entering the United States, but some students and businessmen were allowed in on a temporary basis.

▲ 'Welcome to all' – a cartoon of 1880 which shows immigration to the USA. The cartoonist, Joseph Keppler, was, himself, an immigrant. How useful is this cartoon as evidence of attitudes towards immigration in the USA?

Even English immigrants did not escape criticism. The *New York Herald Tribune* wrote in 1879 that English workmen 'must change their habits if they are to make good in the United States'. In the 1880s, magazines such as *Harper's* and *Atlantic Monthly* included a great number of ethnic jokes, all prejudiced against newcomers. The Scots were depicted as mean and the Irish as ugly, brawling drunkards. All Italians, it was assumed, were involved in organised crime.

However, no group received as much abuse as the Jews. Anti-Semitism was not new to the USA as Jews had been barred from voting until the mid-nineteenth century. Social ostracism continued with the most famous example being the exclusion of the Jewish banker, Joseph Seligman, from the Grand Union Hotel in Saratoga, New York, in 1877. Hotels, clubs and colleges then began to turn Jews away. Some even displayed signs such as 'No Jews or dogs admitted here'.

Nativism

Indeed, immigration during these years increasingly divided US society. A great gulf was opening between a predominantly native plutocracy and a predominantly foreign working class. The USA was becoming two nations separated by language and religion, residence and occupation. Not only was the new tide of immigration depressing wages but also the closure of the frontier and settlement of available land in the West, sealed off the traditional escape route for discontented easterners (see pages 63–65). Thus, Americans began to lose confidence in the process of immigration and integration. The outcome was 'nativism'. Nativist agitation was the work of three groups: unions that regarded unskilled immigrants as a threat to organised labour; social reformers who believed the influx of immigrants exacerbated the problems of the cities; and Protestant conservatives who dreaded the supposed threat to Nordic supremacy.

Skilled workers had most to fear from immigration. After skilled Belgian and British glass workers were brought under contract to work for lower wages in Baltimore and in Kent, Ohio, the two unions of glass workers amalgamated. The new union, Local Assembly 300, set up in 1882, pledged to oppose contract labour. In 1885, a bill was passed by Congress which put a ban on foreign contract labour although this did not extend to skilled workers needed for new industries.

Moreover, Protestant extremists joined secret societies pledged to defend the school system against the enrolment of increasing numbers of Catholic school children, many of whom were from immigrant families. The most powerful was the American Protective Association set up in Clinton, Iowa, in 1887 by a lawyer, Henry F. Bowers.

> **Native plutocracy** – Wealthy, white Americans who controlled the government of the USA.
>
> **Nativism** – The policy of protecting the interests of native-born or established inhabitants against those of immigrants.
>
> **Nordic** – This relates to a group or physical type of the Caucasian race characterised by their tall stature, long head, light skin and hair, and blue eyes originating in Scandinavia.

WORKING TOGETHER

1 To what extent was it more pull than push factors that led to increased immigration to the USA in these years? Discuss this question in groups.

2 In order to gain a fuller understanding of reactions to immigrants, in your groups begin to itemise the different concerns. Write each one on a post-it note. Each group should then attach these to the wall or whiteboard. Compare the points raised by each group. Discuss what seem to be the key issues.

KEY DATES: IMMIGRATION

1882 Chinese Exclusion Act.

1885 Bill was passed by Congress which put a ban on foreign contract labour.

1886 Unveiling of Statue of Liberty in New York harbour.

1887 Setting up of the American Protective Association.

The lives of African Americans, 1877–90

To what extent did African Americans make progress in the years 1877–90?

After the end of Reconstruction in 1877 the civil rights that had been granted to African Americans were vulnerable to a growing racist tide of opinion that was at its most intense and virulent in the South but which also had an impact on the growing number living in the North. Poverty was still the norm for the majority of African Americans and the development of institutionalised segregation in the South ensured that civil rights were reduced rather than increased in this period. However, a minority of African Americans did make economic progress.

Migration and work

Emancipation did give African Americans the freedom to move to another plantation or another region. Between 1870 and 1900, the USA's black population almost doubled from 4.4 million to 7.9 million. The majority of African Americans remained in the South, with substantial numbers moving within the region. Primarily seeking higher income jobs, African Americans generally went south and west from the border states, with Alabama, Arkansas, Georgia, Louisiana, Mississippi, South Carolina and Texas registering the main gains. They found employment in farming, building railroads, making turpentine and lumbering.

Most African Americans in the South were tied to farming. Sharecroppers received artificially low prices for their produce and their 'masters' insisted that they continue to grow cotton or tobacco. It was an advantage to have cheap workers for such labour intensive crops. This gave many freedmen a living, but also meant that they suffered more than most when the boll weevil reached the southern states in 1892 and damaged the cotton crop.

However, there was a slow movement towards more landownership among African Americans although the vast majority were still sharecroppers. By 1910, 25 per cent of black farmers owned their land and their standard of living was rising.

Migration North

At the same time, the black population in the North and West practically doubled from about 460,000 to over 910,000, with migration accounting for half the increase. The flow of African Americans northwards during the Gilded Age had the effect of intensifying Northern white American awareness of and negative reactions to African Americans. A small group of African Americans moved into the New York district of Harlem in the 1880s and the first black ghetto began to develop. African Americans were frequently barred from trade unions and returned from work to poor quality housing.

In the North, African Americans did not find legally determined segregation but they frequently experienced discrimination and their range of employment opportunities, quality of housing, low level of education and effective confinement to specific areas meant that their quality of life did not significantly improve. However, there was the greater possibility of the franchise in the North and a strong black culture was developing.

NOTE-TAKING

Using a spider diagram (see page x), make notes on the following topics on African Americans: migration and work, formal segregation, the loss of the franchise, education.

Labour intensive crops – Cotton and tobacco required more workers than other crops because machinery could not always be used.

Boll weevil – An insect that attacked the cotton crop, eating its buds and flowers.

Ghetto – A densely populated area of a city inhabited by a socially and economically deprived minority.

Formal segregation in the South

Segregation in the South was developing even before the end of Reconstruction in 1877 and was especially noticeable in the states most heavily populated with African Americans. Jim Crow laws developed rapidly between 1887 and 1891, when eight states introduced formal segregation, three of them extending this to waiting room facilities.

The movement of African Americans to southern towns increased the fear of white Americans that African Americans would demand equality. The perception at the time was that African Americans were the underclass and there they must stay. This instinct was re-enforced by the increasingly popular theories of racism in the later nineteenth century. Theories of Social Darwinism asserted a hierarchy of races and provided some apparent justification for discrimination and segregation. The popular press often portrayed African Americans as lazy, intellectually weak and easily provoked to violence. White Southerners were persuaded that separation would reduce the clear racial tension of the time and avoid bloodshed. Separate facilities for the different races were provided and were supposed to be of the same standard. In reality, those provided for African Americans were of poorer quality.

The justices of the US Supreme Court in the 1880s 'shared with other whites a fundamental perception of Negroes as different'. For example, in 1883 the Court denied in *The Civil Rights Cases* that individuals' access to places of public accommodation such as hotels and theatres deserved statutory protection against racial discrimination.

The North
While in the South the Jim Crow laws became constitutionally justified, Northern states tried to rectify the situation. Massachusetts (1865), New York and Kansas (1874) already had civil rights statutes on their books. In 1884, Ohio and New Jersey passed civil rights laws and seven more states followed suit in 1885. By 1895, seventeen states had civil rights legislation on their books. Unfortunately, the statutes were weak, with few penalties and often lax enforcement.

> **Civil rights** – Having the vote in free elections; equal treatment under the law; equal opportunities, e.g. in education and work; freedom of speech, religion and movement.

The loss of franchise

National politics after Reconstruction showed a rapidly declining interest in African Americans on the part of the Republican Party. President Garfield believed that education would close the chasm between the races but did not live long enough to test this theory. His successor, Arthur, had little interest in African Americans. The 1884 election victory of Cleveland, a Democrat, disinclined to offend the white South, contributed to the diminishing enthusiasm for black equality.

White Americans in the South were determined to limit the political rights of African Americans. Many were furious that African Americans had gained the right to vote during the period of Reconstruction and some had even achieved political office. The Fifteenth Amendment of 1870 had outlawed voting discrimination on grounds of race. However, it had not outlawed discrimination because of gender or property ownership. Therefore, Southern states devised complex rules and imposed additional voting requirements (see page 86). By 1910, the near elimination of the African American vote was all but complete in the South.

Ida B. Wells (1862–1931)

Born to slave parents in Mississippi, Ida B. Wells' campaign against discrimination began in 1884 when she refused to give up her seat on a train to a white man. She was removed by force but then sued the railroad company. She showed great courage in publicly opposing lynching after some friends were lynched for so-called 'rape'. Wells also strongly supported women's rights and especially votes for women. Given the reforming atmosphere of the Progressive era she was frequently received sympathetically. However, she failed to gain any commitment from Congress or the President for a federal anti-lynching law so that the problem could be tackled in federal courts. The defence in the South, that a federal anti-lynching law would interfere with states' rights, always won the day.

KEY DATES: AFRICAN AMERICANS

1882 Senator Henry W. Blair of New Hampshire first introduced an education bill.

1883 The Supreme Court decision in *The Civil Rights Case*.

1892 An article by Ida B. Wells exposed the evils of lynching.

Oppression

Lynching had become commonplace during Reconstruction, often being encouraged and carried out by members of the Ku Klux Klan. The Gilded Age also saw the height of the lynching campaign against African Americans. The *Chicago Tribune* began to publish statistics about lynching in the early 1880s. Between 1882 and 1899 over 2,500 men and women were lynched. Accusations of rape, attacks on white women, and occasionally murder, were the usual excuses for a lynching, along with a host of lesser allegations. Ida B. Wells, a black newspaperwoman in Memphis, attacked the lynching fever in 1892 in a black newspaper, defending black males against a rape charge and exposing the lawlessness of lynching. She was run out of town for her article, and a mob destroyed the newspaper's office.

Lynching was often regarded as a public event, which even children occasionally attended. Southern governments and police forces did little to stop it. Cases were rarely brought to court and, if they were, the all-white juries would not convict.

Education

The education of African Americans was an issue that would not disappear during the Gilded Age. In 1882, Senator Henry W. Blair of New Hampshire first introduced an education bill that would have provided millions of dollars to southern black and white schools. The bill was rejected by Congress. For whites in the South, the danger was the extent to which an educated black community would upset the caste structure and destroy its labour system. 'We must have colored servants', an Alabama minister complained in 1891, 'for there is no other laboring class.'

The number of black students in school throughout the USA had doubled between 1877 and 1887, but still only two-fifths of eligible black children were enrolled. Schools, especially in rural areas, were often dirt-floored log houses without the bare essentials of desks and blackboards. When schools existed, they might stay open for a month or two then close so the children could pick cotton. White schools had much longer terms and better financing. State subsidies for African American schools were small and parents often had to make up the difference.

In the North, the pattern varied with mostly integrated schools in the Northeast and both separate and integrated schools in Pennsylvania and the Midwest. By the 1890s, segregated schools were slowly disappearing, most high schools accepted black applicants and colleges and universities admitted small numbers of African Americans.

WORKING TOGETHER

1 Working with a partner:
  ● One of you should identify any evidence of progress for African Americans in these years.
  ● The other should identify evidence of lack of progress.
2 Overall, to what extent did African Americans make progress in this period?

3 The end of the frontier and continued isolation

This section will explore the end of the frontier and the continued path of isolation during this period.

There was continued expansion Westward in the later 1870s and 1880s which brought further settlement on the Plains and significant developments in the lives of Native American Indians. However, in 1890 the Bureau of Census announced that the frontier was closed, that is, that there was no longer any discernible demarcation between frontier and settlement.

The lives of Native Americans, 1877–90

To what extent did the lifestyle of Native Americans on the Plains change in the years 1877–90?

By 1880, most Native Americans were settled on reservations and seven years later they held some 138 million acres, although much of it was unsuitable for agriculture. During the Gilded Age, there were significant attempts to integrate the Native Americans into the 'American' way of life.

Americanisation

The US government did attempt to reduce the problems of Native American mistreatment. For example, under Hayes renewed efforts were made to reform the Bureau of Indian Affairs and prevent corruption. However, even organisations sympathetic to the Native Americans, such as the Indian Rights Association, did not support the continuation of the Native American way of life. Instead, they encouraged the idea of 'Americanisation' and the end of the tribal culture. This would be achieved by getting Native Americans to learn English, become Christians and learn farming. Education was seen as essential to this process, with Congress providing funds to set up boarding schools where Native American children could be taught American skills and attitudes away from the influence of their parents. By 1899, $2.5 million was being spent each year on 148 boarding and 225 day schools for 20,000 children.

The Dawes Act

The climax of this integrationist policy came with the Dawes General Allotment Act of 1887. This was named after Senator Henry Dawes of Massachusetts and gave legal form to a piecemeal practice of many years' standing. It broke up reservation land into small units held by individuals or families. Each head of family could receive 160 acres (65 hectares) of farmland (or 320 acres of grazing land), each single male adult, 80 acres. Native Americans who accepted the allotments and 'adopted the habits of civilised life' were to be granted US citizenship after 25 years.

At the time it was praised by many reformers as a significant achievement as it would end tribal relationships. However, it has subsequently come in for heavy criticism. The Act assumed that Native Americans could be turned into farmers. Moreover, it was doomed to failure at a time of agricultural depression. Besides, no care was taken to provide Native Americans with arable land. After the awards were made, the surplus land was sold commercially. Most Indians had little understanding of what the Act entailed, since the idea of private property was alien to their culture. Within a very short time, most had sold or lost their land to whites and fallen into poverty.

NOTE-MAKING

Using the 1–2 method (see page x) make notes on the following topics: Americanisation, the Dawes Act and the Battle of Wounded Knee.

LOOK AGAIN

Look back at pages 25–7 in Chapter 1.

Remind yourself of the changes that took place to the lifestyle of Native Americans in the years after Civil War.

Bureau of Indian Affairs – Also known as the Office of Indian Affairs, set up in 1824 to centralise the work with Native Americans within the War Department.

In 1891, an amendment to the Dawes Act ended the policy of awarding 160 acres to heads of families. In the future, individual Native Americans were to be awarded 80 acres each, regardless of status. After the Dawes Act conditions on Native American reservations deteriorated rapidly and became nothing short of scandalous.

Source F From a speech by Chief Joseph in 1877. He was leader of the Nez Percé tribe who were forced onto a reservation in Oklahoma in 1877. From *The Gilded Age Perspectives on the Origins of Modern America*, C. Calhoun (ed.), (Rowman and Littlefield), 2007, p.171.

I have heard talk and talk, but nothing is done. Good words do not last long unless they amount to something. Words do not pay for my country, now overrun by white men. Good words will not give my people good health and stop them from dying. Good words will not get my people a home where they can live in peace and take care of themselves. I am tired of talk that comes to nothing. You might as well expect the rivers to run backwards as that any man that was born a free man should be contented when penned up and denied liberty to go where he pleases.

Source G An extract from *The Indian Heritage of America* by the historian M. Josephy Jr, published in 1968. From *America in the Gilded Age* by S. Cashman, (New York University Press), 1993, p.300.

Indian life was marked by poverty, squalor, disease, and hopelessness. In general, Indians received little or no education and were still treated as wards, incapable of self-government or making decisions for themselves. Whatever revenues the tribes received from land sales was dissipated, with virtually none of them going to assist the Indians to create sound foundations for the development of the human and economic resources of the reservation.

The Battle of Wounded Knee

The final tragedy for the Indians and triumph for the army came in 1890 when despairing Sioux in South Dakota rallied to the teachings of Wovoka who promised that if they took up a ceremonial dance their lands and power would be restored. The Ghost Dance craze spread rapidly and with such fervour that it soon alarmed white authorities. An effort to arrest Sitting Bull, one of the chiefs encouraging the Ghost Dance, led to his death. Bands of Lakota Sioux fled their reservations with the army in pursuit. In December 1890, nervous Seventh Cavalry fired into a group of Sioux at Wounded Knee. Some 200 Sioux – many of them women and children – died.

So did 31 soldiers. The 'battle' was an accident: neither side had really wanted to fight. The whole affair, an accident born of mutual distrust, misunderstanding and fear, epitomised relations between Plains Indians and Americans in the late nineteenth century.

Different views

Historians have differed in their views about the treatment of the Plains Indians. Some, such as M. Josephy Jr who wrote a series of sympathetic works in the 1960s and 1970s, have strongly criticised the destruction of the way of life of the Native Americans and their conditions on the reservations. In less than two decades, the Plains Indians' political, cultural, social and economic systems had been destroyed. The reservation policy led to physical disease, alcoholism, dependency and poverty. By 1900, only about 100,000 of the 240,000 Native Americans who had inhabited the Plains in 1865 remained. They had lost their land, their freedom, their pride and their self-respect.

1 What can you learn from Source F about the impact of Western expansion on Native Americans?

2 What does Source G suggest about life for Native Americans on the reservations?

3 How far does Chief Joseph support the views given in Source G?

Far from transforming them into Americans, it condemned them to become a people without a distinctive identity. They were and remained the poorest group of people in the USA.

By 1900, the Native Americans were left without the lands they had been given to them by treaty in the 1860s. They faced the kind of prejudice experienced by other ethnic groups in the US, particularly African Americans, when it came to exercising the right to vote.

However, other historians including Donald L. Parman, have defended the policy of the federal governments towards the Plains Indians. For those willing to adjust to the white man's expectations, reservations offered chances for economic self-sufficiency. Others found off-reservation jobs. Most notable were Native American performers who toured with the Wild West shows. Buffalo Bill hired between 75 and 100 Native Americans during the 1880s.

In addition, there were so many different views about how to deal with Native Americans it was difficult to agree a consistent policy. Some favoured suppression and others favoured Americanisation. Furthermore, there has been a tendency to glorify the Plains Indians. However, they also fought brutally, slaughtering white settlers, sometimes torturing their captives to death. No prisoners were taken at the Little Bighorn. Even with the benefit of hindsight, it is difficult to come up with a better solution than a reservation policy – given American settlers' determination to occupy the West.

1 Make a copy of and complete the scales.

Criticisms of treatment of Native Americans

Defence of the treatment of Native Americans

2 To what extent do you believe the treatment of Native Americans has been exaggerated?

KEY DATES: THE LIVES OF NATIVE AMERICANS

1887 The Dawes Act.

1890 Massacre at Wounded Knee.

NOTE-MAKING

Using bullet points (see page x) make notes on the key features of settlement in the West.

Settlement in the West, 1877–90

What changes took place in the West in this period?

Westward expansion was greatly facilitated by the development of railways with significant developments in farming and ranching during the Gilded Age.

The impact of the railways

The opening of the Pacific Railway had an important impact on the movement west. However, by the 1890s, there were four other transcontinental lines.

- The Northern Pacific, completed in 1883, stretched from Duluth, Minnesota to Portland, Oregon.
- The Southern Pacific, linking New Orleans with San Francisco, was also completed in 1883.
- The Atchison, Topeka and Santa Fe, linking Kansas City with Los Angeles and San Diego, was completed in 1884.
- The Great Northern, extending westwards from St Paul, Minnesota reached the Pacific coast at Seattle, in 1893.

All these transcontinental railroads built numerous branch lines and by 1900 the West accounted for nearly half the national total. All these railways were partly financed by generous land grants from the federal government – 70 million hectares of land in total. In addition, the states helped financially by advancing $200 million as well as land grants totalling 19 million hectares.

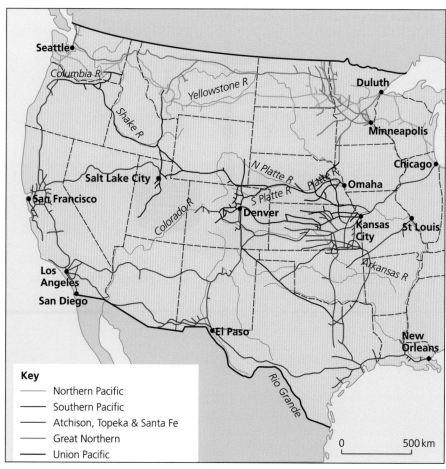

Key
—— Northern Pacific
—— Southern Pacific
—— Atchison, Topeka & Santa Fe
—— Great Northern
—— Union Pacific

0   500 km

▲ **Figure 2** A map showing the main railroad lines in the West.

There was corruption involved with most railroad companies bribing state and federal politicians. It was the price that had to be paid for opening up the West. The railways did bring substantial benefits both nationally and to the West:

- The alternate sections of land it retained along the railroad tracks fetched twice the normal price of $1.25 an acre and government traffic on the land-grant lines enjoyed a 50 per cent discount.
- They revolutionised the West, ensuring that a flood of people (and goods) moved in and an abundance of raw materials moved out.
- The railroads greatly stimulated the growth of the iron, steel, lumber and other capital goods industries.
- The new West of cattlemen and farmers was largely the product of the railroads.

Life on the Plains

Most settlers who went westwards earned their living from the land. A few were ranchers, cowboys and shepherds. But most depended on crops for their livelihood. The Plains presented huge challenges to new settlers.

- The nearest neighbours were often miles away, a problem for women who were about to give birth.
- While the soil was rich, pioneer families fought a constant battle with the elements – tornadoes, hailstorms, droughts, prairie fires, blizzards and pests. Swarms of locusts would sometimes cover the ground 15cm deep, consuming everything in their path.
- If land was relatively cheap, horses, livestock, wagons, wells, fencing and seed-sand fertilisers were not. Freight charges and interest rates on loans were often cripplingly high.

Agriculture

Most of the problems of Plain's agriculture were overcome sufficiently to make farming possible and even, occasionally, profitable. This was helped by important new inventions and processes. Dry farming methods enabled farmers to grow particular types of corn and wheat even when there was scant rainfall. American factories turned out an ever-increasing quantity of farm machinery including reapers, threshing machines, binders and combine harvesters – making possible wheat and maize farming on a colossal scale. In 1873, Joseph Glidden produced the first effective barbed wire, making it possible to fence land cheaply. Deep-drilled wells and steel windmills provided much-needed water.

The results of this newly expanded agriculture were truly phenomenal. American production of wheat increased from 211 million bushels in 1867 to 599 million bushels in 1900. The Department of Labor calculated that whereas it took 35 hours of labour in 1840 to produce fifteen bushels of wheat, it took only fifteen hours in 1900. American wheat exports rose from 6 million bushels in 1867 to 102 million in 1900.

However, this soon became boom and bust agriculture, very heavily dependent on exports and the fluctuating price of wheat. Western farmers were thus unable to determine the price of things they bought and sold, and most suffered in the 1870s as cereal prices tumbled as a result of a glut on the American and world markets. Corn, which sold for 78 cents a bushel in 1867, fell to 31 cents a bushel by 1873. Farmers who had borrowed heavily to finance their homestead and to purchase machinery went bankrupt.

The situation for farmers improved in the late 1870s as cereal prices rose. But over the next two decades economic boom and bust was the norm on the Plains. In the bust years of the late 1880s and early 1890s many hard-hit Plains' farmers were almost in open revolt against big business and state and federal governments. Most supported the Populist – or People's – Party (see page 73). The Populists called for government control of transport and communications, a graduated income tax, regulation of monopolies and utilities and more silver in the currency, ensuring there was more money in circulation. Populist presidential candidate James B. Weaver won a million votes in 1892.

Cattle and ranching

At the end of the Civil War the ranching frontier was based in Texas. Its climatic conditions were ideal for raising cattle and its new land use policies drafted during the administration of Governor John Ireland enabled individuals to accumulate land. It allowed its ranchers to acquire grazing land at 50 cents an acre. In 1867, Joseph McCoy devised a route whereby cattle could be driven north from southern Texas to Abilene, Kansas, along the Chisholm Trail to the west of any settlement. The journey was known as the Long Drive. From Abilene, the Kansas and Pacific Railroad transported cattle to the slaughterhouses of Chicago. Between 1866 and 1885 a total of 5.71 million cattle went north by this route.

In 1868, Philip D. Armour established a meatpacking business in Chicago, and he was followed by Gustavus Swift and Nelson Morris. Meatpacking made use of the assembly-line process long before it was adopted in industry. Each worker had a particular task on the line. *The Jungle*, a novel written in 1906 by the American journalist and novelist Upton Sinclair, vividly portrays the harsh conditions and exploited lives of immigrants in the meatpacking business of Chicago.

As the railroads and farming frontiers extended further westwards, new trails came into being, new railheads eclipsed Abilene, and new cattle towns – Ellsworth, Wichita and Dodge City – developed. Other herds were driven on a second long drive to be fattened or to stock the ranches of Colorado, Wyoming, Montana and the Dakotas.

The Chisholm Trail

The Chisholm Trail was a trail used in the post-American Civil War era to drive cattle overland from ranches in Texas to Kansas railheads. The portion of the trail marked by Jesse Chisholm went from his southern trading post near the Red River, to his northern trading post near Kansas City, Kansas. Texas ranchers using the Chisholm Trail started on that route from either the Rio Grande or San Antonio, Texas, and went to the railhead of the Kansas Pacific Railway in Abilene, Kansas, where the cattle would be sold and shipped eastward.

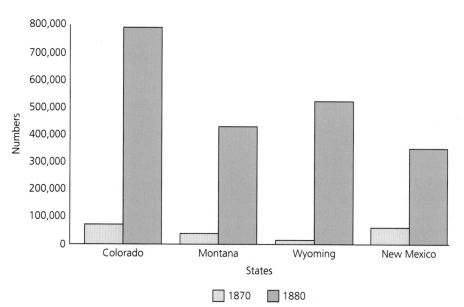

▲ **Figure 3** A graph showing the growth in numbers of cattle in states in the West, 1870–80.

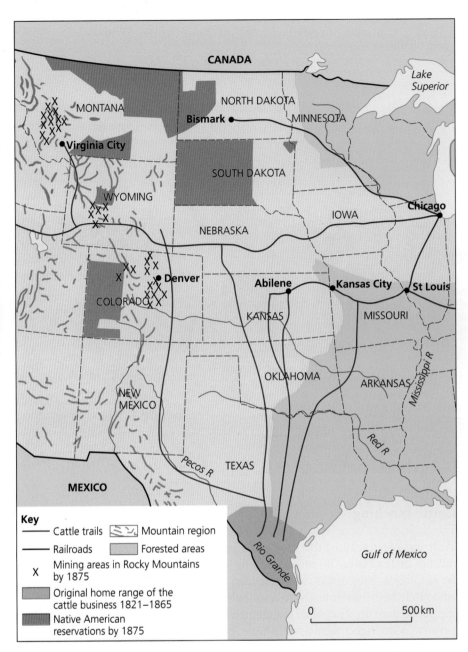

▲ **Figure 4** A map showing the main cattle trails and railroads in the late 1800s.

Cowboys

During the heyday of the long drive and open range, cowboys were the kings of the road. In the twenty years after the Civil War 40,000 cowboys roamed the Plains. Most were in their teens or early twenties. They came from diverse backgrounds. Some were ex-Confederate soldiers seeking adventure. Perhaps a third were Mexican, African Americans, Asian or Native American. Almost all were expert horsemen, an essential skill given that cowboys virtually lived on horseback for the two months that most cattle drives took.

Cowboy life was rarely as glamorous as the dime novel of the time or cinema and television since has depicted it. For a wage of only $25–30 a month, the average cowboy worked an eighteen-hour day, mostly in the saddle, trying to coax forward a sprawling mass of cattle, coping with a continuous cloud of dust, and facing a variety of other potential hazards – floods, poisonous snakes and scorpions, blizzards, stampedes, rustlers and occasionally Native Americans. At journey's end, cowboys not surprisingly whooped it up in the cattle towns.

BRANDING CATTLE ON THE PRAIRIES OF TEXAS—MIRAGE IN THE BACKGROUND.—FROM A SKETCH BY JAMES E. TAYLOR.—SEE PAGE 237.

▲ Cowboys branding cattle on the prairies. This is a woodcut made from a sketch by James E. Taylor, 1867.

Cattle-ranching

The cattle drives were relatively short lived. As railroad lines spread across the West, cattlemen realised that they could best function by establishing cattle ranches on the Plains. By 1880, ranching had spread northwards from Texas as far as Canada. Huge tracts of grazing land were quickly appropriated by ranchers who rarely bothered (initially) to acquire legal title to what was still almost wholly the public domain. They then maintained their position by force, fraud and perjury. Water rights were usually more important than land rights: whoever controlled the water effectively controlled the land. Disputes over land and water rights and rustling of livestock were endemic, often leading to violence between ranchers. Vigilante systems quickly sprang up, providing a measure of order.

Leading ranchers also banded together to form livestock associations which developed a code of rules defining land and water rights and the recording of cattle brands. The associations operated reasonably effectively in most cases but they were by no means universally popular. Some behaved arbitrarily and sometimes unjustly, often favouring big ranchers at the expense of small.

The greatest boom in the open range cattle trade came in the early 1880s when Eastern and European investors poured money into the 'Beef Bonanza'. By 1883, British companies owned or controlled nearly 8 million hectares of western grazing land. By the mid-1880s the open range cattle business thus resembled the kind of large-scale corporate enterprise characteristic of US industry in the late nineteenth century. The Swan Land & Cattle Company of Wyoming, for example, owned a huge area of land on which roamed 100,000 head of cattle. Cowboys, in effect, became farmhands, riding only that part of the range that was owned (or controlled) by their employer.

The end of the open range

Two exceptionally severe winters between 1885 and 1887, straddling a summer drought, resulted in the deaths of millions of western cattle (possibly 90 per cent of the total). Thousands of cattlemen (including the Swan Land & Cattle Company) were ruined. Most of those who survived retreated into the security of smaller, fenced-in ranches (using barbed wire to enclose land actually owned), equipped with shelter for their animals against the elements. Such methods ensured that cattle could be more scientifically bred. By 1890, the days of the open range and the cowboy were effectively over. But the rise of the open range cattle industry, aided by the extension of the railroads and the development of the refrigerator carriage (introduced in 1875), had changed the nation's eating habits: Americans became a primarily beef-eating rather than a pork-eating people.

The end of the frontier

Settling the West meant losing the wilderness and that 'uncivilised' part of the American continent. To some Americans this meant losing the essence of America – freedom. In 1890, the US Census Bureau declared:

'Up to and including 1880 the country had a frontier or settlement, but at present the unsettled area has been so broken into isolated bodies of settlement there can hardly be said to be a frontier line. In the discussion of its extent, its westward movement, etc., it cannot, therefore, any longer have a place in census reports.'

So officially there was no longer a frontier. For the first time in American history there was no large tract of unsettled land.

The Turner essay

One individual to have a strong impact on American history and philosophy, illustrating the key issue of the significance of individuals in this period, was Frederick Jackson Turner. In 1893, Turner, a young historian, presented a conference paper entitled *The Significance of the Frontier in American History*. Turner had grown up in Wisconsin, where the pioneering life was still remembered, but in contrast, had been educated in the East at Johns Hopkins University in Baltimore, where the influences of European manners and expectations were still strong. Turner's key points aroused much debate. He claimed:

- at the deepest root of America's past had been 'the existence of an area of free land'
- that accessible land, as in the West, acted as a safety valve against social discord and violence
- the harshness of the frontier created self-reliant individuals, who were invaluable in a nation like the USA
- that America's development had been different from that of Europe as it had no hierarchy or aristocracy relying on privileges of birth to create social class
- that the USA had a unique form of democracy. It was the abundance of nature and its resources, so visible in the West, that made America free.

Source H An extract from Turner's conference paper of 1893.

Thus American development has exhibited not merely advance along a single line, but a return to primitive conditions on a continually advancing frontier line, and a new development for that area. American social development has been continually beginning over again on the frontier. This ... fluidity of American life, this expansion westward – with its few opportunities, its continuous touch with the simplicity of primitive society, furnish the forces dominating American character. The true point of view in the history of this nation is not the Atlantic coast, it is the Great West. Even the slavery struggle, which is made so exclusive an object of attention ... occupies its important place in American history because of its relation to westward expansion.

In what ways does Turner stress the importance of the West to the development of the USA (Source H)?

Turner's ideas encouraged people, and notably the presidents of the time, to think that if frontiers and all they represented had made the USA unique, then perhaps the USA should have new frontiers, frontiers that were outside the geographic boundary of the nation. Turner's ideas also helped to create an idea or myth of the frontier lands – that the 'West' was different. It was essential to the image of a strong America.

Turner was simply proposing a new way of looking at American history. However, his frontier thesis has subsequently come in for much heavy criticism.

- In 1942, in *The Frontier and American Institutions: A Criticism of the Turner Thesis*, Professor George Wilson Pierson debated the validity of the Turner thesis, stating that many factors influenced American culture besides the looming frontier. Although he respected Turner, Pierson strongly argues his point by looking beyond the frontier and acknowledging other factors in American development.
- Ray Allen Billington in *Westward Expansion, a History of the American Frontier*, published in 1949 notes that Turner never actually defines the frontier and challenges the view that the frontier was some sort of safety valve for urban dwellers. Subsequent research has demonstrated that most of the free land of the West was bought up by land speculators, and that most of the migration in the nineteenth century was to the cities, not to the frontier.
- More recently Glenda Riley has argued that Turner's thesis ignored women. She argues that his context and upbringing led him to ignore the female section of society, which directly led to the frontier becoming an exclusively male phenomenon.
- Many other criticisms were levelled at the thesis, including that it rested on hasty generalisations, that it ignored the role of immigrants and Indians, and that it promoted provincialism.

Source I From 'The Turner Thesis: A Historian's Controversy' by J. A. Burkhart in *The Wisconsin Magazine of History, Vol. 31, No. 1*, September 1947, (Wisconsin Historical Society Stable), pp.70–83.

Nonetheless, some of the aspects of Turner's writing stand corrected and other phrases require further study and exploration. It is quite likely that the West was not ... a safety valve for the oppressed industrial laborer after the Civil War. Moreover, it appears that Turner generalized too much for the whole West on the basis of his knowledge of the Old Northwest. He probably emphasized too strongly the peculiaristic [distinctive] character of the American experience, and he may have overshadowed the influence of other forces with his constant insistence on the significance of the frontier in American life and history. Undoubtedly this is true in respect to democracy. Turner did not credit sufficiently European influences in accounting for the growth and development of American democratic institutions. Finally, it appears that Turner was a bit too enthusiastic for the frontier as a character and personality.

1 In what ways does the article in Source I criticise the Turner essay?
2 To what extent do you agree with these criticisms?

KEY DATES: SETTLEMENT IN THE WEST

1867 Joseph McCoy devised a route whereby cattle could be driven north from southern Texas to Abilene.

1868 Philip D. Armour established a meatpacking business in Chicago.

1893 The Turner essay.

WORKING TOGETHER

Set up a class debate to assess whether Turner gave an accurate interpretation of the significance of the frontier for American history. You could use the motion:

'This class believes that Turner gave an accurate view about the importance of the frontier in American history'.

Foreign and imperial policies

To what extent did the USA remain isolationist in this period?

There was limited interest in foreign policy and imperial expansion in the 1870s and 1880s with isolationism continuing to dominate. However, there was increasing support for an expanded navy to protect US possessions and guarantee America's position as a world power.

Navy

During Arthur's administration politicians began to show a greater interest in foreign policy and called for an expanded navy to demonstrate American willingness to back it up with force if necessary. A nation without a navy, they argued, could make little headway in world affairs in an age of sea power. As early as 1882 the Secretary of the Navy, William H. Hunt, was advocating naval expansion after a review he commissioned found that, of 140 ships on the naval list, only 42 were operational, and the navy still mainly comprised wooden sailing vessels as opposed to more modern steamships. Of only seventeen steamships, fourteen dated from the Civil War period. Representative John D. Long of Massachusetts described it as 'an alphabet of floating tubs'.

The most famous advocate of naval expansion was Captain Alfred Thayer Mahan who wrote two hugely influential books, *The Influence of Sea Power Upon History* in 1890 and *The Influence of Sea Power Upon the French Revolution and Empire* two years later. Mahan argued that history proved that nations with powerful navies and overseas bases to maintain them would grow in strength. He advocated building a modern steam fleet, building coaling stations and bases in the Caribbean and Pacific Ocean and cutting a canal across Latin America in order to facilitate communication and trade.

Hawaii

During the eighteenth century, the United States became interested in the Hawaiian Islands as a way station and provisioning point for shippers, sailors and whalers trading with Asian nations. Since 1875, the USA had imported Hawaiian sugar free of duty in return for the Hawaiian Government refusing concessions such as the importation of manufactured goods to other countries. This meant that Hawaii was effectively reliant on the USA economically. In 1887, the Senate agreed to the renewed and expanded form of the 1875 treaty of friendship with Hawaii negotiated by Secretary of State Thomas F. Bayard. Bayard had secured a new concession, permission to establish a naval base at Pearl Harbor on the island of Oahu.

Latin America

In the 1880s, American politicians expressed particular interest in Latin America. President Garfield's Secretary of State, James Blaine, first advocated a Pan-American conference in 1881. He believed that the USA should act both as a leader across the continent to prevent future wars and conflicts, and that all countries would benefit from greater trade links. His proposal came to nothing due to Garfield's short-lived presidency. However, it was resurrected when Blaine became Secretary of State under Benjamin Harrison.

Delegates from eighteen countries met in Washington in October 1889 with two main aims – a customs union offering free trade across the continent and a system for international arbitration to avoid future wars. Delegates eventually settled for reciprocity agreements and a weak arbitration system which was signed by less than half of them and gave signatories an opt-out clause if they

NOTE-MAKING

Using a spider diagram (see page x) summarise the key developments in foreign and imperial policy in these years.

Concessions – Favourable trading rights.

Pan-American – Relating to all countries on the American continent.

Arbitration – Where two opposing sides go to a neutral body for a judgement in their dispute.

KEY DATES: FOREIGN AND IMPERIAL POLICIES

1887 Acquisition of Hawaii as a naval base.

1889 Pan-American Conference.

1890 Publication of Mahan's book *The InfluenceofSeaPowerUponHistory*.

felt arbitration would threaten their right to independent action. However, they did agree to setting up an International Bureau of American Republics, also known as the Pan-American Union, to organise future conferences. The Conference and its agreements had, at least, set the precedent for future conferences and co-operation.

Chapter summary

- The Gilded Age was the name given by Mark Twain due to the corruption and greed of this period.
- Successive presidents did try to reduce corruption, particularly through reform of the civil service.
- The economy was dominated by wealthy industrialists and financiers who were described as the 'robber barons'.
- The economy continued to expand partly due to inventors such as Edison and Bell.
- This period saw the first serious attempts at labour organisation.
- There was mass immigration to America due to push and pull factors.
- Segregation and discrimination against African Americans, especially in the South, became firmly established.
- The Native Americans of the Plains were Americanised and confined to reservations.
- Settlement in the West led to growth in agriculture and cattle ranching.
- 1890 marked the end of the frontier and, three years later, Turner's famous essay on the significance of the West.

▼ Summary diagram: The Gilded Age c.1877–90

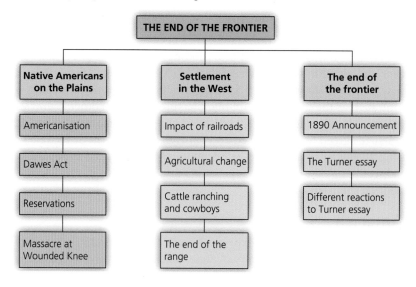

Working on essay technique: analysis

Analysis is a term that covers a variety of high level skills including explanation and evaluation. In essence, analysis means breaking down something complex into smaller parts. This means that a clear structure which breaks down a complex question into a series of paragraphs is the first step towards writing an analytical essay.

Explanation

The purpose of explanation is to account for why something happened, or why something is true or false. An explanatory statement requires two parts: a *claim* and a *justification*.

EXAMPLE

Imagine you are answering the following A-level practice question:

'The most important reason for expansion West in the years 1865–90 was the development of the railroads.' Assess the validity of this view.

(25 marks)

You might want to argue that one important example was the impact of the railroads on the cattle industry. Once you have made this point, and supported it with relevant detail, you can then explain how this answers the question.

For example, you could conclude your paragraph like this:

Railroads were the most important ●────── Claim
reason for expansion West because ●────── Relationship
they encouraged the development and
Justification ──● growth of the cattle industry as well as
encouraging land settlement.

The first part of this sentence is the claim while the second part justifies the claim. 'Because' is a very important word to use when writing an explanation, as it shows the relationship between the claim and the justification.

Evaluation

The purpose of evaluation is to weigh up and reach a judgement. Evaluation, therefore, needs to consider the importance of two or more different factors, weigh them against each other, and then reach a judgement. Evaluation is a good skill to use at the end of an essay because the conclusion should reach a judgement which answers the question.

EXAMPLE

Consider the following A-level practice question:

'The greatest threat to the position of African Americans in the South in the years 1865–90 was formal segregation.' Assess the validity of this view. (25 marks)

If you were answering this question you might want to weigh up the extent to which formal segregation was the greatest threat against other threats such as the Ku Klux Klan, violence and lynching.

For example, your conclusion might read:

Clearly, formal segregation was the greatest threat because of the introduction of the Jim Crow laws which developed rapidly between 1887 and 1891, when eight states introduced formal segregation, three of them extending this to waiting room facilities. However, more physically threatening were the activities of the Ku Klux Klan which led to often extreme violence against African Americans including a significant growth in the number of lynchings of African Americans during these years. Therefore physical threats were a significant threat to the lives of African Americans.

In this example the evaluation is helped by using a series of words (highlighted) that help to weigh up the importance of the factors. 'However' and 'Nonetheless' are useful words as they can help contrast the importance of the different factors.

ACTIVITY

Consider the practice question in the example above.

1 Using your notes from this chapter, write a paragraph about the threat posed by formal segregation. Make sure the paragraph:
   • begins with a clear point that clearly focuses on the question
   • develops the point with at least three pieces of accurate detail
   • concludes with explanation: a claim and a justification.
2 Write a conclusion to the essay in which you weigh up at least two factors (i.e. formal segregation and at least one other factor) and reach a judgement about the threat posed by formal segregation by comparing that factor with the other(s).

A-LEVEL PRACTICE QUESTION

'The main effect of increased immigration to the USA in the years 1865–90 was the growth of nativism.' Assess the validity of this view.
(25 marks)

Use the above question to practise all of the essay techniques that you have learnt so far.

Working on interpretation skills

Section A of the exam paper is different from Section B (see page 32). Unlike Section B, it contains extracts from the work of historians, and the questions are compulsory with no choices. Significantly, this section tests different skills. In essence, Section A tests your ability to analyse different historical interpretations. Therefore, you must focus on the interpretations outlined in the extracts. The advice given in this chapter on interpretations is for both the AS and the A-level exams.

- For the AS exam, there are two extracts and you are asked which is the more convincing interpretation (25 marks).
- For the A-level exam, there are three extracts and you are asked how convincing the arguments are in relation to a specified topic (30 marks).

An interpretation is a particular view on a topic of history held by a particular author or authors. Interpretations of an event can vary, for example, depending on how much weight an historian gives to a particular factor and whether they largely ignore another factor.

The interpretations that you will be given will be largely from recent or fairly recent historians.

Interpretations and evidence

The extracts given in the exam will contain a mixture of interpretations and evidence. The mark scheme rewards answers that focus on the *interpretations* offered by the extracts much more highly than answers that focus on the *information or evidence* mentioned in the extracts. Therefore, it is important to identify the interpretations.

- *Interpretations* are a specific kind of argument. They tend to make claims such as 'Big businessmen of the Gilded Age were robber barons'.
- *Information or evidence* tends to consist of specific details, for example about the political and economic dominance and control of businessmen such as Carnegie in this period.

Analysis of an interpretation

We start by looking at an individual extract and seeing how we can build up skills. This is the essential starting point for both the AS and the A-level style of question on interpretations. The AS mark scheme shows a very clear progression of thought processes:

Level 5	Answers will display a good understanding of the interpretations given in the extracts. They will evaluate the extracts thoroughly in order to provide a well-substantiated judgement on which offers the more convincing interpretation. The response demonstrates a very good understanding of context. *21–25 marks*
Level 4	Answers will display a good understanding of the interpretations given in the extracts. There will be sufficient comment to provide a supported conclusion as to which offers the more convincing interpretation. However, not all comments will be well-substantiated, and judgements may be limited. The response demonstrates a good understanding of context. *16–20 marks*
Level 3	The answer will show a reasonable understanding of the interpretations given in the extracts. Comments as to which offers the more convincing interpretation will be partial and/or thinly supported. The response demonstrates an understanding of context. *11–15 marks*
Level 2	The answer will show some partial understanding of the interpretations given in the extracts. There will be some undeveloped comment in relation to the question. The response demonstrates some understanding of context. *6–10 marks*
Level 1	The answer will show a little understanding of the interpretations given in the extracts. There will be only unsupported, vague or generalist comment in relation to the question. The response demonstrates limited understanding of context. *1–5 marks*

Now study Extract A and the practice question below, which is about big business during the Gilded Age.

With reference to the extract [A] and your understanding of the historical context, how convincing do you find the extract in relation to the impact of big business in the years 1865–90?

To help you answer this type of question you need to assess the interpretation in the extract. Carry out activities 1–5 below to help you do this.

Extract A

No income tax impeded the swift accumulation of private fortunes; no labor laws or workmen's compensation acts interfered with their profits; no government officials told them how to run their business. Political power and social prestige naturally gravitated to big business, to the corporations. As a matter of course they exerted a decisive influence on politics and parties. They controlled newspapers and magazines, subsidized candidates, bought legislation and even judicial decisions. The greatest of them such as John D. Rockefeller or J. P. Morgan, treated state governors as servants, and Presidents as equals, in the exercise of power. Wealth dominated the political, economic and social scene.

Adapted from *The Growth of the American Republic* by S. Morison, H. Commager and W. Leuchtenburg, (Oxford University Press), 1969.

Extract B

During the Gilded Age there appeared the big businessmen such as Rockefeller and Carnegie and the powerful and influential institution – the corporation. The new giants of business embraced and began to shape technology and science to nourish and serve the culture of consumption that defines modern America. Big business and more especially the corporations drove American economic growth. It is also important to note that the change did not occur mostly or merely as a result of conspiracies or uncontrolled greed. The 'robber barons' explanation is too simple and too convenient.

Adapted from *The Gilded Age: Perspectives of the Origins of America* by C. W Calhoun, ed., (Rowman and Littlefield), 2007.

ACTIVITY

1 What is the argument for the interpretation in Extract A? (Is it arguing that big business had a positive or negative influence?)
2 What evidence can you find in the extract to support the argument? (What examples are mentioned to support the interpretation?)
3 What do you know (that is, contextual knowledge) that supports these claims?
4 What contextual knowledge do you have to contradict these claims?

5 Using your judgement, are the arguments in support stronger than the arguments against, or vice versa?

Look back at the mark scheme on page 69, and see how your answers might match up to the levels shown there.

In relation to Extract A's assertions about big business, you should be able to find arguments both to support and to contradict. Remember, you can apply this approach when responding to other similar questions.

Comparing two interpretations

As part of the building up of skills, we move on to comparing two interpretations. Activity 6 is the format of the AS question, but will also be useful in the process of gaining confidence for A-level students.

ACTIVITY

6 Consider the AS-level practice question below.

With reference to these extracts and your understanding of the historical context, which of these two extracts provides the more convincing interpretation of the impact of business on the USA in the years 1865–90?   (25 marks)

Follow the same five steps for Extract B as you did for Extract A in the activity on page 70 then compare the results of the two and come to a conclusion about which extract provides the must convincing interpretation.

Then compare your results. Do you have more in support for Extract A and/or Extract B for Question 3 than Question 4? Or is it the other way round? Is it the same for both extracts?

This should give you the direction of your overall conclusion and judgement about which of the extracts is more convincing.

Remember that the top two levels of the mark scheme refer to 'supported conclusion' (Level 4) and 'well-substantiated conclusion' (Level 5). For Level 4, 'Supported conclusion' means finishing your answer with a judgement that is backed up with some accurate evidence drawn from the extract(s) and your knowledge. For Level 5, 'well-substantiated conclusion' means finishing your answer with a judgement that is very well supported with evidence and, where relevant, reaches a complex conclusion that reflects a wide variety of evidence.

There is no one correct way to write the answer! However, the principles are clear. In particular, contextual knowledge should be used *only* to back up an argument. None of your knowledge should be 'free-standing', i.e. in the question in Activity 6, there should not be a paragraph saying what you know about the topic (in this case big business), unrelated to the extracts. All your knowledge should be used in context. For each extract in turn:

- Explain the evidence in the extract, backed up with your own contextual knowledge. In this example, for the negative impact of big business.
- Explain the points in the extract where you have evidence that contradicts the negative impact of big business.

Then write a conclusion that reaches a judgement on which is more convincing as an interpretation.

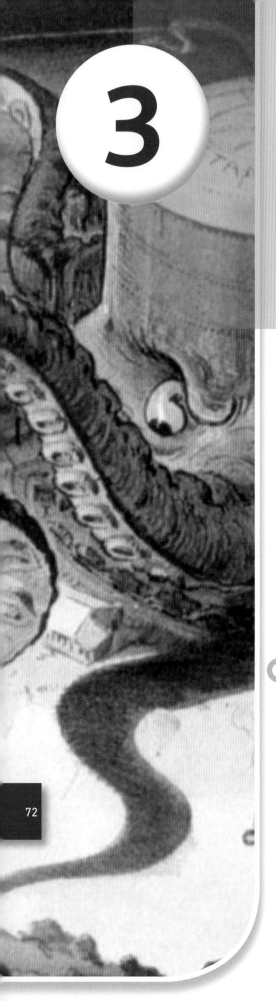

3

Progressivism and Imperialism, the USA 1890–1912

This chapter covers developments in the USA from 1890 to 1912, when Woodrow Wilson won the presidential election. It deals with a number of areas:

- The Populist movement.
- The emergence of Progressivism and its significance.
- Economic and social change.
- Foreign and imperial policies.

When you have worked through the chapter and the related activities and exercises, you should have detailed knowledge of all those areas, and you should be able to relate this to the key breadth issues defined as part of your study, in particular: How did the role of the USA in world affairs change in this period and how important were ideas and ideology? For the period covered in this chapter the main focus can be phrased as a question:

In what ways did the role of the USA in international affairs change in this period?

The focus of the issue is on the motives for imperial policy and the importance of the Spanish–American War of 1898.

CHAPTER OVERVIEW

There were profound political, economic and social changes during this period. Politically, the Populist Party and the Progressive Movement greatly influenced the policies of Presidents Roosevelt and Taft. Economically, despite continued industrial growth, the USA experienced a second major depression in 1893. Mass immigration, stimulated by economic expansion, had a major impact on the racial and ethnic mix as well as the living conditions of many towns and cities, especially in the more industrialised North. African Americans continued to experience institutionalised segregation and discrimination in the South while those that moved North to seek work in industry suffered from inferior living and working conditions. This was also a period of significant change in American foreign and imperial policies particularly in the years that followed the Spanish–American War of 1898.

1 The Populist movement and political protest

In the 1890s a new political party, the Populists, developed in the southern and western parts of the USA.

Reasons for the emergence of the Populists

Why did the Populist Party emerge in the 1890s?

There were many who did not benefit from the economic growth of the USA. In 1893, there was a depression that bankrupted many businesses. Moreover, most farmers felt that they were not benefiting from American prosperity. A Populist movement emerged which consisted of farmers, working people and supporters of silver. This new party was opposed to 'big business', especially in north-west America, which was getting an increasingly bad press.

Silver

Traditionally, the USA followed the Gold Standard. The coinage was minted from gold and paper currency had to be convertible into gold. However, bimetallists felt silver should be used in the production of coinage as well as gold. World production of gold had decreased between 1865 and 1890 whereas there had been a rapid growth in the production of silver in the USA after its discovery in Nevada and other Rocky Mountain states, from just over $150,000 dollars in 1860 to $57 million 30 years later. Pressure from the silver industry led to the Sherman Silver Purchase Act of 1890 which meant that the government would buy 4,500,000 ounces of silver each month at market price and use it in the production of coinage.

To the conservatives this reform was abhorrent. It threatened to undermine the economy, isolate the USA from Europe and increase government interference in business. Therefore, in 1896, President Grover Cleveland removed this measure, believing that the confidence of the business community had been lost because of the use of silver in the coinage. This angered the supporters of silver who were based mainly in the western areas of the USA.

Agricultural discontent

There was much discontent among farmers. This was partly because of falling prices, especially in wheat and cotton. In 1860, wheat was sold at $1.60 a bushel and had fallen to 60 cents by 1890. In the same period, cotton fell from 30 cents a bushel to 6 cents. Moreover, high tariffs on foreign goods meant that foreigners would not buy US agricultural products and the USA faced increasing competition for European markets from Australia, Russia and Canada. To make matters worse, harvests deteriorated from the later 1880s due to poor weather conditions.

Formation of the Populist Party, 1892

In July 1892, the Populist Party was formed at a convention in Omaha from an alliance of silver and farming interests to fight against the traditional Democrat and Republican candidates. This was very much a 'people's party' and they chose James B. Weaver to stand for president in that year. Although they did not do very well compared to the two main parties, Weaver did poll one million votes.

NOTE-MAKING

Using the 1–2 method (see page x) make notes on this section. For example on the left-hand side write 'Reasons for emergence of the Populist movement' and, on the right-hand side, a bulleted point list of the reasons.

Gold Standard – Where the value of money is based on the amount of the nation's gold reserves.

Bimetallists – Those who wanted both silver and gold used in the coinage.

Aims

The Party fought the 1892 presidential election with the following programme:

- The regulation of railways, particularly the freight prices that many felt were artificially high.
- Far more government regulation of farm prices.
- A graduated income tax that would take away dependence on tariffs as the main source of government income. This would ensure that the rich were taxed more heavily and encourage more exports, especially for farmers.
- The direct election of senators to ensure that all citizens would be able to choose two senators from each state who went to Congress and directly represented their interests.
- A maximum eight-hour working day.
- To alter the basis of the currency, which was traditionally based on gold.

Source A From a speech given in 1892 by Ignatius Donnelly, a leading member of the Populist Party. From *The Growth of the American Republic* by S. Morison, H. Commager and W. Leuchtenburg, (Oxford University Press), 1969, p.173.

We meet in the midst of a nation brought to the verge of moral, political and material ruin. Corruption dominates the ballot-box, the legislatures, Congress and even the judiciary. The people are demoralised. The newspapers are largely subsidised or muzzled and public opinion silenced. Land and industry is concentrated in the hands of a few capitalists. Industrial workers are denied the right of organisation for self-protection and immigration brings down wages. The profits from the work of the millions are stolen to build up the colossal fortunes of a few. We now breed two great classes – tramps and millionaires.

Bryan and 1896 election

The Populist Party had sufficient support to have a decisive voice in the nomination of the Democrat candidate to fight the presidential election campaign of 1896. They chose William Jennings Bryan who was a supporter of silver coinage and farming interests and wanted to improve conditions for the urban working class.

The 1896 election was the first where modern campaigning methods and financing were employed, including dirty tricks. For example, a wealthy businessman, Mark Hanna, spent $3 million supporting the Republican candidate, William McKinley, using some of it to smear the reputation of Bryan. McKinley was the popular Governor of Ohio who won much support, especially from the working classes, because he supported a strong tariff to protect American industry. For example, Hanna sent 1,500 speakers into electoral areas where voters seemed undecided which candidate to vote for and paid for millions of pieces of campaign literature. Most of the national newspapers, including the influential *New York Times,* supported McKinley.

Bryan was unable to call upon such financial support and used more traditional methods of campaigning. He travelled over 28,000 km and gave 600 campaign speeches. McKinley won 7,036,000 of the popular vote to Bryan's 6,468,000, and 273 of the electoral college votes to the 176 of his rival.

McKinley's victory was not due simply to the backing of Hanna. Bryan was unable to win a single state in the populous North-east where workers feared the free silver idea as much as their bosses. The economy of 1896 was also on the upswing. Had the election occurred during the economic depression of 1893, the results may have differed.

What can you learn from Source A about the reasons for the emergence of the Populist Party?

William Bryan (1860–1925)

William Jennings Bryan was born in 1860 in Salem, Illinois. He eventually studied law at Union College Chicago, qualifying as a lawyer and working in Jacksonville from 1883–87 before moving to Lincoln, Nebraska. In 1890, he was elected as a Democrat to the US House of Representatives. Over the next few years he showed his great ability as an orator when campaigning in favour of the silver interests. Moreover, he tried to ensure that the Democratic Party reflected the aims of the Populist Party and built a reputation as a champion of Populism. He ran unsuccessfully as a presidential candidate on three occasions – 1896, 1900, when he ran as an anti-imperialist, and again in 1904. Bryan received a total of 493 electoral college votes – the most by any candidate in American history who never won the presidency. From 1912–14 he served as Secretary of State for Woodrow Wilson and, in later years, campaigned for Prohibition. He died in 1925.

How important was Populism?

Since the 1890s historians have vigorously debated the nature of Populism. Some historians see a close link between the Populists of the 1890s and the Progressives of 1900–12 but, for the most part, the link was reactionary. 'Progressives' feared popular democracy as represented by Populism and most of the leading Progressives such as Theodore Roosevelt and Woodrow Wilson strongly opposed it. Some historians see the Populists as forward-looking liberal reformers and others view them as reactionaries trying to recapture an idyllic and utopian past based on farming.

The Populist Party never recovered from the events of 1896. By 1900, membership had fallen and Populist activists had either retired from politics or joined one of the major parties. However, it did have importance in the politics of the USA:

- The Progressives adopted many of the aims of the Populist Party.
- The Party also had electoral successes. Besides electing eleven governors and numerous other state and local officials, approximately 45 members of the Party served in the US Congress between 1891 and 1902.

WORKING TOGETHER

Working in pairs, compare the notes you have made on this section. Add anything that you have missed and check anything that you have disagreed on.

KEY DATES: POPULISM

1890 The Sherman Silver Purchase Act.

1892 The Populist Party is established.

1896 Bryan loses the presidential election campaign to McKinley.

2 Progressivism

Historians often refer to the first two decades of the twentieth century as 'the Progressive era'. There has been a long-standing debate, which continues to the present day, about when the Progressive era started or finished and how much the Progressive Movement actually achieved. Indeed, some historians even challenge the whole idea of a Progressive era or movement.

The emergence of Progressivism

Why did Progressivism emerge?

What became known as the Progressive Movement emerged in the USA in the 1890s.

The meaning of Progressivism

Progressivism was a loose grouping of many individuals and organisations, with no easily identifiable leaders and no clear set of aims. It was not confined to one of the main parties as, at presidential level, Theodore Roosevelt and Taft, who were both Republican, and Wilson, a Democrat, were seen as Progressives. One of the first historians of Progressivism, De Witt, whose book *Reflections on Progressivism* was published in 1913, thought that the Progressive Movement was concerned with the regulation of big business, political reform and social reform. More recently, Chambers defined Progressivism as interventionism – the belief that direct intervention at state and federal level could bring about improvements to society.

Over time the movement developed in different ways – from political reform and the regulation of working hours through to votes for women and major constitutional changes. The Progressives were responsible for a number of significant achievements including amendments to the Constitution, radical reforms and changes to the role of the federal government which would have far-reaching implications for the twentieth century.

NOTE-MAKING

1 Using a spider diagram (see page x) summarise the main reasons for the emergence of Progressivism. Rank order these reasons, beginning with the most important at 12 o'clock, moving clockwise to the least important.

2 Compare your spider diagram and rank order with that of a partner. How far do your rank orders differ?

Why did it emerge?

There was no single reason for the emergence of Progressivism.

Economic problems

A recession struck in 1893, leading to high unemployment in industrial cities, which remained at twelve per cent for the rest of the 1890s. Businesses cut wages to sustain profits, which led to a fall in living standards. Many banks collapsed during the recession, which meant many people lost their savings. Moreover, agriculture continued to decline due to falling prices. The small farmers of the North-east could not compete with the large-scale farming of the West.

Social problems

Many Americans lived in desperate poverty. Living conditions were terrible in many cities where there was overcrowding and totally inadequate sewage disposal and a lack of clean water. Working conditions were also often very poor with no restriction on working hours, with a six-day, 72-hour working week commonplace. Moreover, there was no welfare system in the USA – no unemployment or sick pay or compensation for accidents.

The need for political reform

There was growing dissatisfaction with the two main political parties. The Democrats, strong in the South, were deeply conservative. The Republicans, who dominated Congress, seemed to have become the party of big business and banks. Moreover, Progressives were opposed to corrupt party machines and big business domination of the political process.

The need to regulate big business

In the late nineteenth century large businesses, in particular trusts, became so powerful that they threatened to establish monopolies in particular industries, which meant they could fix prices without fear of competition. There was increasing hostility towards individuals such as Rockefeller, Morgan and Carnegie who seemed to put their own profits before the interests of the masses. There was a growing demand for government regulation to control big business, especially trusts, although Progressives could not agree on how they should be brought under control.

The influence of the media

In the early twentieth century, there was a huge increase in newspaper and magazine circulation. By 1904, *McClure's* magazine was selling 750,000 copies and eight years later *Collier's* magazine had reached 1 million sales per edition. The press was to play a major role in exposing the evils in American society, beginning in 1902 with *McClure's* magazine which exposed political and business corruption in most of America's cities. Other writers and journalists such as Ida Tarbell, Lincoln Steffens and Upton Sinclair wrote a whole series of what became known as 'muckraking articles', which greatly influenced public opinion and accelerated reform.

Fear of revolution

Some Americans were concerned about the growth of socialism and radicalism and felt that unless there was reform there could well be revolution. Trade unions grew in strength with more and more workers supporting more militant actions such as strikes which often turned violent, such as the 1892 steelworkers strike in Pittsburgh. Many of those who feared revolution were from the middle class. Indeed, Progressivism is often seen as a middle-class movement. Most Progressive leaders were middle-class professionals such as lawyers and doctors who were desperate to bring about reform to create a more efficient and stable society.

Aims

The Progressive Movement had a wide variety of political, economic and social aims.

Political aims

Progressives wanted a range of political reforms:

- Changes to the Constitution including allowing women to vote and ensuring that senators were more accountable by making them directly elected rather than being chosen by state legislatures.
- A much greater role for federal government in the economy and society in particular to regulate big business and intervene on the side of the workers.
- Radical reform of the management of towns and cities which were often controlled by corrupt officials. The Progressives wanted a more open and democratic system for electing mayors and other public officials.
- Changes to the political parties which seemed to be dominated by a few wealthy businessmen who controlled candidate nomination at local, state and even presidential level. One demand was for the open primary election.

Economic aims

The Progressives wanted government to play a much greater role in regulating business, to ensure that it was run in the interests of the whole community and not just a few rich individuals. They believed that government should have much more control of banks, insurance companies and the stock market.

They also wanted new legislation which would ensure that employers recognised trade unions, regulated hours of work and provided compensation for injury at work as well as introducing insurance schemes for unemployment, sickness and old age. In addition, laws to provide consumer protection against adulterated food, which was quite widespread at the time, rigged prices and monopolies.

Finally, they wanted to change the currency, which was based on gold and introduce a silver coinage which Progressives believed would help to raise prices for farmers and reduce the power of the trusts and big business.

Social aims

These included a broad range of reforms which would provide a better quality of life for a great number of Americans including:

- Female emancipation. In 1890, the National American Suffrage Association was set up to campaign for the vote for women.
- Many Progressives were shocked at the poor living and working conditions and the extent of poverty in the USA and wanted the government to provide a safety net to help those who were too poor to help themselves through state-funded welfare benefits, such as those introduced in Germany and France.
- Progressives also supported the abolition of the manufacture and sale of alcohol. In 1893, the Anti-Saloon League was founded as a pressure group to campaign for Prohibition by publicising the damage that alcohol did to society.
- Reforms to help African Americans who, having moved to the North to escape the poverty of the South, were often treated as second-class citizens and experienced poor living standards.

Robert La Follette (1855–1925)

Much of the work of the Progressive Movement was done at state or local level by individuals such as La Follette who, as governor of Wisconsin between 1901 and 1906, fought corruption and brought in a whole series of Progressive reforms. These included the first workers' compensation system, railroad rate reform, open government and the open primary system where a registered voter may vote in any party primary regardless of his own party affiliation, as well as a minimum wage and progressive taxation. He also developed what became known as the Wisconsin Idea with the University of Wisconsin, which promoted the idea of basing all legislation on thorough research (using the university) and expert involvement.

Primary election – An early stage of voting in which the whole electorate can choose a political party's candidates for election, rather than having the candidates chosen for them by the party.

Prohibition – The prevention by law of the manufacture and sale of alcohol.

NOTE-MAKING

Using the 1–2 method (see page x) create notes on the domestic achievements of Theodore Roosevelt using the following side headings:

● Anti-trust measures
● Labour relations
● Conservation measures

You should consider the following question as you make these notes:

'To what extent was Theodore Roosevelt a progressive president?'

State of the Union Address – The US President's message to the country at the start of a new session of Congress.

In what respects can this speech (Source B) be seen as 'Progressive'?

The Sherman Anti-Trust Act, 1890

Any trust that restricted trade between states or between foreign nations was declared illegal. However, the Act's terms were vague and very early on it was weakened by a Supreme Court ruling of 1895, *United States v. E. C. Knight.* The Supreme Court held that the American Sugar Refining Company had not broken the law by taking over a number of competitors.

Theodore Roosevelt and Progressivism (1901–08)

How Progressive was the presidency of Theodore Roosevelt?

Theodore Roosevelt became president in 1901 after the assassination of the Republican President William McKinley. Some historians see him as a reactionary who supported reforms in order to prevent revolution. Others believe that he gave much publicity and impetus to the Progressive Movement. He felt that the federal government had a role in the economy and should intervene where and when necessary. He was criticised by liberals for being too cautious and by many in his party for being too radical.

Progressive measures

Roosevelt wasted little time in introducing significant reforms. In his first State of the Union Address to Congress in December 1901, he made it clear that he was going to take on big business.

Source B From Theodore Roosevelt's first State of the Union Address to Congress.

The first essential in determining how to deal with the great industrial combinations is knowledge of the facts – publicity. In the interest of the public, the Government should have the right to inspect and examine the workings of the great corporations engaged in interstate business. Publicity is the only sure remedy which we can now invoke. What further remedies are needed in the way of governmental regulation, or taxation, can only be determined after publicity has been obtained, by process of law, and in the course of administration. The first requisite is knowledge, full and complete – knowledge which may be made public to the world ... There should be created a Cabinet officer, to be known as Secretary of Commerce and Industries, as provided in the bill introduced at the last session of the Congress. It should be his province to deal with commerce in its broadest sense; including among many other things whatever concerns labor and all matters affecting the great business corporations and our merchant marine.

Anti-Trust measures

Roosevelt was determined to make the Sherman Anti-Trust Act of 1890 more effective. As early as 1902, Roosevelt instructed his attorney-general, Philander C. Knox, to start proceedings against the Northern Securities Company, a vast holding company which controlled several railroads in the north-east of the USA. This involved taking on powerful businessmen such as Rockefeller and J. P. Morgan, who appeared to be using the company's monopoly to create excess profits. After a long battle, the Supreme Court decided in 1904 that the Company was illegal and it was dissolved. This encouraged Roosevelt to embark on 44 anti-trust prosecutions, among them American Tobacco and Standard Oil (see page 45 for more on Standard Oil).

The 1903 Department of Commerce and Labor Act created a new Department of Commerce with a Cabinet secretary. It was given the power to collect data from any business that dealt in interstate commerce which would be vital in identifying the need to regulate business if it showed monopoly or price fixing. Roosevelt played a very important role in getting this legislation passed by Congress, encouraging the public to put pressure on their Senators and Congressmen to get the Bill passed.

The 1906 Hepburn Act gave a federal government commission the power to inspect books of railroad companies and to lay down the maximum rates they could charge. This was to try to protect the public from exploitation.

▲ A cartoon of 1904 which shows the Standard Oil Company as an octopus. The octopus uses its tentacles to ensnare (from top left to right): Congress; the state legislatures; taxpayers; and is reaching out to try to ensnare to White House.

Labour relations

Roosevelt was prepared to intervene in industrial disputes such as the anthracite coal strike of 1902. Employers had locked out miners who went on strike for better wages and an eight-hour day. Roosevelt summoned both sides to Washington and told the employers that unless they agreed to arbitration he would send troops in to work the mines. The employers settled, raising wages and offering a nine-hour day. Previous presidents had always taken the side of the employers. Roosevelt had been seen to expand the role of government to obtain justice and fair play – one of the key elements of Progressivism. While this action made Roosevelt very popular with the working classes, the employers had not conceded very much and simply raised prices to cover the pay rise.

Conservation

Roosevelt was also far ahead of his time on conservation issues. He was possibly the first president to realise that natural resources were not infinite. He ordered 150 million acres of forest to be placed on federal reserves and strictly enforced laws concerning grazing, mining and lumbering. In 1908, Roosevelt organised the National Conservation Conference which led to many states creating commissions to look after the environment. By supporting conservation, he seemed to be supporting the 'people' against mining, timber and oil 'interests'.

Roosevelt also extended the role of the federal government in food consumption. An Act of 1906 led to a federal programme of meat inspection. In the same year he introduced the Pure Food and Drug Act which started the process of ending food adulteration.

Roosevelt's State of Union Address, 1908

Roosevelt's State of Union Address in 1908 included inheritance and income taxes. In addition, he advocated further regulation of interstate business and railroads and a more effective system of dealing with labour disputes. He also wanted an eight-hour working day, compensation for injuries at work and stock market regulation.

To what extent would you agree with the view in Source C about Roosevelt's presidency?

NOTE-MAKING

Using bullet points (see page x) make notes on the achievements of Taft. These notes should include reforms, opposition from Roosevelt and the 1912 presidential election.

Roosevelt's achievement

In the last few years of his second administration (1906–08), Roosevelt continued to take action against big business and also continued to support conservation measures. Some 120 million acres were taken into the public domain between 1905 and 1909. In his final State of the Union message in 1908, he laid down an agenda that his Democrat successors should put into practice. He seemed to show a genuine concern for the underdog and he placed on the nation's agenda many of the issues that were of greatest concern to the Progressives and kept them there. Moreover, he brought the presidential office of the USA firmly into the arena of economic and social reform.

However, Roosevelt was unable to persuade Congress to pass more in the way of Progressive reform. He was not helped by the fact that there was a growing divide in the Republican Party between conservatives and Progressives.

Source C An extract from an article in the *Independent Magazine* in 1909 entitled 'An Assessment of Theodore Roosevelt's Presidency'. From *History of the USA 1840–1941* by P. Bowring and P. Walsh-Atkins, (Cambridge University Press), 2013, p.125.

The notable thing about his two presidential terms is the multitude of things he has said and done from the initiative of his own brain ... He dared tackle the combinations of wealth and compelled them to cease their unfair competition ... He has demanded a square deal, and we loved him for the enemies he has made. It would have been vastly easier to keep quiet but he wanted the just thing done. He has purified the civil service as well as business methods, protected our forests, ended conflict with miners and investigated agricultural conditions.

KEY DATES: ROOSEVELT AND PROGRESSIVISM

1902 Roosevelt intervened in the anthracite coal strike.

1903 The Department of Commerce and Labor Act created a new Department of Commerce.

1904 The Supreme Court decided in 1904 that the Northern Securities Company was illegal and it was dissolved.

1906 The Hepburn Act gave a federal government commission the power to inspect the books of railroad companies.

The Presidency of Taft, 1909–12

Did Progressivism continue under Taft?

Roosevelt was very popular in 1908 and, had he been prepared to stand again, he would almost certainly have won. However, he respected the two-term tradition established by George Washington and refused to run for a third term as president. His successor was William Taft. Taft fought the presidential election campaign against the Democrat, William Bryan. Taft polled 321 of the electoral votes and 7,678,90 of the popular vote to the 162 and 6,409,104 of his opponent

Taft's achievements

On the one hand Taft did continue Roosevelt's ant-trust policies. His administration initiated 80 anti-trust suits under the Sherman Anti-Trust Act, twice as many as Roosevelt, and introduced an eight-hour day for government employees as well as mine safety legislation. He also gave power to the Interstate Commission to set railroad rates, introduced a federal income tax and corporation tax, both of which later had significance in covering increased government spending, and brought in the direct election of senators by the people rather than being appointed by state legislatures.

However, as a lawyer, he was concerned with what he saw as Roosevelt's overuse of presidential authority. He respected the rights of Congress to oppose his ideas and was determined to act within the limits of the Constitution. He also lacked the political skills of his predecessor and failed to handle the Progressive–conservative divisions among Republicans. Moreover, he earned the opposition of many Progressives by sacking Gifford Pinchot, the great conservationist who had originally been appointed by Roosevelt.

Taft seemed to increasingly align himself with the conservative wing of the Republican Party particularly over the issue of tariff reform. In 1909, Taft's convention of a special session of Congress to debate tariff reform legislation spurred the Republican protectionist majority to action and led to the passage of the Payne–Aldrich Act, which did little to lower tariffs. Though more progressive Republicans (such as Roosevelt) expected Taft to veto the bill, he signed it into law and publicly defended it.

Opposition from Roosevelt

Concerns about Taft's reluctance to carry out further reform were communicated to Roosevelt in 1910 while he was taking part in a safari in Africa. Roosevelt returned to America to act as an opponent to Taft. He made an important speech at Osawatomie in which he attacked the trusts, urged the need for social reform and supported even greater federal power, launching his policy of New Nationalism. In 1911, he determined to run against Taft for the presidential election nomination, but Taft controlled the Party machine and was able to dominate the convention.

Roosevelt now claimed that the Republican Party no longer represented the wishes of the people and in 1912 left to form a new party, which was called the Progressives, to fight the 1912 presidential election. This new party split and weakened the Republicans and contributed greatly to their defeat in the 1912 presidential election.

Source D An extract from *The Growth of the American Republic* by S. Morison, H. Commager and W. Leuchtenburg, (Oxford University Press), 1968, p. 268.

Against the crowding evils of the time there arose a full-throated protest which distinguished American politics and thought from approximately 1890 to World War 1. It demanded the centralization of power in the hands of a strong government and the extension of regulation or control over industry, finance, transportation, agriculture, labor and even morals. It found expression in a new concern for the poor and the underprivileged, for women and children. It called for new standards of honesty in politics and business. It formulated a new social and political philosophy which rejected *laissez-faire*. The new progressivism had a distinctly moral flavor with Bryan, Roosevelt and Wilson its moral crusaders.

WORKING TOGETHER

There has been much debate and discussion between historians about the achievements of Progressivism in this period. Set up a class debate to assess the achievements of Progressivism, with one group arguing 'for' Progressivism, and another 'against'. You could use the motion:

'This class believes that Progressivism was very successful in this period'.

William Taft (1857–1930)

Taft was born into a powerful family in Ohio in 1857. After college, he went to law school and became a successful prosecutor. He was promoted to a series of prominent roles in the US judiciary and from 1901 to 1903 he served as the USA's governor-general in the Philippines. In 1904, Roosevelt appointed him as Secretary of War. At first Taft was reluctant to run as president as his ambition was to serve on the Supreme Court. After his presidency he became the chief judge of the Supreme Court. Taft has been criticised by historians for being unimaginative, conservative and lacking in energy. As he was by profession a lawyer, he often thought very carefully before coming to decisions. This made him appear to be indecisive.

How far do you agree with the interpretation of Progressivism given in Source D?

KEY DATES: PRESIDENCY OF TAFT

1908 Taft wins the presidential election.

1911 Roosevelt sets up a new party – New Nationalism.

1912 Taft loses the presidential election to Woodrow Wilson.

3 Economic and social change

The 1890s and first decade of the twentieth century was a period of economic and social change in the USA with continued industrial growth, agricultural discontent and even greater immigration.

Economic developments

To what extent did the economy continue to expand in the years 1890–1912?

This was a period of industrial expansion although the USA did experience a second major depression in 1893.

Industrial growth

Industry continued to expand, particularly oil and steel. Iron production rose from 920,000 tons in 1860 to 10.3 million tons by 1900. The city of Pittsburg, in Pennsylvania, became the centre of the iron industry. It was highly centralised with 38 steel plants along 42 km of navigable rivers.

Modern oil production began in January 1901 with the success of the Lucas Well in Spindlehop, Texas. This well produced 70,000–110,000 barrels per day for nine days before being capped. Further 'gushes' were discovered throughout the Southwest. Indeed, by 1907 Oklahoma was the leading oil producer and, six years later, was producing 25 per cent of the nation's oil.

Trusts and monopolies also continued to develop. By 1904, the largest 4 per cent of US companies produced 57 per cent of the total industry of the USA. Between 1898 and 1902, there were 319 major consolidations. For example, the firm of Dupont controlled 85 per cent of the nation's electric power. The Carnegie Steel Corporation, which had been set up by Andrew Carnegie, was sold to J. P. Morgan in 1901. It was renamed US Steel and became the world's first billion-dollar corporation.

The Depression of 1893

The Depression of 1893 sparked a stock market crash that turned into the worst depression in American history up to that time. The financial panic began when the Reading Railroad declared bankruptcy. Soon afterwards, 'Industrial Black Friday' hit, and 24 businesses failed per day in May alone. The crisis sparked a four-year depression in which 15,000 companies and 600 banks closed and the national unemployment rate approached 20 per cent. The unemployment rate in Pennsylvania hit 25 per cent, in New York 35 per cent, and in Michigan 43 per cent. Soup kitchens were opened to help feed the destitute.

President Grover Cleveland was among the last of the conservative Democrats who supported limited federal government and believed, like most people of both major parties, that the business cycle was a natural occurrence and should not be tampered with by politicians. He was a supporter of a sound monetary system based on gold. As such, he opposed many in his party by calling for the repeal of the Silver Purchase Act. Cleveland persuaded enough members of Congress to pass the Repeal of the Silver Purchase Act in October 1893. This helped boost business confidence and gradually stemmed unemployment.

Perhaps most importantly, the panic of 1893 and the subsequent depression alienated many people from both the economy and the political process and led to the rise of Progressivism. The panic of 1893 and other factors had a lasting impact. The effects of the Depression lasted until 1897. One response to the series of failures and bankruptcies was an upsurge in business consolidations.

NOTE-MAKING

Make notes on the key economic and social developments in this period. Your notes should consider the following questions:
- To what extent did industry continue to expand in this period?
- What were the effects of the economic depression of 1893?
- How much progress was made by labour unions in these years?

LOOK AGAIN

Look back at pages 17–19 in Chapter 1.

Why was there rapid industrial expansion after the Civil War?

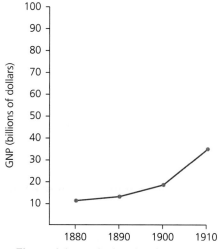

▲ Figure 1 A graph showing Gross National Product (the total value of all final goods and services produced within a nation in a particular year) from 1880–1910.

The poorer elements of society believed they had been ignored during the hard times and then were left at the mercy of the trusts. This encouraged the rise of Progressivism.

Agricultural discontent

Farmers in the South and West did not share the prosperity and expansion experienced by industry. Moreover, they objected to the power of bankers and corporations. Farmers traditionally saw themselves as independent and self-sufficient, but many relied on loans to get them through the farming year. However, falling agricultural prices, together with higher prices charged for grain storage and transportation, meant less income for repaying loans. Many farmers blamed the railroads and bankers for their problems.

They joined together into Farmers' Alliances, creating unity for themselves through co-operation and mutual self-respect. These Alliances led to the Populist Party and support for the Democrats in the presidential election of 1896.

Trade unions

Labour unions representing different crafts were set up in the years following the Civil War. In 1885, The American Federation of Labour (AFL) was created to represent these labour unions, speaking on behalf of all member unions and encouraging mutual support between unions. It tried to bring about better working conditions and better wages with its main weapon being strike action. In 1886, there were 1,400 strikes involving 500,000 members.

Employers were generally hostile to trade unions and would often sack workers who joined trade unions and use blackleg labour to break strikes, as shown during two significant labour conflicts of the 1890s.

The Pittsburgh steelworkers' strike of 1892

At Carnegie's Homestead Steelworks plant the manager, Henry Clay Frick, cut wages in 1892 and refused to accept union negotiation. In an attempt to break the power of the union, the Amalgamated Association of Iron and Steel Workers, private detectives were used to smuggle in strike-breakers, who were then attacked by the strikers. The Company called in the militia, armed with rifles and machine guns. However, after five months without wages, the strikers were starving and their action collapsed. This defeat set back union power considerably.

The Pullman strike of 1894

This was the first national strike in the USA and it paralysed the railway system. The Pullman company had cut wages but refused to lower rents for the houses where employees were required to live. When the workers went on strike, the American Railway Union (ARU) run by Eugene Debs refused to handle any trains carrying Pullman cars including mail trains. The railway owners asked President Cleveland for support and he agreed to send in troops to keep the trains running. Rioting was followed by the troops firing into the crowd and killing four people. The strike gradually ended in failure with the rents remaining as they were. The federal government had shown itself hostile to unions and willing to shoot its own citizens. The Omnibus Indictment Act, used against the ARU, permitted the legal banning of strikes and remained in force until the 1930s.

It was this belief that federal government did not care about the less well off in society that was to turn many of the industrial classes towards the more radical ideas of the Populist Party.

Labour unions – US term for a trade union formed to look after the interests of its members.

Blackleg labour – Strike-breakers.

KEY DATES: ECONOMIC DEVELOPMENTS

1892 The Pittsburgh steelworkers' strike.

1893 The Depression.

1894 The Pullman strike.

NOTE-MAKING

Make notes summarising the main effects of mass immigration on the USA.

LOOK AGAIN

Look back at pages 48–50 in Chapter 2.

What were the main reasons for mass immigration to the USA in the second half of the nineteenth century?

Mass immigration

What were the effects of mass immigration to the USA in the years 1890 to 1912?

Massive immigration to the USA in the second half of the nineteenth century was to have profound effects on American society.

Effects of mass immigration

Between 1860 and 1900, at least 14 million immigrants arrived in the USA. The number of immigrants reached an all-time high in the years 1901 to 1910. By 1900, New York had more Italians than Naples, and twice as many Irish as Dublin. Moreover, by 1914, the Jewish population was 1.4 million out of a city

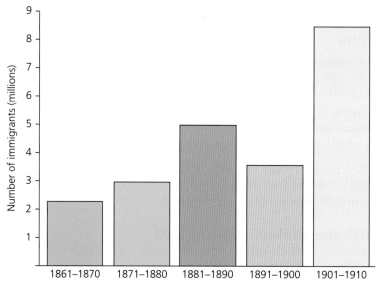

▲ **Figure 2a** A graph showing the numbers of immigrants arriving in the USA, 1861–1910.

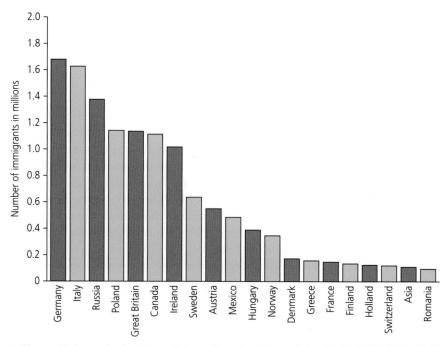

▲ **Figure 2b** A graph showing origins of immigrants arriving in the USA, 1861–1910.

population of 4.7 million. The immigrants from Europe disembarked in New York and headed for the cities where they provided the cheap labour needed for industrial growth or headed west to farm in the new territories. Chinese and Japanese immigrants usually arrived in San Francisco. By 1890, one-tenth of the population was Chinese.

Immigration was a major reason why the USA was able to progress as quickly as it did with industrialisation. Immigrants came as workers but, just as importantly, they came as consumers. Agencies matched immigrants to jobs so efficiently that many had employment within a few hours of arrival. By and large the immigrants assimilated well into US society. They formed the unskilled workforce in the rapidly growing industries.

The migrant was grateful for a job, an opportunity and a roof over his or her head. It was estimated that by 1900 over two-thirds of those who had arrived in the USA in the previous twenty years existed below subsistence level. Indeed, the reality of life in America was often a shock to new arrivals who were surprised to find that the streets were not paved with gold. Settling in this new country was hard, especially for those moving from a peasant outdoor life, unregulated by clocks, to a disciplined, machine-controlled life. Low wages often meant that wives and children had to work.

Reactions

While many immigrants were welcomed by employers as cheap and willing labour, they were an easy target for Americans who were fearful and resentful about the rapid changes brought about by industrialisation. This was because immigrants were often used as strike-breakers; brought in by employers as blacklegs to replace striking workers, they contributed to overcrowding in towns and cities and increased racial and ethnic conflict. It was easy for opponents to see their cultural and religious interests as un-American. These opponents argued that immigrants from southern and eastern Europe did not assimilate into US culture as easily as their northern counterparts, and brought with them dangerous political ideas such as socialism and anarchism.

In 1887, the American Protective Association was set up to try to put pressure on the government to limit immigration. The Association suggested that the Anglo-Saxon, Protestant 'traditions' that dominated American culture were being undermined. The anti-immigration forces had limited success before the First World War, although the 1882 Chinese Exclusion Act stopped immigration from China and, in 1908, immigration from Japan also ceased.

Source E From an eye-witness account of the Bowery district of New York City, written in 1898. From *America 1870–1975* by J. O'Keeffe, (Longman), 1984, p.20.

A short alley in the Fourth Ward [local electoral district] in 1885 had 140 families living on it, of whom 100 were Irish, 38 Italian and 2 German. It was typical of New York. A huge Italian quarter was growing up west of the Bowery, along Mulberry and Mott Streets. The Jews were dotting the Bowery, Baxter Division, Grand and other streets with their favorite businesses – clothing, jewelry, pawn-broking. Crowded in between the Italians and Chatham Square, Chinatown was growing rapidly. Most of the inhabitants still wore the pigtail, silken blouse, baggy trousers, and thick-soled shoes of the old country. More immigrants were coming than industry could decently support and in the crowded slums many of them were driven to desperate toil to keep body and soul together. The children of such families began working as soon as their little fingers could master a detail. Other children began roaming the streets, living by begging or prostitution.

Anarchism – Belief in no government, no private ownership and the sharing out of wealth.

Using Source E, can you suggest any reasons why some Americans disliked these new immigrants?

KEY DATES: IMMIGRATION

1887 The American Protective Association was set up.

1900 One-tenth of the population of San Francisco was Chinese.

NOTE-MAKING

Using the 1–2 method (see page x), make notes on the position of African Americans in this period using the following side headings:
- Economic and social position
- Segregation
- Voting rights
- Booker T. Washington
- Du Bois

The position of African Americans

Was there any progress in the position of African Americans in this period?

During this period there was little progress in the position of African Americans, especially in the South, and, in some cases, it became worse.

Economic and social conditions

The majority of African Americans, whether in the North or South, still lived in poverty although a minority did make economic progress.

Segregation in the South

In 1887, a railroad company in Florida was the first to introduce segregated railway carriages and over the next four years seven more Southern states brought in segregation on trains. This was gradually extended to cover public places. Segregation was reinforced by the *Plessy v. Ferguson* case.

The *Plessy v. Ferguson* case, 1896

Homer Plessy was light-skinned but was legally classed as an African American because he had one-eighth black ancestry. He deliberately challenged the Louisiana state law, requiring railroad companies to provide separate facilities on their trains for black and white Americans, by refusing to leave a 'white' carriage. He was arrested and put on trial with Plessy insisting that his rights were being violated under the Fourteenth Amendment. Ferguson, the local judge, ruled against Plessy whose case was then taken to the Supreme Court. Seven of the eight Supreme Court judges ruled that segregation was legal because 'separate but equal facilities' were sufficient to be within the law.

The ruling was a disaster for black civil rights since states could now interpret 'equal' in whatever way they wanted. In 1899, in *Cumming v Board of Education*, the separate but equal ruling was extended to schools which in practice meant under-funded, poor quality schools for African Americans were allowed to continue.

Voting rights

Many Southern states were also determined to ensure that African Americans did not exercise their right, according to the Fifteenth Amendment, to vote. To achieve this, state governments devised complex rules as well as additional voting qualifications.

- Georgia introduced a poll (individual) tax of up to $2 on citizens wanting to vote. Most African Americans were too poor to have such money available.
- In 1898, Louisiana introduced the 'grandfather clause'. The franchise was granted to adult males but only if their fathers or grandfathers had voted before 1 January 1867, the date when African Americans gained the vote.
- Some states also introduced rules which meant that only those who owned their own homes were allowed to vote.
- In 1890, Mississippi introduced a literacy test in order to register to vote which effectively excluded many illiterate African Americans. This process could be arranged so that the questions for uneducated white Americans were simpler than those for their African American counterparts.

By 1910, very few African Americans were able to vote in the South. Therefore, few of them became political leaders at local, state or national level. Many African Americans accepted the situation as being too difficult to change, especially as there seemed little or no support at national level. Furthermore, the period 1880–1910 saw the height of the lynching campaign against African Americans with an average of one hundred each year. Cases were rarely brought to court and, if they were, all-white juries would not convict.

Booker T. Washington (1865–1915)

Booker T. Washington was born a slave in Virginia with a black mother and a white father whom he never knew. After emancipation, he was able to attend college and became a teacher. In 1881, he set up the Tuskegee Institute in Alabama. This became a model for education linked to vocational training for black students. Washington believed that African Americans, in order to progress, had to acquire skills first through education. Later, he helped to set up the National Urban League to help black workers adjust to industrial, urban life. He was convinced that hard work and financial success would weaken discrimination.

In a speech in Atlanta, Georgia in 1895, Washington argued that if white Americans could regard African Americans as potential economic partners rather than as a threat to their political control, the race question would be resolved. He suggested that African Americans should focus on education and economic progress rather than trying to remove segregation and discrimination and achieving voting rights, and that change would be a slow process.

His critics called the speech the Atlanta Compromise and attacked his attempts at accommodation with white Americans in the South. However, the speech established Washington as the leader of the African Americans in the South.

> **Accommodation** – Acceptance of economic, political and social circumstances not of your own making or liking.

Source F An extract from Booker T. Washington's speech in Atlanta in 1895. From http://historymatters.gmu.edu/d/39/.

The wisest among my race understand that the agitation of questions of social equality is the extremest folly, and that progress in the enjoyment of all the privileges that will come to us must be the result of severe and constant struggle rather than of artificial forcing. No race that has anything to contribute to the markets of the world is long in any degree ostracized. It is important and right that all privileges of the law be ours, but it is vastly more important that we be prepared for the exercise of these privileges. The opportunity to earn a dollar in a factory just now is worth infinitely more than the opportunity to spend a dollar in an opera-house.

> Using evidence from Source F, consider whether Washington's critics were justified in describing Washington's beliefs as 'accommodation'.

Washington's achievements

There has been much debate both during his lifetime and in subsequent years about the contribution made by Washington to the cause of civil rights for African Americans. His critics have insisted that he seemed to accept the idea of white supremacy, made no attempt to challenge the second-class social position of African Americans and did little for civil rights. He seemed to focus on working within the system, rather than trying to change the system itself. Moreover, he underestimated the importance of the vote for improving the position of African Americans.

However, he did have some achievements. He provided a role model for African Americans because of the way he progressed from slave to college principal, along with his strict standards of behaviour and self-discipline. He also developed valuable contacts for African Americans within the white-dominated political world of the USA. One of his greatest achievements was to gain the interest of Theodore Roosevelt. Roosevelt frequently consulted Washington on African-American issues and invited him to tea at the White House.

NAACP

The National Association for the Advancement of Colored People (NAACP) was set up by Du Bois and other leading African American campaigners in 1909. Du Bois was keen to attract white people, if possible, to join the movement. The aims of the NAACP were to investigate racism, publicise it, suggest possible solutions and to take legal action to enforce the law against it. The NAACP adopted a constitutional approach to lawsuits, believing that many of the measures taken against African Americans were violations of the constitutional amendments brought in during Reconstruction. Du Bois played a very important role in the NAACP, editing its magazine for twenty years. However, his frustration at the slow pace of change eventually resulted in him moving to Ghana where he died in 1963.

KEY DATES: AFRICAN AMERICANS

1895 Booker T. Washington's speech at Atlanta, Georgia.

1896 The *Plessy v. Ferguson* case.

1905 Du Bois helped to found the Niagara movement.

1909 The setting up of the NAACP.

W. E. B. Du Bois (1868–1965)

Du Bois came from a very different background to that of Washington. After gaining degrees at Fisk, a college for African Americans, Berlin and Harvard University, he became a lecturer in philosophy. At first he supported Washington's ideas of slow but gradual change but by 1900 he was arguing for more active resistance to discrimination. He urged the use of legal and political processes through unceasing agitation.

The Niagara movement

Du Bois helped to found the Niagara movement in 1905, which developed from a meeting held in Canada, in the city of Niagara Falls. The movement rejected Washington's cautious approach and put the emphasis on protest to demand civil rights, especially the restoration of civil rights and the abolition of discrimination. Niagara never developed into a mass movement. Du Bois and his followers were too academic and the movement lacked money and organisation. Nevertheless, Niagara provided impetus to the growing number of African Americans who wanted to challenge the views of Washington. Du Bois also played an important role in the setting up of the NAACP.

The position of African Americans in 1912

African Americans were, more than ever, second-class citizens, especially in the South. The active political role at lower levels of government that some African Americans had gained in the South during Reconstruction had disappeared. There were no African Americans in Congress or even in state legislatures. Moreover, the right of African Americans to vote had been systematically removed in the South by a series of state laws. This lack of political power made it extremely difficult to challenge white political domination, especially in the South.

As blacks disappeared from voting registers they lost any rights to serve on juries and give their own race any chance of legal equality. Moreover, segregation laws had formalised and increased the separation of races in the South. African Americans were often faced with inferior facilities, especially in education.

On the other hand, chances of receiving a formal education did increase during this period and African Americans were free to leave the South and migrate North, which they did in increasing numbers. By the end of this period a civil rights protest movement had begun to be developed with the NAACP.

WORKING TOGETHER

1 Working with a partner, divide your paper in two. One of you should identify improvements for African Americans in the years 1890–1912. The other should note any examples of lack of progress.

2 To what extent do you agree with the view that the position of African Americans improved in the years 1890–1912?

4 Foreign and imperial policies

In the years after the Civil War the USA had, for the most part, pursued a policy of isolationism with very little interest in imperial expansion. However, the USA became more involved abroad from 1890–1914 in the Spanish–American War of 1898, as well as becoming a colonial power when the USA took over the Philippines and Hawaii.

NOTE-MAKING

Make notes on this section using the 1–2 method (see page x).

Motives for imperialism

Why were there changes in US foreign and imperial policies in the years 1890–1914?

There has been much debate among historians as to what motivated US imperialism at the end of the nineteenth century which brought changes in American foreign and imperial policies. The policies followed by the USA during this period together with the changes they brought about will be explained over the following section.

Accidental empire

Some historians, such as Harold Evans in his book *The American Century* (1998), have argued that the USA never actually sought an empire at all. He argues that the decision to annex the Philippines was due to the deciding vote of Vice-President Garrett Augustus Hobart. Evans insists that, for economic reasons, the USA did not need an empire because it was carrying out a huge amount of trade with Britain.

Progressive imperialism

The historian Walter McDougall in *The American Encounter With the World Since 1776* (1997) suggests that US imperialism was motivated by a desire to improve the lives of non-Americans, shown for example in the removal of yellow fever in Cuba and the building of hospitals and schools. In other words, the export of American values to less well-developed countries. Indeed, some historians go further and suggest that the USA became an imperial power because it wanted to dominate the world by creating countries in its own image – believing that other countries would benefit from the pursuit of Americans to civilise the world.

This was linked to the missionary work undertaken by Americans. The impetus to do this work was linked to the belief that White Anglo-Saxon Protestants (WASPS) were a superior peoples who had a duty to help members of 'lesser races' improve their lives by following their example. Missionaries were often followed by colonists, as was the case in the Philippines and Hawaii.

Need for markets

The need for markets was the primary motive according to William A. Williams in his book *The Tragedy of American Diplomacy* written in the 1950s. However, the USA believed that this need for markets could be met by the 'Open Door' policy rather than actual territorial expansion. Another historian, Niall Ferguson, in his book *American Colossus* published in 2003, also stressed this economic motive with the Depression of 1893 stimulating a desire to see new markets. Moreover, the USA faced surpluses in farm produce and needed markets to absorb these.

'Open Door' – This was a term first used to guarantee the protection of equal privileges among countries trading with China. The policy proposed to keep China open to trade with all countries on an equal basis; thus, no international power would have total control of the country.

The end of Westward expansion

Some historians have argued that Westward expansion in the second half of the nineteenth century was a form of imperialism and that once this ended America could then turn its attention to foreign adventures. These views were first expressed by the historian Frederick Jack Turner in 1893 in his thesis *The Significance of the Frontier in American History*.

Preclusive imperialism

The term 'preclusive imperialism' was first used by the historian William Langer. It refers to the idea that countries take colonies to prevent others from doing so. Moreover, it links with the idea that the USA wanted to copy the example of European powers such as Britain, France and Germany which had built up empires in Africa and Asia in the later nineteenth century. Therefore, the USA took advantage of its predominant position in Latin America as well as the Monroe Doctrine (see page 28) to expand in Central America and the Caribbean.

Source G From a speech by Henry Cabot, a Republican Senator, about the Anglo-Saxon race in the 1890s. From *Modern America: the USA, 1865 to the Present* by Joanne de Pennington, (Hodder), 2005, p.55.

The great nations are rapidly absorbing for their future expansion and their present defense, all the waste places of the world. It is a movement which makes for civilization and the advancement of the race. As one of the great nations of the world the US must not fall out of line of the march.

> What motive is being suggested by Cabot in Source G?

WORKING TOGETHER

Motives for imperialism

At this point it would be useful to explore further the possible motives for imperialism. Below are a number of suggested explanations or factors. Divide into pairs or small groups and allocate one factor per group; research and develop your factor and feed back to the rest of the group. Each factor is presented as a heading:
- Preclusive imperialism
- Progressive imperialism
- Need for markets
- Accidental empire
- The end of Westward expansion

US foreign and imperial policy in the 1890s

Why did the USA become involved in war with Spain in 1898?

During this decade the USA extended its influence in the Pacific and Latin America and fought a war against Spain which was a major turning point in American foreign and imperial policy.

Pacific

The USA became increasingly involved in the Pacific in the 1890s.

Samoa

US actions in Samoa were an example of preclusive imperialism. America's interest in Samoa first began in 1872 when the King of Samoa offered the USA the naval base of Pago Pago on the eastern island of Tutuila. Although this was refused, the USA was aware of increasing German and British interests in the

> **NOTE-MAKING**
>
> Using a spider diagram (see page x) summarise the causes, events and results of the Spanish–American War.

area, with the German Trading and Plantation Company turning Samoa into the most important trading post in the Pacific.

During a civil war in Samoa in 1898, the Americans and British supported the opposing side to that of the Germans. The following year the three powers abolished the Samoan monarchy and signed the Tripartite Convention in which Britain relinquished all rights to Samoa, the USA established a protectorate in Eastern Samoa while Western Samoa became a German colony. The British relinquished all rights to Samoa in return for being given other Pacific island chains formerly belonging to Germany.

Hawaii

In 1898, the USA annexed Hawaii. Hawaii was important as a stopping station on the way to Japan and China and US missionaries had settled there. Moreover, since 1875 the USA had imported Hawaiian sugar duty free and Hawaii became increasingly dependent on the US economy. By the 1890s, there were 3,000 American sugar growers out of the 90,000 Hawaiians living on the island.

In 1887, the USA established its first major Pacific naval base at Pearl Harbor in Hawaii. In 1890, the McKinley Tariff removed duties on raw sugar so the Hawaiian growers lost their trading advantage and began to suffer as a result of competition from other sugar interests, especially in Cuba. In 1891, the Hawaiian king died and the new queen, Liliuokalani, led a rebellion and American residents called for help from the USA. The marines arrived and

Protectorate – A state that is controlled and protected by another. For example, after the United States Navy took possession of Eastern Samoa on behalf of the United States, the existing coaling station at Pago Pago Bay was expanded into a full naval station. In 1911, the US Naval Station Tutuila, which was composed of Tutuila, Aunu'u and Manu'a, was officially renamed American Samoa.

Annex – To incorporate a territory into an existing political unit such as a country, state, county or city.

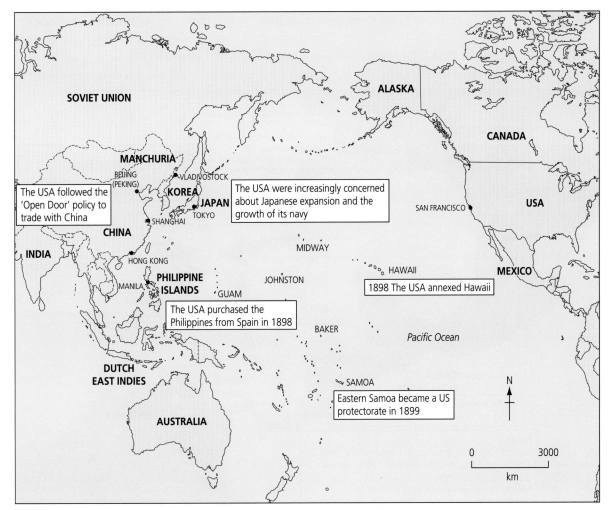

▲ **Figure 3** A map showing US involvement in the Pacific.

OPPOSITION IN THE USA

In the USA, the opposition to the annexation of the Philippines was led by the Anti-Imperialist League, an organisation of different groups set up in 1898 that opposed US imperial expansion. The opponents of annexation argued that the Filipinos would lose the right to govern themselves and that the USA would have nothing to gain from the Philippines. In 1897, the Philippines had received less than one per cent of US exports. In his 1899 book *The Conquest of the United States by Spain*, William Graham Sumner suggested that annexation would ruin the US financially as it had helped to ruin Spain.

within three days the rebels surrendered. The USA now planned to annex Hawaii because of its important location but was opposed by those who feared that America would become an imperial power, no better than the Europeans. However, the war with Spain in Cuba strengthened the arguments for annexation, which took place in July 1898.

The Philippines

As part of the Treaty of Paris, 1898, which ended the Spanish–American War (see page 95), the USA was allowed to purchase the Philippine Islands from Spain for $20 million. There were various reasons for this purchase:

- Many felt that the USA would be able to civilise the islanders through converting them to Christianity as well as 'superior' American ideals.
- In addition, there was preclusive imperialism. The fear was that the Philippines might be taken over by Britain, Germany or Japan.
- The islands could not be returned to Spain and the Filipinos, even though they wanted independence, seemed incapable of ruling themselves effectively.

There was strong opposition to the annexation of the islands both in the Philippines and in the USA. The Filipinos had been fighting for independence from Spain and assumed that once the Spanish were defeated, they would be given their independence. The USA had to fight a four-year war of subjugation, costing around $600 million and, by 1904, 126,000 troops were stationed in the Philippines.

Latin America

The USA looked to extend its influence in Latin America in terms of political influence and developing trade links. While there was no intention of annexing regions, US business interests sought to exploit South and Central America and in doing so raise their standards of living and quality of life.

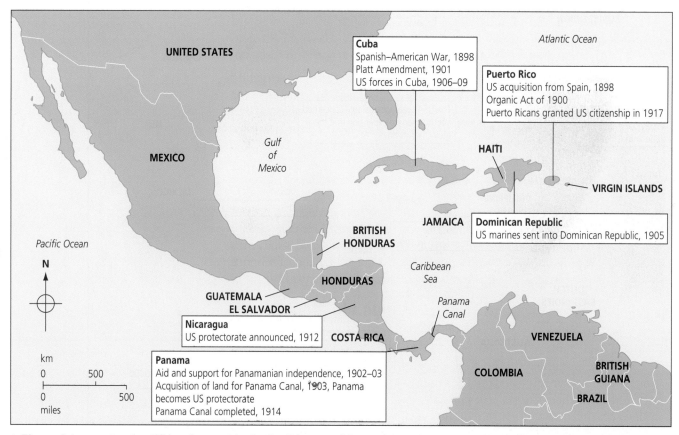

▲ **Figure 4** A map showing US involvement in the Caribbean and Central America.

Puerto Rico

This island was a Spanish colony but had been given a degree of independence before the outbreak of the Spanish–American war in 1898. It was invaded in 1898 by American troops and, after a little fighting, the Spanish surrendered and withdrew. Under the Organic Act of 1900, Puerto Rico was to be administered by the USA.

Venezuela

In 1895, Britain and Venezuela were in dispute over Venezuela's border with the British colony of Guiana. President Cleveland demanded that the British agree to send the dispute to arbitration, a demand which was, at first, rejected by Salisbury, the British Prime Minister. The British eventually backed down when the USA threatened to send 54 vessels to the disputed area. Arbitration eventually decided in favour of Venezuela.

The Spanish–American War, 1898

In 1898, the USA went to war with Spain, which most historians agree marked a change to a more active foreign and imperial policy. Cuba was on America's doorstep and according to the Monroe Doctrine, was in the USA's sphere of interest. However, Cuba was controlled by Spain but Cuban revolutionaries were demanding independence. Spain did offer the Cuban rebels concessions but not enough. The USA was unsure about how to react to either Spain or the rebels until two incidents resulted in war with Spain. A private letter from the Spanish minister in Washington DC was stolen and printed. It accused President McKinley of being a 'weak bidder for the admiration of the crowd' in his Cuban policy. McKinley and the American public found this very insulting. This was followed by the 'Maine' incident.

The 'Maine' incident

While on a 'friendly' visit to Havana Harbour, the American battleship *Maine* exploded, with the loss of 266 crew. Immediately the US press accused the Spanish of sabotage. The Spanish did investigate the incident but came to the conclusion that the explosion had been caused by a fault on the ship. However, an American investigation concluded that it was caused by a mine. The incident certainly inflamed US public opinion as well as the press and encouraged Roosevelt to order a blockade (surrounding and blocking) of Cuba. Later impartial investigations found that the explosion was caused by a known design problem in the ship – a coal bunker fire close to where the shells were stored.

▼ A contemporary lithograph which shows the explosion of the *Maine* in Havana Harbour, Cuba, 15 February 1898.

'**Yellow Press**' – The term used to describe the sensationalist journalism of the 1890s. Journalists such as William Randolph Hearst and Joseph Pulitzer competed with each other to print stories about apparent Spanish atrocities in Cuba including the ill-treatment of female prisoners. It became known as the Yellow Press after a cartoon character called the Yellow Kid, from Pulitzer's *New York World*.

Great Powers – The most powerful countries such as Russia, Britain and Germany.

Reasons for US involvement

There has been much debate about the reasons for the outbreak of the Spanish–American War. The historian Carl Degler, writing in the 1950s, suggested that it was due to economic reasons, with America seeking new markets in response to the 1893 Depression. Most historians stress the impact of the Yellow Press as well as the desire of the USA to join the ranks of the Great Powers.

Others have emphasised the role of President McKinley who was elected with a pledge to protect US interests and, with so much interest in Cuban sugar, it was essential to maintain stability in Cuba. There has been debate about the significance of the part played by McKinley. Traditionally, he has been seen as being reluctant to go to war, having wrestled with his conscience and, ultimately, only being persuaded by Congress. However, more recently historians such as Walter LaFeber have argued that McKinley favoured war as it was in the interests of the USA. Spain would be defeated quite easily and the USA would benefit from greater investment in Cuba as well as increased trade.

Overall, there were several reasons for US intervention:

- It was partly inspired by an aggressive and patriotic press campaign that inflamed public opinion, known as the 'Yellow Press'.
- In addition, there were economic motives. This was partly to protect US business interests in Cuba but also to offer a deliberate distraction from the Depression of the 1890s.
- In many respects, intervention was inevitable given the misrule of the Spanish, the geographical closeness of Cuba and the Monroe Doctrine. The USA had to intervene to restore order.
- Moreover, there were real fears in the USA that they would not be able to control an independent Cuba which, in turn, would threaten American interests on the island.

Source H From a speech given by President McKinley, 1898.

… Third, the right to intervene may be justified by the very serious injury to the commerce, trade, and business of our people, and by the wanton destruction of property and devastation of the island.

Fourth, and which is of the utmost importance, the present condition of affairs in Cuba is a constant menace to our peace, and entails upon this government an enormous expense. With such a conflict waged for years in an island so near us and with which our people have such trade and business relations; when the lives and liberty of our citizens are in constant danger and their property destroyed and themselves ruined; where our trading vessels are liable to seizure and are seized at our very door by warships of a foreign nation, all these and others that I need not mention, with the resulting strained relations, are a constant menace to our peace.

1 What motives are suggested by McKinley (Source H) for US intervention in Cuba?
2 How far does McKinley successfully justify US intervention?

Defeating Spain

In April 1898, US forces launched a double attack on Spanish territories. The navy attacked Spain in the Philippines and defeated its fleet outside Manila. The navy also played an important role in Cuba with one fleet under Rear Admiral Sampson blockading Santiago and the northern approaches to Cuba and a second fleet, under Commodore Winfield Schley, blockading the southern approaches to the island.

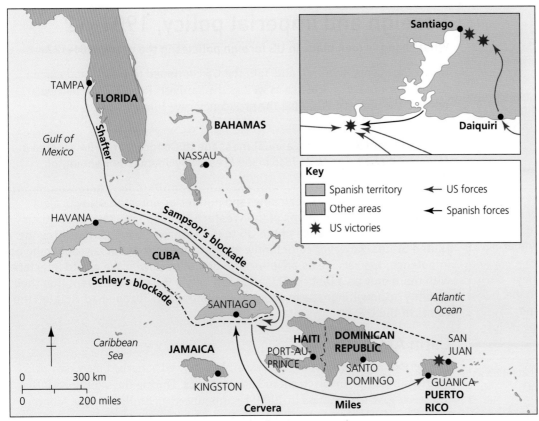

▲ **Figure 5** A map showing the Spanish–American War.

Meanwhile, 17,000 American troops under General William Shafter landed near Santiago. The combination of land forces and the naval blockade forced the surrender of the Spanish troops after less than three weeks of fighting. In the action on Cuba, 379 US soldiers were killed and over 5,000 suffered from yellow fever. Moreover, there was a lot of hostility between the Cuban freedom fighters and US troops. The Cuban General Calixto Garcia with his army of 5,000 played an important role in the defeat of the Spanish on the island. However, the USA ignored the contribution of the Cubans and maintained that it was a purely American victory.

The results of the war

The USA therefore did not include or even seriously consider the Cubans in the final peace settlement with Spain, the Treaty of Paris, which was signed with Spain in August 1898. The Treaty stated that:

- Cuban independence was recognised but the USA was allowed possession of Guantanamo Bay.
- Spain lost the last parts of its American empire by ceding Puerto Rico in the Caribbean to the USA.
- The USA was able to purchase the Philippines for $20 million (see page 92).
- Spain also ceded the Pacific island of Guam to the USA.

The USA had demonstrated its areas of interest as set out in the Monroe Doctrine. Moreover, it had protected and provided for the expansion of its economic interests in Cuba. Under Roosevelt, the USA was also to achieve much greater political control over the island.

> **KEY DATES: FOREIGN AND IMPERIAL POLICY IN THE 1890s**
>
> **1895** The settlement of the Venezuela Boundary dispute.
>
> **1898** The Spanish–American War.
>
> The USA annexed Hawaii.
>
> The USA bought the Philippine Islands from Spain.

1 What can you learn from Source I about Roosevelt's aims in foreign and imperial policy?
2 To what extent are they similar or different to the aims of US foreign and imperial policy in the 1890s?

Corollary – A statement that follows on from another statement.

Roosevelt Corollary

The Roosevelt Corollary sanctioned US armed intervention in Latin America when it felt necessary to prevent financial and/or political collapse. This was used by Roosevelt and his successors to justify much more US military involvement in Latin America. Indeed, Roosevelt insisted that countries in Latin America had to pay off their debts from loans that they had previously received from the USA and act responsibly. In this sense, he was setting up the USA as a sort of police force throughout the Americas, both to protect countries from foreign interference and also to ensure responsible behaviour. This marked a very significant shift in US foreign policy, which was to have repercussions for the future.

Foreign and imperial policy, 1901–12

What changes took place in US foreign policies in the years 1901–12?

Under Presidents Roosevelt and Taft, the US continued to protect and extend its influence in Latin America as well as the Far East. Roosevelt, in particular, relished the opportunities that the presidency gave him for control of foreign and imperial affairs.

Source I From Roosevelt's annual message to Congress in 1904. Quoted in *Modern America: The USA, 1865 to the Present* by Joanne de Pennington, (Hodder), 2005, p.60.

It is not true that the US feels any land hunger or entertains any project as regards the other nations of the Western Hemisphere save as for their welfare but the adherence of the US to the Monroe Doctrine may force the United States, however reluctantly, in flagrant cases of such wrongdoing or impotence, to exercise as an international police power. We would interfere with them only as a last resort, and then only if it became evident that their inability or unwillingness to do justice at home and abroad had violated the rights of the US.

Latin America

The period after the Spanish–American War showed a marked increase in US interest and direct involvement in Latin America. During the same speech that Roosevelt gave to Congress in 1904, he announced a corollary to the Monroe Doctrine, which became known as the Roosevelt Corollary.

Cuba

Once the Spanish had been defeated and withdrawn from Cuba, a major debate started in the USA about what to do with Cuba. It could be given its independence and left alone. On the other hand it could become a colony or protectorate of the USA. In April 1898, just prior to war with Spain, Congress had passed the Teller Amendment which stated that the USA would not annex the island, which would be given its independence.

However, the war led to a change of opinion in the USA where there was a belief that the Cubans were not ready to rule themselves. Moreover, independence might threaten American commercial interests on the island. As a result, in 1901 Congress passed the Platt Amendment.

Cuba's final treaty with the USA was signed in 1903, which imposed a new political system on the country and made its economy heavily dependent on the USA. For example, Cuban sugar and tobacco were tied to the US markets through preferential tariffs, while US goods entered Cuba at reductions varying from 25 to 40 per cent. A far-reaching takeover of Cuban land by Americans followed and American businesses began to move into Cuba on a large scale.

US forces, which had occupied the island since the war of 1898, left in 1902. However, these forces returned in 1906 and remained until 1909 as a result of unrest that began during the presidential elections of 1905. The USA invaded again in 1912 with marines to help the Cuban Government put down a revolt of former slaves.

Panama Canal

The USA had long supported the building of a canal to connect the Atlantic and Pacific Oceans. The journey round the tip of South America was long and often dangerous by sea. As early as the 1860s, US Secretary of State William Seward had tried to begin negotiations with the government of Colombia, which at that time controlled Panama, for a canal, but he was stopped by the Senate.

In 1881, a French company, under the French engineer Ferdinand de Lesseps who had built the Suez Canal in Egypt, began to build a canal in Panama but ran into financial difficulties. An American Company, the New Panama Canal Company, encouraged by President Roosevelt, took over the rights to build the canal. However, Colombia demanded $15 million from the government of the USA and $10 million from the New Panama Canal Company to build the canal across Panama. Roosevelt refused to pay.

However, in 1903 the Panamanians staged a national revolt for independence from the rule of Colombia and were supported by the USA who sent a battleship and a regiment to support the rebellion. Panama achieved independence and accepted a US offer of $10 million for a strip of land 16 km wide through which the canal would be built. The canal was completed in 1914 with the passage of the *SS Ancon* through it. Within a year over 1,000 ships were using it annually.

Platt Amendment

This gave the United States control of Cuban foreign, financial and commercial affairs. It limited Cuban sovereignty and gave the USA the right to intervene in Cuban affairs. It also gave the USA certain naval bases in Cuba. The Amendment was named after Senator Orville H. Platt who introduced it into Congress in February 1901.

Nicaragua
Nicaragua was of importance to the USA because of its proximity as well as the possible Atlantic/Pacific canal site and a high level of economic investment in the country. These interests were threatened by Nicaragua's anti-American president, Jose Santos Zelaya, who, in 1909, cancelled the economic privileges previously granted to US mining concerns. President Taft sent in the marines to install a pro-American president, Adolfo Diaz, and his Secretary of State, Philander C. Knox, extended American influence in Nicaragua by providing huge loans and, in return, the USA controlled the Nicaraguan National Bank. Within three years, the USA once again had to send in 3,000 troops when the position of Diaz was threatened by revolution. The USA now set up a protectorate and occupied the country for a further ten years.

Dominican Republic
The Dominican Republic was an example of the USA using its 'police' power in Central America. In 1903, the Republic defaulted on the repayment of American loans worth $40 million. Roosevelt was reluctant to invade and, instead, in 1904, took control of the customs revenue of the Dominican Republic, using it to pay off the debt. The President described this as his 'big stick' policy.

The USA and the Far East

The USA had become interested in China and Japan in the second half of the nineteenth century for economic reasons – they were anxious to develop the vast potential of the markets of these countries.

China
The USA, unlike Britain, Russia and Germany, had no desire to expand territorially into China. US Secretary of State John Hay realised that many Americans would oppose any acquisition of territory and, instead, in 1899 he introduced the Open Door policy with the first Open Door note asking states to respect each other's trading rights in China, even in each other's spheres of interest.

In 1900, an uprising known as the Boxer Rebellion, directed largely against foreigners, broke out in China. The USA sent a small number of troops to assist other countries in the rescue of foreign embassies in Peking. At the same time Hay announced an extension of the Open Door policy with a second Open Door note, asserting the principle of equal and impartial trade in all parts of China, not just in the existing foreign spheres of interest. It also asserted that in future the US government would protect the lives and property of US citizens living in China.

Japan

Relations with Japan were tense at the turn of the century. There had been substantial Japanese immigration into both Hawaii and the USA but legislation in 1900 had put a stop to this. The openly racist nature of these laws upset the Japanese, as did the annexation of the Philippines. On the other hand, the USA felt threatened by the growth of a large Japanese navy as well as Japan's ambitions in China.

These threats increased when Japan defeated Russia in the Russo–Japanese War of 1904–05. Roosevelt helped to negotiate the end of the war with the Treaty of New Hampshire in which Japan was given a free hand in Korea. However, the Japanese blamed Roosevelt for the decision not to force Russia to pay a war indemnity.

Roosevelt, increasingly concerned about Japanese imperialism, was keen to develop better relations and, in 1908, the Root–Takahira Agreement was signed. The two countries agreed to respect each other's interests in China and to maintain the current situation in the Pacific. The Open Door policy was confirmed for the USA who, in return and without consulting the Koreans, agreed to the Japanese 'right' to annex Korea.

American foreign and imperial policy had undergone significant changes during the years 1890 to 1912. At the beginning of this period the USA was mainly isolationist with minimal intervention abroad. There was limited support for imperial expansion. However, by 1912, the USA had become involved in its first major external conflict in nearly one hundred years. Moreover, there was much greater support for imperial expansion with the USA extending its influence in the Pacific, particularly the Philippines and Samoa, the Far East, especially China, and Latin America including Cuba.

> **War indemnity** – Compensation from a defeated nation to the victors following a war.

KEY DATES: USA FOREIGN AND IMPERIAL POLICY 1901–12

1904 Roosevelt announced a corollary to the Monroe Doctrine.

1908 The USA signed the Root–Takahira Agreement with Japan.

1909 President Taft sent in the marines to the Dominican Republic.

1914 Opening of the Panama Canal.

WORKING TOGETHER

1 Having made notes on this section, swap them with a partner. Compare your notes and give each other feedback.

2 Make a copy of and complete the following table with a brief summary of each of the motives you select for each event.

	Accidental empire	Progressive imperialism	Need for markets	End of Westward expansion	Preclusive imperialism	Monroe Doctrine	Roosevelt Corollary
Samoa							
Hawaii							
Philippines							
Spanish–American War							
Cuba							
Panama Canal							
Nicaragua							
Dominican Republic							
China							

3 To what extent did the motives for these policies change during these years?

Chapter summary

- In the 1890s a new political party, the Populists, developed in the southern and western parts of the USA.
- Progressivism emerged due to a combination of economic, social and political factors.
- Both Roosevelt and Taft introduced a series of Progressive reforms.
- The US economy continued to develop despite the Depression of 1893.
- Massive immigration to the USA in the second half of the nineteenth century was to have profound effects on American society.
- African Americans remained as second-class citizens especially in the Southern states.
- Both Booker T. Washington and William Dubois made important contributions to civil rights during this period.
- American imperial expansion was motivated by a variety of economic, moral and political influences.
- The Spanish–American War of 1898 was to establish American influence over Cuba and was a turning point in US foreign policy.
- The USA increased its influence over Latin America due to the Roosevelt Corollary.

▼ Summary diagram: Progressivism and imperialism, the USA 1890–1912

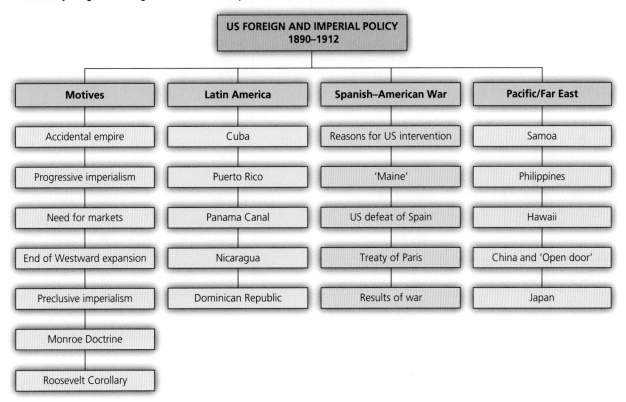

Working on essay technique: argument, counter-argument and resolution

Essays that develop a good argument are more likely to reach the highest levels. This is because argumentative essays are much more likely to develop sustained analysis. As you know, your essays are judged on the extent to which they analyse. The mark scheme opposite is for the full A-level. It is virtually the same for AS level. Both stress the need to analyse and evaluate the key features related to the periods studied. It distinguishes between five different levels of analysis (as well as other relevant skills that are the ingredients of good essays).

The key feature of the highest level is sustained analysis: analysis that unites the whole of the essay.

You can set up an argument in your introduction, but you should develop it throughout the essay. One way of doing this is to adopt an argument, counter-argument structure. A counter-argument is an argument that disagrees with the main argument of the essay. Setting up an argument and then challenging it with a counter-argument is one way of weighing up, or evaluating (see page 67) the importance of the different factors that you discuss. Essays of this type will develop an argument in one paragraph and then set out an opposing argument in another paragraph. This approach will be very relevant on certain topics and questions where there are different opinions. We will first look at techniques for developing sustained analysis and argument before looking at the counter-argument technique.

Argument and sustained analysis

Good essays will analyse the key issues discussed in the essay. They will probably have a clear piece of analysis at the end of each paragraph. This will offer a judgement on the question and is likely to consist of little or no narrative.

Outstanding essays are more likely to be analytical throughout. As well as the analysis of each factor discussed above, there will probably be an overall analysis. This will run throughout the essay and can be achieved through developing a clear, relevant and coherent argument.

High-level arguments

Typically, essays examine a series of factors. A good way of achieving sustained analysis is to consider which factor is most important as in the example on page 101.

Level 5	Answers will display a very good understanding of the full demands of the question. They will be well organised and effectively delivered. The supporting information will be well-selected, specific and precise. It will show a very good understanding of key features, issues and concepts. The answer will be fully analytical with a balanced argument and well substantiated judgement. *21–25 marks*
Level 4	Answers will display a good understanding of the demands of the question. It will be well-organised and effectively communicated. There will be a range of clear and specific supporting information showing a good understanding of key features and issues, together with some conceptual awareness. The answer will be analytical in style with a range of direct comment relating to the question. The answer will be well balanced with some judgement, which may, however, be only partially substantiated. *16–20 marks*
Level 3	Answers will show an understanding of the question and will supply a range of largely accurate information, which will show an awareness of some of the key issues and features, but may, however, be unspecific or lack precision of detail. The answer will be effectively organised and show adequate communication skills. There will be a good deal of comment in relation to the question and the answer will display some balance, but a number of statements may be inadequately supported and generalist. *11–15 marks*
Level 2	The answer is descriptive or partial, showing some awareness of the question but a failure to grasp its full demands. There will be some attempt to convey material in an organised way, although communication skills may be limited. There will be some appropriate information showing understanding of some key features and/or issues, but the answer may be very limited in scope and/or contain inaccuracy and irrelevance. There will be some, but limited, comment in relation to the question and statements will, for the most part, be unsupported and generalist. *6–10 marks*
Level 1	The question has not been properly understood and the response shows limited organisational and communication skills. The information conveyed is irrelevant or extremely limited. There may be some unsupported, vague or generalist comment. *1–5 marks*

EXAMPLE

Consider the following A-level practice question:

To what extent was the growth of imperialism in the years 1890–1912 due to the search for new markets? (25 marks)

Introduction 1 addresses the question but does not develop an argument:

Introduction 1

Clear focus on the question

During this period there was an economic depression in 1893 which encouraged the search for new markets abroad in order to help recovery and stimulate further growth. However, there were also other reasons why there was a growth in imperialism. These include 'progressive imperialism', which meant a desire to improve the lives of non-Americans as well as the end of the frontier. This was a form of imperialism and once this ended America could then turn its attention to foreign adventures.

Wide range of factors

Recognises that can't just cover named factor

This introduction could be improved by the introduction of an argument. An argument is a type of explanation. It makes a claim about the question and supports it with a reason.

A good way of beginning to develop an argument is to think about the meaning of the words in the question. With the question above, you could think about the words 'how far'.

Here is an example of an introduction that begins an argument:

Introduction 2

During this period there was an economic depression in 1893 which encouraged the search for new markets abroad in order to help recovery and stimulate further growth. However, this was not the main reason for the growth of imperialism. 'Progressive imperialism' meant a desire to improve the lives of non-Americans, for example the removal of yellow fever in Cuba and the building of hospitals and schools. In other words, the export of American values to less well-developed nations. But the most important reason for the growth of American imperialism was the end of Westward expansion. This was a form of imperialism and once this ended America could then turn its attention to foreign adventures.

The introduction begins with a claim

Introduction continues with another reason

Concludes with outline of argument of most important reason

This introduction focuses on the question and sets out the key factors that the essay will develop. However, it also sets out an argument that can then be developed throughout each paragraph, and then rounded off with an overall judgement in the conclusion. It also introduces an argument about which factor was most significant in the growth of American imperialism. This means that Introduction 2 would start the essay at a higher level than Introduction 1.

Counter-argument

You can set up an argument in your introduction as we have seen above, but you should develop your argument throughout the essay. One way of doing this is to adopt an argument, counter-argument structure. A counter-argument is an argument that disagrees with the main argument of the essay. Setting up an argument and then challenging it with a counter-argument is one way of weighing up, or evaluating (see page 68), the importance of the different factors that you discuss. Essays of this type will develop an argument in one paragraph and then set out an opposing argument in another paragraph.

(see page 68)

ACTIVITY

Imagine you are answering the following A-level practice question:

'The main reason for the growth of the Progressive Movement in the years 1890–1912 was because of the need to regulate big business.' Assess the validity of this view.

(25 marks)

Using your notes from this chapter:

1 Divide your page as follows:

How the need to regulate big business led to the growth of the Progressive Movement	Other reasons for the growth of the Progressive Movement

2 Consider the following points and place them either in the left- or right-hand column:
- Large businesses established monopolies in particular industries.
- A recession struck in 1893 which led to high unemployment in industrial cities.
- Many Americans lived in desperate poverty.
- Monopolies meant they could fix prices without fear of competition.
- There was growing dissatisfaction with the two main political parties.
- The press was to play a major role in exposing the evils in American society.

- There was increasing hostility towards individuals such as Rockefeller, Morgan and Carnegie who seemed to put their own profits before the interests of the masses.
- There was a growing demand for government regulation to control big business.
- Some Americans were concerned about the growth of socialism and radicalism and felt that unless there was reform, there could well be revolution.

3 Now write a short argument that addresses the question of how important the need to regulate big business was in explaining the growth of the Progressive Movement. Remember, your argument should contain a statement and a reason.

4 Begin with the side of the argument that you agree with. Write two sentences that explain this side of the argument.

5 Now write two sentences for the side of the argument that you don't agree with. This is your counter-argument. Remember that it has to consist of a claim and a reason.

6 Use your original argument and counter-argument as the basis for writing two paragraphs in answer to the question.

Remember, you can apply this approach when responding to other, similar, questions.

Resolution

The best written essays are those which contain sustained analysis. We have seen that one way of achieving this is to write an essay that develops a clear argument (see page 101) and counter-argument (see above).

(see page 101)

Next you should resolve the tension between the argument and the counter-argument. One way of concluding an essay is to resolve this debate that you have established between the argument and the counter-argument as in the example on page 103.

example on page 103.

EXAMPLE

Imagine you are answering the following practice question:

To what extent was the regulation of big business the most important achievement of the Progressive Movement in the years 1890–1912? **(25 marks)**

A possible way to tackle this question would be to write one clear paragraph arguing that the regulation of big business was the most important achievement of the Progressive Movement, and two paragraphs arguing against this. In an essay of this type you could then resolve the tension by weighing up the argument and counter-argument in the conclusion. In so doing, you can reach a supported overall judgement. For example, a possible conclusion could look like this:

Begins with main argument

Resolves tension

Counter-argument contrast

Limitations of counter-argument

In conclusion, the most important achievement of the Progressive Movement was the reform of big business. These included a series of anti-trust measures, particularly the Sherman Anti-Trust Act of 1890 and further reforms by Theodore Roosevelt which brought much greater regulation of their activities. However, the Progressive Movement did also encourage political reform, especially the increased role of the federal government. But although Theodore Roosevelt was more active in social and economic policies during his presidency, this was short-lived with his successor, Taft, being more circumspect about extending the powers of the presidency. Therefore, it can be argued that the regulation of big business was the most long-lasting achievement of the Progressive Movement. Both Roosevelt and Taft introduced a series of measures which ensured that there was much greater federal control and regulation of the activities of the big trusts and corporations.

This conclusion evaluates the argument and counter-argument. It resolves the tension by identifying a problem with the counter-argument, and reaching an overall concluding judgement in relation to the question.

The process of evaluating the argument and the counter-argument is helped by the use of words such as 'However' and 'Nonetheless', indicating that the paragraph is weighing up contrasting arguments.

ACTIVITY

Imagine you are answering the following A-level practice question:

'The main reason for the growth of the Progressive Movement in the years 1890–1912 was because of the need to regulate big business.' Assess the validity of this view. **(25 marks)**

Use the ideas on pages 101–3 and look at the work you did on this question in order to complete the activities.

1 Answer the following questions:
   • Which is stronger, the argument or the counter-argument? Why is it stronger?
   • What are the flaws in the weaker argument?
   • What strengths does the weaker argument have?

2 Having answered these questions write a conclusion that weighs up the argument and the counter-argument in order to reach an overall judgement. You could use the words 'However', 'Nonetheless', and 'Therefore' to structure the paragraph.

Working on interpretation skills: extended reading

What was new about American politics in the Progressive Era (1890–1920)?

Lecturer Dr Katharina Rietzler considers the changes in American politics during the Progressive Era.

Historians have long emphasised the diversity of Progressivism, an era of American history that saw a host of reformers compete with one another to shape public policy. Whether they campaigned to shorten the working hours of women and children, fight infectious diseases in the nation's crowded urban tenement houses, protect the environment, educate immigrants and the rural poor or curb the excesses of corporate power, what united them all was an urgent desire to solve the great problems of American society outside of traditional party politics. Party loyalties and voter participation suffered a sharp decline in the Progressive Era and American electoral politics was turned upon its head. 10

This was most apparent in the presidential election of 1912. In a rare four-way contest former President Theodore Roosevelt and the sitting President William Howard Taft split the Republican vote and made way for the Democrat Woodrow Wilson. Coming in last place was the fourth contender, Eugene Debs, polling nearly one million votes and attaining 15 the second-highest result for a Socialist candidate in American history. Shortly before the election Roosevelt had founded a national Progressive Party because of disagreements with Taft over the direction government should take in reform. Roosevelt himself had been a vigorous 'trust-buster' during his seven and a half years in office. His government used 20 the Sherman Anti-Trust Act to bring suits against forty-four corporations, including Standard Oil and the American Tobacco Company. In an age of 'bigness', growing cities and a consolidating economy, Roosevelt promised ordinary Americans control over monopolistic businesses, pure food and drugs and measures to conserve the natural environment for future 25 generations. Taft, his successor, pursued even more large corporations under the Sherman Act and succeeded in making way for a federal income tax. Woodrow Wilson, the first Democratic President to significantly disrupt the Republicans' dominance after the Civil War, also described himself as a Progressive. Under the banner of a 'New Freedom' Wilson sought 30 to protect workers and consumers from the influence of big business by further strengthening the anti-trust law regime and imposing labour regulations.

Most Progressive reform measures, however, were implemented at the state and local level. This was an age when energetic reformers with 35 an appealing agenda could secure political office comparatively easily. Progressive governors such as Robert La Follette in Wisconsin experimented with innovative policies in an attempt to extend democracy. La Follette secured laws for railroad regulation, a state income tax and restrictions on lobbying. Wisconsin was the first state to introduce the direct primary 40 in 1903, allowing voters to choose party candidates themselves. Cities also became hubs for reform. Toledo boasted free childcare facilities, public

5

parks and playgrounds. Cleveland's mayor Tom L. Johnson campaigned for public ownership of streetcars and food inspection standards, making his home town 'the best-governed city in America', according to the 'muckraker' journalist Lincoln Steffens. Significantly, change often began in places far away from the Eastern seaboard. Campaigns for one of the most successful causes of the Progressive era, women's suffrage, took off west of the Mississippi river. By 1914, eleven Western states had granted women the right to vote. At the end of the Progressive Era, in 1920, the states ratified the Nineteenth Amendment, extending women's suffrage across the nation. Electoral change, however, also revealed the limits of many Progressive reforms, often based on race. While white women gained the ballot, African Americans were systematically disenfranchised in the South between 1890 and 1910, and literacy tests and registration requirements restricted the franchise among the poor.

Progressivism had a remarkable international reach, underlining the extent to which the dynamics of American social politics had changed. Americans had always looked to Europe for inspiration in cultural and social matters but by the 1890s the Atlantic became a veritable turntable for the circulation of reform models. One of these was the settlement house, a housing development where middle-class reformers lived among the poor and provided healthcare and education. Toynbee Hall in London's East End pioneered the scheme and famous settlement houses were set up in Chicago and New York City by Jane Addams and Lillian Wald. These experiments were not free of the era's typical paternalism but innovative for their time.

Progressives understood that they had entered an era in which American politics was transformed. To meet the challenges of this transformation and to fulfil the promise of American democracy, many voices needed to be united in a common purpose. This goal remained elusive but it gave the era its peculiar dynamism.

Dr Katharina Rietzler, Lecturer in American History, University of Sussex.

ACTIVITY

Having read the essay, answer the following questions.

Comprehension

1 What does the author mean by the following phrases?
   a) 'excesses of corporate power' (line 6)
   b) 'trust-buster' (line 19)
   c) 'literacy tests' (line 55)

Evidence

2 Using paragraphs 2 and 3, list the ways in which the author evidences Progressive policies.

Interpretation

3 Using your knowledge from your study of Progressivism list evidence to support the author's view that 'politics was turned upon its head' (line 10).

Evaluation

4 Write an essay explaining how far you agree with the author's view about what was new in American politics in the Progressive Era.
   ● The author suggests that Progressivism had a major impact at national level. To what extent were these changes also due to Populism?
   ● To what extent were there changes to the way elections at national and local levels were conducted and to the two main political parties during this period?

4

Emergence on the World Stage, 1912–20

This chapter covers developments in the USA from 1912 to 1920, including the presidency of Woodrow Wilson. It deals with a number of areas:

- Progressivism and Wilson's New Freedom
- The First World War: neutrality and entry
- Economic and social change

When you have worked through the chapter and the related activities and exercises, you should have detailed knowledge of all those areas, and you should be able to relate this to the key breadth issues defined as part of your study, in particular: how did the role of the USA in world affairs change? For the period covered in this chapter the main points can be phrased as a question:

Why did the USA move from isolationism in the early 1890s to involvement in the First World War?

The focus of the issue is the change in US policy and commitments abroad culminating in the declaration of war on Germany in 1917.

CHAPTER OVERVIEW

Woodrow Wilson served two terms as president of the USA. His first term saw a series of important progressive reforms in banking, finance and the economy as well as continuing the anti-trust legislation of his predecessors. There was limited reform during his second administration mainly due to American involvement in the First World War. Wilson's policies abroad were very much influenced by his own views of moral diplomacy – his ideas of what was right and wrong. He was prepared to intervene in Latin American countries, especially Mexico, if he felt the government was corrupt and/or evil. He maintained US neutrality during the first three years of the war although America became increasingly anti-German due to the sinking of ships, including the *Lusitania*, by German U-boats. In April 1917, the USA declared war on Germany partly because of the resumption of unrestricted U-boat warfare. American forces, although relatively slow to arrive in Europe, eventually played an important role in the defeat of Germany. Involvement in the war led to changes in the USA itself including war production, employment and to the position of African Americans. Wilson, with the publication of his Fourteen Points in 1918, hoped to have a decisive influence on the peace conference.

1 President Wilson and the New Freedom

President Wilson, who served two terms, began a programme of reform that was quite similar to that proposed by the progressive Republicans. The phrase 'the New Freedom' was used by Wilson to describe his general purpose – to create conditions of greater economic opportunity for labour, farmers and small business.

WORKING TOGETHER

Working with a partner, make a copy of and complete the following table. One of you should complete the Progressive column and the other the Limitations column.

Reforms	Progressive	Limitations
Banking		
Economic and financial		
Social		
African Americans		
Constitutional		

Progressive reforms, 1912–20

To what extent were Wilson's reforms progressive?

The election to the presidency gave Wilson an opportunity no Democrat in the previous 50 years had been given. A huge majority of voters in the electoral college had given him their votes and, with them, a mandate from the people to reform government. Armed with support from the Democratic Party, the bipartisan support of progressives, and with both the House of Representatives and the Senate under Democratic control, Wilson was able to initiate and carry out his reforms with little political opposition. He worked closely with Congress, being the first president, for example, to have a direct telephone link with the Legislature.

Soon after his election, the new President declared that he intended to make good on his promises of reform. His domestic progressive policies, which became collectively known as the New Freedom, included reduction of the tariff on imported goods, reform of the inept national banking system and strengthening of the Sherman Act to combat trusts.

Source A An extract from a campaign speech by Woodrow Wilson in 1912. From *History of the USA 1840–1941* by P. Browning and P. Walsh-Atkins, (Cambridge), 2013, p.128.

Politics in America is a case which sadly requires attention. The system set up by our law and our usage doesn't work, or at least it can't be depended on; it is made to work only by a most unreasonable expenditure of labor and pains. The government, which was designed for the people, has got into the hands of bosses and their employers, the special interests. An invisible empire has been set up above the forms of democracy.

The 1912 presidential election

There were four candidates – Taft (Republican), Woodrow Wilson (Democrat), Roosevelt (Progressive) and Eugene Debs (Socialist). However, the main contest was between Wilson and Roosevelt. Wilson triumphed, winning 435 electoral college votes and 6,283,019 popular votes to the 88 electoral college votes and 4,119,507 popular votes of Roosevelt. The Democrats benefited from the split in the Republican Party and won majorities in both Houses of Congress. Wilson became the first Democrat president since 1897.

Bipartisan – Supported by members of two parties.

1 What can you learn from Source A about Wilson's aims?
2 As you work through Wilson's reforms, decide to what extent he fulfilled these aims.

Federal Reserve Board – A centralised system that allowed banks to run their own affairs with only limited government interference.

Rediscount rates – The interest rate at which banks borrow money from the Federal Reserve Banks.

Inflation – Rise in prices due to more money being in circulation

Deflation – Fall in prices and goods.

Banking reform

The Federal Reserve Act of 1913 was an Act typical of Wilson, as it maintained a balance between the interests of big business and the needs of the wider community. The Act created the first central banking system in the USA. Twelve banking districts were created, each under the supervision of a **Federal Reserve Board**. All national banks and any state bank that wished to participate in the system had to invest six per cent of their capital and surplus in the reserve bank. The Federal Reserve Banks could lend money to member banks at **rediscount rates**. The system meant that the supply of money was no longer dependent on the amount of gold. The Federal Reserve Bank in Washington was at the centre of the system and appointed the majority of directors of the other Federal Reserve Banks.

This system enabled the reserve banks to control the money supply in the USA. When **inflation** threatened, the banks could increase the rediscount rates, discouraging borrowing and therefore reducing the amount of money in circulation. Where there was **deflation** the banks could lower the rediscount rate and therefore encourage borrowing so that there was more money in circulation. By 1923, roughly 70 per cent of the nation's banking resources were part of the federal reserve system. One of Wilson's most enduring achievements, this system still serves as the basis of the nation's banking system.

Anti-trust measures

Wilson was also determined to ensure that measures aimed against trusts were applied effectively. In 1914, Congress passed two important laws affecting trusts and giant corporations:

Federal Trade Commission

This was formed to investigate corporations and stop unfair practices, although the word 'unfair' was not defined. It was a regulatory body for business that covered every possible dubious business action. Many felt that it was not strong enough, but it established an important principle of federal regulation. Under Wilson, the FTC administered almost 400 cease-and-desist orders to companies engaged in illegal activity. Still in effect today, the FTC also prosecutes dishonest stock traders and regulates internet sales.

Clayton Anti-Trust Act

This gave more powers to those enforcing the Sherman Anti-Trust Act. It made certain business practices illegal such as price discrimination to foster monopolies, 'tying arrangements' which forbade retailers from handling rivals' products and the creation of interlocking directorates to control companies that appeared to be in competition. Samuel Gompers, president of the American Federation of Labor (AFL), saw great value to workers in the Clayton Act. He called it a Magna Carta for labour, referring to the English document, signed in 1215, in which the English king recognised that he was bound by the law and that the law granted rights to his subjects.

Economic and financial reforms

Wilson also introduced a series of financial and economic reforms including the first ever income tax. The Department of Labor had been created by Wilson's predecessor, Taft. Woodrow Wilson appointed its first secretary, William Wilson, who was a former miner and union leader who played a large part in helping resolve disputes between capital and labour. Woodrow also reorganised

LOOK AGAIN

Look back to Chapter 3. What were the key aims of the Progressive Movement? Split into groups and begin to list its key aims. Write each one on a post-it note. Each group should then attach these to the wall or whiteboard. Compare the aims raised by each group. Discuss what seem to be the key aims.

the Department of Agriculture to assist all those involved in farming, ensuring better credit and distribution networks for farmers. In addition, the Federal Farm Loan Act of 1916 provided low-cost loans to farmers.

Underwood Tariff

In October 1913, the Underwood Tariff significantly reduced many duties and freed certain items from them entirely. These included food, wool, iron and steel, shoes and agricultural machinery, all of which could be produced more cheaply in the USA than abroad and so did not need protection from foreign competition. Loss of government revenue was compensated by the introduction in 1913 of federal income tax. This necessitated a change to the Constitution (the Sixteenth Amendment). Many people regarded this as an attack on big business, which favoured high tariffs, and an aid to smaller businessmen and farmers.

Income tax

Income tax was intended to replace the government income lost when tariffs were reduced or abolished. Initially, income tax only had to be paid by those with an income of over $4,000, which at the time was over four times a good industrial wage. The income tax gave the federal government a major source of income. Moreover, the Revenue Act of 1916 continued the plan of taxing the rich and redistributing wealth, expanding into the taxation of business profits and estates as well. Initially, few Congressmen realised the potential of the income tax, but by 1917 the government was receiving more money on the income tax than it had ever gained from tariffs. Today, income taxes on corporations and individuals represent the federal government's main source of revenue.

Social reform

Wilson also introduced a series of social reforms. The first Federal Child Labor Act of 1916 made a start in dealing with the 2 million children under sixteen who were known to be in work and were often deprived of education. It also barred goods made by child labour from inter-state commerce. However, two years later the Act was ruled unconstitutional by the Supreme Court of the United States.

Also in 1916, a Workmen's Compensation Act ensured that federal employees who were absent from work because of injury or illness received financial assistance and the Adamson Act laid down a maximum eight-hour day for railroad workers.

However, Wilson showed little sympathy towards or support for trade unions. For example, in 1913, coal miners went on strike in Ludlow, Colorado. The company refused their demands and evicted workers from company housing. Workers set up tents outside the company. The Colorado National Guard was called. The Guardsmen fired on the tents and killed 26 people. Wilson sent federal troops to restore order and break up the strike.

African Americans

Despite Wilson's economic and political reforms, he disappointed Progressives who favoured social reform. In particular, on racial matters Wilson appeased conservative Southern Democratic voters but disappointed his Northern white and black supporters. He placed segregationists in charge of federal agencies, thereby expanding racial segregation in the federal government, the military and Washington DC.

Woodrow Wilson (1856–1924)

Woodrow Wilson was born in 1856. His father was a strict Christian minister and Woodrow Wilson was brought up in a household associated with such beliefs. He was educated at Princeton and then at the University of Virginia and Johns Hopkins University. In 1890, he was appointed a professor at Princeton, a position he held until 1902. From 1902 to 1910, Woodrow Wilson was president of Princeton. In 1910, he was elected governor of New Jersey for the Democrats. He swiftly achieved national fame for his social reforms in New Jersey and in 1912 won the presidential election. He was president of the USA until 1919 when he collapsed from a stroke, and his political career ended suddenly. He was an invalid for the rest of his life and died in 1924.

WORK TOGETHER

Set up a class debate to assess whether Wilson's period as president deserves the title of the 'New Freedom', with one group arguing 'for' and another 'against'. Use the notes you made from the Activity on page 107. You could use the following motion to structure your debate:

'This class believes that Wilson's presidency deserves the title of the New Freedom.'

KEY DATES: PROGRESSIVE REFORMS

1913 The Federal Reserve Act.
The Underwood Tariff Act.

1914 The Clayton Act.
The Federal Commission Act.

1916 The first Federal Child Labour Act. Wilson re-elected president.

During the presidential campaign of 1912, he won the support of the NAACP's black intellectuals and white liberals by promising to treat blacks equally and to speak out against lynching. As president, however, Wilson opposed federal anti-lynching legislation, arguing that these crimes fell under state jurisdiction. He appointed to his cabinet fellow white Southerners who extended segregation. Secretary of the Navy Josephus Daniels, for example, proposed at a cabinet meeting to do away with common drinking fountains and towels in his department. According to an entry in Daniels' diary, President Wilson agreed because he had 'made no promises in particular to negroes, except to do them justice'. Segregated facilities, in the President's mind, were just. African Americans and their liberal white supporters in the NAACP felt betrayed.

Wilson's second term as President, 1917–21

Wilson served as president for a second term, from 1917–21.

The 1916 presidential election

The presidential election of 1916 occurred when most Americans, while leaning towards the Allied forces, wanted to remain neutral. Wilson tapped into this desire for neutrality with the campaign slogan 'He kept us out of war'. The Republican Party nominated Supreme Court Justice Charles Evans Hughes. He was a moderate candidate chosen because he appealed to both conservatives and progressives in the Republican Party; thus, he would hopefully be able to heal the 1912 split. The Progressive Party tried to run Theodore Roosevelt for president, but he declined his nomination in favour of supporting Hughes, leading to the collapse of the Progressives.

The Republicans campaigned against Wilson's pacifist stance, arguing for a programme of greater mobilisation and preparedness, and attacked Wilson's interventions in the Mexican Civil War. Wilson narrowly won the election, becoming the first Democrat since Andrew Jackson to serve a second presidential term.

This second term was dominated by the involvement of the USA in the First World War and the measures taken by Wilson during the war, particularly greater federal control of the economy and workforce.

How progressive was Wilson?

Wilson did introduce a series of economic and welfare reforms in the early years of his administration. He had introduced significant changes to the Constitution which extended the role of the federal government. He continued the work of his predecessors in anti-trust legislation. There were also highly significant financial reforms including the first ever income tax as well as the federal reserve system.

However, by 1914, he seemed satisfied with his achievements and there were few reforms for the next six years. Many Americans thought he had not gone far enough. Little had been done on the welfare front, largely because Wilson thought this was the responsibility of individual states rather than the federal government. Nor was there any real attack on big business. He opposed federal child labour and anti-lynching legislation and he did not fight segregation, in fact it actually increased during his presidency. Despite Wilson's original aims, there were very limited changes to the powers of the presidency and the federal government.

2 The US entry into the First World War

There were significant changes in foreign policy under Wilson, with the USA moving from neutrality in the first three years of the First World War to declaring war on Germany in 1917 and direct involvement in the First World War.

US neutrality, 1914–17

To what extent did the USA adopt a policy of neutrality?

Wilson and moral diplomacy

President Wilson and his Secretary of State William Jennings Bryan genuinely believed that the USA had a responsibility to improve the lives of foreign peoples through US example. They spoke of a 'moral diplomacy' in which the desire to do good would govern US policy. They believed that contact with the USA could only benefit others; that the USA was morally superior to other nations and that its diplomacy was governed by noble and benevolent principles. This description of his ideological perspectives on foreign policy is also known as Wilsonianism.

To this end, the USA gave Colombia $20 million in reparations for the role the USA had played in encouraging the Panamanians to rebel from Colombian rule in 1903. Nevertheless, Wilson went on to intervene many times in Latin America. In this sense he continued and indeed extended the policies of Roosevelt and Taft, which he had opposed before taking office.

Wilson's idealism

Wilson declared, on taking office, that future co-operation in Latin America would only be possible with 'just' government, the implication being that he would oppose military dictatorships or revolutionary governments. This took the Roosevelt Corollary (see page 96) to a new level. The goal in Latin America became 'to support the orderly processes of just government based upon law and not upon arbitrary or irregular forces'. Indeed he went further, saying 'I am going to teach the South American Republics to elect good men'. One of his envoys, Walter H. Page, actually went further still, saying, presumably in an unguarded moment, that US forces would 'shoot men until they learn to vote and rule themselves'.

All this may seem naïve in the world of international relations. However, Wilson's idealism did achieve some successes:

- He fought against special concessions – he insisted that Congress, for example, repeal the 1912 law exempting US coastal shipping from paying tolls to the Panama Canal.
- US interests built highways, bridges, airfields, hospitals and schools and set up telephone services throughout Latin America.

However, Wilson involved the USA more than any president in its history thus far in foreign affairs.

The onset of war, 1914

At the onset of war in August 1914, the USA apparently adopted a policy of neutrality which was maintained until April 1917, when it entered the war as an

> **NOTE-MAKING**
>
> Using a spider diagram summarise US neutrality in the years 1914–17. Your spider diagram should include the following:
> - Reasons for neutrality
> - Tensions concerning neutrality
> - Support for the Allies
> - Unrestricted U-boat warfare

> **Reparations** – War damages to be paid by a defeated country.

> ### Wilson's intervention in Latin America
>
> Wilson ordered interventions in Latin America because he felt the countries the USA intervened in were badly governed or corrupt. He genuinely felt the USA had a moral obligation to force them to improve or else to take them over for the benefit of the local populations. He ordered intervention in Haiti after a revolution in 1915. The USA invaded, restored order and effectively supervised the running of the country, remaining in Haiti until 1934. Following various revolutions, the Dominican Republic was placed under US military government in 1915. This was, Wilson implied, the least bad solution. Troops remained there until 1924. He maintained the US presence in Nicaragua. In fact, the US military occupation continued from 1912–25 and 1926–33.

Associated power – Power not formally allied to other countries fighting against a common enemy, therefore having independence as to military strategy and the subsequent peace settlement.

Allies – The countries fighting against Germany including Britain, France, Belgium and Russia.

associated power on the side of the **Allies**. During the 1916 presidential elections, Wilson campaigned to keep the USA out of war; and yet a few months after his electoral victory he had joined the conflict.

Reasons for neutrality

There are various reasons why the USA attempted to remain neutral in August 1914 including the weight of public opinion and Wilsonianism.

Public opinion

The prevailing mood in the USA was that the war in Europe had nothing to do with them. There was a widespread feeling that wars were wrong and achieved little. On 29 August 1914, 1,500 women marched down Fifth Avenue in New York in black robes to the beat of drums to protest the war. Various influential leaders including Wilson's Secretary of State William Jennings Bryan began to organise campaigns against the war.

Wilsonianism

Wilson himself sought neutrality. He regarded himself as an honest broker who could negotiate a peace settlement. This was consistent with Wilsonianism, the phrase that describes how he tried to impart moral and Christian principles to his diplomacy.

To succeed in this and gain the trust of all parties he had to be above reproach in terms of neutrality. In his Declaration of Neutrality of 19 August 1914 he offered to mediate. This was a declaration to Congress in which he warned US citizens against taking sides in the First World War. He was desperate not only for the USA to stay out, but for the conflict to end. Wilson, it must be remembered, was guided by a sense of Christian morality which found war abhorrent – despite the number of times he had intervened in Latin America. Wilson also feared the war could escalate and the USA be sucked in so he was anxious from the start to support moves to end the conflict. If the USA was to have influence in peace-making, it would need to be beyond reproach in its neutrality.

Tensions concerning neutrality

There were, however, problems with neutrality including pro-British and anti-German sentiments, issues of trade and issues around freedom of the seas.

Pro-British feeling

While Wilson genuinely sought neutrality he, and many of his advisers, actually favoured the Allies, and the British in particular. This was in part due to Wilson's natural preferences for British culture and customs. He maintained all his life fond memories of cycling around the English Lake District as a young man and saw Britain as a centre of civilisation and decency.

Anti-German feeling

More seriously, however, Wilson agreed with his advisers, particularly his close friend Colonel Edward House and Robert Lansing (Legal Advisor to the State Department, and, from June 1915, Secretary of State) that Germany posed a threat to US interests and it would be better to help the Allies fight the Germans now than have the USA possibly have to fight them alone one day. The USA had had confrontations with Germany in Samoa in 1889 and Wilson worried about Germany's growing interests in Latin America, especially Mexico.

In his message to Congress in December 1915, Wilson attacked German-Americans for disloyalty to the USA.

I am sorry to say that the gravest threats against our national peace and safety have been uttered within our own borders. There are citizens of the United States, I blush to admit, born under other flags but welcomed under our generous naturalization laws to the full freedom and opportunity of America, who have poured the poison of disloyalty into the very arteries of our national life; who have sought to bring the authority and good name of our Government into contempt, to destroy our industries wherever they thought it effective for their vindictive purposes to strike at them, and to debase our politics to the uses of foreign intrigue . . . They have formed plots to destroy property, they have entered into conspiracies against the neutrality of the Government, they have sought to pry into every confidential transaction of the Government in order to serve interests alien to our own.

There was also considerably anti-German propaganda in the popular press. Stories of German atrocities on the Western Front in Europe abounded such as raping nuns in Belgium, spearing babies on bayonets and wholesale murder of civilians. That there was little truth in any of these allegations hardly mattered; the Hun was depicted as cruel and bestial.

To a certain extent Wilson's partiality affected the judgement of his administration. So, despite the genuine desire for US neutrality and a fair peace settlement, Wilson's policies were never really neutral as such and always favoured the Allies.

Trade

The Allies also benefited more than the Central Powers from trade with the USA.

By 1914, the USA was one of the world's major trading nations. In that year it exported $549 million worth of goods to Britain and showed a trading surplus of over $300 million. It also sold over $344 million worth of goods to Germany, with a trading profit of $154 million. Some Americans favoured the prevention of trade with any of the countries at war because of the complications it could cause. Others argued its continuation would bring prosperity to the USA as all sides needed to buy US goods because of the demands of war. The government wanted to maintain trade if only because it received 40 per cent of its revenues from the tariff and loss of trade could see a $60 to $100 million deficit in government spending over income.

Wilson followed the rules of international law, which basically said that neutrals could sell to countries at war. Trade favoured the Allies much more than the Germans, in part because of the effectiveness of the British blockade of Germany. Trade with the Allies, much of which was in munitions, stood at $3.2 billion by 1916. This was ten times that of trade with the Central Powers. By 1916, US trade with Germany was only one per cent of what it had been in 1914. In its trade policies therefore the USA could hardly be seen to be neutral – it was selling far more to the Allies than to the Central Powers.

In addition, the Allies had, by the end of hostilities in 1918, borrowed nearly $7 billion from the USA – which after the war they would need to repay. Eventually, by the time of the peace settlement, Allied war debts to the USA amounted to $10.5 billion.

Freedom of the Seas

The laws of the sea allowed countries at war to blockade enemy ports, as the British were doing to German ports, and seize cargo classified as 'contraband',

> What dangers is Wilson alerting his audience to (Source B)?

Hun – Derogatory term for Germans, derived from Huns, a warlike tribe renowned for their cruelty and barbarism in the fifth century.

Central Powers – Germany and its allies such as Austria–Hungary and Turkey.

British blockade of Germany – British naval blockade to prevent goods leaving and entering German ports.

Munitions – Weapons and ammunition.

which could be loosely defined as anything useful to the enemy. At first this caused conflict between Britain and the USA because, during the early stages of the war, Britain began seizing US ships and confiscating their cargoes destined for neutral ports even on occasion when they only carried foodstuffs. Britain declared many commodities, including food and textiles, as contraband and blacklisted foreign firms who traded with the Central Powers. The situation seemed similar to the British blockade during the Napoleonic wars, which had led to the 1812 war between Britain and the USA.

Wilson could justifiably have made far more of a protest because British actions of seizing neutral ships verged on illegality. However, Wilson faced the dilemma that, while the British actions might have been unfair on neutral nations, he nevertheless wanted the Allies to win the war. It was true also that American crews were treated with courtesy, and there was no loss of life. This was in contrast with the German development of submarine warfare in which vessels might be attacked without warning and loss of life was considerable.

Unrestricted submarine warfare, February–August 1915

In February 1915, Germany declared British waters a war zone and reserved the right to sink any ships en route to Britain – including those flying the flags of neutral countries. They would deploy their new submarine fleet to destroy merchant ships containing essential supplies as they crossed the Atlantic Ocean. This policy of unrestricted submarine warfare was Germany's attempt to break the deadlock of trench warfare in Western Europe, through wresting control of the seas from Britain and starving her into surrender.

Wilson immediately responded by warning Germany he would hold them responsible for the loss of any American lives on ships sunk by Germany. Nevertheless, at the time, some Americans felt unrestricted submarine warfare was a reasonable tactic, and the answer was to ensure that US ships and civilians weren't heading to Britain. Wilson's Secretary of State, William Jennings Bryan, actually said that merchant ships carrying war supplies couldn't rely on the presence of women and children to protect them from attack – by which he meant they could not expect to be safe from attack simply because they carried women and children, almost as defensive shields. Ships were vulnerable to attack whoever might be among their passengers. The German Embassy took out advertising campaigns in the USA to warn Americans not to travel to Britain.

Nevertheless, after another British ship, the *Arabic*, was sunk in August 1915, with the deaths of two Americans, Germany agreed to abandon unrestricted submarine warfare. From now on submarines would only attack the ships after giving due warnings and ensuring their crew and passengers had been placed in lifeboats.

Unrestricted submarine warfare – Attacking any ship en route to an enemy port.

Trench warfare – The defensive network on the Western Front in which millions died.

The *Lusitania*

The controversial policy of unrestricted submarine warfare came to a head with the sinking of the British ship the *Lusitania* in May 1915, with 128 Americans among the 1,200 dead. Wilson issued a strong protest, demanding that Germany abandon the policy. Bryan resigned as Secretary of State over the uneven handling of the issue. He argued that Wilson did not protest British violations in seizing neutral ships as described above – although many historians have noted that these did not result in American deaths. Germany was surprised by Wilson's vehemence, particularly after their well-publicised warnings.

114

KEY DATES: US NEUTRALITY, 1914–17

1915 Feb Germany introduces unrestricted U-boat warfare.

1915 May The sinking of the *Lusitania*.

1915 Aug Germany called off unrestricted U-boat warfare.

WORKING TOGETHER

1 Work with a partner on US neutrality in the years 1914–17.
   • One of you find evidence of US neutrality
   • The other find evidence on US intervention.
   • Compare your findings.
2 To what extent do you agree that the USA adopted a policy of neutrality in the years 1914–17?

US entry into the war

Was it inevitable that the USA entered the war in 1917?

While earlier Wilson had seen US neutrality as the key factor in giving the USA the respect of all the countries at war in promoting peace-making, he increasingly saw US involvement as the best guarantee of the right of the USA to influence the post-war peace settlement. For this reason, Wilson was speaking of a post-war world even before US entry into the war.

An end to war

Wilson was increasingly considering a post-war world in which there could be no more war. As early as 1912, he had spoken of four ideas necessary for the survival of humanity:

- some sort of international association for nations to join
- a guarantee of the rights of all peoples
- internationally agreed sanctions for aggressors
- the removal of the manufacture of munitions from profit-making private concerns to governments.

In May 1916, Wilson gave a speech in which he outlined the factors that lead to war such as secret diplomacy, which led to distrust between nations, and increasing expenditure on armaments. He went on to speak of the need for the consent of the peoples affected before territories could be transferred and the need for an international organisation to keep the peace.

Source C An extract from Wilson's 'Peace Without Victory' speech to the Senate, 22 January 1917. From *Emergence of the USA in Global Affairs, 1880–1929* by P. Clements and P. Benson, (Hodder Education), 2013, p.100.

Victory would mean peace forced upon the loser, a victor's terms imposed upon the vanquished. It would be accepted in humiliation, under duress, at an intolerable sacrifice, and would leave a sting, a resentment, a bitter memory upon which terms of peace would rest, not permanently, but only as upon quicksand. Only a peace between equals can last. Only a peace, the very principle of which is equality and a common participation in a common benefit. The right state of mind, the right feeling between nations, is as necessary for a lasting peace as is the just settlement of vexed questions of territory or of racial and national allegiance.

Wilson was, in other words, formulating what would become his Fourteen Points as a basis for a lasting peaceful settlement in which the USA would set the example of international relations to which all nations would aspire. Referring to Wilson's 'Peace Without Victory' speech, French premier Georges Clemenceau said, 'Never before has any political assembly heard so fine a sermon on what human beings might be capable of accomplishing if only they weren't human'.

Failure of peace initiatives

However, by April, the USA had cast neutrality aside and entered the war. Wilson realised that if the USA did join the war he would lose credibility as a peacemaker, but no one seemed interested in his efforts to broker peace anyway. He had sent his envoy Colonel Edward House twice to Europe in 1915 and 1916 to negotiate a truce but neither side responded very enthusiastically.

NOTE-MAKING

Make notes on this section using bullet points (see page x). You will need a heading for each reason that explains US entry into the war, and then a bulleted point summary.

What can you learn from the speech (Source C) about Wilson's aims for any eventual peace settlement?

Reasons for the USA's entry into the war

In April 1917, the USA entered the war on the Allied side. Various reasons have been offered for this:

Resumption of unrestricted submarine warfare

On 31 January 1917, Germany gave eight hours' notice that it intended to sink all ships found within the war zone around British waters. The German government believed they were in a position where they could starve Britain into surrender by intensifying the U-boat campaign. If the USA declared war as a result, the German gamble was that the Allies, both lacking foodstuffs and war materials imported from the USA and other American countries, would surrender before the Americans could cross the submarine-infested Atlantic in sufficient numbers to make any difference.

While Wilson privately considered the Kaiser as insane, and on 3 February broke off diplomatic relations with Germany, he still hoped to avoid entry into the war. However, during February and March 1917 several US ships were sunk by German U-boats.

German activities within the USA

We have already seen that Wilson distrusted many German-Americans and accused them of espionage and sabotage. Some Germans were undoubtedly spying and committing acts of espionage within the USA. While the extent and impact of their activities may have been exaggerated, the presence of internal traitors undoubtedly fuelled further resentment against Germany.

Zimmerman Telegram

The Zimmermann Telegram was a coded telegram from German Foreign Secretary Arthur Zimmermann sent to the German Ambassador to Mexico, Heinrich von Eckhart, on 16 January 1917. It told Heinrich to propose to the Mexican government a secret alliance with Germany in which, if they went to war with the USA, Mexico would receive back Texas, Arizona and New Mexico. In February 1917, the US Ambassador in Britain sent to the State Department an intercept of the telegram. The German Ambassador in Mexico had not in fact acted on the instruction, and Mexico knew nothing of it. With a civil war raging there they were hardly in a position to make full-scale war on the USA. Nevertheless, Wilson was affronted by this telegram and it afforded him a further pretext for war.

Declaration of War

In April 1917, Wilson asked Congress for the authority to make war on Germany. He realised quite simply that he had little choice; the USA had been provoked until its credibility was threatened. The Allies, moreover, were in trouble. In February and March 1917, 1 million tons of Allied shipping was sunk by U-boats. Wilson feared their defeat was increasingly likely if US involvement wasn't forthcoming. He, by now, realised that only belligerents could possibly have any influence in negotiating the post-war settlement.

Different interpretations

Historians have emphasised differing reasons for the entry of the USA into the war and in this debate we will reflect on some of the perspectives from which they argue.

The economic and isolationist debate

During the inter-war period between 1918 and 1941, when reaction to the horrors of the First World War had set in, many commentators such as

Black Tom's munitions plant

Black Tom's munitions plant in Jersey City Harbor mysteriously exploded on 30 July 1916, causing $20 million worth of damage and smashing windows as far as sixteen miles away. Some fragments from the explosion lodged in the Statue of Liberty. It has been estimated that as much as 2 million pounds of ammunition went up in the explosion. German saboteurs were blamed for the explosion although no one was ever brought to trial.

Belligerents – Countries engaged in warfare.

C. Hartley Grattan and Walter Mills saw Wilson as a dupe, someone who had been swayed by a special relationship with big business including bankers and munitions manufacturers into going to war, so these powerful and wealthy interests could continue to enjoy huge profits. They cite evidence such as how exports to the Allies brought the USA out of Depression in 1914 and that Bryan resigned because he felt loans and exports were compromising neutrality. Charles Beard developed the argument further, stressing that the pressures for entry into war came from ordinary business interests.

Many of these historians supported isolationism during the inter-war years; they deployed their arguments to reason that entry into the war had been wrong and the USA should not repeat this. Given the subsequent rise of Nazi Germany and the entry of the USA, belatedly, many felt, into the Second World War, their arguments became somewhat discredited after that conflict. Of late, however, historians such as Benjamin O. Fordham have reconsidered them, using more refined economic data to suggest they may have validity. US exports doubled as a percentage of the GNP between 1914 and 1916, and 70 per cent of them went to Europe. Within this context, the German renewal of unrestricted submarine warfare was a real catalyst for war.

However, historians no longer tend to see economic reasons as significant. By 1916, the US economy was so healthy as a result of jumping into markets no longer met by the belligerents that, even if Allied trade had been severed, it wouldn't have made a significant difference to US prosperity.

The moral crusade

President Wilson himself saw self-interest as unimportant in his declaration of war. Since the mid-twentieth century, historians have tended to view US involvement in terms of variations on this theme. Writing in the 1950s, for example, Carl N. Deger argued Wilson's main reason for involvement was legalistic. Wilson's concept of neutrality rights followed established international law and asserted that the USA should be free to trade non-contraband goods with any belligerent it chose and American citizens should be safe to sail in any ships. Wilson saw unrestricted submarine warfare as illegal in international law – in fact a crime against humanity.

In the 1990s, Harold Evans argued that Wilson followed a moral principle, believing that the USA needed to fight in order to make the world a better place. He contrasted Wilson with Theodore Roosevelt who, he argues, would have gone to war earlier than Wilson in order to defeat the aggressor nation Germany, remedy US grievances and restore the balance of power. Wilson, however, went to war to destroy the old forms of diplomacy and introduce a new world order based on rights and respect for all peoples.

Ross Kennedy, writing in 2008, developed this theme. He argued that Wilson blamed the old European reliance on the balance of power for the military expansion which had led to war. However, Wilson also recognised that the collective security he favoured could only come about if countries trusted each other. He believed in particular that Germany must return the lands it had taken and become a democracy before it could be trusted to maintain the peace. Therefore, argues Kennedy, Wilson shared the Allied war aims. Indeed, there was always a contradiction in Wilson's earlier neutrality because he favoured the Allies over Germany.

In the 1960s, Hugh Brogan felt the Germans left Wilson no choice but to go to war. He argued that Wilson's alleged neutrality was anything but, and eventual involvement of the USA was inevitable. He went on to suggest that the actual timing of the entry of the USA lay with Germany. In February 1917, Germany

Gross National Product (GNP) – The total value of all final goods and services produced within a nation in a particular year.

Legalistic – Following the letter of the law.

Mobilisation – Gearing the country for war, including recruiting, equipping and transporting the military.

War bonds – Debt securities issued by a government to finance military operations and other expenditure in times of war.

took the decision to renew unrestricted submarine warfare, hoping it would result in the defeat of Britain and France before the USA was ready to fight. This gamble failed. Once it entered the struggle, however, the aims of the USA became wider. It was fighting for a better world, where there would be no more war, rather than simply to defeat Germany and its allies. According to Brogan, the USA did not necessarily share the Allies' war aims. Brogan quotes one editor who argued that the Allies were thieves and the Germans murderers: 'On the whole we prefer the thieves but only as the lesser of two evils'.

Niall Ferguson, whose book *Colossus* appeared in 2003, felt that Wilson the idealist sought to construct an entirely new international order based on fairness and justice for all peoples. As early as December 1914 he had asserted that any peace settlement 'should be for the advantage of the European nations regarded as peoples and not for any nation imposing its governmental will upon alien people'. In May 1915 he went further: 'every nation has a right to choose the sovereignty under which they shall live'. While the sinking of the *Lusitania* and unrestricted submarine warfare were undoubtedly triggers, Wilson had something more sublime in mind when he declared war.

KEY DATES: US ENTRY INTO THE WAR

1916 Black Tom's munitions plant explosion.

1917 Jan Resumption of U-boat warfare and Zimmermann Telegram.

1917 Apr US declaration of war.

The USA during the war

In what ways did the USA change during the war?

Having reluctantly gone to war, Wilson oversaw an effective mobilisation both for the war effort and to unite Americans in its support. American armed forces were to play a very significant role in the conflict itself and the war speeded up changes in the USA.

The War economy

The USA was not prepared for massive war production as it would be in the Second World War. The gigantic Hog Island Shipyard in Philadelphia, for example, employed 3,400 workers and failed to complete its first vessel before the war ended. Of the 8.8 million artillery rounds fired by US troops, fewer than 8,000 had been manufactured in the USA. However, the economy was prepared for the conflict.

Paying for the war

The war cost $33.5 billion in addition to the $7 billion lent to the Allies, which was expected to be recouped after the conflict. Two-thirds of this cost was raised by loans such as Liberty and Victory Loans whose drives were very successful. There were five war bond issues between April 1917 when the USA joined the war, and April 1919, six months after it ended. Movie stars such as Charlie Chaplin, Mary Pickford and Douglas Fairbanks Jnr were deployed to encourage people to buy bonds and the Army Signal Corps organised aerial displays during drives in particular places. The country was plastered with bills and posters – for the third loan issue in April 1918, 9 million posters and 5 million window stickers were issued. The government also collected $10.5 billion in taxes in part through a steeply graded income tax with a top level of 75 per cent. A 25 per cent inheritance tax was also introduced.

War Industries Board

Wilson created the War Industries Board in July 1917 to co-ordinate the tasks of finance and supplies. It had power to direct scarce resources, standardise production and fix prices but still allow firms to make large profits. US Steel, for example, made half a billion dollars in two years and led to accusations of war profiteering in the post-war years.

> **War profiteering** – Making excess profits during war time, for example by charging artificially high prices.

Railroads

The railroads were run as a single centralised system to co-ordinate and simplify what was a vital transport system for the movement of goods and troops during wartime. As Director-General of the Railroads, William G. McAdoo pooled all railway equipment, standardised accounting practices, raised wages for employees and increased passenger rates.

▲ American troops being welcomed in London in 1917.

Agriculture

Wilson appointed Herbert Hoover as his Food Administrator after the entry into the war in 1917. Hoover had co-ordinated relief efforts in Europe for refugees in the first years of the war. In 1917, the Lever Food and Fuel Control Act gave him the power to:

- set wheat prices at $2.20 per bushel to encourage production
- establish a government corporation to buy US and Cuban sugar to maintain supplies
- organise a voluntary campaign to eat sensibly, thereby avoiding the need for rationing – for example 'Wheatless Mondays' and 'Meatless Thursdays'. Chicago residents were so successful in using leftovers that the amount of garbage in the city fell from 12,862 to 8,386 tons per month.

Food production increased from 12.3 million to 18.6 million tons per year and farmers' incomes grew by 30 per cent between 1915 and 1918.

Workers

Various government agencies were set up to facilitate industrial relations and effective working arrangements.

- The National War Labor Board was set up in April 1918 to settle industrial disputes, considering over 1,200 cases until its demise in May 1919.
- The War Labor Policies Board set wages and standards of employment. Wages doubled in the steel industry. As it consulted labour unions as well as employers, it gave greater influence and acceptance to unions, which had found it difficult to establish themselves in the USA. Union membership rose by 2.3 million during the war years, an increase of per cent.

Although conditions for many workers improved during the war years, women and African Americans still experienced problems within the workforce.

Women

Most women supported the war but they were not mobilised into war production as they would be in the Second World War. While one million men were called up, comparatively few women replaced them in munitions production and only 6,000 women were engaged in aircraft manufacture. Their role was seen mainly as encouraging people to buy war bonds and sending comforts to the troops abroad. Labour unions did not support the hiring of women because they thought they depressed wages. Indeed, women did suffer unequal pay, poor promotion prospects and little job security. Those who had found jobs in wartime production or in replacing men recruited into the armed forces were generally discharged when the war ended.

African Americans

US involvement in the war also brought further changes to the position of African Americans.

Migration of African Americans

The period saw a flood of African American migrants from the South to northern cities such as Chicago – as many as 500,000 migrated between 1914 and 1918. The African American population of New York grew from 92,000 to 152,000 and that of Detroit from little more than 5,000 to 41,000 between 1914 and 1918. However, while pay in industrial plants in the North was considerably better than in the cotton fields of the South, discrimination continued and there were serious riots against the African American presence in several northern cities such as East St. Louis in the summer of 1917 when 39 African Americans were killed. The military, meanwhile, was strictly segregated with most of the 200,000 African American troops confined to labour battalions. Nevertheless, their experience of less racist attitudes, particularly among the French, led to changes in their own perceptions and was to add to considerable racial tensions as they returned home.

Patriotism of African Americans

The patriotism of African Americans in wartime could not reasonably be questioned – over 360,000 volunteered for service, of whom 200,000 served abroad. The propaganda disseminated by men like Emmett Jay Scott, however, was clearly skewed and was easily seen through. By July 1918, most African American organisations were supporting the war. However, their experiences abroad did help develop a sense of black consciousness and determination to improve conditions on their return.

Suppression

Many American politicians feared African Americans would not support the US in a war 'to make the world safe for democracy' when they clearly faced prejudice and discrimination at home. Few African Americans in the South could vote; how could they be expected to fight for the rights of foreigners who could?

The government was prepared to give credence to rumours that German agents were about to subvert the loyalty of African Americans and authorised the Bureau of Investigation of the Justice Department, and military intelligence, to track down pro-German feelings among African Americans. These investigations focused particularly on the Black Press. The Black Press included about 200 weekly papers and six monthly magazines embracing a wide variety of styles and viewpoints from the conservative *New York Age* to the more radical *Crisis* and the *Cleveland Gazette*. The latter stressed that African-Americans were expected to be patriotic and support the war yet faced unfair and unequal treatment at home.

The periodical of the National Association for the Advancement of Colored People (NAACP), *The Crisis*, came in for particular attention, in part because it was the most influential radical African American mouthpiece – between 1917 and 1918 its circulation increased from 41,000 to 74,000. It was warned 'to publish only facts and constructive criticism' and avoid anything that might cause dissatisfaction among African-American troops.

Source D Excerpt from 'Returning Soldiers', by W. E. Du Bois, in *The Crisis*, XVIII, May, 1919, p. 13. From *Emergence of the Americas in Global Affairs, 1880–1929* by P. Clements, (Hodder Education), 2013, p.113.

We return

We return from fighting

We return fighting.

WORKING TOGETHER

Share the tables you have created on the changes that occurred in the USA during the First World War (see page 118). Discuss what you think was the greatest change brought about by the First World War in the USA. Give reasons for your judgement.

Labour battalions – Troops who worked in construction or loading or transportation of equipment rather than serving in combat.

Black Press – A term used to describe newspapers, magazines and periodicals aimed at a largely black audience.

What might Source D suggest about African American attitudes in post-war America?

KEY DATES: THE USA DURING THE FIRST WORLD WAR

1917 Jul War Industries Board set up.

1918 Apr National Labor Board set up.

1918 Nov The armistice was signed.

3 Renewed isolationism 1919–20

Woodrow Wilson was heavily involved in the peace conference in Paris at the end of the First World War. However, this direct US involvement, particularly in the affairs of Europe, was not to last, as the Senate voted against American membership as the USA reverted to a policy of isolationism.

The Fourteen Points

How important were the Fourteen Points in influencing the peace settlement?

Wilson wanted a peace settlement that would bring lasting peace. To this end, he proposed a settlement based on his 'Fourteen Points'. The Fourteen Points were roughly grouped into three categories. The first five considered general principles to maintain orderly relations between countries, based in part on what had gone wrong and led to war. In particular, there should be no more secret agreements between nations as these led to insecurity and double-dealing – diplomacy should be open and above board.

The next eight dealt with matters of self-determination, with borders being redrawn according to the wishes of local populations. Included in this was the restoration of Alsace-Lorraine to France and renewed guarantees for Belgian independence. The fourteenth point announced the setting up of a League of Nations, an international organisation for peacekeeping and mutual co-operation which all signatories of the treaties should join.

It is a myth that the peace settlement was ever fully based on the Fourteen Points. Ideas such as self-determination couldn't please everyone – some nations would necessarily lose land and populations. Nevertheless Wilson's efforts did win him the 1919 Nobel Peace Prize.

The Peace Settlement

Why was the USA against joining the League of Nations?

The peace settlement was dominated by three leaders – Clemenceau, the French prime minister, Lloyd George, the British prime minister, and Wilson.

The Peace Conference

A peace conference convened in Paris in January 1919 to create a lasting peace settlement. Wilson made the decision to go to Paris himself. This was momentous, not least because no previous president had even left the United States while in office. Wilson was so determined to see a lasting settlement that he gambled with his own health. He had the first of the strokes that would finally incapacitate him on 3 August, but before this he was already showing signs of extreme stress and paranoia, working eighteen-hour days squatting uncomfortably over huge maps spread out on the floor, with areas and regions cut out like jigsaw pieces, and being obsessed with French spies.

Wilson's idea of a lasting peace settlement based on fairness and moral principles did not necessarily receive a sympathetic audience within this atmosphere. Most decisions were made by the 'Big Three': the USA, Britain and France. Each had a different agenda. The war on the Western Front

Alsace-Lorraine – Area of France taken by Germany after the 1871 Franco–Prussian War.

KEY DATES: FOURTEEN POINTS

1918 Speech by Wilson announcing the Fourteen Points.

1919 Wilson awarded the Nobel Peace Prize.

NOTE-MAKING

Make notes on the part played by Wilson at the Paris Peace Settlement, including the Peace Conference and the Peace Settlement.

had largely been fought on French soil. France therefore sought a harsh settlement both so Germany would have to pay for its reconstruction and never be strong enough to attack her again. The British leader, David Lloyd George, saw the problems and resentment from Germany that would accrue if the settlement was too harsh but the British population largely wanted some form of revenge.

Wilson's priority was to gain acceptance of the League of Nations. In order to achieve this he would have to compromise over other issues such as self-determination and German war guilt. Wilson was not totally sympathetic to Germany as he had a profound dislike of German militarism. He believed that Germany should be punished but in a way that would lead to European reconciliation as opposed to revenge.

The USA and the League of Nations

The League of Nations was the brainchild of Woodrow Wilson, one of his Fourteen Points and part of the Versailles peace settlement in 1919. Wilson returned to America after the peace settlement in order to drum up support for the League.

Why Wilson failed

A document condemning the League of Nations and suggesting it should be delayed was signed by 37 Republican senators. Wilson's campaign for US membership of the League failed for two main reasons.

● Wilson decided, against doctors' orders, to tour the USA in September 1919 in order to win support for membership of the League. He was followed by opponents of the League who spoke equally convincingly against membership. The tour was very exhausting, with Wilson making 37 speeches in two days and, on 25 September, Wilson collapsed after a speech in Pueblo, Colorado. His campaign was over.

● Wilson refused to compromise. There were some in the senate known as the middle and strong reservationists who were not totally opposed to membership and were willing to negotiate and compromise over membership of the League. Lodge introduced a compromise bill in the Senate in November which Wilson told the Democrats to oppose. It therefore failed, by 53 to 38 votes.

When, in March 1920, the original peace settlement was presented to the Senate, it was passed by 49 to 35 votes. However, this was seven short of the two-thirds majority needed for approving treaties.

Source E From *The Strangest Friendship in History* by G. S. Viereck, published in 1933. In *America 1870–1975* by J. O'Keefe, (Longman), 1984, p.32.

On September 3rd the battered, broken, one-eyed Covenanter sets forth upon his crusade. He made a notable speech in Columbus, Ohio. However, in Pueblo, on September 25, fever assails his body. Tumulty finds the President fully dressed but with tears streaming down his cheek. His left arm and leg no longer function. Mrs Wilson now takes command of the situation and the train turns homeward to Washington.

On November 18, the President is permitted to sun himself on the south lawn of the White House. From the windows of the Cabinet Room, the members of the Cabinet can see the President in his wheelchair. They could see him but could not reach or communicate with him. Senator Gilbert Hitchcock is equally unlucky. He leads the fight for the Treaty that is most dear to Wilson's heart, but the sick room is locked against him.

Knox–Porter Resolution

The Covenant of the League of Nations was attached to all peace treaties and, by rejecting membership of the League, the USA was effectively refusing to sign the peace treaties. This problem was solved by the Knox–Porter Resolution in October 1921. This declared that the war was over and the Senate passed the peace treaties except for the Covenant of the League of Nations.

WORKING TOGETHER

There had been much change in foreign policy under Wilson in the years 1912–20. Using a flow chart, show how and when these changes occurred.

To what extent does this account (Source E) suggest that Wilson's illness was the most important reason for the refusal to join the League of Nations?

KEY DATES: THE PEACE CONFERENCE

1919 Jan The peace conference began in Paris.

1919 Jun The signing of the Treaty of Versailles.

1919 Aug Wilson suffered the first of his strokes.

1919 The Senate rejects membership of the League.

The USA by 1920

By 1920, the USA had become the most powerful nation in the world, economically and industrially.

Economy

By 1920, the USA was the world's leading industrial nation partly due to the impact of the First World War. The USA did not enter the First World War until 1917. Its economy benefited greatly from the war. Indeed, by 1918 the USA was the world's leading economy.

The war was fought in Europe and badly affected the economies of leading countries such as Britain, France and Germany, which had to divert their resources to the war effort. These countries bought much needed supplies from the USA. Money poured into the USA for food, raw materials and munitions. This led to the growth of US industry and agriculture.

Moreover, many countries ended up borrowing huge sums of money from the USA. American bankers and businessmen increasingly invested in Europe and made money once the economies of these countries recovered in the 1920s.

> **Mechanisation** – The use of machines.

In addition, during the war, European countries were unable to maintain their pre-war exports. US manufacturers and farmers took over European overseas markets and further expanded. For example, the USA took over from Germany as the leading producer in the world for fertilisers and chemicals. Finally, the war had stimulated technological advances, particularly in mechanisation as well as the development of new raw materials such as plastics. The USA led the world in new technology.

By 1920, the USA produced and consumed 70 per cent of the world's oil and was its leading producer of coal and steel. On the Great Plains of the Midwest, large, efficient farms supplied the rest of the world with nearly a third of its wheat and over two-thirds of its corn.

America was, without doubt, a wealthy country. The standard of living for many American families was much higher than that of their European counterparts, especially as the USA had not been directly affected by the ravages of war as had most of Europe. However, wealth in the USA was unevenly distributed and millions of Americans did not have a share in the nation's prosperity in this 'land of the free'. Many industrial workers found themselves at the mercy of the large business corporations that employed them but refused them any negotiating rights over working hours or rates of pay. Low wages forced them to live in slum areas of towns.

Small farmers were also facing financial difficulties as they struggled to compete with larger agricultural enterprises and competition from Argentina, Canada, Australia and New Zealand.

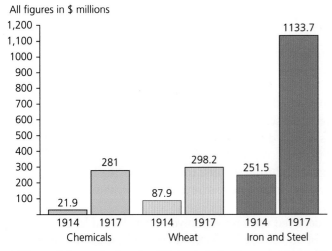

All figures in $ millions

▲ Figure 1 A graph showing US exports in the years 1914–17.

Society

American society was diverse and multicultural. At its core were the ancestors of the original white, English Protestant settlers, but they had been joined in America by Germans, Poles, Italians, Irish, Chinese, Russian Jews and other immigrants who came in search of the 'American dream'. The first two decades of the twentieth century saw further waves of immigrants, though the reality they experienced was often poverty and exploitation. By adding their cultural dimensions to the American scene, they created a society unlike any other in the world. It aggravated the racial tension that existed in America despite the end of slavery.

Moreover, the USA remained a divided and unequal society. African Americans, especially in the South, were very much second-class citizens due to discrimination, segregation and intimidation. Native Americans had lost their lands and original way of life and were now confined to life on reservations.

Politics

There had been some expansion in the role of the president and the federal government under a series of presidents during the Progressive Era, particularly Theodore Roosevelt and Woodrow Wilson, and especially in the regulation of business, finance and social reform. However, the role of both remained limited as many Americans, especially in Congress, championed a *laissez-faire* society, upholding the principle of individual liberty, with minimal government control.

In world affairs, the USA had moved from isolationism to involvement in the First World War with its president, Wilson, playing a leading role in the peace conference and the setting up of the League of Nations. However, the prevailing mood in the USA by 1920 was for far less involvement, especially in Europe, and for a return to isolationism.

Chapter summary

- Woodrow Wilson brought in a series of progressive reforms during his first period as president.
- These reforms included more anti-trust measures, banking, economic and financial reform, especially the first ever income tax in the USA.
- Wilson was re-elected for a second term as president in 1916.
- There was much less reform during his second period as president due to his preoccupation with the First World War.
- The USA remained neutral during the first three years of the First World War, although Wilson was increasingly sympathetic to Britain, France and Russia.
- The USA eventually declared war on Germany in April 1917 due to the German resumption of unrestricted U-boat warfare and the Zimmermann Telegram.
- US forces played a significant role in the eventual Allied victory on the Western Front in 1918.
- American involvement in the war led to changes in war production, finance, the workforce and the position of African Americans.
- Wilson introduced his Fourteen Points, which he hoped would provide the basis for the peace conference. He had limited influence at the conference.
- Wilson failed to convince a majority of the Senate to support the League of Nations as the USA resumed its policy of isolationism.

▼ Summary diagram: The USA and the First World War

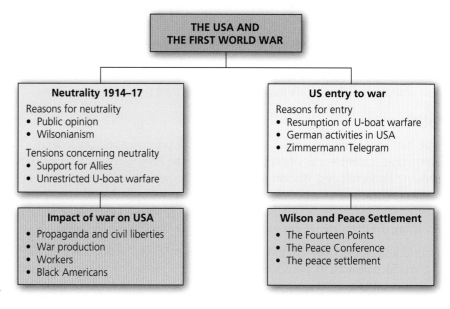

Working on essay technique: evaluation and relative significance

Reaching a supported overall judgement is an important part of writing good essays. One very important way to do this is by evaluating the relative significance of different factors, in the light of valid criteria. Relative significance means how important one factor is compared to another. This section examines how to evaluate and how to establish valid criteria.

Evaluation

The purpose of evaluation is to weigh up and reach a judgement. This means that you need to consider the importance of two or more different factors, weigh them against each other, and then reach a judgement. Evaluation is a good skill to use at the end of an essay, because it helps support your overall judgement.

EXAMPLE

Look again at the following A-level practice question from Chapter 3 (page 103):

To what extent was the regulation of big business the most important achievement of the Progressive Movement in the years 1890–1912? **(25 marks)**

A possible way to tackle this question would be to write one clear paragraph arguing that the regulation of big business was the most important achievement of the Progressive Movement, and two paragraphs arguing against this. In an essay of this type you could then resolve the tension by weighing up the argument and counter-argument in the conclusion. In so doing, you can reach a supported overall judgement. For example, a possible conclusion could look like this:

Begins with main argument → In conclusion, the most important achievement of the Progressive Movement was the reform of big business. These included a series of anti-trust measures, more especially the Sherman Anti-Trust Act of 1890 and further reforms by Theodore Roosevelt which brought much greater regulation of their activities. However, the Progressive Movement did also encourage political reform particularly in the increased role of the federal government. ← *Counter-argument contrast*

Limitations of counter-argument → But although Theodore Roosevelt was more active in social and economic policies during his presidency, this was short-lived with his successor, Taft, more circumspect about extending the powers of the presidency. Therefore, it can be argued that the regulation of big business was the most long-lasting achievement of the Progressive Movement. ← *Resolution of the arguments*

In this example the evaluation is helped by using arguments with precise evidence that help to weigh up the importance of the different factors – anti-trust laws, extending the powers of the federal government, and social reform. This conclusion provides an example of what could be high level work (if written in full with appropriate details) because it reaches an overall judgement and supports this through evaluating the relative significance of different factors in the light of valid criteria.

Relative significance

Clearly, the arguments above about big business can be based on new evidence and new interpretations. The best essays will always make a judgement about which was most important based on valid criteria.

It is up to you to come up with valid criteria. Criteria can be very simple – and will depend on the topic and the exact question.

The following criteria are often useful:

- **Duration:** which factor was important for the longest amount of time?
- **Scope:** which factor affected the most people?
- **Effectiveness:** which factor achieved most?
- **Impact:** which factor led to the most fundamental change?

For example, for the essay title above you could compare the factors in terms of their duration and their impact.

ACTIVITY

Use the technique on page 127 to address the following A-level practice question:

'Wilson was the most progressive of the American presidents in the years 1890–1920.' Assess the validity of this view. (25 marks)

1 Think about the following when planning your answer to this question. The same points can be taken into consideration for other questions of this type:
   - How will you define progressive?
   - Compare Wilson to at least two other presidents – probably Taft and Roosevelt.
   - Decide on the criteria with which you show how progressive they were – volume of reform, significance of their reforms.
2 Write an argument in a sentence that summarises Wilson's claim to be the most progressive president of the period.
3 Support this by writing additional sentences that are specific to the areas you have chosen.

Use words such as 'however' and 'nonetheless' to weigh contrasting points.

Working on interpretation skills

The advice given here builds on the help given at the end of Chapters 1 or 2 (see pages 34 or 69).

For the AQA A-level exam, Section A gives you three extracts, followed by a single question. The wording of the question will be something like this:

'Using your understanding of the historical context, assess how convincing the arguments in these three extracts are in relation to ...' (30 marks)

The A-level mark scheme opposite is very similar to the AS one on page 69.

Notice that there is no reference in the mark scheme to *comparing* the extracts or reaching a judgement about which of the extracts is the most convincing.

Here is an A-level practice question (Extracts B and C are on page 130):

Using your understanding of the historical context, assess how convincing the arguments in these three extracts are in relation to the reasons why the USA became more involved in foreign affairs in the years 1890–1917.

Extract A

In the 25 years before World War I, the United States involved itself in international politics in many new ways, acquiring overseas colonies, building a battleship fleet, and intervening increasingly often in Latin America. The widespread belief that foreign markets were necessary for the country's prosperity contributed to this new foreign policy, but continuing demands to protect the home market from foreign competition also influenced it. The politically dominant Republican Party was strongly committed to trade protection. This commitment led Republican policy makers to focus on less developed areas of the world that would not export manufactured goods to the United States rather than on wealthier markets in Europe.

Adapted from 'Protectionist Empire: Trade, Tariffs, and United States Foreign Policy' by Benjamin O. Fordham, *North American Review*, 1911.

Level 5	Shows a very good understanding of the interpretations put forward in all three extracts and combines this with a strong awareness of the historical context to analyse and evaluate the interpretations given in the extracts. Evaluation of the arguments will be well-supported and convincing. The response demonstrates a very good understanding of context. *25–30 marks*
Level 4	Shows a good understanding of the interpretations given in all three extracts and combines this with knowledge of the historical context to analyse and evaluate the interpretations given in the extracts. The evaluation of the arguments will be mostly well-supported, and convincing, but may have minor limitations of depth and breadth. The response demonstrates a good understanding of context. *19–24 marks*
Level 3	Provides some supported comment on the interpretations given in all three extracts and comments on the strength of these arguments in relation to their historic context. There is some analysis and evaluation but there may be an imbalance in the degree and depth of comments offered on the strength of the arguments. The response demonstrates an understanding of context. *13–18 marks*
Level 2	Provides some accurate comment on the interpretations given in at least two of the extracts, with reference to the historical context. The answer may contain some analysis, but there is little, if any, evaluation. Some of the comments on the strength of the arguments may contain some generalisation, inaccuracy or irrelevance. The response demonstrates some understanding of context. *7–12 marks*
Level 1	Either shows an accurate understanding of the interpretation given in one extract only or addresses two/three extracts, but in a generalist way, showing limited accurate understanding of the arguments they contain, although there may be some general awareness of the historical context. Any comments on the strength of the arguments are likely to be generalist and contain some inaccuracy and/or irrelevance. The response demonstrates limited understanding of context. *1–6 marks*

Extract B

The belief in the necessity of expansion abroad in order to sustain national prosperity was only one reason for the popularity of imperialism. Race had long been the center of this American 'world-view'. From the time of the revolt against Great Britain, American policy-makers had deemed non-whites inferior and therefore less able to govern or to use land and other resources productively. Following the Civil War, Social Darwinism, with its emphasis on competition and survival of the fittest, provided an ostensibly scientific rationale for prospective ventures abroad. Domination of others was thought to be the inevitable fate of a superior race such as that of white Americans.

Adapted from 'Phases of Empire: Late Nineteenth Century US Foreign Relations' by J. A. Fry in *The Gilded Age* Ed. C. W. Calhoun, (Rowman and Littlefield), 2007.

Extract C

American imperialism in the late nineteenth and early twentieth centuries was both a fulfilment and a betrayal of American traditions. It was a logical extension of the Monroe Doctrine, by which the United States claimed the right to preserve the New World from the Old, and a natural development of the Manifest Destiny. Although the United States had acquired much of its continental territory, such as Florida and Alaska, by purchase, it had also acquired much by war – Texas, New Mexico, California and Arizona from Mexico, and Cuba from Spain. However, the notion of holding colonies was alien to the principles of the Revolution and the Constitution. Because the Spanish–American War of 1898 was fought overseas, it set precedents in strategy, tactics and diplomacy.

Adapted from *America in the Gilded Age* by S. D. Cashman, (New York University Press), 1993.

Possible answer

First, make sure that you have the focus of the question clear (see page 129) – in this case, the reasons for the US becoming more involved in foreign affairs.

Then you can investigate the three extracts to see how convincing they are.

You need to analyse each of the three extracts in turn. A suggestion is to have a large page divided into nine blocks.

Extract's main arguments	Knowledge to corroborate	Knowledge to contradict or modify
A		
B		
C		

- In the first column list the main arguments each uses.
- In the second column list what you know that can corroborate the arguments.
- In the third column list what might contradict or modify the arguments. (NB 'Modify' – you might find that you partly agree, but with reservations.)
- You may find, of course, that some of your knowledge is relevant more than once.

Planning your answer – one approach

Decide how you could best set out a detailed plan for your answer. You could, for example:

- Briefly refer to the focus of the question.
- For each extract in turn set out the arguments, corroborating and contradictory evidence.
- Do this by treating each argument (or group of arguments) in turn.
- Make comparisons between the extracts if this is helpful. The mark scheme does not explicitly give credit for doing this, but a successful comparison may well show the extent of your understanding of each extract.
- An overall judgement is not required, but it may be helpful to make a brief summary, or just reinforce what has been said already by emphasising which extract was the most convincing.

Remember that in the examination you are allowed one hour for this question. It is the planning stage that is vital in order to write a good answer. You should allow sufficient time to read the extracts and plan an answer. If you start writing too soon, it is likely that you will waste time trying to summarise the *content* of each extract. Do this in your planning stage – and then think how you will *use* the content to answer the question.

Then the actual writing!

● Think how you can write an answer, dealing with each extract in turn, but making cross-references or comparisons, if this is helpful, to reinforce a point.
● In addition, make sure your answer:
  • shows very good understanding of the extracts
  • uses knowledge to argue in support or to disagree
  • provides a clear argument which leads to a conclusion about each extract, and which may reach a conclusion about the extracts as a whole.

Extracts that have an argument and counter-argument

Sometimes an extract will give opposing views within a paragraph – that is, an attempt at providing balance. The extract may reach a conclusion on which argument is stronger, or it may leave an open verdict. Look at extract D.

Extract D

After the Civil War, the two traditional policies in American foreign relations – the Monroe Doctrine and expansion in the Pacific area – persisted. American interest in the Pacific and the Far East dated back to the old China trade and became vital with the acquisition of Oregon and California. These interests became increasingly centred on Hawaii. However, others see a distinct change in American foreign policy, especially in the 1890s, due to less traditional factors. This change to greater involvement synchronised with the passing of the frontier, the shift from the 'old' to the 'new' immigration and the rise of big business and industry. This emergence of the USA as a world power was not an isolated phenomenon, for the closing years of the nineteenth century witnessed everywhere an international struggle for new markets and sources of supply. The USA began to compete with Britain, Germany and France for these new markets.

The Growth of the American Republic by S. Morison, H. Commager and W. Leuchtenburg, (OUP), 1969.

This extract presents:

● an argument in the first half that represents the traditional view of US expansionism
● information that gives a counter-argument (in the second half).

If this extract was being studied, your plan could highlight the balance within the extract, and could seek to find evidence to support and refute both sides.

This would have to be reflected in your answer in relation to how convincing the arguments are. An extract that includes counter-argument as well as argument *could* be more convincing, but not necessarily so. It will depend on the context – and your own knowledge that you are using in order to reach a judgement.

Key Questions: From Civil War to World War, 1865–1920

The specification on the USA states that it requires the study in breadth of issues of change, continuity, cause and consequence in the period through six key questions. These have been either featured or mentioned at various points in the four chapters you have studied. The questions set in the examination (both the interpretation question and the essays) will reflect one or more of these Key questions. It is very useful to pause to consider developments across the wider time period you have studied so far, as this will help you to see and analyse change and continuity with a sense of perspective.

KEY QUESTION 1:
How did government, political authority and political parties change and develop?

'government': does this refer to government at federal and/or state level?

'political authority': this refers to the extent of power exercised at national and state level. In what ways did their powers change in this period?

'political parties': this refers to changes in the Democrats and Republicans. However, did any other parties/movements emerge?

'change and develop' suggests whether or not and how far government, political authority and political parties were extending or increasing. How far can you relate it to the period 1865–1920?

Questions to consider

- To what extent did the Civil War affect the powers of government and the political parties?
- During Reconstruction, the presidency was challenged by Congress. In addition, the mainly Republican North dominated this period at the expense of the Democrat South. To what extent did this continue throughout this period?
- During the Progressive period presidents Roosevelt, Taft and Wilson extended the role of federal government. In what ways? Were there any changes in the powers used by state governments, e.g. the work of Robert La Follette?
- In the period 1890–1920, a new Populist Party emerged and Roosevelt created his own party. How far did these threaten the dominance of the traditional parties?

Working in groups

Considering the period, 1865–1920:

1 Discuss the ways in which the powers of the presidency changed.
2 Discuss any changes in the position of the two leading parties – the Democrats and Republicans.
3 Discuss the emergence of new parties in the Progressive period.

KEY QUESTION 2:
In what ways did the economy and society of the USA change and develop?

'economy': what does this include? Think about the differing economies of the South, North and West.

'society': this can include living and working conditions, immigrants and the emergence of trade unions.

'change and develop' suggests extending or increasing. How far can you relate it to the period 1865–1920?

Questions to consider

- There was rapid industrial development in the North during and after the Civil War. Why did these changes take place? Remember that industry was badly affected by the depressions of 1873 and 1893. The organisation of industry changed with corporations and trusts.
- The mainly agricultural South was badly affected by the Civil War. There were changes after the Civil War with the growth of sharecroppers but agriculture did not expand and prosper in the same way as industry. Why was this?
- Rapid industrial growth led to similar growth in industrial cities and towns, even more so with mass immigration, but this led to poor working and living conditions. Trade unions emerged but were often given a hard time by both the government and employers. Why was there such strong opposition to trade unions?

Working in groups

Considering the period, 1865–1920:

1 Discuss to what extent the USA changed from a predominantly agricultural to a mainly industrial economy in this period.
2 Discuss the different interpretations of the reasons for industrial expansion during this period.
3 Discuss the reasons for and impact of immigration on the US economy and society.

KEY QUESTION 3:
How did the role of the USA in world affairs change?

'the role of the USA': implies that the USA was involved in affairs abroad.

'world affairs': this could include involvement in all the major continents, especially America, Asia and Europe, including peaceful involvement as well as wars.

'change' suggests extending or increasing but also some continuity. How far can you relate it to the period 1865–1920?

Questions to consider

- The traditional US policy in the nineteenth century was isolationism. What was meant by isolationism?
- Remember the significant changes in American attitudes towards imperialism in the 1890s and the early years of the twentieth century. What different motives were there for this change?
- The USA kept clear of external conflicts throughout most of the nineteenth century and yet, between 1865 and 1920, became involved in two wars – the Spanish–American War and the First World War. Why did the USA become involved in these wars?

Working in groups

Considering the period, 1865–1920:

1 Discuss the extent to which the USA was isolationist during these years.
2 Discuss the different interpretations of the motives for greater interest in and support for imperialism in this period.
3 Discuss the implications of US involvement in Latin America, the Pacific and the Far East.
4 Discuss the significance of US involvement in two wars – the Spanish–American War and the First World War.

KEY QUESTION 4:
How important were ideas and ideology?

'how important' means you have to make a judgement on significance of these ideas and ideology.

'change and continuity': some of these ideas or ideology could have brought about change and others could have prevented such change and maintained the status quo – continuity.

'ideas and ideology' refers to beliefs – these could be political, economic, social, racial or religious.

Questions to consider

- What was new about Populism and Progressivism?
- Consider the importance of ideas such as the Manifest Destiny. How did this influence Westward expansion?
- Racial ideas during and after Reconstruction: how far did these ideas influence the treatment of African Americans and Native Americans as well as American imperial policies?
- You may also consider ideas about the role of government – especially *laissez-faire*. How far did this encourage economic and social change or continuity?
- What differences were there in the ideas/ideologies of the North and South?

Working in groups

Considering the period, 1865–1920:

- Discuss the influence of Progressivism and Populism on US politics, presidents and society in the years after 1890.
- Discuss the impact of the Monroe Doctrine on Westward and imperial expansion. How influential was Turner's essay on the ending of the frontier?
- Discuss the different ideas and ideologies of North and South and how they influenced the Civil War and the period of Reconstruction that followed.

KEY QUESTION 5:
How united were the states during this period?

'how' is asking you to make a judgement on the extent of unity.

'united' means being in agreement, joined together socially, economically, and politically.

'the states' refers to the states that constituted the USA during these years.

Questions to consider

- What effects did the Civil War and Reconstruction have on the unity of the North and the South?
- Consider the years after Reconstruction. What differences were there between the North and South and how did these differences affect unity?
- African Americans were given emancipation and some rights due to the various constitutional amendments but suffered segregation, discrimination and even violence, especially in the South, in the years after the Civil War. What differences were there in the treatment of African Americans in the North and South?
- How did Westward expansion affect unity between Native and white Americans?
- Examine the impact of mass immigration on the unity of the USA. What impact did this have on the unity of the USA?

Working in groups

Considering the period, 1865–1920:

1 Discuss the impact of North and South differences on the unity of the USA throughout this period.
2 Discuss how changes in the position of African Americans in both the South and the North during this period affected the unity of the USA.
3 Discuss the extent to which the states were united in this period.

KEY QUESTION 6:
How important was the role of key individuals and groups and how were they affected by developments?

| 'how important' means making a judgement on the importance of individuals to American history in this period. | 'role': what part was played by these individuals and groups – what contribution did they make? | 'key individuals': who was most prominent in bringing about political, economic or social change or influencing US foreign and imperial policies? | 'developments' refers to economic, political and social changes. | 'groups': this could include organisations and societies. |

Questions to consider

- What contribution was made by individuals (particularly presidents) in Reconstruction? For example, what contribution was made by Johnson?
- Then consider which presidents made a significant contribution in the years that followed Reconstruction. For example, how important was the role of Roosevelt in domestic and foreign policies?
- How far did the key individuals associated with the Popular Party and the Progressive Movement influence change?
- Remember the work of William Du Bois and Booker T. Washington for black civil rights. Did they make a significant contribution to the position of African Americans?
- In foreign and imperial policy you may wish to consider the part played by key individuals. For example, what part was played by President McKinley in US involvement in the Spanish–American War?
- Examine the role of groups such as the Ku Klux Klan and the NAACP. How did developments in the position of African Americans affect these groups?

Working in groups

Considering the period, 1865–1920:

1 Discuss the significance of any other key individuals to the development of the USA at home and abroad.
2 Discuss overall the significance of individuals in bringing about change in this period.
3 Discuss the group or groups which brought about the greatest change in this period.

5

The return to 'normalcy', 1919–32

This chapter covers developments in the USA from the end of the First World War to the election of Roosevelt as president in 1932. It deals with a number of areas:

- The domestic and foreign policies of the Republican presidents
- Reasons for the boom in the US economy in the 1920s
- Key social and cultural changes in the 'Jazz Age'
- The causes of the Wall Street Crash and the impact of the Depression

When you have worked through the chapter and the related activities and exercises, you should have detailed knowledge of all those areas, and you should be able to relate this to the key breadth issues defined as part of your study, in particular: how did the economy and society of the USA change and develop? For the period covered in this chapter the main issues can be phrased as a question:

Was the Wall Street Crash the main reason for the Great Depression of 1929–32?

The focus of the issue is on social and economic developments and of causal factors that contributed to that development, as set out briefly below.

CHAPTER OVERVIEW

The Republicans dominated this period of American history with three presidents, Harding, Coolidge and Hoover. For most of the years, 1919–29, the USA experienced an unprecedented boom in the economy due to the benefits of the First World War as well as the impetus provided by developments in the car industry. The 1920s was nicknamed the 'Age of Jazz' with many people enjoying a much better lifestyle and significant changes in entertainment and the role of women. However, not everyone enjoyed this prosperity. There was increasing hostility towards immigrants and growing support for the Ku Klux Klan. The boom years ended with the Wall Street Crash of 1929 which was followed by the Great Depression and massive unemployment. Hoover's limited attempts to deal with the Depression led to the election of Roosevelt as president in 1932.

1 The domestic and foreign policies of Harding and Coolidge

The Republicans monopolised the White House in the 1920s with three successive presidents. They were:

- Warren Harding: 1921–23
- Calvin Coolidge: 1923–29
- Herbert Hoover: 1929–33

Domestic achievements

How successful were Harding and Coolidge?

Harding and Coolidge have generally been given a bad press by historians because of the lack of domestic reform and reversion to a policy of isolationism.

Warren Harding 1921–23

Harding was a surprising choice as Republican candidate for the presidential election campaign of 1920 but won a landslide victory. Harding's victory remains the largest popular-vote percentage margin (60.3 per cent to 34.1 per cent) in presidential elections after the so-called 'Era of Good Feelings' ended with the victory of James Monroe in the election of 1820.

> **Warren Harding**
>
> Harding was raised in a small town in Ohio and, as a young man, he brought a nearly bankrupt newspaper, the *Marion Star*, back to life. He won a seat in the Ohio State Senate, serving two terms before becoming a US senator for Ohio in 1914. During his term as senator, Harding missed more sessions than he attended, being absent for key debates on prohibition and women's suffrage.
>
> Harding faced an equally surprising Republican opponent. Former President Theodore Roosevelt had been the favourite for the Republican nomination but he died in January 1919. The Democrats chose an outsider, newspaper publisher and Governor James M. Cox. Cox launched an energetic campaign against Senator Harding, and did all he could to defeat him but Harding virtually ignored Cox and essentially campaigned against Wilson, calling for a return to 'normalcy', or a return to the nineteenth century with very little government intervention at home and in foreign affairs. Harding said 'We want less government business and more government in business'.

Harding's achievements

Harding had several achievements as president:

- He made a number of able appointments including Andrew Mellon as Secretary of State for the Treasury, Herbert Hoover as Secretary of Commerce and Charles Hughes as Secretary of State.
- The Sheppard–Towner Maternity Aid Act was passed which provided federal aid to states to encourage them to build infant and maternity health centres.
- Harding was successful in making cuts to government spending. For example, the Budget and Accounting Act made departments present budgets to the president for approval. Government spending, which totalled $5,000 million in 1920, had fallen to $3,333 million by 1922.

NOTE-MAKING

Using the 1–2 method (see page x), make notes on the presidencies of Harding and Coolidge. For example, write 'Harding's achievements' on the left-hand side and a bulleted point list of his achievements on the right-hand side.

Teapot Dome scandal

This involved the secret leasing of federal oil reserves by the Secretary of the Interior, Albert Bacon Fall, during Harding's presidency. In April 1922, Fall secretly granted to Harry F. Sinclair of the Mammoth Oil Company exclusive rights to the Teapot Dome (Wyoming) reserves. When the affair became known, Congress forced Harding to cancel the leases. In addition, the Supreme Court declared the leases fraudulent and ruled illegal Harding's transfer of authority to Fall. Harding was not directly implicated in the scandal although it did take a toll on his health. The scandal, however, had little effect on the popularity of the Republicans, reflected in the overwhelming victory of Coolidge in the 1924 presidential election. Nevertheless, like Watergate in the 1970s, 'Teapot Dome' became synonymous with scandal and corruption in government.

- He did try to make government more efficient. For example, he addressed Congress on several occasions calling for an increased federal government role in the economic and social life of the nation.
- His belief in very limited federal government intervention reflected the popular mood of the nation at that time.
- Harding also achieved his aim, which was to return to a situation where there was as little government as possible – the return to normalcy.

Harding's shortcomings

Harding is, however, often described as one of the weakest and least effective presidents. His own personal reputation was tainted by extramarital affairs, at least two of which were made public. He achieved very little due to his belief in 'normalcy' and a return to the very limited government intervention of the nineteenth century. Harding made some very dubious appointments including some of his 'Ohio Gang' cronies. In 1923, it emerged that there had been extensive corruption during Harding's administration. For example, the Head of the Veterans' Bureau had misappropriated or wasted $250 million and the Alien Property Custodian had accepted bribes. The most infamous example was the Teapot Dome scandal.

Calvin Coolidge, 1923–29

Harding died on 2 August 1923 and Coolidge, who had been his vice-president, was sworn in as president. In the presidential election of the following year, Coolidge won a decisive victory. He was given credit for a booming economy at home and isolationist policy abroad which had begun under Harding and continued under Coolidge in his first year as president. Coolidge was helped by a split within the Democratic Party. The regular Democratic candidate was John W. Davis, a little-known former congressman. However, Davis was a conservative, which encouraged many liberal Democrats to leave the party and back the third-party campaign of Wisconsin Senator Robert M. LaFollette, Sr., who ran as the candidate of the Progressive Party.

Calvin Coolidge, 1872–1933

Calvin Coolidge was born in 1872 in the village of Plymouth, Vermont. He qualified as a lawyer in 1891 and nine years later became the Republican town mayor of Northampton, Vermont.

His rise in politics continued as he was elected governor of Massachusetts in 1919 and then in 1921 became vice-president to Harding after serving as his running mate in the previous year's presidential election campaign.

When Harding died in 1923 Coolidge took his place as president. He served for one term only, deciding not to run again in 1928. He died in Northampton, Massachusetts, in 1933 from a heart attack.

Coolidge's qualities

Coolidge liked to be thought of as a man of the people, especially those of small-town America. He had very nineteenth-century views, believing in as little government intervention as possible. 'The business of America is business', he said. Although criticised for doing and saying very little during his term in office, he made more speeches and met more people than any of his predecessors.

Coolidge enjoyed being seen in public and was a popular president because he exuded confidence and appeared calm and unflappable. He was honest and incorruptible, unlike other presidents, and did not smoke, drink or chase women. He was seen as the dependable pilot at the helm. His election victory of 1924 led to an extension of Republican pro-business policies, with low taxation, low interest rates and minimum government spending.

Coolidge's failings

Historians have criticised Coolidge for his low work rate. He slept a lot and said very little, being nicknamed 'Silent Cal'. Some believe that he suffered a severe depression in 1924 after the death of his son. To some he had a superiority complex and, although acknowledging that the USA had problems, did very little to address them. As president he was determined to do less, rather than more, than his predecessor. Coolidge refused to stand as president in 1928 due to health concerns.

Source A From a speech by Coolidge at the Fifteenth Meeting of the Business Organisation of the Government, 11 June 1928. (From the website: 'America in Class: Becoming America; America in the Twenties': http://americainclass.org/sources/becomingmodern)

I have rejoiced in keeping down the annual budget, in reducing taxes, and paying off the national debt, because the influence of such action is felt in every home in the land. It has meant that the people not only have greater resources with which to provide themselves with food and clothing and shelter, but also for the enjoyment of what was but lately considered the luxuries of the rich. We call these results prosperity. They have come because the people have been willing to do their duty. They have refrained from waste, they have shunned extravagance.

> To what extent does the speech (Source A) show why many Americans would have considered Coolidge a successful president?

KEY DATES: HARDING AND COOLIDGE

1920 Harding wins the presidential election.

1921 Beginning of Harding presidency.

1921 Budget and Accounting Act.

1922 Teapot Dome scandal.

1923 Death of Harding. Coolidge becomes president.

1924 Coolidge wins the presidential election.

1928 Coolidge decides not to stand as president.

US foreign policy in the 1920s

To what extent was the USA isolationist in the 1920s?

In 1920, the US Senate (see page 123) refused to join the League of Nations. This has led some historians to believe that the USA followed a policy of isolationism in the 1920s. Others have suggested that in reality, the USA was too powerful and influential to be completely isolationist and became involved in European affairs, particularly with the Dawes and Young Plans, as well as international disarmament with the Washington Naval Disarmament Conference.

Aims of US foreign policy

The USA had several aims in foreign policy:

- Firstly, the USA was convinced that the First World War was caused by the selfish rivalries of the European powers and wanted to avoid involvement in any further conflicts.

> **NOTE-MAKING**
>
> Using a spider diagram (see page x) summarise the key features of the US foreign policy in the 1920s including international agreements and involvement in Europe.

LOOK AGAIN

Look again at page 96 in Chapter 3.

How important was the Monroe Doctrine in influencing US policy in Latin America between 1890 and 1912?

What evidence is there in the speech in Source B that Harding supports a policy of isolationism?

- Moreover, there was a growing fear of the spread of Communism after the Bolshevik Revolution in Russia in October 1917. This was seen as a threat to the economic and political ideology of the USA.
- Furthermore, the USA wanted to maintain the status quo in naval power and the Far East. The USA had the most powerful navy in the world and wanted to stop any further naval arms race, especially the growth of the Japanese navy.
- The USA also wanted to protect their interests, especially trade, in the Far East by maintaining the status quo and particularly the 'Open Door' policy. (These were increasingly threatened by Japanese expansionist policies.)
- The USA was also determined to maintain the Monroe Doctrine and its economic and political interests in Latin America.

Source B From a speech by Warren Harding during the presidential election campaign of 1920. From *AQA History USA, 1890–1945* by C. Rowe, (Nelson Thornes), 2008, p.71.

America's present need is not heroics but normalcy; not revolution but restoration; not internationality but nationality. It's one thing to battle successfully against world domination by a military autocracy, but it is quite another thing to try to revise human nature. My best judgement of America's needs is to steady down, to get squarely on our feet, to make sure of the right path.

International conferences

The USA took the initiative in promoting disarmament, especially the Washington Disarmament Conference of November 1921 and the Kellogg–Briand Pact of 1928.

Reasons for the Washington Conference

The Washington Conference was attended by the United States, Great Britain, Japan, France and Italy. The USA was keen on this conference for several reasons:

- The USA wanted to prevent the renewal of the Anglo–Japanese Alliance in 1922. Britain was keen to renew this to secure Japanese support for her interests in the Far East. The USA, however, feared the spread of Japanese influence in the Far East, especially China, and wanted to detach them from their ally.
- The USA wished to maintain the status quo in China, particularly the Open Door policy which favoured US trading interests.
- President Harding left foreign affairs in the control of Secretary of State, Charles Evans Hughes, who was a keen supporter of disarmament.
- The most important reason was US fear of growing Japanese influence in the Far East. Japan had acquired German colonies in the Pacific and posed a potential threat to communication links between Hawaii and other US possessions in Guam and the Philippines. Moreover, Japan threatened China, which was increasingly vulnerable due to civil war.

Achievements of the Washington Conference

On the one hand the conference appeared to be a great success. It was the first agreement on arms limitation and brought stability and peace in the Pacific. The disarmament agreement was made between four powers: the USA, Britain, Japan and France, with Italy signing in 1922. Each agreed to reduce the tonnage of battleships for ten years, persuading Japan to accept less tonnage than Britain and the USA in an approximate ratio of five for USA and Britain, three for Japan and 1.75 for Italy and France respectively.

In addition, they signed the Four Power Treaty in which they agreed to respect each country's interests in the Far East as well as to maintain the Open Door policy in China. Furthermore, Japan promised to remove its troops from the Chinese province of Shantung and the USA agreed not to strengthen its military presence in Guam.

However, the conference had several limitations. It imposed no limits on the size of armies or air forces. The naval limitations only applied to battleships and aircraft carriers. The agreement was 'toothless' with no method of enforcing the limitation agreement. No sanctions were to apply to those who broke the agreement. While Japan abided by the treaty for several years, she began to expand her influence in the 1930s.

The Kellogg–Briand Pact, 1928

The Kellogg–Briand Pact was an international agreement set up by Frank B. Kellogg, the US Secretary of State, and Aristide Briand, the French Foreign Minister.

This pact was signed for two main reasons. The French were keen on an alliance with the USA. However, America did not want any commitments in Europe and used the pact as a means of placating the French. Moreover, there was a strong movement for peace in the USA in the 1920s with growing support for peace societies.

> **Peace societies** – Various groups set up in the USA in the 1920s to encourage support for peace. One example was the World Peace Association.

The pact was signed by fifteen countries which agreed not to wage war except in self-defence and to seek peaceful means to resolve disputes. However, it was another toothless agreement with no sanctions to deal with any country that broke the agreement. The Senate ratified the pact by 85 votes to one, but the Senate Foreign Relations Committee insisted that the pact did not actually sanction the use of war even if attacked, or commit the USA to help any country that was threatened.

The USA and Europe

The USA also found it impossible to avoid involvement in Europe partly due to the effects of the Versailles peace settlement, in particular reparations.

Loans

The USA was prepared to lend money to countries after the war to restore prosperity and prevent the spread of Communism – but not to the USSR and China. They insisted that all war debts had to be repaid. Indeed, the USA used debt repayments as a threat to European powers, particularly when Britain tried to force up the price of rubber by restricting supplies in the British Empire. The USA retaliated by threatening harsher repayment terms for war debts.

The Dawes and Young Plans

The USA was also keen on a stable Germany to prevent a Communist revolution and was directly involved with the Dawes and Young Plans. Under the Dawes Plan of 1924 Charles G. Dawes, an American banker, was asked by the Allied Reparations Committee to investigate the fact that Germany could not afford to pay the original reparations instalments and had defaulted on its payment in 1923. His report, published in April 1924, proposed a plan for instituting annual payments of reparations on a fixed scale. He also recommended the reorganisation of the German State Bank and increased foreign loans. The plan that was drawn up reduced German payments to $250 million a year with these payments increasing over the next five years as the German economy improved. Germany was also given an immediate loan of 800 million marks, with US bankers providing half and the rest coming from foreign bankers.

The Young Plan

The Young Plan of 1929 was drawn up by Owen Young, head of the General Electric Company. This scaled down reparation payments to $26 billion, to be paid over a period of 59 years.

Overall, the USA was lending money to Germany which was using these loans to pay reparations to the Allies who, in turn, were using these payments to repay loans to the USA. In other words, the USA was effectively paying itself back with its own money. The situation became even more confused with the Dawes and Young Plans scaling down German reparation payments. Germany was paying less to the Allies who, in turn, paid less to the USA.

Involvement in Latin America

Although the USA, for the most part, did revert to isolationism, they did continue to pursue and protect their interests in Latin America. There was increased involvement by the USA in Latin American in the 1920s. This was partly due to the Monroe Doctrine as well as the emergence of the Good Neighbor Policy which cultivated good relations with Latin America. Much of this increased involvement was economic which, in turn, often encouraged more political and military intervention in order to safeguard these economic interests.

Economic involvement

US investment in Latin America doubled in the years 1924–29 from $1.5 billion to $3 billion. This included automobile firms such as General Motors which manufactured vehicles in Argentina, Brazil and Uruguay. In 1923, General Electric set up the American and Foreign Power Company and controlled the provision of electricity in eight Latin American countries. In addition, US companies dominated the media such as the movies and radio.

The State Department even hired economists such as Edwin Kemmerer to develop plans for countries that requested US investment. The Kemmerer Plans helped to stabilise and develop the economies of such countries by offering advice on sound currency and central banks.

However, such investment did bring problems and increase US involvement in order to protect these investments. For example, it would intervene to prevent US loans being spent by corrupt officials on luxuries. However, the USA was reluctant to sanction military intervention because it was expensive and unpopular with taxpayers.

Settling disputes

During the 1920s, where possible, the US settled disputes with troops. These were often replaced by loyal local militia.

- The USA gave Colombia $25 million in compensation for its support for the independence of Panama in 1903.
- There was an ongoing dispute with Mexico after the latter defaulted on its international debts, much of which were from the USA, in 1914. In 1922, the Mexican Government agreed to repay $500,000 and, in the following year, the Bucareli Accords provided compensation for damage caused to foreign property during the Mexican Revolution.
- In 1925, US troops were withdrawn from Nicaragua in order to improve relations between the two countries. However, the following year 5,000 troops were sent back in due to the outbreak of civil war. A US diplomat, Henry Stimson, organised the Peace Treaty of Tipitapa which led to the election of Juan Bautista Sacasa in 1928.

WORKING TOGETHER

1 Working with a partner, make a copy of and complete the following table, with one of you completing the evidence for isolationism and the other evidence of involvement in foreign affairs.

Evidence of isolationism	Evidence of involvement in foreign affairs

2 Compare your findings and discuss the question: 'To what extent was the USA isolationist in the 1920s?'

2 Reasons for the boom in the US economy in the 1920s

During the 1920s, the USA experienced an economic boom. There is much debate among historians as to why this boom took place. Some historians stress the importance of more long-term factors such as the First World War, while others give emphasis to more immediate factors including the policies of the Republican governments and the impact of the growth of the car industry. Details of the economic effects of the First World War were covered in Chapter 4, page 124. Here, we focus on the short-term reasons for economic success in the USA.

Short-term factors

How important was the growth of the car industry in the economic boom of the 1920s?

More immediate factors included the policies of the Republican governments, technological change, consumerism and the availability of credit and confidence.

The policies of the Republican governments and 'rugged individualism'

Republican presidents dominated politics in the 1920s and successive presidents were greatly influenced by Treasury Secretary Andrew Mellon, a firm believer in a free economy.

Laissez-faire

President Coolidge held the view of many Americans, that governments should be involved as little as possible in the day-to-day running of the economy. If businessmen were left alone to make their own decisions, it was thought that high profits, more jobs and good wages would be the result. This was the policy of *laissez-faire* – the only role for the government was to help business when it was asked to.

Under Harding and Coolidge, the Republican economic policy of *laissez-faire* contributed to the prosperity of the USA. Low taxes and few regulations meant that businessmen were able to chase profits without fear of interference. Indeed, laws concerning price fixing were often ignored.

Rugged individualism

Successive Republican presidents believed in 'rugged individualism'. This was a term used by Republican presidents such as Hoover who believed that people achieved success by their own hard work. It originated with the early Americans who moved to the West and made a new life for themselves through their own efforts.

Source C A speech delivered by the Republican President Herbert Hoover in 1928. Quoted in *USA 1919–41* by S. Waugh and J. Wright, (Hodder Education), 2009, p. 11.

During the war, we turned to the government to solve every difficult economic problem. When the Republican Party came to power, it restored the government to its position of umpire instead of a player. For these reasons the American people have gone forward in progress. Our opponents propose that we must thrust government into business. It would stifle initiative and invention.

NOTE-MAKING

Using bullet points (see page x) make notes on the reasons for the economic boom of the 1920s.

Boom – When the economy of a country is rapidly developing.

Andrew Mellon

Andrew W. Mellon (1855–1937) was appointed Secretary of the Treasury by President Warren G. Harding in 1921, and he continued to serve under Presidents Calvin Coolidge and Herbert Hoover. Mellon's philosophy was one of debt reduction, tax reduction and a balanced budget. His tax reform scheme, known as the Mellon Plan, reduced taxes for business.

What does Source C suggest about the role of government in the economy?

Protectionism

Republican governments put tariffs on imported goods in order to limit the competition from foreign imports. Imports became more expensive compared with American-made goods. This, in turn, encouraged the purchase of American goods and helped US-based producers. The Fordney–McCumber Tariff (1922) raised import duties on goods coming into the USA to the highest level ever, thus protecting American industry and encouraging Americans to buy home-produced goods.

In addition, a reduction of income tax rates left some people with more cash to spend on consumer goods. This, in turn, provided the cash to buy the home-produced goods. Mellon handed out tax reductions totalling $3.5 billion to large-scale industrialists and corporations.

Technological change and new business methods

New business methods ensured that technological advances were fully exploited.

Technological change

The USA led the world in changes in technology. The development of electricity was fundamental to this advancement. It provided a cheaper, more reliable and flexible form of power for factories and other industries. Moreover, it stimulated other associated electrical goods industries such as refrigerators, vacuum cleaners and radios.

Other key developments included the conveyor belt and mass production techniques adopted by the car industry, which speeded up industrial

▶ *The Builder* by the American artist Gerrit Beneker, painted to symbolise the rising prosperity of America.

production, improved productivity and led to greater profits. These were already established in some industries, for example, in the manufacture of firearms, sewing machines and railroad engines. They were later extended to the production of clocks, typewriters and bicycles.

Plastics like Bakelite were developed and used in household products. Other innovations included glass tubing, automatic switchboards and concrete mixers. New materials enabled the construction of new types of buildings. The skylines of the great cities were transformed by skyscrapers.

New business methods
There was a significant growth in huge corporations that made use of more scientific business methods. By 1929, the largest 200 corporations possessed twenty per cent of the nation's wealth. They dominated industry in various ways:

- They operated as cartels to fix prices. The government turned a blind eye to these practices.
- Some corporations such as US Steel were so big that they were able to dictate output and price level throughout the industry.
- The large corporations also created holding companies. For example, Samuel Insull built up a vast empire based on electrical supply. He eventually controlled as many as 111 companies.

Management science led to the development of different management roles such as specialisms in production, design, marketing or accounts. There was a significant growth of business schools with as many as 89 by 1928 training 67,000 students. There were new 'scientific' theories put into practice, particularly the work of Frederick Taylor and his followers.

Consumerism and advertising
The economic boom of the 1920s was partly encouraged by the growth of consumerism.

Reasons for consumerism
Increased demand for consumer goods was due to several factors. By 1927, two-thirds of US homes had electricity. In 1912, only sixteen per cent of the American people lived in electrically-lit homes. By 1927, the number had risen to 63 per cent. The growth of electric power encouraged a much more widespread use of electrical goods. During this period, consumption of other energy sources also grew, for example the amount of oil used doubled and gas quadrupled.

The growth in female employment also increased the need for labour-saving devices such as washing machines and vacuum cleaners and hire purchase schemes made it easier to buy goods on credit. Furthermore, the popularity of entertainment meant more and more Americans bought radios and gramophones. For the majority of workers in industry, wages increased. Between 1923 and 1929, the average wage rose by eight per cent. In other words, workers had more spare money to spend on consumer goods.

Advertising
Various advertising techniques developed rapidly during the 1920s. Before then advertisements had mainly comprised the use of the printed word telling the customer about the attributes of the product. But now companies needed to expand demand for their products so they began to hire psychologists to design campaigns and target specific groups such as young women. Lucky Strike, for example, encouraged women to smoke in

Cartel – A group of companies agreeing to fix output and prices in order to reduce competition and increase profits.

Holding company – Where one very large company obtains a controlling interest in smaller companies in order to control the market.

Consumerism – An increase in the production of consumer goods on the grounds that high spending is the basis of a sound economy.

Hire purchase – A system of credit whereby a person may purchase an item by making regular payments while already having the use of said item.

Frederick Taylor
Frederick Taylor (1856–1915) was a mechanical engineer and one of the first management consultants. He promoted greater efficiency in business and industry in his book *The Principles of Scientific Management*. He believed in the theory of 'time and motion', a system in which production techniques are allocated set times for completion and production targets laid on this basis. His ideas underpinned the use of the assembly line, especially in the car industry.

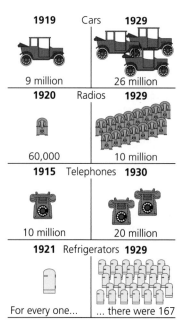

▲ Figure 1 The growth in the sales of consumer goods. Can you suggest other industries that would benefit from the growth in sales of these items?

public with their cigarettes marketed as 'torches of freedom'. Advertising campaigns began to emphasise slogans, brand names, celebrity endorsements and consumer aspirations. There was a constant need to create demand. The growth in industrial production required a continuous market. It was no longer enough to sell a durable unchanging product that might last the purchaser for life, as Ford had done with his Model T. Now, to fuel the boom, it was necessary for people to buy new things frequently. They had to be convinced that they could not do without the latest model of an electrical appliance or the new design in clothing.

For many consumers advertising techniques worked. Not only did they associate products with a slogan, but they also believed they could not manage without the advertised product. The *Kansas City Journal-Post* was hardly exaggerating when it wrote, 'Advertising and mass production are the twin cylinders that keep the motor of modern business in motion'. By 1929, companies were spending $3 billion annually on advertising, five times more than in 1914.

Media and advertising

The new mass media, especially the cinema and the radio, brought about a revolution in advertising. By 1928, there were 17,000 cinemas in the USA. These provided enormous potential for commercials being shown between the two main films. By 1929, there were 618 radio stations throughout the USA with an audience estimated at 50 million. Advertisers again saw the potential and began to sponsor programmes in return for air time for commercials.

Credit

The growth of credit made it much easier for people to buy goods even though they did not have enough cash to pay for them immediately. This was due to the development of hire purchase whereby goods were paid for in instalments. The goods were owned once the last installment was paid. About half the goods sold in the 1920s were paid for by hire purchase.

The car industry

The car industry played a very important role in the boom of the 1920s, often leading the way in technological change as well as stimulating the growth of other industries. It grew dramatically in the 1920s and by the end of the decade there were 4.5 million cars on the road, the largest industry in the USA.

The assembly line

In 1913, Ford introduced a much more efficient method of producing cars, the assembly line or 'magic belt'. He had seen how efficiently this was used in meat-packing factories and slaughterhouses. An electric conveyor belt carried the partly assembled car at the same speed past workers who stood at the same spot and did the one job such as fitting on the wheels or doors. This saved time as the tools and equipment were brought to the worker rather than him having to waste time walking about for these. In 1913, the Ford factory in Detroit was producing one car every three minutes. By 1920, the same factory was producing the same car every ten seconds.

Workforce

Ford believed in hard work and would walk round his factory each day encouraging his workers to do their job properly. However, he had quite a turnover of workers who found the assembly line boring and monotonous.

Henry Ford

Henry Ford was born in Greenfield Township, Michigan, but he moved to Detroit to learn about engineering and became an electrical engineer, building his first car in a rented brick shed. In 1903, he founded the Ford Motor Company in Detroit. In 1908, he introduced his Model T. Ford which was nicknamed the 'tin lizzie'. Existing car manufacturers built several different car models in a range of colours, but Ford showed the benefits (and reduced costs) of manufacturing one standard model that was 'any colour as long as it was black'.

Therefore, in 1914 Ford announced that he would double the wages to $5 a day, which was far more than anyone else paid for the equivalent job. Workers rushed to Detroit to work for him. He also reduced the length of the working day to eight hours and introduced a third shift, so the factory was operating a three-shift system and working 24 hours each day.

Owing to his business methods and new technology, Ford brought down the price of cars and made them affordable to many Americans. In 1914, a Model T cost $850. By 1926, the price had dropped to $295. Ford also led the way in introducing hire purchase as a method of credit.

Benefits of the car industry

The car industry revolutionised American industry. It used so much steel, wood, petrol, rubber and leather that it provided jobs for more than five million people. Around 90 per cent of petrol, 80 per cent of rubber and 75 per cent of plate glass produced in the USA was consumed by the car industry by the late 1920s. The car industry transformed buying habits, making hire purchase a way of life for most Americans because it enabled an average family to buy a car. It promoted road building and travel, which in turn led to motels and restaurants being built in places that had been considered out of the way. The production of automobiles rose dramatically from 1.9 million in 1920 to 4.5 million in 1929. The three main manufacturers were the giant firms of Ford, Chrysler and General Motors.

Source D From *Only Yesterday: An Informal History of the Nineteen Twenties*, by an American journalist, Frederick Lewis Allen. (America in Class: Becoming America; America in the 1920s at: http://americainclass.org/sources/becomingmodern/prosperity/text1/text1.htm)

To my mind, the largest single force has been the motor car. The automobile was something which people really wanted with a desire that amounted to a passion. The effect was two-fold. It stimulated business, and it suffused the country with the visible *appearance* of a prosperity in which everybody seemed to share. Other prosperous periods have been stimulated by foreign trade, or by the seeping of gold into the community. But this particular period was stimulated by a large, active, noisy, and inescapable article visible on every road. You could see, hear, smell the monster for miles. (Some 25,000 unfortunates are touched by it each year, never to breathe again.) Something in the nature of 500 millions of horsepower was given over to the ultimate consumer in a remarkably short space of time the biggest single block of power, by many-fold, which the world has ever delivered. It sent the credit structure spiralling upward, and it certainly made us look prosperous.

> Why does the journalist in Source D believe the car industry was an important factor in the boom?

Road building

Breaking with the policy of *laissez-faire*, the federal government expended a great deal of energy on road building in the 1920s. The Federal Highway Act of 1921 gave responsibility for road building to central government and highways were being constructed at the rate of 10,000 miles per year by 1929. But this was not enough. New roads could not keep pace with the growth of traffic. Congestion was common, particularly in the approaches to large urban centres. In 1936, the Chief Designer in the Bureau of Public Roads reported that between 25 and 50 per cent of modern roads built over the previous twenty years were unfit for use because of the amount of traffic that was quite simply wearing them out.

Motor vehicles also created the growth of new service industries such as garages, motels, petrol stations and used car salerooms. They gradually changed the landscape alongside the highways of the USA.

Improved transportation also afforded new opportunities for industry. For example, goods could be much more easily moved from factories to their markets. The number of truck registrations increased from less than 1 million in 1919 to 3.5 million by 1929, when 15 billion gallons of petrol were used and 4.5 million new cars were sold.

The stock market boom

In the 1920s, the stock market seemed to be the link to the prosperity of the USA. The values of stocks and shares rose steadily throughout the decade until they rose dramatically in 1928 and 1929. Moreover, the amount of buying and selling of shares grew substantially until it was a common occurrence for ordinary working people to become involved – the accepted image of the 1920s is that 'even the shoeshine boy' was dealing in shares.

Most companies' shares seemed to rise, and so people were prepared to risk their money on buying shares – after all, their value would rise. The USA began to speculate. Even if people did not have enough money to pay the full amount, they would make a deposit, borrow to pay the rest and then sell the shares in a couple of weeks when their value had risen and a profit had been made. The speculator would then pay off his debt and still have made money on the deal. (This was called 'buying on the margin'.)

The number of shares traded in 1926 was about 451 million, increasing to 577 million the following year. By 1928, with share prices rising fast, there was a bull market on the Wall Street Stock Exchange and, in 1929, there were more than 1.1 billion shares sold. Up to 25 million Americans became involved in the frenzy of share dealing in the last years of the decade.

Stocks and shares – Certificates of ownership in a company.

Bull market – A time when share prices are rising.

KEY DATES: SHORT-TERM FACTORS

1908 Ford launched the Model T.

1913 Ford introduced the assembly line.

1922 The Fordney–McCumber tariff.

1927 Two-thirds of the USA had electricity.

1929 4.5 million cars were produced in the USA.

WORKING TOGETHER

1 Was the car industry the most important reason for the boom in the US economy? Make a copy of the following grid. Give a rating for each factor, with a brief explanation for your choice. 'Decisive' means the boom would not have happened without this factor.

	Quite important	Important	Decisive
First World War			
Republican policies			
Consumerism			
Car industry			
Technological change			
Credit			
Confidence			

2 Do you agree that the car industry was the most important reason for the boom of the 1920s?

3 Key social and cultural changes in the 'Jazz Age'

There were rapid social changes in the USA in the 1920s and the period is often referred to as the 'roaring twenties' or the 'Jazz Age'. This included developments in the status of some women, particularly the flappers. The radio and the cinema revolutionised entertainment. Hollywood became the centre of the film industry. However, there were also more negative developments with Prohibition encouraging the growth of organised crime and the re-emergence of the Ku Klux Klan.

The position of women in the 1920s

To what extent was there progress in the position of women in the USA in the 1920s?

Women were very much second-class citizens in the USA before 1917. They played no part in politics and did not have the vote. Their social position was restricted and there were limited employment opportunities. There is much debate about the changes in the position of women in the USA in the 1920s, particularly the impact of the flappers.

Changes after 1917

There were some changes in the position of women in the 1920s, which were partly influenced by the First World War.

The impact of the First World War

The USA's entry into the First World War in 1917 provided greater opportunities for women. By the end of the war, 2.8 million men had been drafted into the armed forces and over a million women helped with the war effort. Approximately 90,000 served in the US armed forces in Europe. For example, the Navy and Marine Corps enlisted women as clerks, radio electricians, chemists, accountants and nurses. The Army, unlike its sister services, was more conservative in the jobs it permitted women to fill in its ranks, enlisting more than 21,000 as clerks, fingerprint experts, journalists and translators. Women also worked in jobs traditionally done by men such as heavy industry, engineering works and transport. The war proved women could do the jobs just as well as men and encouraged greater freedom, especially in social habits such as smoking and drinking in public and going out unchaperoned. Their participation also made a powerful argument for women's voting rights, weighing heavily in the passing of the Nineteenth Amendment giving American women the right to vote in 1920. This gave them greater political power and encouraged some to campaign for further change.

The 1920s saw a series of changes to the position of women. These were influenced by the consumer boom of the 1920s, which provided exciting opportunities for women. Labour-saving devices, such as vacuum cleaners and washing machines, provided extra time which enabled some women to go into employment, and gave others more opportunity for leisure and recreational activities.

The 'Jazz Age' brought changes in entertainment and leisure. The popularity of the cinema, radio and dance halls provided further opportunities for women. For example, Mary Pickford and Clara Bow became stars of silent movies and were so successful that they joined two other stars in setting up their own film

NOTE-MAKING

Using the 1–2 method (see page x) make notes on this section. For example, on the left-hand side you could put a side heading such as 'Impact of the First World War on women' and on the right-hand side a bulleted list of reasons.

company. Mae West, Gloria Swanson and Jean Harlow became stars of the 'talkies' and role models for many younger girls.

Employment

There were other changes in the position of women. There was certainly progress in the number of women in employment. By 1930, 2 million more women were employed than had been ten years earlier. However, these tended to be in unskilled low-paid jobs. Despite the fact that a third of university degrees were awarded to women in 1930, only four per cent of university professors were women. Medical schools allocated only five per cent of places to women. Consequently the number of women doctors actually declined in the 1920s.

Men were still paid a lot more than women for doing the same job. Women received no support from the Supreme Court, which banned all attempts to set minimum wages for women. In 1927, the government took the side of the employers when women textile workers in Tennessee went on strike for better pay. The strikers were arrested by the local police. There were some new career opportunities for women but this was in so-called 'women's jobs' such as librarians and nurses.

Jobs	1900	1930
Professional and technical workers	8	14
Managers and officials	1	3
Clerical and sales workers	8	28
Skilled craftspeople	1	1
Workers and labourers	26	19
Domestic servants	29	18
Other service workers	7	10
Farmers	6	2

▲ **Figure 2** A table showing the percentage of women in certain jobs in the years 1900–30.

> Does the table in Figure 2 suggest that there was progress in the position of women in the USA in the 1920s?

Politics

Women were given the vote in 1920. A few women did make progress in gaining political power. For example, Nellie Tayloe Ross of Wyoming became the first woman to be elected governor of a state in 1924. Two years later, Bertha Knight Landes became the first female mayor of a city, Seattle.

However, these were the exception and women made little progress in politics itself. Political parties wanted their vote but did not see them as realistic candidates for political office. By 1920, there were only a handful of female politicians. Most women, in any case, had little interest in politics. The women's movement failed in its attempt to get the Equal Rights Amendment Act passed, which would have given them equality in law with men.

Women and birth control

Margaret Sanger drew attention to the plight of poor women through her work as a nurse. Often lacking any means of contraception, women were forced into dangerous back-street abortions, which may have killed as many as 50,000 women per year. She began to write articles on contraception. However, widespread dissemination was difficult because the Comstock Act of 1873 banned the distribution of both written articles on contraception and items through the US mail. Arrested in 1916 for opening the first contraception clinic in the USA, in 1921 Sanger founded the American Birth Control League.

Many supporters of eugenics supported birth control because they felt the poor should be discouraged from breeding because to do so would threaten race degeneration. This was particularly apposite regarding non-white ethnic

Eugenics – The study of, or belief in, the possibility of improving the qualities of the human species or a human population.

groups. Sanger herself began to promote sterilisation for mentally handicapped people, and the birth control movement has undoubtedly been criticised for its associations with eugenics.

The flapper

The greatest change in the position of females was experienced by women known as the flappers. In the 1920s, a number of women, generally from middle- and upper-class families living in the Northern states, decided to challenge the traditional attitudes to and appearance of women. These women became known as the flappers. They tried to show a greater independence and freedom in their appearance and social life.

However, in some respects, the flappers did not further the cause of women's rights in the 1920s. They were seen as too extreme by many traditional groups, especially in rural areas, with strong disapproval from religious societies. Many of the older generation criticised the lifestyle of the flappers and formed Anti-Flirt Leagues. Others saw the flappers as simply pleasure-seeking women with few other attributes.

Moreover, to a certain extent the focus on flappers conceals the realities for most women in the 1920s. Writing in 2007, Lucy Moore contrasts the post-war opportunities for young women with those of the past and gives examples of how these could liberate them – while including the proviso that most were expected to give up work when they married. Other historians have been less optimistic. Writing in the 1990s, Michael Parrish argued that even the flappers' movement was a form of exploitation which reinforced gender stereotypes as women seemed to focus on indulgence and beauty rather than serious issues. William Leuchtenberg, in the 1950s, was even more critical, showing that the numbers of women in the workforce and higher education actually diminished during the decade and women had little interest in voting. More recently, however, Lynn Dumenil has redressed the balance, showing how, despite the problems they faced, both white and African-American women activists could be influential at state and local level, focusing, for example, on social reforms.

The flapper

The flappers cut their hair short and wore make-up, short skirts and very bright clothes. They smoked and drank in public and went out to speakeasies and to the cinema without a chaperone. Flappers openly danced with men in public, especially the new craze, the Charleston, and listened to controversial new music known as jazz. Many drove cars and even motor bikes and wore very revealing swimming costumes on public beaches. Actress Joan Crawford was the most famous flapper of them all. She kissed, drank, smoked and danced the Charleston in films such as *Our Modern Maidens* (1929).

KEY DATES: THE POSITION OF WOMEN IN THE 1920s

1920 The Nineteenth Amendment gave American women the right to vote.

1924 Nellie Tayloe Ross of Wyoming became the first woman to be elected governor.

1926 Bertha Knight Landes became the first female mayor of an American city, Seattle.

1930 Two million more women in employment than in 1920.

WORKING TOGETHER

With a partner, divide your paper into two.
- One of you should identify evidence of progress for women in the USA in the 1920s.
- The other should identify evidence of lack of progress.

Overall, to what extent would you agree that women had made progress in the USA in the 1920s?

NOTE-MAKING

1 Using a spider diagram (see page x) summarise in what ways entertainment in the USA changed in the 1920s.
2 Which do you think was the greatest change? Give reasons for your answer.

New forms of entertainment

In what ways did entertainment in the USA change in the 1920s?

There was a growth in many forms of entertainment in the USA in the 1920s including sport, radio, the cinema and music. Labour-saving devices for the home, such as washing machines, gave people more free time. Mass production meant people worked less. Americans began to look for ways to fill their spare time, especially as many were better paid.

Sport

In the early 1920s, sport became a very important part of the lives of many US citizens and it was made even more popular as a result of the radio. Indeed, the 1920s was officially named the 'Golden Age of Sport'. Baseball, football, horse racing and tennis captured the imagination of many people. Baseball was the most popular game and Babe Ruth was the most popular sporting star of the time; he had a major influence on the younger generation because he was not shy about drinking and smoking in public.

Spectators flocked to see sporting events. In 1924, 67,000 watched the football match between Illinois and Michigan in the Memorial Stadium in Baltimore, Maryland. In 1926, some 145,000 saw the boxing match between Jack Dempsey and Gene Tunney.

Baseball

The decade is particularly associated with baseball success, partly because it saw a significant number of supremely gifted players – Babe Ruth and his New York Yankee team-mate Lou Gehrig, for example. The game had been popular since the 1870s because it was easy to play on any patch of waste land but during the 1920s it captured the public imagination to the extent that massive stadia could be built such as West Side Grounds in Chicago. Many historians of the game agree the transformation of baseball was largely down to the charisma associated with Babe Ruth. On a more prosaic note, however, it may be equally due to the introduction of a cork-centred ball that was easier to hit hard. This transferred emphasis away from pitchers to hitters like Babe Ruth – hence the fascination with spectacular home runs.

1920 saw the formation of the Negro National Baseball League, a testament to the fact that sport was still largely segregated and African-American players were excluded from the major league teams. Ironically, African-American teams toured the USA playing games to mixed crowds. The high point of the season, the East–West All Star game, could attract crowds of 30,000. The players earned less than half of the salaries of their white counterparts, and committed themselves to exhausting circuits, some years playing up to three times a day every day. Nevertheless, the Negro leagues were among the biggest African-American-owned businesses in the USA.

The radio

Radio grew dramatically from the time of the establishment of the first commercial radio station. KDKA in Pittsburgh was set up in 1920 and by 1922 there were 500 stations dotted across the USA. The first national network, NBC, was set up in 1926 with CBS following in 1927. Some critics argued that invisible energy flying through the air must be dangerous and cited dead birds as evidence. However, for most, the radio brought a new world into people's living rooms. An estimated 50 million people listened to the 1927 boxing match between Gene Tunney and Jack Dempsey. People held 'radio parties' where friends and family could listen together in their home.

Radios weren't cheap. A typical model cost $150, usually paid for on credit. They were often big pieces of cabinet-like furniture. By 1927, 33 per cent of all money spent on furniture was spent on radios. Between 1923 and 1930, 60 per cent of all American families purchased one. Sales grew from $60 million in 1923 to $842 million six years later.

As we have seen (see page 145), radio held huge attraction for advertising and sponsorship, which often paid for programmes. In August 1929, for example, the toothpaste company Pepsodent began to sponsor the popular comedy series *Amos 'n' Andy* on NBC; in the next few years the audience for this show would rise as high as 40 million. Programmes ranged across the spectrum from comedies to westerns to detective serials to music and comedy. While some felt the content of programmes should be uplifting and educational, most realised people wanted entertainment – and if it came in the form of serials they would be hooked. The power of radio to broadcast important sporting events should not be forgotten either – it brought the nation together for the first time. Through the power of radio Americans could listen to the same songs, laugh at the same jokes and thrill to the same sporting events at the same time.

The cinema

Cinema was even more significant. While moving picture shows had been around since the early years of the century, often as a novelty feature in a variety show, the 1920s saw their development as possibly the pre-eminent US contribution to world culture. By the 1920s, the cinema industry, centred in Hollywood, Los Angeles, was the fourth largest in terms of capital investment. It employed more people than either Ford or General Motors.

Going to the movies wasn't simply a form of escapism. Often movies were shown in elaborate picture palaces that could hold thousands of customers – in any one day there could be in excess of 10 million people in 20,000 cinemas. The most glamorous picture palaces were on a truly epic scale. The Roxy in New York, which cost in the region of $7–$10 million to build, had three organs, a huge chandelier, a red carpet valued at $10,000 and a 118-piece orchestra.

Movies offered escape, excitement and a chance to imagine oneself in a different world peopled by heroes. Actors became huge stars, the first real celebrities, and included:

● exciting actresses such as Clara Bow, the 'It girl' who symbolised the modern liberated woman, and Theda Bara, the 'vamp' exuding a dangerous sexuality
● action heroes like Douglas Fairbanks
● comic geniuses such as Buster Keaton and Charlie Chaplin.

The first sound film, *The Jazz Singer*, appeared in 1927; it served to make cinema even more popular.

Jazz music

The 1920s is known as the 'Jazz Age' because the popular music of the time was jazz. Jazz was not new. It originated with black slaves who were encouraged to sing in order to increase production. They used washboards, cans, pickaxes and percussion to produce their own distinctive brand of music. Their music was given various names including 'blues', 'rag' or 'boogie-woogie'. By changing the beat and creating particular rhythms, it was changed into jazz. However, these words were taken from black sexual

Hollywood

Hollywood became the centre of movie making in the USA in the 1920s. The first film shot in the Hollywood area was called *In Old California* in 1910. In the following year the first studio was opened by the New Jersey-based Centaur Company which wanted to make Western films in California. By 1915, the majority of American films were being made in the Los Angeles area. Four major film companies – Paramount, Warner Bros, RKO and Columbia, had studios in Hollywood. Five years later 1 million people were employed in the area in making films. Movie stars themselves moved to the Los Angeles area and began building themselves luxury homes. For example, Gloria Swanson had a 22-room mansion in Beverly Hills. Charlie Chaplin and Buster Keaton both lived in the area.

KEY DATES: ENTERTAINMENT IN THE 1920s

1920 The first film shot in the Hollywood area.

1926 145,000 saw the boxing match between Jack Dempsey and Gene Tunney.

1927 The first 'talkie' was made, making the cinema even more popular.

slang terms and, at first, were not popular among white people because of their links to sex, and were renamed Jazz.

Jazz, however, became popular with the white middle-class youth, especially the flappers, of the 1920s, and was seen as another sign of a fall in moral standards. For example, in 1921 the *Ladies Home Journal* published an article with the title 'Does Jazz put the Sin in Syncopation?' Some cities, including New York and Cleveland, prohibited the public performance of jazz in dance halls. However, this only made it more exciting to the young and increased its appeal. Jazz became the great attraction of the night clubs and speakeasies and was brought into homes through radio broadcasts.

> **Syncopation** – The off-beat rhythms that characterise jazz music.

Prohibition and gangsters

To what extent was Prohibition a 'noble experiment'?

Prohibition

There has been much debate among historians about the impact of Prohibition on the USA. During the nineteenth century, many groups had supported the idea of prohibiting the sale of alcohol. Their campaign played an important part in the introduction of Prohibition in the USA in 1919, which was described by Herbert Hoover as the 'noble experiment'. However, it created as many problems as it solved – in particular, by encouraging a rise in gangsters and organised crime.

Why was Prohibition introduced?

The idea of Prohibition goes back to the nineteenth century, when many groups supported the idea of prohibiting alcohol for moral reasons. Groups such as the Women's Temperance Association and the Anti-Saloon League campaigned against the devastating effects of excessive drinking. Momentum for Prohibition built up in the early years of the twentieth century with 26 states passing laws limiting the sale of alcohol.

- Female reformers had argued for years that there were clear links between the consumption of alcohol and wife beating and child abuse.
- Industrialists such as Henry Ford were concerned that drinking reduced efficiency and output at work.
- Many religious groups saw alcohol as the root of the sin and evil values of American people.
- It was felt that Prohibition would enhance the traditional, encouraging people to be hard-working and thrifty.
- America's participation in the First World War encouraged further support as many brewers were of German origin and Prohibition was seen as patriotic. As anti-German feeling grew in the USA, beer consumption was seen as a betrayal of the USA and beer was given the nickname of 'Kaiser's brew'.

In 1918, President Wilson banned beer production until the war ended. In January 1919, the Prohibition Amendment, which stopped the 'manufacture, sale or transportation of intoxicating liquors' was ratified by Congress and became known as the Volstead Act.

Why did Prohibition fail?

Prohibition failed to prevent the consumption of alcohol as it simply drove drinkers underground. Huge numbers of people were prepared to break the law not only to produce alcohol but to go to private bars to consume it. Within a short time after the introduction of Prohibition there were more speakeasies than there had been legal saloons. For example, in New York alone, there were

> **NOTE-MAKING**
>
> Using bullet points (see page x) summarise the main developments in Prohibition and gangsters under the following side-headings:
> - Reasons for Prohibition
> - Reasons for the failure of Prohibition
> - Achievements of Prohibition
> - Organised crime.

> **Speakeasy** – An illegal drinking shop.

more than 30,000 speakeasies. Prohibition was a classic case of a law being passed that was impossible to enforce.

One reason was geographical difficulties in enforcing Prohibition. The USA has 18,700 miles of coastline and land border and so it was difficult to prevent smuggling. This was so successful that it was estimated that in 1925, agents only intercepted about five per cent of alcohol coming into the country illegally.

Moreover, the Internal Revenue Service, set up to enforce Prohibition, never had more than 2,500 agents and some of them became paid hands of the gang leaders (see page 156). Between 1920 and 1930, about ten per cent of Prohibition agents were fined for corruption with many more escaping prosecution.

Many people, known as 'bootleggers', went into business as producers and distributors of illegal alcohol, which was often called 'moonshine' because it was manufactured in remote areas by the light of the moon. As the 1920s progressed, the mood of the nation changed. For many Americans, especially those living in the cities, their main aim in life was having a good time. Illegal drinking in gangster-run speakeasies became very popular in urban areas.

The end of Prohibition
By the early 1930s, there was clear and growing opposition to Prohibition. In 1928, the Democratic presidential candidate, Al Smith, advocated the abolition of Prohibition. Hoover, who defeated Smith in the election, set up the Wickersham Commission to investigate Prohibition. It reported that it was impossible to enforce but it recommended a continuation of Prohibition. It was Hoover's successor, Roosevelt, who finally abolished the measure in 1933. This was during the Depression with many feeling that if Prohibition was removed, the legal brewing industry would create jobs. People would pay more in taxes and duties, thus helping people to combat the effects of the Depression.

Was Prohibition a total failure?
Prohibition had mixed effects for Americans.

Benefits of Prohibition	Shortcomings of Prohibition
• Deaths from alcoholism had fallen by 80 per cent by 1921. Male deaths from cirrhosis of the liver fell from 29.5 per 100,000 in 1911 to 10.7 per 100,000 in 1929. • Prohibition reduced the number of people killed on the roads and the incidence of drink-related accidents at work also fell. • Alcohol consumption fell from an average of 2.6 gallons per person in the years before 1917 to one gallon by the 1930s. • Arrests from drunkenness fell.	• About 50,000 people died from poisoned alcohol and doctors reported an increase in deaths. • Prohibition helped to create organised crime (see pp. 160–61). Between 1927 and 1930 alone, there were 227 gangland murders in Chicago with only two killers ever convicted. Some argue that had it not been for Prohibition, such large criminal gangs would not have developed in the first place. • Illegal drinking made criminals of a good percentage of the population. • The brewing industry suffered badly due to Prohibition. For example, St Louis had 22 breweries before Prohibition. Only nine re-opened after Prohibition ended in 1933.

Source E From evidence given in 1926 by a New York politician, Fiorello LaGuardia, to the Senate Judiciary Hearings Committee on Prohibition. Quoted in *USA History 1890–1945* by C. Rowe, (Nelson Thornes), 2008, p. 60.

It is impossible to tell whether Prohibition is a good thing or a bad thing. It has never been enforced. At least a million quarts of liquor are consumed each day in the United States. I believe that the percentage of whisky drinkers in the United States is now greater than in any country in the world. Prohibition is to blame for this. A billion dollars a year is being lost to the federal government and the state in lost customs duties. The money goes instead into the pockets of bootleggers and corrupt public officials.

Using the evidence from Source E and your own knowledge, to what extent do you agree that Prohibition was a 'noble experiment'?

Gangsters and organised crime

There were criminal gangs in the USA before Prohibition. However, there is no doubt that Prohibition led to a huge growth in gangsters and crime. Mobsters controlled territories by force and established monopolies in the manufacture and sale of alcohol. The gangs bought out hundreds of breweries and transported liquor in armoured lorries. Gang leaders saw themselves as businessmen and, when faced with competition, took over their rivals. However, these takeovers were often carried out violently and usually ended with the murder of the opposition. Gangs also became involved in rackets such as protection, prostitution and 'numbers' (illegal lottery).

Gangsters were easily able to control politicians. For example, 'Big Bill' Thompson, the Mayor of Chicago, did little or nothing to control the activities of gangsters in his city. Al Capone was the most notorious of the gangsters. When Capone finally went to jail in 1932, for income tax evasion, it was estimated that his gang had made over $70 million worth of illegal business.

Al Capone

The son of Italian immigrants, Al Capone left school at an early age and became involved in small-time criminal activities. He was given the nickname 'Scarface' following a fight when he was a bouncer at a New York club. He eventually succeeded John Torrio who had run the illegal alcohol business in Chicago. Capone soon established his position as one of the leading gangsters in Chicago by bribing local officials. He controlled the mayor and senior police officers and was able to fix local elections. He also controlled speakeasies, gambling houses, brothels, nightclubs, distilleries and breweries.

Capone was also a man of violence. He built up an army of 700 gangsters who committed over 300 murders in Chicago. On 14 February 1929, five of his men dressed as policemen, 'arrested' seven of the rival 'Bugs Moran' gang and machine-gunned them to death. This became known as the 'St Valentine's Day Massacre'. Capone himself was in Florida with the perfect alibi.

Despite his criminal activities, Capone was seen by many as a glamorous person. He moved in the highest social circles and was the first to open soup kitchens after the 1929 Wall Street Crash.

KEY DATES: PROHIBITION AND GANGSTERS

1919 Prohibition is introduced.

1920 The Volstead Act.

1929 'The St Valentine's Day Massacre'.

1932 Capone arrested for tax evasion.

1933 Prohibition abolished.

NOTE-MAKING

Using the 1–2 method (see page x), make notes under the following side headings: 'Sacco and Vanzetti Case', 'KKK' and 'Monkey Trial'. Compare your notes with others and expand upon what each of you has written.

Intolerance in US society in the 1920s

Why was there growing opposition to immigrants?

Many people living in the USA suffered from racism and intolerance. There was a great deal of intolerance towards foreign-born immigrants, African Americans and those whose beliefs, whether religious or political, seemed to challenge traditional American attitudes. This resulted in famous court cases such as Sacco and Vanzetti and the 'Monkey Trial' as well as the re-emergence of the Ku Klux Klan.

Immigration

In the years after the First World War, there was growing opposition to immigration leading to measures to restrict policies.

Changing attitudes towards immigrants

Immigrants became less welcome in the years after 1900 because they provided competition for jobs and brought different customs and attitudes. In addition,

US involvement in the First World War fuelled anti-German feelings and encouraged support for restrictions on immigration. For example, German was banned in schools in several states.

Furthermore, most Americans did not want to be dragged into another major war. They blamed the First World War on rivalries between countries in Europe and wanted the USA to isolate itself from events in Europe. This included restrictions on immigration from these European countries. Many of the new immigrants were poor labourers with little formal education. Immigrant ghettos began to appear in the big northern cities of America. These were often dangerous places with high incidences of drunkenness and violence. Many Americans believed that the immigrants were to blame for these problems.

Changes in immigration policy

Immigration was restricted by a series of measures:

- The 1917 Literacy Act – all foreigners wishing to enter the USA had to take a literacy test. They had to prove that they could read a short passage in English. Many people from poorer countries, especially in Eastern Europe, could not afford to take English lessons and failed the test.
- The Immigration Quota Act of 1921 – this introduced a quota system. New immigrants were allowed in as a proportion of the number of people of the same nationality who had been in America in 1910. The figure was set at three per cent per year. For example, if there had been 100 Italian immigrants in the USA since 1910, then three were allowed in. This therefore reduced the number of immigrants from Eastern Europe because relatively few had emigrated before 1910.

Further measures

The 1924 National Origins Act reduced the quota to two per cent of the 1890 census. In other words, since there had been a lot more people from Northern Europe in 1890, proportionately more of these groups were allowed to enter. Five years later, the Immigration Act restricted immigration to 150,000 per year. There were to be no Asians at all. Northern and Western Europeans were allocated 85 per cent of places. By 1930, immigration from Japan, China and Eastern Europe had virtually ceased.

The Sacco and Vanzetti case

On 5 May 1920, two Italian labourers – Nicola Sacco and Bartolomeo Vanzetti – were arrested and charged with the murder of Fred Parmenter. Parmenter was the paymaster of a factory in South Braintree. He, together with a security guard, was shot by two armed robbers on 15 April 1920. The security guard and Parmenter died but not before he had described his attackers as slim foreigners with olive skins.

Their trial began in May 1921 and lasted 45 days. It took several days to find a jury of twelve men who were accepted by both the prosecution and defence because of the strong publicity given to the case. In fact, 875 were called to the court. On 14 July 1921, the jury delivered a verdict of guilty. There were demonstrations all over the USA in support of the two men. Their case was taken to appeal in higher courts but all failed. The last appeal was in 1927. The two men were executed by electric chair on 24 August 1927.

> ## 'WASP'
> For many Americans in the 1920s, the ideal citizen was a 'WASP' – a White, Anglo-Saxon Protestant. Asian immigrants were not white, while many recent European immigrants were Catholics, Greek Orthodox or Jewish. Finally, the 'Red Scare' fuelled even more feelings against immigrants. Many Americans feared that immigrants would bring with them dangerous political beliefs, especially Communism.

Importance of the case

The Sacco and Vanzetti case was important because the trial was reported all over the world and showed the intolerance of US society. As Italian immigrants, the two men were victims of racial discrimination and were denied rights entitled to them. It exposed the unfairness of the American legal system. The two men were convicted on flimsy evidence although subsequent evidence suggests that Sacco may have been guilty. In the 1970s, the Governor of Massachusetts granted Sacco and Vanzetti a formal pardon and agreed that a mistrial had taken place.

The Ku Klux Klan

A key factor in changing attitudes within the USA during the years after the First World War was the revival of the Ku Klux Klan (KKK).

Reasons for the revival of the KKK

The Ku Klux Klan (KKK) had been set up in the 1860s by former soldiers after the American Civil War. It was revived for several reasons:

- The release of a film, *The Birth of a Nation,* in 1915 which was set in the South after the Civil War and showed the Klan saving white families from gangs of African-Americans intent on raping and looting. The film attracted huge audiences and seemed to reinforce the idea of white supremacy.
- After the First World War, labour tensions rose as veterans tried to re-enter the workforce. In reaction to these new groups of immigrants and migrants, the membership of the Klan increased.
- Increasing industrialisation, which brought more and more workers to towns and cities. The Klan grew rapidly in cities such as Memphis and Atlanta, which had high growth rates in the years after 1910.
- Many of these workers were immigrants from Eastern and Southern Europe or African Americans migrating from the Southern states to the urban centres of the North.
- Southern whites also resented the arming of African-American soldiers during the First World War.

Source F From 'Reviving the Ku Klux Klan' by Walter F. White, published in the *Forum*, April 1921. (America in Class: Becoming America; America in the 1920s – The Ku Klux Klan, at: americainclass.org/sources/becomingmodern/prosperity/text1/text1.htm).

But what, many ask, is behind the attempt to establish this movement in the North? The answer is easy. Drawn on the one hand into the North during the war by industrial opportunity, and driven out of the South on the other hand by oppressive conditions there, between 750,000 and 1,000,000 Negroes have migrated since 1925. As a result, the South has felt keenly the losing of this labor and has suffered heavy financial losses. Among a small percentage of Southern employers there is a realization that the old order of Negro oppression has passed and definite steps are being taken to eradicate some of the evils. But, unfortunately, there is a larger element which still holds to the doctrine of 'keeping the negro in his place'. The Ku Klux Klan, by spreading its propaganda in Northern industrial centers, seeks to oust Negroes from employment, thinking that they will be forced to return to the South. Having served America faithfully during the War, and with the prospect of a tide of immigration from Europe furnishing a great mass of cheap labor for Northern industries, Negroes are to be driven by unemployment and starvation back to the land of lynchings.

LOOK AGAIN

Look again at pages 15–16 in Chapter 1.

Why was the KKK set up in 1865?

What reasons are suggested in Source F for the growth of the Klan in northern cities?

Organisation and activities of the KKK

The new Klan was founded in Atlanta by a Methodist preacher, William Simmons. The Klan members were WASPS. They were fighting for 'native, white, Protestant supremacy'. They were anti-Communist, anti-blacks, anti-Jew, anti-Catholic and against all foreigners. The members dressed in white sheets and wore white hoods. This was to hide the identity of the original Klan members who often attacked their victims at night. The white colour symbolised white supremacy. They carried American flags and lit burning crosses at their night-time meetings. Their leader was a dentist called Hiram Evans, who was known as the Imperial Wizard. Officers of the Klan were known as Klaliffs, Kluds or Klabees.

In 1920, the Klan had 100,000 members. By 1925, it claimed to have over 5 million. It attracted members all over the USA, but especially in the Southern States, and generally white, Protestant and racist. Oregon and Oklahoma had governors who were members of the Klan.

Members of the Klan carried out lynchings of African Americans and beat up and mutilated anyone they considered to be their enemy. They stripped some of their victims and put tar and feathers on their bodies. For example, in 1921 Chris Lochan, a restaurant owner, was run out of town because he was accused of being a foreigner. His parents were Greek.

Decline of the KKK

The Klan declined after 1925 when one of its leaders, Grand Wizard David Stephenson, was convicted of a sexually motivated murder. When the Governor of Indiana refused to pardon him, Stephenson produced evidence of illegal Klan activities. This discredited the Klan and led to a decline in membership. There were also divisions about tactics among Klan leaders and some politicians, who had originally supported the Klan, were quick to dissociate themselves when public opinion began to turn the other way, against the activities of the KKK.

The Monkey Trial, 1925

The Monkey Trial was a famous trial that showed the great differences between the beliefs of rural and urban Americans at the time.

Most people living in the towns and cities of the USA accepted Charles Darwin's theory of evolution, which suggested that over a period of millions of years human beings had evolved from ape-like creatures. However, these views were not accepted by many people in rural areas, especially the so-called 'Bible belt' states such as Tennessee. Many in these areas were known as Fundamentalists. They held strong Christian beliefs, including the belief that the biblical account of the creation in which God created humans on the sixth day, was literally true.

Six US states, led by William Jennings Bryan, a leading member of the Democrats, decided to ban the teaching of Darwin's theory of evolution in their schools. A biology teacher called John Scopes decided to challenge this ban. He deliberately taught evolution in his class in Tennessee in order to be arrested and put on trial.

Both sides hired the best lawyers for a trial, which took place in July 1925, and captured the imagination of the public. Scopes was convicted of breaking the law. However, the trial was a disaster for the public image of the Fundamentalists. Bryan was shown to be confused and ignorant while the media mocked the beliefs of those who opposed the theory of evolution.

Bible belt – Area of southern USA where strict fundamentalist Protestant (particularly Baptist) Christianity is strong.

KEY DATES: INTOLERANCE IN US SOCIETY IN THE 1920s

1921 Immigration Quota Act.
1921 Trial of Sacco and Vanzetti.
1925 The Monkey Trial.

4 The Wall Street Crash and the Great Depression

In October 1929, the American stock market on Wall Street crashed and this was followed by the Great Depression. There has been much debate among historians as to the reasons for the Crash and the part played by the Crash in causing the subsequent Depression. However, both events were the consequence of long-term problems in the economy.

Problems in the economy

What were the long-term reasons for the Wall Street Crash and the Great Depression?

The Great Depression, which began in 1929, was due partly to long-term structural problems within the US economy as well as the repercussions of the Wall Street Crash.

Falling demand for consumer goods

The construction boom of the 1920s came to an end in 1928. This had a knock-on effect, slowing down spending and investment. The great boom in car ownership slowed sharply. By 1929, most Americans who could afford a car already had one. Industrial production fell in the two months before the Wall Street Crash.

The fall in demand for consumer goods was partly due to the unequal distribution of wealth. The new-found wealth of the 1920s was not shared by everyone. Almost 50 per cent of American families had an income of less than $2,000 a year, the minimum needed to survive. They could not afford to buy the new consumer goods. Some manufacturers did not see that there was a limit to what could be bought, and so they continued to produce goods. The result was overproduction.

In addition, the USA could not sell its surplus products to other countries, especially in Europe. Some European countries owed the USA huge amounts of money and were struggling with repayments. The US government had put high tariffs on foreign goods in the 1920s. Many foreign governments responded by doing the same to American goods and consequently US businessmen found it very difficult to sell their goods abroad. Therefore, an ideal outlet for their overproduction was blocked.

The instability of 'get-rich-quick' schemes

While many people saw easy credit as a strength in the economy, there were also considerable drawbacks. 'Get rich quick' was the aim of many Americans in the 1920s. They invested in hugely speculative ventures and inevitably many lost their money. This situation provided golden opportunities for confidence tricksters and crooks. In the early 1920s, for example, Charles Ponzi, a former vegetable seller, conned thousands of gullible people into investing in his ventures. He promised a 50 per cent profit within 90 days. When sentencing him to prison, the judge criticised his victims for their greed. Ponzi had not forced people to part with their money. The period saw other more large-scale speculations, notably during the Florida land boom and on the stock exchange in the latter part of the decade.

NOTE-MAKING

Using a spider diagram, summarise the main problems in the US economy in the 1920s. On your spider diagram show links between these problems, for example, you could link overproduction to the problems of farming.

The Florida land boom

While on bail awaiting trial, Ponzi found employment selling land in Florida. This was a venture well suited to his talents. Until this time, Florida was a relatively undeveloped state with a small population. Between 1920 and 1925, the population of the state increased from 968,000 to 1.2 million. There were large-scale coastal developments. Parcels of land began to be sold to wealthy Northerners on the basis of glossy brochures and salesmen's patter. People began to invest their money in unseen developments, hoping to sell and make a quick profit. The land boom could be sustained only as long as there were more buyers than sellers. But demand tailed off in 1926. There were scandals of land advertised as within easy access of the sea that was really many miles inland or in the middle of swamps. Then nature played its part, with hurricanes in 1926 killing 400 people and leaving 50,000 homeless. With thousands of people bankrupted, the Florida land boom collapsed, leaving a coastline strewn with half-finished and storm-battered developments.

Problems with agriculture

The farming industry had benefited from the First World War with prices rising by as much as 25 per cent. However, after the war, falling demand led to falling prices with wheat dropping from $2.5 to $1 a bushel. Farmers were producing more food than America needed. Moreover, demand fell further due to the growth of synthetic fibres, which lessened the market for natural ones such as cotton. Prohibition cut the demand for grain previously used in the manufacture of alcohol. Paradoxically, technical advances meant that more crops could be produced on the same or even reduced acreage. Greater use of tractors meant fewer horses were necessary, which in turn meant less demand for animal food.

The situation was no better abroad. During the war, farmers had been able to sell their surplus abroad. After the war, European farmers were able to grow enough to meet their own demands. Moreover, there was stiff competition from Canadian, Australian and Argentinian farmers who were supplying a vast amount of grain to the world market.

Town and country

There was a distinct division between the town and the countryside. While many towns and cities, especially in the North, experienced economic growth and prosperity during the 1920s, this was not the case with rural areas, especially in the South and West, due to problems with agriculture. This led, for the most part, to much lower living standards and even poverty in these areas of the USA. The countryside did not really benefit from the improved lifestyle of many urban Americans who had electricity and running water, and wages were very low. By 1928, half of all US farmers were living in poverty.

Problems with the old industries

Several staple industries faced long-term difficulties in the 1920s. Coal mining and the textile industry were stagnating or in decline. Demand for coal fell in the 1920s as gas and electricity were more widely used and there was more foreign competition, especially cheap coal from Poland. This led to the closure of a great number of mines and many miners were made redundant.

The textile industry also experienced problems. The lowering of the tariffs on wool and cotton in 1913 meant that the US textile industry faced stiff competition from abroad. It also faced the challenge of a new product – rayon. This man-made fibre was far cheaper to produce than wool, cotton or silk. Textile mills in the North, for example in Massachusetts, closed down, or moved south where there was cheap labour.

Source G From *The American Nation*, written by the American historian John A. Garraty and published in 1991.

While most economic indicators reflected an unprecedented prosperity, the boom rested on unstable foundations. The problem was mainly one of maladministration of resources. Productive capacity raced ahead of buying power. Too large a share of profits were going into too few pockets. The 27,000 families with the highest income in 1929 received as much money as the 11 million with annual incomes of under $1500, the minimum sum required to maintain a family decently. High earnings and low taxes permitted huge sums to pile up in the hands of individuals who did not invest the money productively.

To what extent is Source G a valid interpretation of the problems of the US economy in the 1920s?

NOTE-MAKING

Using bullet points (see page x), make notes on the causes, events and results of the Wall Street Crash.

The Wall Street Crash

To what extent was overspeculation the main reason for the Wall Street Crash?

The Wall Street Crash was one of the turning points of the twentieth century both for the USA and the world. The Crash was widely regarded as the trigger for the Great Depression, but few economic experts agree that it was the main cause.

Reasons for the Crash

Finding an adequate explanation for the Crash is not that straightforward. This is because the stock market crash of 1929 was not unique. There had been many previous financial panics in the USA since 1873 and this did not seem notably worse.

The banking system

The US banking system was out of date by the 1920s. Twelve regulatory reserve banks were headed by the Federal Reserve Board, with seven members appointed by the president. The system allowed the banks to regulate themselves without the government having to interfere. However there were problems:

- The Reserve Banks acted in the interests of bankers rather than the nation as a whole.
- Local banks were not part of the centralised system. In the 1920s, there were over 30,000 banks in the USA. Most were very small and unable to cope with financial problems.
- The Federal Reserve Board wanted to keep the market buoyant so it favoured low interest rates. This encouraged the easy credit that was one of the causes of the Crash. In 1927, it lowered interest rates from four to three and a half per cent, which many believe encouraged the 'bull market'.

Over-speculation on the stock market

During the 1920s, more and more Americans bought shares on the stock exchange and prices kept rising, thus creating a bull market. The amount of trading grew, particularly after Hoover's victory in the presidential election of 1928.

In 1928, however, shares did not rise as much as in previous years. This was because many companies were not selling as many goods, so their profits fell. Fewer people were willing to buy their shares and there was a drop in confidence in the market. This was a warning but when share prices began rising again, greed took over and speculation recurred. The complete lack of stock market regulation by the government or any other agency encouraged more and more speculation. Successive Republican presidents stuck to their beliefs in *laissez-faire*. In 1925, the stock market value of stocks stood at $27 billion but by October 1929, it had reached $87 billion. By the summer of 1929 there were 20 million shareholders in the USA and prices continued to rise.

Availability of easy credit

The growth of credit made it much easier for people to buy goods even though they did not have enough cash to pay for them on the spot. Firms arranged for customers to pay in instalments on hire purchase. This included the practice of buying shares on credit, 'on the margin'. This practice was further encouraged by the easy credit policies on the part of the Federal Reserve Board.

This worked well as long as prices were rising. However, when the price rise started to slow down or prices fell, problems set in. Seventy-five per cent of the purchase price of shares was borrowed. This, in turn, created artificially high prices.

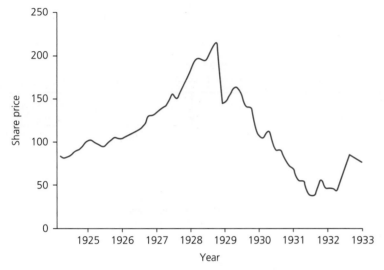

▲ **Figure 3** A graph showing the changes in the price of shares in the USA in the years 1925–33.

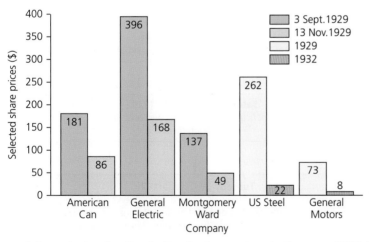

▲ **Figure 4** A graph showing the decline in share values in the years 1929–32.

Loss of confidence

The market structure was maintained largely by the confidence that people had in it. When, in the autumn of 1929, some experts started to sell their shares heavily before their value fell even further, small investors panicked. They saw the fall in prices and rushed to sell their own shares – as can be seen in Figure 3. This led to a complete collapse of prices and thousands of investors lost millions of dollars.

Historians point to various reasons for this loss of confidence. There were rumours that the Federal Reserve Bank was about to tighten credit facilities by making it more difficult to borrow. Moreover, rumours spread that many of the men who had made fortunes on the stock market, such as Bernard Baruch, were selling their stock.

Events leading to the Crash

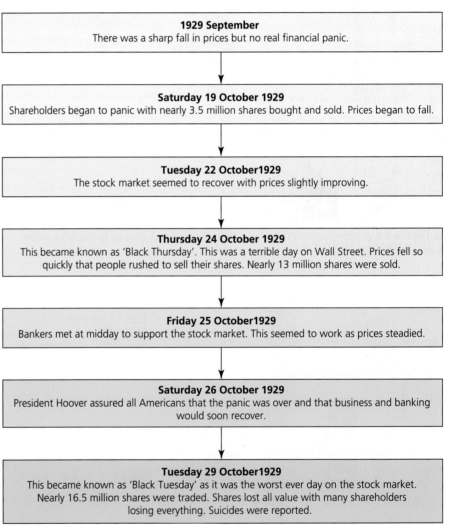

1929 September
There was a sharp fall in prices but no real financial panic.

Saturday 19 October 1929
Shareholders began to panic with nearly 3.5 million shares bought and sold. Prices began to fall.

Tuesday 22 October 1929
The stock market seemed to recover with prices slightly improving.

Thursday 24 October 1929
This became known as 'Black Thursday'. This was a terrible day on Wall Street. Prices fell so quickly that people rushed to sell their shares. Nearly 13 million shares were sold.

Friday 25 October 1929
Bankers met at midday to support the stock market. This seemed to work as prices steadied.

Saturday 26 October 1929
President Hoover assured all Americans that the panic was over and that business and banking would soon recover.

Tuesday 29 October 1929
This became known as 'Black Tuesday' as it was the worst ever day on the stock market. Nearly 16.5 million shares were traded. Shares lost all value with many shareholders losing everything. Suicides were reported.

▲ **Figure 5** Timeline of the Crash.

▲ A photograph showing depositors outside a bank in New Jersey. They are trying to get into the bank to withdraw their deposits on Black Tuesday, 29 October 1929.

Effects of the Crash

It is worth remembering that even after October 1929 prices still stood higher than they had done at any time during the previous year. What had been wiped out were the spectacular gains of the previous year.

It is often popularly believed that the Wall Street Crash led to the Great Depression. However, many historians have argued that it was simply one sign of a depression already well on its way. Nevertheless, the Crash was an important trigger in worsening the Depression.

- It led to the collapse of many businesses with individuals losing billions. Thousands were bankrupted and there were a number of suicides. For example, the President of Union Cigar plunged to his death from the ledge of a New York hotel when stock in his company fell from $113.50 to $4 in a single day.
- People who had lost so much could not afford to consume or invest. As workforces were laid off there was even less money within the economy for spending. This, in turn, led to a further slowing of the economy as it moved into depression.
- The Crash led to the collapse of credit with loans called in and new ones refused. This, in turn, led to a credit squeeze and a fall in demand and business activity.
- Above all else, the Crash destroyed confidence in the US economy. Wall Street was the symbol of the prosperity of the 1920s and had seemed safe and secure. Those who warned of the dangers of over-speculation and 'buying on the margin' had been largely ignored. People had listened to the confident voices of Coolidge and Hoover. These voices were now ignored as national confidence sank to rock bottom. This, in turn, deepened the Depression.

WORKING TOGETHER

Working as a group, discuss to what extent you agree that over-speculation was the main reason for the Wall Street Crash.

KEY DATES: WALL STREET CRASH AND DEPRESSION

1927 Federal Reserve Board lowered interest rates.

24 October 1929 'Black Thursday' on Wall Street.

29 October 1929 'Black Tuesday' on Wall Street.

NOTE-MAKING

Using a spider diagram (see page x) make notes on Hoover and the Depression.

Herbert Hoover (1874–1964)

Hoover was born to a Quaker family in the small town of West Branch, Iowa, in 1874. He graduated from Stanford University as a mining engineer and, in 1908, began his own very successful mining business. In 1917, when the USA entered the First World War, he was appointed National Food Commissioner and, three years later, became Secretary of Commerce in Warren Harding's government. In 1928, he won the presidential election but, four years later, he lost a second election to Roosevelt. He wrote his memoirs in 1952 and died in 1964.

Hoover was a very shy individual who often shunned publicity. He was more of an administrator than a politician but his presidency was dominated by the Great Depression. He worked tirelessly to combat its worst effects, very long hours, every day, but lost credibility as the effects of the Depression worsened. He gained an unfair reputation as an uncaring president. For example, in 1927 Hoover organised large-scale relief when the Mississippi burst its banks over a huge area.

Hoover and the Depression

How successful was Hoover in dealing with the Depression?

Herbert Hoover was president during the Depression. The traditional view, expressed by historians such as Charles P. Kindleberger and Robert Sobel, is that he did little to help, instead actually making the situation worse. More recently historians have been more sympathetic to Hoover, believing he was a victim of his own beliefs and of a terrible crisis. Hoover's achievements were reassessed in the 1980s, during the presidency of Ronald Reagan, who followed similarly conservative economic policies.

Hoover's beliefs

In the 1928 presidential election campaign, Hoover claimed that 'the USA is nearer to the final triumph over poverty than ever before in the history of any land'. Within a few years, these words would come back to haunt him. Hoover had certain beliefs that he acquired at an early age and which greatly handicapped his attempts to deal with the worst effects of the Depression. He believed that people should be responsible for their own welfare and that government should not intervene to try to solve people's problems. The role of government was to give people the ability to solve their problems themselves. 'Economic wounds must be healed by producers and consumers', said Hoover.

Hoover was also a firm believer in 'rugged individualism', which he wrote about in his book *American Individualism*, published in 1922. He was a self-made man and felt that everyone could achieve what he had achieved through hard work and initiative. He placed great emphasis on the role of the individual. Overall, he believed in self-help and voluntary co-operation to solve problems. People should help themselves and help each other. 'A voluntary deed', he said, 'is infinitely more precious to our national ideal and spirit than a thousand deeds poured from the Treasury.'

However, voluntarism and self-help were never going to be enough to deal with the problems created by the Great Depression. Hoover's problem was that he could never abandon these fundamental beliefs and accept a greater (if temporary) role for federal government. He was convinced that the economy would right itself. To be fair to Hoover, there were few theories at the time about how to solve the Depression.

Hoover's policies

One the one hand Hoover has been criticised for doing too little too late to deal with the Depression and that some of his policies, especially increasing tariffs, actually made the situation worse. Indeed, by 1932, he was being widely ridiculed in the USA. His name became a term of abuse with the new shanty towns set up on the edge of cities by the unemployed nicknamed 'Hoovervilles', and newspapers that homeless people used to cover themselves called 'Hoover blankets'. However, a British historian, Paul Johnson, has suggested that Hoover should not have done more but less and that the economy would have righted itself had he done so.

Agriculture

Hoover assisted farmers with the Agricultural Marketing Act of 1930. This Act enabled the government to lend money to farmers through special marketing groups which stabilised prices and tried to ensure that produce was sold at a profit.

The Grain Stabilisation Corporation, introduced in the same year, tried to guarantee fair prices by buying wheat so that it could be stored until the price went back up again. However, prices continued to plunge.

Hoover's agricultural policies failed because he was paying farmers artificially high prices. In addition, farming was badly affected by the introduction of tariffs through the Hawley–Smoot Tariff Act of 1930. This protected US farmers by increasing import duties on foreign goods. In retaliation, other countries refused to trade with the USA.

Industry

Hoover tried to balance the budget by reducing federal spending and opposing relief schemes that were suggested by Congress. Instead, he relied on voluntary action. He hoped to persuade businessmen and state governments to solve the Depression by voluntary efforts.

- He met businessmen and implored them not to cut their workforce or wages. He encouraged state governments to begin new public works programmes. In 1932, he gave an additional $500 million to help various agencies to provide relief.
- The Reconstruction Finance Corporation (RFC) of January 1932 was the most radical measure introduced by Hoover to deal with the Depression and was a forerunner of Roosevelt's New Deal policies. It lent up to $2 billion to rescue banks, insurance companies, railroads and construction companies.
- The Emergency Relief Act in July of the same year gave $300 million to state governments to help the unemployed.
- The Home Loan Bank Act of 1932 was to stimulate house building and home ownership. Twelve regional banks were set up with a fund of $12 million.

The Bonus Marchers

Hoover's treatment of the Bonus Marchers made him even more unpopular. The Bonus Marchers were veterans of the First World War who had been promised a bonus for serving in the war, payable in 1945. The veterans felt that they could not wait that long. In May and June 1932, a Bonus Expeditionary Force, made up of over 12,000 unemployed and homeless veterans from all over the USA, marched to Washington DC to voice their support for a bill that would allow early payment of the bonuses. They brought their wives and children and built a Hooverville outside the capital. To pay the bonus would have cost $2.3 million, and Hoover felt that it was simply too much. Five thousand Bonus Marchers refused to leave and Hoover then called in the army to control the situation. The armed forces, led by Douglas MacArthur, Army Chief of Staff, razed the Hooverville to the ground. More than 100 were injured and a baby died of tear gas poisoning. This event left a bitter taste in the mouth of many Americans who were more convinced than ever that Hoover did not care. It finally destroyed the credibility of the President.

WORKING TOGETHER

1 Firstly, compare the notes that you have made on Hoover (see page 166). Add anything that you have missed and check anything that you have disagreed on.
2 Next, divide your paper into two. One of you should identify the achievements of Hoover as president. The other should note his shortcomings.
3 After you have finished, combine your findings.
4 To what extent do you think that Hoover's policies were successful in dealing with the immediate effects of the Depression?

KEY DATES: HOOVER AND THE DEPRESSION

1929 Hoover wins the presidential election campaign.
1930 The Agricultural Marketing Act and the Hawley–Smoot Tariff Act.
1932 The Reconstruction Finance Corporation (RFC) and the Bonus Marchers.

The impact of the Depression

Why was the impact of the Depression so widespread?

Economic effects

The Depression had profound and severe social and economic effects. With unemployment reaching 16 million, few people were left unaffected. The Depression hit men and women, all races and classes and almost all geographical areas of the USA: towns, cities and the countryside. Its effects on people were profound, painful and long-lasting.

There are no fully accurate statistics but official figures show that unemployment increased from 3.2 per cent in 1929 to 25.2 per cent in 1933 with 12,830,000 out of work. The Labor Research Association insisted that these figures were underestimates and suggested that the figure was nearer 17 million.

Unemployment was unevenly distributed throughout the country.

- New York State had 1 million unemployed. In Toledo, there was 80 per cent unemployment.
- Unemployment was four to six times greater among African Americans. Employment opportunities in northern cities, which had opened up for them in the 1920s, were now generally closed to them.
- There was also much higher unemployment among working-class women. Those in unskilled jobs were likely to be laid off before men.

The growth rate of the US economy went into decline, from 6.7 per cent in 1929 to minus 14.7 per cent in 1932. In the coal industry, production in 1932 was the lowest since 1904 with 300,000 made unemployed. Iron and steel production fell by 59 per cent.

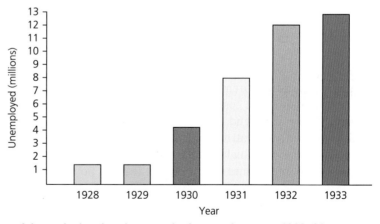

▲ Figure 6 A graph showing the growth of unemployment, 1929–32.

Social effects

The human cost of the Depression was enormous.

Depression in the cities

Once the crisis began in October 1929, it was not long before factories began to close down. People stopped spending and, as this trend continued, production had to slow down or stop. The industrial cities saw a rapid rise in unemployment and by 1933 almost one-third of the workforce was out of work. Once a person became unemployed, it was practically impossible to secure another job.

Those Americans who lost their homes as a result of becoming unemployed moved to the edges of towns and cities. They built homes of tin, wood and cardboard. These became known as 'Hoovervilles'. There was even a Hooverville in Central Park, New York.

Many of the unemployed in cities wandered the streets. They slept in doorways or cardboard boxes or lived in the parks where they slept on the benches. Some drifted across the USA as hobos. They caught rides on freight trains in search of work. It was estimated that in 1932 there were more than 2 million homeless.

Depression in the countryside

As the Depression took hold, farmers experienced several problems. Bankruptcy among farmers grew because they were unable to sell their produce. In many cases, food was left to rot in the ground. The drought of 1931 compounded the farmers' problems as reduced prices and falling output meant there was no hope of breaking even financially. Crops were damaged not only by the dry weather but also by high temperatures, high winds and sometimes attacks from grasshoppers and other insects.

The states worst affected by the drought were Oklahoma, Colorado, New Mexico and Kansas. Poor farming methods had exhausted the soil, and in the drought the soil turned to dust. Therefore, when the winds came, there were dust storms. The affected area, about 20 million hectares, became known as the 'dust bowl'.

These issues forced more than 1 million people to leave their homes and seek work in the fruit-growing areas of the west coast. Farmers and their families packed what they could, tied it to their cars, and set off for the West. Those from Oklahoma were nicknamed 'Okies' and those from Arkansas 'Arkies'.

KEY DATES: EFFECTS OF THE DEPRESSION

1929 Just over 1 million out of work.

1931 Beginning of drought in countryside.

1932 Over 13 million out of work.

Chapter summary

- Harding and Coolidge were presidents during most of the 1920s and have generally been given a bad press by historians.
- In foreign policy Harding and Coolidge reverted to the more traditional isolationist policies of the USA, although America did become involved in Europe as well as Latin America.
- The 1920s was a period of economic growth and innovation due to more long-term factors such as the First World War and the impact of the car industry.
- Prohibition failed in its attempts to ban the sale of alcohol and encouraged the growth of organised crime.
- There was continued intolerance in American society of African Americans as shown by the re-emergence of the KKK, as well as increasing hostility towards immigrants and immigration.
- There were some changes in the position of women with some involved in politics and the impact of the flappers. However, for the most part, they still remained as second-class citizens.
- The 1920s was known as the 'Jazz Age' with massive changes in recreation and entertainment, including the popularity of the cinema, radio, jazz music and sport.
- The Wall Street Crash was due to long-term structural problems as well as over-speculation and led to loss of confidence in banking and the economy.
- The Great Depression led to massive economic and social changes, with rapid growth in unemployment and the emergence of Hoovervilles.
- Hoover has generally been criticised by historians for doing too little, too late to deal with the Depression, although some historians suggest it would have been better if he had done less.

▼ Summary diagram: The return to normalcy

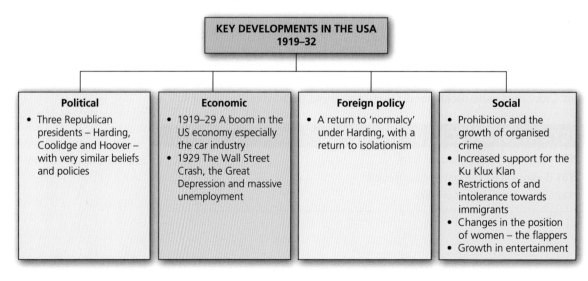

Working on essay technique: writing an essay

Remember the skills that you built up in Chapters 1–4 on essay writing.

The main headings were:

- *Focus and structure* Be sure what the question is on and plan what the paragraphs should be about.
- *Focused introduction to the essay* Be sure that the introductory sentence relates directly to the focus of the question and that each paragraph highlights the structure of the answer.
- *How to use detail* Make sure that you show detailed knowledge – but only as part of an explanation being made in relation to the question. No knowledge should be 'free-standing'.

- *Explanatory analysis* Think of the wording of an answer in order to strengthen the explanation.
- *Argument and counter-argument* Think of how arguments can be juxtaposed as part of a balancing act in order to give contrasting views.
- *Resolution* Think how best to 'resolve' contradictory arguments.
- *Relative significance and evaluation* Think how best to reach a judgement when trying to assess the relative importance of various factors, and possibly their inter-relationship.

ACTIVITY

Consider the following A-level practice question:

'The main reason for the growth of the US economy, 1900–30, was technological change.' Assess the validity of this view. **(25 marks)**

1 On the top of a large sheet of paper write out the title.
2 On the left-hand side jot down the main topic areas (in this case, causes of the growth of the economy) that you might cover in an answer.
3 On the right-hand side transform these ideas into a basic plan for an answer. Think of the structure. In outline, what evidence is there that the growth in the US economy was down to changes in technology? What were these changes? What other factors played a role in the growth of the economy at the time?

4 Then look at the list of essay-writing skills above. See how they can fit in to your plan. Some, such as an introduction, will be there automatically.
- Introduction – Is it simple or could it be complex? Does it do more than introduce? Does it highlight the structure of the answer?
- Where can you add specific details to your plan so that you show a range of knowledge?
- Does your plan successfully feature analysis and evaluation? Are you sure it will not lead to a narrative or descriptive approach?
- Can you balance arguments and counter-arguments?
- Can you reach a judgement that 'resolves' any conflicting arguments, and that assesses the relative importance of the various factors?

Working on interpretation skills

In earlier chapters of the book you were given the opportunity to develop skills in answering Interpretations questions. It is probably a good idea to re-read the advice given at the end of Chapters 2 and 4 (pages 69–70 and 129–30) before you answer the following practice question.

Using your understanding of the historical context, assess how convincing the arguments in these three extracts are in relation to the development of the US economy between 1910–30. (30 marks)

Extract A

The prosperity of the Coolidge era was huge, real, widespread but not ubiquitous [found everywhere] and unprecedented. It was not permanent – what prosperity ever is? But it is foolish and unhistorical to judge it insubstantial because we now know what followed later. At the time it was as solid as houses built, meals eaten, automobiles driven, cash spent and property acquired. Prosperity was more widely distributed in the America of the 1920s than had been possible in any community of this size before, and it involved the acquisition, by tens of millions of ordinary families, of an economic security that had been denied them throughout all previous history.

Adapted from *A History of the American People* by Paul Johnson, (Phoenix), 1998.

Extract B

Already the forces which were to destroy Coolidge prosperity were at work. Indeed, the first signs of trouble came as early as 1926, when the sale of new housing began to slacken. This had various causes, among them the collapse of a land boom in Florida, where thousands of sun hungry Northerners had been hoaxed into buying pieces of swamp, miles from the sea, in the belief that they were getting valuable property near the beach ... A more serious cause of the housing slowdown was the fact that the market was becoming saturated, like the market for farm products. Of course there were still tens of millions of Americans who needed better housing than they were ever likely to get, but they had no money. By 1926, those who had money had usually already acquired their houses or mortgages; and though new buyers came on to the market every year, they were not numerous enough to sustain the boom.

Adapted from *The Penguin History of the United States of America* by Hugh Brogan, (Penguin), 1985.

Extract C

The second and third decades of the twentieth century, like the decade after the Civil War, featured conservatism in politics and in social philosophy. In both eras the Republican Party enjoyed almost undisputed control of national affairs. It supported the philosophy of laissez faire as well as 'rugged individualism', especially with the economy, and, in practice, made government an instrument of large corporations. Both decades saw a rapid rise in manufacturing and business techniques and an extravagant but badly distributed industrial prosperity as well as agricultural distress in the countryside. This economic growth was to be followed, at the end of the second decade, by a serious and prolonged depression in both industry and agriculture.

Adapted from *The Growth of the American Republic Sixth Edition* by Samuel Eliot Morrison, Henry Steele Commager & William E Leuchtenburg (Oxford University Press) 1969.

New Deals and new directions in international relations, 1933–45

6

This chapter covers developments in the USA during the presidency of Roosevelt, including his New Deal and US involvement in the Second World War. It deals with a number of areas:

- The impact of the New Deal and the Second World War on the economic recovery
- Conflict of ideas over the role of the federal government
- FDR and the end of isolationism and the Second World War
- The social impact of the Second World War

When you have worked through the chapter and the related activities and exercises, you should have detailed knowledge of all those areas, and you should be able to relate this to the key breadth issues defined as part of your study, in particular in what ways did the economy and society of the USA change and develop, and how did the role of the USA in world affairs change and how did political authority develop? For the period covered in this chapter the main focus can be phrased as a question:

How successful was the New Deal in the years 1933–41?

CHAPTER OVERVIEW

This period was dominated by the four terms of President Roosevelt and his New Deal policies. These policies brought in significant measures with the aim of bringing about reform, recovery and relief and led to profound economic and social developments. However, they also aroused influential opposition from the left and right in politics as well as from the Supreme Court. In foreign policy Roosevelt continued the 'Good Neighbor' and isolationist policies with a series of Neutrality Acts. However, Roosevelt and the USA, although still technically neutral, increasingly supported Britain in the early years of the Second World War in Europe. Rivalry with Japan culminated in the Japanese attack on Pearl Harbor and the USA's declaration of war. US forces were to play a very important role in the War in the Pacific and Europe and the Second World War itself brought significant economic and social developments.

Franklin Delano Roosevelt (1882–1945)

Roosevelt was born in 1882 at Hyde Park, New York into one of the most distinguished and wealthy families in the USA. As a young man he preferred socialising to hard work. In 1905, he married Eleanor Roosevelt, a distant cousin, and five years later was elected to New York State Senate. His political career soon made progress when he was made Assistant Secretary of the Navy in 1913 and, seven years later, became Democratic nominee for vice-president. However, in 1921 he suffered a setback when polio left him crippled. He refused to allow this to curtail his political progress and in 1929 he became Governor of New York.

In 1929, during the Depression, Roosevelt became a reforming governor of New York and implemented policies he would further develop in the White House. Roosevelt was elected president in 1932 and began his 'New Deal' programme, being re-elected in 1936 and again in 1940. In 1941, he brought USA into the Second World War after the Japanese attack on Pearl Harbor and was re-elected for a fourth term of office three years later but died, still in office.

1 Roosevelt's New Deals

Roosevelt served as president no less than four consecutive times. He was president during the 1930s when his New Deal transformed the USA, and became its war leader during the Second World War when he died still in office. Roosevelt always displayed dynamic energy. Under his leadership the federal government grew to an unprecedented degree, and in this context it changed American life. Roosevelt is widely regarded as one of the greatest presidents of the USA.

Roosevelt and the presidential election of 1932

Why did Roosevelt win the 1932 presidential election?

Roosevelt won the 1932 presidential election partly because of his own promises of a New Deal but also due to the failings of the Hoover administration.

Roosevelt was by far the strongest Democratic nominee for president. Hoover was the only possible Republican nominee unless the party changed its policies. However, Hoover was too busy fighting the Depression to campaign effectively. The members of his re-election team were themselves short on ideas. One slogan they thought up but dared not suggest use was 'Oh boy! Wasn't that some Depression!'

Hoover generally had poor relations with the press: Roosevelt courted them. Hoover lacked charisma: Roosevelt exuded it. However, many historians have argued that there was little to choose between the candidates in terms of economic policies. Certainly, Roosevelt did not promise government action to solve economic problems. In fact, he even made a speech on 19 October attacking Hoover's 'extravagant government spending' and pledging a 25 per cent cut in the federal budget.

The most important factor was that Hoover expected to lose, while his opponent was determined to win. Many of Roosevelt's promises were vague and even contradictory. In San Francisco, he made a speech advocating economic regulation only as a last resort while, at Oglethorpe University, Georgia, he spoke of 'bold experimentation' to beat the Depression and of a redistribution of national income. However, Roosevelt did say things that captured the public imagination. In a national radio address in April 1932, before his nomination, he called for government to help 'the forgotten man'.

Roosevelt used the radio to great effect. It was as though he was speaking directly to individuals and he won by the biggest majority since Abraham Lincoln in 1864. However, it was not an overwhelming victory: 57 per cent of the popular vote is little more than half. Moreover, few really knew what Roosevelt stood for. Political columnist Walter Lippmann was possibly close to the truth when he wrote that Roosevelt was 'a pleasant man who, without any important qualifications for the office, would very much like to be president'.

However, Americans were voting above all for change. Whatever Roosevelt may have stood for, this, crucially, is what he seemed to offer.

Source A From *Depression and the New Deal*, by R. Smalley, (Longman), 1960.

Roosevelt showed confidence. The Democratic candidate's smile and optimism proved far more popular with the electorate than Hoover's grim looks. This difference in presentation was important because in some ways the two candidates seemed to have similar policies.

The First New Deal, 1933–35

To what extent did the first New Deal achieve its aims?

Following his inauguration, President Roosevelt called Congress into a special session that lasted for 100 days and saw the development of the First New Deal. This resulted in a considerable amount of emergency legislation and the setting up of many 'alphabet agencies'. Many historians have categorised the measures into those intended to bring about 'relief, recovery or reform', but as we shall see it is dangerous to assume Roosevelt had a blueprint to transform American life greatly.

Source B From Frances Perkins, Roosevelt's Secretary for Labor after 1933, writing in 1946 about the 1932 election campaign. From *The Roosevelt I Knew* by F. Perkins, (Viking), 1946.

In the campaign, Roosevelt saw thousands of Americans. He liked going round the country. His personal relationship with the crowds was on a warm simple level of friendly neighborly exchanges of affection.

The Hundred Days

Roosevelt saved the capitalist system in the USA through his New Deal programme. The New Deal may by no means have been a cohesive programme; indeed, it often seemed contradictory. It may even be misleading to call it a programme at all. Possibly, it might best be seen as a series of measures to deal with specific crises, with little overall plan. Certainly, it is most easily categorised with the hindsight of history. Historians can look back to see common strands running through the legislation and its implementation. They can see where it led and how its ideas were later developed. There is little doubt that at the end of the New Deal legislation, the USA was changed forever and the role of government greatly increased. However, whether this was intentional is a point for debate. It is no exaggeration to say that, intentionally or not, at the end of the Hundred Days the USA had been transformed.

Roosevelt's priority was to create economic improvement, which he attempted not merely through measures to effect recovery but also to improve the infrastructure, for example in banking and finance. This was to ensure the system would be modern and sophisticated enough to promote and stimulate a modern economy and, if necessary, able to address any downturn in the future. Roosevelt was very charismatic and used his personality to good effect. He spoke directly to the electorate via the radio in his 'fireside chats' in which he explained his policies. His reassuring voice helped restore confidence and made people feel recovery was on the way.

Agriculture

Agricultural recovery was given a higher priority than industrial recovery. This was for a variety of reasons. Thirty per cent of the labour force worked in agriculture. If agricultural workers could afford to buy more, industry would be stimulated.

Agricultural Adjustment Act, May 1933

Overproduction had been the greatest problem of American agriculture. The main principle behind the Agricultural Adjustment Act was that the

NOTE-MAKING

Create a table to note down the achievements and short comings of the following as you work through the section on the New Deal:
- Agricultural Adjustment Act (AAA)
- Tennessee Valley Authority (TVA)
- Emergency Banking Act (EBA)
- National Recovery Administration (NRA)
- Federal Emergency Relief Administration (FERA)
- Civilian Conservation Corps (CCC).

Inauguration – The ceremony that begins the president's term of office.

What reasons are suggested in Sources A (page 174) and B for Roosevelt's victory?

Government would subsidise farmers to reduce their acreage and production voluntarily. By producing less, the cost of food would increase, and so would farmers' incomes.

A new agency was set up called the Agricultural Adjustment Administration (AAA). It would pay farmers to reduce their production of 'staple' items, initially corn, cotton, milk, pork, rice, tobacco and wheat. The programme was to be self-financing through a tax placed on companies that processed food. It was assumed that these companies would in turn pass on the increased cost to the consumer.

Reduction of cotton production was perhaps the most pressing need. At the beginning of 1933, unsold cotton in the USA already exceeded the total average annual world consumption of American cotton. Moreover, farmers had planted 400,000 acres more than in 1932. They were, quite simply, paid to destroy much of this. A total of 10.5 million acres were ploughed under, and the price of cotton accordingly rose from 6.5 cents per pound in 1932 to 10 cents in 1933.

However, it was one thing to destroy cotton but it was far more contentious to destroy food when so many Americans were hungry. Six million piglets were bought and slaughtered. Although many of the carcasses were subsequently processed and fed to the unemployed, the public outcry was enormous.

In fact, the AAA destroyed only cotton and piglets. Drought helped to make the 1933 wheat crop the poorest since 1896, and agreements were reached to limit acreage in other crops in subsequent years.

Total farm income rose from $4.5 billion in 1932 to $6.9 billion in 1935. The percentage of farmers signing up for AAA agreements was high at first – 95 per cent of tobacco growers, for example – and the Act was very popular with farmers. Faced by drought, Western ranchers sought to bring beef cattle under the protection of the AAA in 1934. By January 1935, the Government had purchased 8.3 million head of cattle, in return for which ranchers agreed to reduce breeding cows by twenty per cent in 1937. Overall, it would appear that the AAA worked effectively to deal with the crisis of overproduction, although there were problems.

Tennessee Valley Authority (TVA), May 1933

The TVA was set up to deal with the underdevelopment and poverty in the Tennessee Valley. The TVA was one of the most grandiose schemes of the New Deal. It was created to harness the power of the River Tennessee, which ran through seven of the poorest states in the USA. It was hoped that by so doing this region of 80,000 square miles with a population of 2 million people would become more prosperous. The TVA had several major tasks:

● to construct twenty huge dams to control the floods that periodically affected the region
● to develop ecological schemes such as tree planting to stop soil erosion
● to encourage farmers to use more efficient means of cultivation, such as contour ploughing
● to provide jobs by setting up fertiliser manufacture factories
● to develop welfare and educational programmes
● most significantly, perhaps, to produce hydro-electric power for an area whose existing supplies of electricity were limited to two out of every 100 farms.

The TVA effectively became a central planning authority for the region. It was largely responsible for the modernisation and improved living standards that

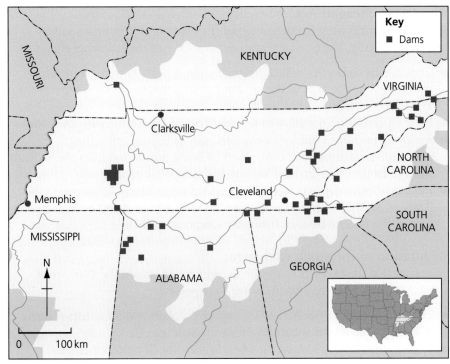

▲ **Figure 1** A map of the Tennessee Valley Area.

saw its residents increase their average income by 200 per cent in the period from 1929 to 1949.

Banking and finance

Alongside agriculture a particularly pressing concern was the collapse of the American banking system. By 1932, banks were closing at the rate of 40 per day. In October 1932, the Governor of Nevada, fearing the imminent collapse of an important banking chain, declared a bank holiday and closed every bank in the state. By the time of Roosevelt's inauguration, banks were closed in many states.

Emergency Banking Relief Act

On 6 March 1933, Roosevelt closed all the banks in the country for four days to give Treasury officials time to draft emergency legislation. The ensuing Emergency Banking Relief Act was passed by Congress after only 40 minutes of debate. Its aim was simply to restore confidence in the American banking system. It gave the Treasury power to investigate all banks threatened with collapse. The Reconstruction Finance Corporation was authorised to buy their stock to support them and to take on many of their debts. In doing so the RFC became in effect the largest bank in the world.

In the meantime, Roosevelt appeared on radio with the first of his fireside chats. He explained to listeners, in a language all could understand, the nature of the crisis and how they could help. The message on this occasion was simple; place your money in the bank rather than under your mattress. It worked. Solvent banks were allowed to reopen and others were reorganised by government officials to put them on a sounder footing. By the beginning of April, $1 billion in currency had been returned to bank deposits and the crisis was over.

Fireside chats

Roosevelt was said to have 'the first great American radio voice'. His fireside chats became so popular that those who did not have a radio would visit with those who did to ensure they did not miss the President. The mass media was still in its infancy. Until Calvin Coolidge went in for being photographed, few Americans had ever seen a picture of their president, let alone heard his voice. Now the reassuring voice of Roosevelt in living rooms throughout the nation restored confidence and helped people to believe that everything was going to be alright. After he told people over the radio to tell him their troubles, it took a staff of 50 to handle his mail, which arrived by the truckload. By contrast, one person had been employed to deal with Herbert Hoover's correspondence.

The Glass–Steagall Act

Roosevelt later drew up legislation to put the banking system on a sounder long-term footing. The Glass–Steagall Act of 1933 had the following effects:

- Commercial banks that relied on small-scale depositors were banned from involvement in the type of investment banking that had fuelled some of the 1920s' speculation.
- Bank officials were not allowed to take personal loans from their own banks.
- Authority over open-market operations such as buying and selling government securities was centralised by being transferred from the Federal Reserve Banks to the Federal Reserve Board in Washington.
- Individual bank deposits were to be insured against bank failure up to the figure of $2,500, with the insurance fund to be administered by a new agency, the Federal Deposit Insurance Corporation (FDIC).

Regulation of the stock exchange

To ensure that the excesses of the 1920s, which had caused the Wall Street Crash, were not repeated two measures were passed:

- The Truth-in-Securities Act, 1933, required brokers to offer clients realistic information about the securities they were selling.
- The Securities Act, 1934, set up a new agency, the Securities Exchange Commission (SEC). Its task was to oversee stock market activities and prevent fraudulent activities such as insider dealing, as in the bull pool.

Industrial recovery

Industrial recovery was a priority for the New Deal. However, it had only limited success due to the scale of the industrial collapse. Although the economy grew ten per cent per year during Roosevelt's first term from 1933 to 1936, output had fallen so low since 1929 that this still left unemployment at fourteen per cent. The problem was that there was no consensus on how to go about ensuring industrial recovery.

Roosevelt's primary aims were to get people back to work and to increase consumer demand. He introduced the National Industry Recovery Act (NIRA) of June 1933. The Act came in two parts:

- National Recovery Administration (NRA)
- Public Works Administration (PWA).

National Recovery Administration

The NRA was set up to oversee industrial recovery. Headed by General Hugh Johnson, it seemed to offer something to all groups involved in industry. Powerful businessmen, for example, benefited from the suspension of anti-trust legislation for two years. The argument behind this was that if industrial expansion was to be promoted, it was crazy to maintain laws that restricted it. Firms were encouraged to agree to codes of practice to regulate unfair competition such as price cutting, and to agree on such matters as working conditions and minimum wages in their industry.

Ultimately the codes did not help economic recovery. This led Johnson to attempt a 'Buy Now' campaign in October 1933 to encourage people to spend and therefore stimulate production. He also advocated an overall ten per cent wage increase and ten-hour cut in the working week. Neither was successful.

Problems with the codes

Problems with most of the operations of the NRA quickly became apparent. Many of the codes, for example, turned out to be unworkable. This was in part because they were adopted so quickly, often without proper thought or planning, but also because they were often contentious. Many large manufacturers, notably Henry Ford, never subscribed to them and yet small firms complained that they favoured big business. Many small firms found it difficult to comply with all the regulations, particularly the minimum wage clauses. It was hoped, for example, that the firms signing the codes would introduce a minimum wage of $11 for a 40-hour week. Few small firms could afford this.

In reality, the NRA codes looked impressive but they could not bring about an economic recovery. Many critics argued that, in practice, they did little except give large firms the opportunity to indulge in unfair practices – the very opposite of what had been intended.

The Supreme Court dealt the death blow in May 1935 when it declared the NRA unconstitutional.

Source C From *Freedom from Fear* by D. M. Kennedy, (Oxford University Press), 1999.

The Blue Eagle [a symbol used by companies to show compliance with NIRA] was meant to symbolise unity and mutuality, and it no doubt did for a season, but Johnson's ubiquitous 'badge of honor' also clearly signified the poverty of the New Deal imagination and the meagreness of the measures it could bring to bear at this time against the Depression. Reduced to this kind of incantation and exhortation for which they had flayed Hoover, the New Dealers stood revealed in late 1933 as something less than the bold innovators and aggressive workers of government power that legend later portrayed.

> To what extent do you agree with the views expressed in Source C?

Public Works Administration

The second part of NIRA set up an emergency Public Works Administration (PWA) to be headed by the Secretary of the Interior, Harold Ickes. It was funded with $3.3 billion and its purpose was 'pump-priming'. It was hoped that expenditure on public works such as roads, dams, hospitals and schools would stimulate the economy. Road building would lead to increased demand for concrete, for example, which would lead the concrete companies to employ more workers, who would therefore have more money to spend, and so on. Eventually the PWA put hundreds of thousands of people to work, building, among other things, nearly 13,000 schools and 50,000 miles of roads.

> **Pump-priming** – The activity of helping a business, programme, economy, etc., to develop by giving it money.

It pumped billions of dollars into the economy and was responsible for massive public works schemes, particularly in the West, where it enabled dams to be built to help irrigate former semi-desert land, electricity to be produced and four vast National Parks to be created.

Civil Works Administration

A further measure to create employment was the Civil Works Administration (CWA). This agency was created in November 1933, with a $400 million grant from the PWA, primarily to provide emergency relief to the unemployed during the hard winter of 1933–34. Although it put 4 million people to work on public works projects, it was closed down in March when the winter was over. However, FERA agreed to fund more public works projects itself.

Despite the fact that many jobs agencies such as the PWA were created, unemployment and attendant social problems persisted and the Federal Government had to turn to relief measures.

Relief

There were millions of needy people in the USA. One major difference between Roosevelt and Hoover was the willingness of the former to involve the Government in direct relief measures. These included the Federal Emergency Relief Act and the Civilian Conservation Corps.

Federal Emergency Relief Act, May 1933

This Act established the Federal Emergency Relief Administration (FERA). It was given $500 million to be divided equally among the states to help provide for the unemployed. Half the money was to be granted to states for outright relief. With the remainder, the Government would pay each state $1 for every $3 it spent on relief.

Roosevelt chose Harry Hopkins to run this programme. He had administered the relief programmes that the President had introduced when Governor of New York. The Act said that each state should set up a FERA office and organise relief programmes. It should raise the money through borrowing, tax rises or any other means. When some states such as Kentucky and Ohio refused to comply, Hopkins simply threatened to deny them any federal monies.

Many states were wedded to the idea of a balanced budget and found expenditure on relief extremely distasteful. It was still felt by many that to be poor was your own fault. Those requiring relief were often not treated well. In many places there could be interminable waits and delays.

In the face of such opposition, FERA's effectiveness was limited. Its workers were refused office space in some states and often their caseloads were numbered in thousands. Its funds were limited, too. In 1935, it was paying about $25 per month to an average family on relief, while the average monthly minimum wage for subsistence was estimated at $100.

However, although its effects were disappointing, it did set the important precedent of federal government giving direct funds for relief.

Civilian Conservation Corps, 1933

Unemployment among young people was a huge problem and Roosevelt understood they needed a special programme to afford them both the experience of work and useful training in community service, co-operation and other skills essential to their growth as useful citizens. Unemployed young men between the ages of 17 and 24 (later 28) were recruited by the Department of Labor to work in the Civilian Conservation Corps (CCC) in national forests, parks and public lands. The Corps was organised along military lines, but its tasks were set out by the Departments of the Interior and Agriculture.

The CCC was originally set up for two years but Congress extended this for a further seven years in 1935, when its strength was increased to 500,000. In the period of its life, the CCC installed 65,100 miles of telephone lines in inaccessible areas, spent 4.1 million man-hours fighting forest fires and planted 1.3 billion trees. The CCC gave countless young men, particularly those from the cities, a new self-respect and valuable experience of both comradeship and life in the 'great outdoors'.

WORKING TOGETHER

1 Compare the notes you have made in your table, from page 175, with a partner.

2 Discuss together the extent to which you think that the measures introduced during the first New Deal were a success.

KEY DATES: FIRST NEW DEAL

1933 The Hundred Days.

1933 May Tennessee Valley Authority.

1933 May Agricultural Adjustment Act, May 1933.

1933 November Civil Works Administration (CWA).

	Unemployed, in millions	Percentage of workforce unemployed
1933	12.8	24.9
1934	11.3	21.7
1935	10.6	20.1

▲ Figure 2 A table showing unemployment between 1933 and 1935.

The Second New Deal

How significant were the achievements of the Second New Deal?

Many historians have argued that the New Deal seemed more radical in the years after 1935, with Roosevelt genuinely trying to favour the poorer classes at the expense of the rich. They point in particular to the measures that made up the Second New Deal as evidence of this, such as the introduction of social security and the legalisation of labour unions.

Reasons for the Second New Deal

Roosevelt had several reasons for introducing the Second New Deal.

- The climate in the new Congress was for action and Roosevelt wanted to prevent this. He did not wish to surrender the initiative in preparing New Deal legislation.
- Roosevelt was increasingly frustrated by the Supreme Court, which was beginning to overturn New Deal legislation. He believed it was opposing him. This in itself made him more radical in outlook.
- Roosevelt was also increasingly frustrated with the wealthy and with the forces of big business, who were opposing him more and more. He was particularly angry when the US Chamber of Commerce attacked his policies in May 1935. He believed he had been elected to save American business and he felt let down by its lack of continued support.

Works Progress Administration (WPA)

The WPA recruited people for public works projects. At any one time it had about 2 million employees and, by 1941, twenty per cent of the nation's workforce had found employment with it. Wages were approximately $52 per month, which was greater than any relief but less than the going rate in industry. The WPA was not allowed to compete for contracts with private firms or to build private houses. However, it did build 1,000 airport landing fields, 8,000 schools and hospitals, and 12,000 playgrounds.

Although it was not supposed to engage in large-scale projects, it did so. Among other things it was responsible for cutting the Lincoln Tunnel, which connects Manhattan Island to New Jersey, and building Fort Knox in Kentucky.

Wagner–Connery National Labor Relations Act (the 'Wagner Act'), July 1935

Roosevelt was reluctant to become involved in labour relations legislation. There are many reasons for this.

- There was a mistrust of labour unions in the USA. This was particularly the case among conservative politicians such as the Southern Democrats whose support he needed.
- He had no more wish to become the champion of unions than to upset big business further – and big business generally loathed unions.

The Act guaranteed workers the rights to collective bargaining through unions of their own choice. They could choose their union through a secret ballot; and a new three-man National Labor Relations Board was set up to ensure fair play. Employers were forbidden to resort to unfair practices, such as discrimination against unionists.

It was the first Act that effectively gave unions rights in law and in the long term committed federal government to an important labour relations role. However, Roosevelt still did not see it that way and preferred to continue to take a back seat in labour relations.

NOTE-MAKING

Using the 1–2 method (see page x) make notes on this section. For example write 'The WPA' on the left-hand side and add a bullet point list of its features on the right-hand side.

Social Security Act, August 1935

Provision made by states for social security was wholly inadequate. For example, only Wisconsin provided any form of unemployment benefit and this was to be paid by former employers as a disincentive to laying-off their workers. Roosevelt had long been interested in a federal system of social security. However, what he came up with was both conservative and limited in its provision. Certainly it was not as generous as a proposal by Townsend, a critic of the New Deal, whose popularity was of concern to Roosevelt and many members of Congress.

The Social Security Act was the first federal measure of direct help as a worker's right and would be built upon in the future. The Act provided for old-age pensions to be funded by employer and employee contributions, and unemployment insurance to be paid for by payroll taxes levied on both employers and employees. While the pension scheme was a federal programme, it was anticipated that states would control unemployment insurance.

However, the Social Security Act was generally inadequate to meet the needs of the poor. Pensions were paid at a minimum of $10 and a maximum of $85 per month according to the contributions that recipients had paid into the scheme. They were not to be paid until 1940 so everyone receiving them had paid something in. Unemployment benefit was a maximum of $18 per week for sixteen weeks only.

Although the Social Security Act had serious flaws, it should not be forgotten that it was a major break with American governmental tradition. Never before had there been a direct system of national benefits. But it is important to stress that this was not relief. Roosevelt refused to allow general taxes to subsidise the system. It had to be self-financing. Recipients had to pay into the system. The pensions were not paid at a flat rate but according to how much the worker had contributed previously. Unemployment benefits were low and paid for a very limited period.

The Banking Act, August 1935

This Act was intended to give the federal government control of banking in the USA. The Governor of the Federal Reserve Board, Marriner Eccles, felt that Wall Street exercised too much power in national finance and sought to repeal the 1913 Federal Reserve Act, which governed the American banking system. The control of banking was removed from private banks to central government and the centre of financial management shifted from New York to Washington.

The Second New Deal saw an important expansion of the role of federal, state and local government. There was much that was new.

- The banking system was centralised.
- Labour unions were given a legal voice.
- The Social Security Act created the first national system of benefits, although individual states operated the parts they had control over very differently.
- There was also further development of existing policies, as with the creation of the WPA to aid both relief and recovery.

WORKING TOGETHER

Working in pairs, compare the First and Second New Deals.

One of you should look at the similarities between the First and Second Deals.

The other should look at the differences.

Share your findings.

KEY DATES: SECOND NEW DEAL

1935 April Works Progress Administration.

1935 July Wagner–Connery National Labor Relations Act.

1935 August The Banking Act.

1935 August Social Security Act.

2 The impact of the New Deal

The New Deal had a profound economic, social and political impact and faced opposition from the left and right in politics as well as the Supreme Court. This was due mainly to a conflict of ideas about the role of the Federal Government.

Opposition to the First New Deal

Why was there opposition to the First New Deal?

The New Deal attracted much opposition, from the political right because it was too radical and from the political left because it was not radical enough. In this section the alternatives put forward by some of these opponents are examined.

The right

Many of the wealthy, who had supported Roosevelt in the darkest days of the Depression as the saviour of capitalism, now turned against him when it seemed that capitalism had been saved. This was in part because of the increases in taxes, which they argued fell too heavily on them. They also tended to oppose what they perceived as too much government involvement in the economy.

The Republican Party, still associated with its failures during the early 1930s, was rebuilding and preparing for the 1936 election, but it was finding it difficult to field a strong candidate, which meant there was a lack of effective opposition to Roosevelt.

Roosevelt also faced opposition from the Liberty League, which was supported by members of the Republican Party as well as his own party, the Democrats.

The left

At the time, Roosevelt was more concerned about threats from the left. This was particularly because left-wing groups might join together to form a third party to challenge him in the next presidential election. The threats varied from those advocating radical schemes such as 'Old Age Revolving Pensions Incorporated' to popular leaders such as Huey Long and Father Charles Coughlin.

End Poverty in California (EPIC)

The novelist Upton Sinclair came up with a scheme whereby the unemployed would be put to work in state-run co-operatives. They would be paid in currency, which they could spend only in other co-operatives. For a time, Sinclair's ideas gained credibility and proved useful recruits for more serious alternative movements as discussed below.

'Share Our Wealth'

In February 1934, Senator Huey Long from Louisiana moved onto the national scene with his 'Share Our Wealth' programme. He advocated that all private fortunes over $3 million should be confiscated and every family should be given enough money to buy a house, a car and a radio. There should also be old-age pensions, minimum wages so that every family would be guaranteed $2,000–$3,000 per year and free college education for all suitable candidates. Long's ideas proved very popular and 'Share Our Wealth' clubs grew to 27,431 in number, with 4.6 million members spread across the states.

NOTE-MAKING

Create your own spider diagram (see page x) to make notes on the following topics: opposition to the New Deal and the achievements of the New Deal.

Liberty Leaguers

The Liberty League was organised in April 1934 by many conservative Democrats as well as Republicans to promote private property and private enterprise unregulated by law. The Liberty Leaguers attacked Roosevelt throughout the New Deal years and formed the basis of right-wing opposition to him. By July 1936, it had 125,000 members; after Roosevelt's victory in the elections of that year, however, it became less significant.

Huey Long

As an energetic governor of Louisiana, Huey Long had ordered massive public works programmes – over 3,000 miles of paved highways were built between 1928 and 1933, besides new public buildings and an airport at New Orleans – and ambitious adult literacy schemes. Long began to talk of joining forces with other radicals to form a third party to oppose Roosevelt in the 1936 presidential election. In 1935, Postmaster General James A. Farley took a secret poll to assess Long's popularity and was shocked to discover that up to four million people might vote for him in 1936. This meant that Long might hold the balance of power in the election. The Louisiana Senator was, in fact, gunned down in September 1935.

Old Age Revolving Pensions Incorporated

Francis Townsend was a retired doctor who advocated old-age pensions with a difference. Everyone over 60 years of age who was not in paid employment should be given $200 per month on the understanding that every cent of it was spent and none saved. The idea was that this would boost consumption and thereby production and so pull the USA out of the Depression. Moreover, encouraging people to retire at 60 would provide more jobs for the young. Soon Townsend Clubs had 500,000 members and Congress was being lobbied to put the plan into operation. It was, of course, totally impractical. Payments to recipients would have amounted to 50 per cent of national income and an army of bureaucrats would have been necessary to ensure pensioners were spending all their $200. Nevertheless, the level of support showed that the movement had to be taken seriously.

Father Charles Coughlin

Charles Coughlin was a priest whose radio programme, *The Golden Hour of the Little Flower*, was enormously influential during the first half of the 1930s. It regularly commanded an audience of 30–40 million, and listeners contributed more than $5 million per year to his parish in Detroit. In 1934, Coughlin founded the National Union for Social Justice with the aim of monetary reform and redistribution of wealth. Roosevelt was afraid of Coughlin's influence, particularly when a possible alliance with Huey Long was mooted. However, Long was assassinated and Coughlin became increasingly anti-Semitic, blaming Jews for both the New Deal and control of Wall Street. This lost him significant support.

Opposition of the Supreme Court

Given Roosevelt's flexible ideas on the workings of the Constitution, it was perhaps inevitable that he would come into conflict with its guardian, the Supreme Court. Although he had not directly attacked the Court during the election campaign, he felt it was in need of reform. While the Court had supported New Deal laws in the days of crisis, it had increasingly declared legislation unconstitutional as Roosevelt's first term of office came to an end. In the 140 years before 1935, the Supreme Court had found only about 60 federal laws unconstitutional; in eighteen months during 1935 and 1936, it found eleven to be so.

Indeed, on one day, 'Black Monday', 27 May 1935, the Supreme Court attacked the New Deal in several ways. For example, it found the Farm Mortgage Act unconstitutional. It argued that the removal of a trade commissioner, which Roosevelt sought, was the responsibility not of the president but of Congress. Most importantly, it found the NRA to be unconstitutional through the 'sick chicken' case.

If the Federal Government could not prosecute individual firms for breaking the NRA codes, it followed that all the codes themselves must be unconstitutional. This was because they were developed by federal government but affected individual firms in individual states. The argument went that the executive had acted unconstitutionally in giving itself the powers to implement the codes in the first place. This was because it had no authority to intervene in matters that were the preserve of individual states. Given that the codes were at the heart of NIRA, it could not survive without them. More significantly, the ruling seemed to imply that the government had no powers to oversee nationwide economic affairs except in so far as they affected inter-state commerce.

The 'sick chicken' case, 1935

This was possibly the Court's most serious decision and it motivated Roosevelt into action. The case involved the Schechter Brothers, a firm of butchers in New York who were selling chickens unfit for human consumption. Prosecuted by the NIRA for breaking its codes of practice, the Schechter Brothers appealed against the verdict to the Supreme Court. It decided that their prosecution should be a matter for the New York courts not the Federal Government, and the poultry code was declared illegal. In effect, the decision meant that federal government had no right to interfere in internal state issues. While recognising that the Federal Government had powers to intervene in inter-state commerce, the Court found that it had no powers to do so in the internal commerce of states.

Judiciary Reform Bill

Roosevelt believed the justices on the Supreme Court were out of touch. Of the nine judges, none were his appointments. He increasingly saw the issue of the Supreme Court as one of unelected officials stifling the work of a democratically elected government, while members of the Supreme Court saw it as them using their legal authority to halt the spread of dictatorship. The scene was set for battle.

On 3 February 1936, Roosevelt presented the Judiciary Reform Bill to Congress. This proposed that the president could appoint a new justice whenever an existing judge, reaching the age of 70, failed to retire within six months. He could also appoint up to six new justices, increasing the possible total to fifteen. The measure had been drawn up in secret, although, ironically, the idea of forcibly retiring judges had first been proposed by one of the existing members of the Supreme Court in 1913.

Roosevelt had stirred up a hornet's nest. Many Congressmen feared he might start to retire them at 70 next. He had also greatly underestimated popular support and respect for the Court. In proposing this measure, Roosevelt was seen as a dictator. In July, the Senate rejected the Judiciary Reform Bill by 70 votes to 20.

▼ A cartoon of July 1935 with the title *Gulliver's travels*. It shows Uncle Sam as Gulliver tied down by New Dealers and their new policies. How does the cartoon criticise the New Deal?

Opposition to Roosevelt

Roosevelt faced significant opposition from big business and wealthy people who increasingly felt the New Deal had gone too far. Some wouldn't even say his name; they called him 'that cripple in the White House'. Roosevelt himself said that everyone was against him but the electorate. However, the relationship with big business was always difficult. Roosevelt knew the economy couldn't recover without its support and big business may have feared the alternative had the New Deal failed completely. However, they hated the Revenue Acts which raised taxes and opposed what they perceived as ever greater government interference.

Republican opponents in Congress were to be joined by more conservative Democrats who also feared the New Deal had gone too far. Roosevelt called for a special congressional session in November 1937 to pass various measures such as an anti-lynching bill, which had been delayed due to the debates on the Judicial Reform Bill. Not one was passed.

KEY DATES: OPPOSITION TO THE NEW DEALS

1934 February Senator Huey Long set up the 'Share Our Wealth' programme.

1934 April The Liberty League was organised.

1935 27 May 'Black Monday', the Supreme Court attacked the New Deal in several ways.

1936 February Roosevelt presented the Judiciary Reform Bill to Congress.

WORKING TOGETHER

There is much discussion about which opponents posed the greatest threat to Roosevelt and the New Deal. Set up a class debate to assess the significance of the opposition of the Supreme Court to the New Deal, with one group arguing it posed the greatest threat, and another group arguing 'against', looking at other threats. You could use the motion:

'This class believes that the Supreme Court posed the greatest threat to the New Deal.'

The achievements of the New Deal

To what extent was the New Deal successful in achieving its aims in the years 1933–41?

Roosevelt spoke of the New Deal's aims as 'relief, recovery and reform' and it is against these that its success should be judged. There has been much debate about the achievements of the New Deal, in particular how it extended the economic and social role of the Federal Government.

Economic effects

Economic recovery was sluggish during the New Deal years, in part because many of its measures were contradictory. Roosevelt believed in a balanced budget. He was, therefore, reluctant to spend excessively on federal projects. He failed to see that massive government expenditure might be necessary to offset the reduction in spending in the private sector. This desire for a balanced budget led to a reduction of the budget deficit over the course of Roosevelt's presidency. In 1938, the deficit was lower than the $2.5 billion deficit Hoover had run up in 1932 and over which Roosevelt had criticised him in the 1932 presidential election.

The actual achievements of the New Deal were rather slender. The national total of personal income stood at $86 billion in 1929 and only $73 billion in 1939. This was despite a population increase of 9 million during the course of the decade. The Government seemed reconciled to a permanent unemployment figure of at least 5 million. Wages averaged $25.03 per week in 1929 and $23.86 ten years later.

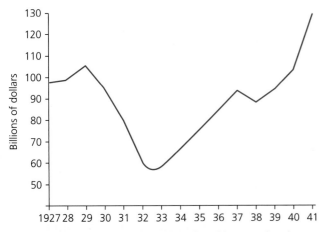

▲ **Figure 3** A graph showing US national income for the years 1927–41.

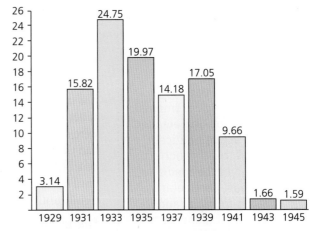

▲ **Figure 4** A graph showing the percentage of the workforce out of work in the years 1929–45.

In 1933, 18 million Americans were unemployed. In 1939, 9 million were still out of work. While there was a reduction in unemployment in the early years of the New Deal, it may largely have been the result of people working in the alphabet agencies. The Roosevelt Recession of 1937 saw a return to higher unemployment with nineteen per cent of the workforce jobless in 1938. Most historians agree that the real reason unemployment fell was the amendment of the 1935 Neutrality Act in November 1939. This meant that belligerents could buy from the USA. Within a year there were orders for 10,800 aircraft and 13,000 aeroplane engines.

Political effects

The New Deal was, when viewed as a whole, a programme of reform. The reforms were economic, political and social and transformed the national infrastructure of the USA.

Economic reforms were mainly intended to rescue the capitalist system from its worst excesses and to provide a more rational framework in which it could operate. Roosevelt allowed labour unions to take their place in labour relations and reluctantly recognised that federal government had a role in settling industrial disputes.

Reluctantly, Roosevelt came to realise that the expansion of government he had created was to be permanent. His attempted reform of the Supreme Court failed, but the Court nevertheless became more sympathetic to New Deal legislation, recognising the political realities of the later 1930s. The New Deal also saw an expansion in the functions of state and local government, for example in terms of welfare provision. The system became more modern and able to address the needs of citizens in the twentieth century.

People increasingly expected that the government would take responsibility for their problems. The Social Security Act and the relief and job creation agencies expanded the role of government considerably.

Social effects

The New Deal did bring about fundamental social changes.

Relief

One of the greatest achievements of the New Deal was in changing the role of federal government. This was particularly true of help for the less fortunate members of society. Relief agencies such as FERA and the

Eleanor Roosevelt (1864–1962)

Eleanor Roosevelt expanded the role of the First Lady from what had largely been seen as one of fulfilling ceremonial functions and looking elegant, into a more active political role. She did this through manipulation of the media to promote ideas, particularly with regards to social and gender issues. Eleanor was anxious to promote gender issues and ensure women stayed within the workforce. She introduced women-only press conferences in the White House where she gave political opinions on public issues. This indirectly enhanced the role of women in journalism: too often women had been given the lifestyle and personal interest stories to cover but now they had the First Lady's spin on weighty matters. She also began a monthly feature entitled 'I Want you to Write to Me' for the *Woman's Home Journal* in which readers could submit questions and suggestions about government policies. Within five months of its first appearance, 300,000 women had done so. Eleanor made extensive visits to see New Deal programmes in operation; she has been called 'the President's eyes, ears and legs'. Eleanor was also active in the question of civil rights and encouraged her husband to consider improving the lives of ethnic minorities.

WPA were set up to offer hope to millions. There were new departures in governmental responsibilities. The Social Security Act was not strictly a relief measure as it was financed through contributions paid by recipients. However, it did set up a national system of old-age pensions and unemployment benefit for the first time.

It is true that the amounts spent were inadequate for the needs of a population suffering from a prolonged depression. Nevertheless, important precedents were set by this legislation. It could be built on in the future. Never before had the Federal Government become involved in granting direct relief or benefits. Roosevelt initially saw relief agencies as only temporary expedients until economic recovery was achieved. In offering direct relief, however, he significantly increased the role of federal government.

This led in turn to a greater role for state and local governments as partners, however unwillingly at first, in many of the programmes.

Women and the New Deal

Women held more important posts in government during the New Deal era than at any time before or after until the 1990s. Mrs Roosevelt was one of the most politically active first ladies. As Secretary of Labour from 1933 to 1945, Frances Perkins was only one of many women holding government office and Ruth Bryan Owen became the first female ambassador (to Denmark) in 1933.

The New Deal itself did little for women. Unlike African Americans, they did not tend to vote as a group. As a result, politicians did not set out particularly to win their support. Much New Deal legislation worked against them:

- In 1933, the Economy Act forbade members of the same family from working for federal government. A total of 75 per cent of those who lost their jobs through this measure were married women.
- NRA codes allowed for unequal wages.
- Some agencies, such as the CCC, barred women entirely.

Women suffered particularly in the professions where, even by 1940, about 90 per cent of jobs were filled by men. Where women did find employment, which many had to do to balance the family budget, it tended to be in low-status, poorly paid jobs. On average during the 1930s, at $525 per annum, women earned half the average wage of men.

African Americans and the New Deal

Roosevelt needed the vote of Southern Democrats and not surprisingly, therefore, the New Deal saw no civil rights legislation. Many measures – the AAA for instance – worked against African Americans.

African Americans suffered particularly badly in the Depression, often being the last to be taken on and the first to be fired. Many poorly paid, menial jobs previously reserved for them were now taken by whites. NRA codes allowed for African Americans to be paid less than whites for doing the same jobs. Some African Americans called the NRA the 'Negro-run-around' because it was so unfair to them. The CCC was run by a Southern racist who did little to encourage African Americans to join: those who did faced strict segregation. Anti-lynching bills were introduced into Congress in 1934 and 1937, but Roosevelt did nothing to support either and both were eventually defeated.

The President did employ more African Americans in government, notably Mary McLeod Bethune at the National Youth Administration (NYA). However, while there were more African Americans in government office, it seems an exaggeration to speak as some did of an 'African-American cabinet' addressing race issues. The civil service tripled the number of African Americans in its employment between 1932 and 1941 to 150,000. There was also some unofficial positive discrimination, notably again in the NYA where African-American officials were usually appointed in areas where African Americans predominated.

Native Americans

The new Commissioner for the Bureau of Indian Affairs, John Collier, was determined to reverse government policy towards Native Americans and abolish assimilation.

The Indian Reorganisation Act of 1934 recognised and encouraged Native American culture in a shift from the former policy of assimilation. Tribes were reorganised into self-governing bodies that could vote to adopt constitutions and have their own police and legal systems. They could control land sales on the reservations, while new tribal corporations were established to manage tribal resources. However, many argued that respect for traditional Native American culture and society undermined efforts to modernise and join mainstream society. Indeed, 75 out of 245 tribes vetoed them when asked to vote on the measures.

These measures in no way relieved Native American poverty. Officials did their best to ensure Native Americans could take advantage of New Deal agencies such as the CCC and PWA to find jobs, but Native American poverty was so great that these measures, for all their good intentions, could have only a very limited effect at best. As New Deal programmes wound down in the 1940s, Native Americans began to set up pressure groups to promote their development, but they often remained among the poorest people in the USA. In 1943, for example, a Senate enquiry found widespread poverty among Native Americans on reservations.

LOOK AGAIN

Look back to Chapter 2, pages 55–6. What changes took place to the lifestyle of the Plains Indians in the 1870s and 1880s?

WORKING TOGETHER

1 Firstly, compare the notes that you have made on the impact of the New Deal. Add anything that you have missed and check anything that you have disagreed on.

2 Next, make a copy of the following table. One of you should identify the achievements of the New Deal and the other its shortcomings.

	Achievements	Shortcomings
Reform		
Relief		
Recovery		
Women		
Native Americans		
African Americans		

3 After you have finished, combine your findings.

4 Overall, do you believe that the New Deal was successful in achieving its aims?

The debate

Historians have differed greatly in their views about the New Deal but it cannot be judged solely on the economy. In the years following the New Deal many historians were supportive. Writing in the 1950s, Carl Degler called it 'a third American revolution' because of the growth in government involvement and the break with *laissez-faire*. However, during the 1960s historians associated with the New Left such as Paul Conkin became more critical, arguing that it was too limited in its scope and that it was a missed opportunity for radical change. More recently, right-wing historians such as Amity Shlaes have been more critical still, arguing that it stifled economic recovery. They argue that high wage rates, partly as a result of union activities, discouraged employers from taking on more workers. The emphasis has shifted from the overview to specifics – too much government involvement, in this case the legalisation of labour unions stifled the private sector's ability to create more jobs.

Source D From an article in the *Economist,* October 1934.

The achievements of the New Deal appear to be small. Relief there has been, but little more than enough to keep the population fed, clothed and warm. Recovery there has been, but only to a point well below pre-depression level. There has been no permanent adjustment of agriculture and very little has been done to iron out the problems of industry. However, its achievements compared with the situation which confronted it in 1933, it is a striking success. Mr Roosevelt may have given the wrong answers to many of its problems, but at least he is the first president of modern America to ask the right questions.

Source E From *The Roosevelt Myth* by John T. Flynn, published in 1944.

Roosevelt did not restore our economic system. He did not construct a new one. He substituted an old one which lives upon permanent crises and an armament economy. And he did this not by a process of orderly architecture and building, but by a succession of blunders, moving one step at a time, in flight from one problem to another, until we are now arrived at that kind of state supported economic system that will continue to devour a little at a time the private system until it disappears altogether.

Source F From *The USA 1917–45* D & S Willoughby Heinemann 2000, p. 239.

The New Deal helped to give birth to the idea within America of the 'semi-welfare' state, that the government had the responsibility to look after the welfare of its citizens. It extended the rights of workers and began for many of them social security payments. It introduced much needed controls on the banking system and began the idea of government having responsibility for regulating the economy. At a time of economic depression it helped to restore national morale.

ACTIVITY

1 To what extent do Sources D and E differ in their views of the New Deal?
2 Which do you think gives the more realistic view?
3 To what extent does Source F challenge the views of Sources D and E?

3 International relations, 1933-41

During these years the USA moved from a policy of isolationism to war with Japan and involvement in the Second World War. There has been much debate among historians about isolationism as well as the reasons the USA went to war with Japan.

The 'Good Neighbor' policy

What were the key features of Roosevelt's 'Good Neighbor' policy?

When Roosevelt became president in 1933, the majority of members of Congress were isolationists. Roosevelt did not intend becoming involved in European affairs. He wanted the USA to follow a policy of friendship towards other countries and thought the USA could act as a 'moral force' for good in the world, especially to his American neighbours.

The introduction of the 'Good Neighbor' policy

Overcoming the economic crisis facing the USA was President Roosevelt's foremost task. He encouraged economic and diplomatic co-operation through the idea of the 'Good Neighbor' policy, which was in a sense a continuation of Hoover's policies of persuasion and economic pressure to exert influence on Latin America. Roosevelt saw his policy as transforming the Monroe Doctrine into arrangements for mutual hemispheric action against aggressors.

Source G Excerpt from President Roosevelt's inaugural speech, 4 March 1933.

In the field of world policy I would dedicate this nation to the policy of the good neighbor, the neighbor who resolutely respects himself and, because he does so, respects the rights of others – the neighbor who respects his obligations and respects the sanctity of his agreements in and with a world of neighbors.

> **Relations between the USA and Latin America**
>
> In accordance with the 'Good Neighbor' policy, US troops left Haiti, the Dominican Republic and Nicaragua. In 1934, Congress signed a treaty with Cuba that nullified the Platt Amendment, which had authorised the US occupation of Cuba. The USA did retain one naval base at Guantánamo. By 1938, the 'Good Neighbor' policy had led to ten treaties with Latin American countries, resulting in huge trade increases for the USA. Hull's policies of low tariffs improved the economies of the Latin American countries, especially in Cuba when the tariff on Cuban sugar was reduced and trade increased accordingly. To show continued goodwill to his neighbours, Roosevelt passed the Reciprocal Trade Agreement Act in 1934. This repealed several of the 1920s isolationist trade policies so the USA could compete better in foreign trade. The 1934 Act began the historic move towards lower trade barriers and greater global engagement.

NOTE-MAKING

Using a spider diagram (see page x) summarise the key features of Roosevelt's 'Good Neighbor' policy.

Good Neighbor – Foreign policy adopted by Roosevelt to mend and improve relations with Latin America.

Hemispheric – Relating to the western or eastern or northern or southern part of the world. In this case, it refers to North and South America.

What can you learn from Source G about Roosevelt's aims in foreign policy?

NOTE-MAKING

Using bullet points (see page x) make notes on the USA's policy of neutrality.

Totalitarianism – When political regimes suppress political opposition and control all aspects of people's lives.

The USA's policy of neutrality

Why did the USA follow a policy on neutrality in the 1930s?

The widespread feeling that involvement in the First World War had been a mistake continued in the USA throughout the 1930s. It was made evident when Congress passed a series of Neutrality Acts, which intended to keep the USA out of future wars. It was felt that the USA had unnecessarily lost men and military equipment, and that Europe was drifting towards further conflict as a result of the growth of totalitarianism.

The Neutrality Acts

The first Neutrality Act of 1935 gave the president the power to prohibit US ships from carrying US-made munitions to countries at war. The Neutrality Act could also prevent US citizens from travelling on ships of those countries at war except at their own risk. This was to avoid situations like the *Lusitania* incident, 1915, (see page 115). The second Neutrality Act, the following year, banned loans or credits to countries at war. The Act set no limits on trade in materials useful for war and US companies such as Texaco, Standard Oil and Ford were thus able to sell such items on credit to General Franco in the Spanish Civil War.

A third Neutrality Act of 1937 forbade the export of munitions for use by either of the opposing forces in Spain. It did, however, permit nations involved in a war to buy goods other than munitions from the USA, provided they paid cash and used their own ships. This became known as 'cash and carry'. The fourth Neutrality Act, of the same year, authorised the US president to determine what could and could not be bought, other than munitions, to be paid for on delivery, and made travel on ships of countries at war unlawful.

Roosevelt and neutrality

In the 1930s, the totalitarian and militaristic states of Germany, Italy and Japan openly built up large armed forces. Roosevelt despised the spread of totalitarianism in Germany and Italy and, by 1937, began to see that the USA might need to become involved in European affairs. His views differed from those of Congress and, most importantly, the majority of the American people. For some, the idea of US involvement in others' problems was completely abhorrent. For others, going to war would end the reforms of the New Deal.

In 1937, a Gallup Poll indicated that almost 70 per cent of Americans thought that US involvement in the First World War had been a mistake and 95 per cent opposed any future involvement in war. Although Roosevelt was aware of public opinion, in October of that year he made a speech in Chicago, warning the people of the USA about the situation in Europe and the Far East and the consequent dangers of war. It became known as the 'Quarantine Speech'. He had been appalled by the Nationalist bombing of civilians in Spain and the aggressive nature of Japan in declaring war on China in 1937. He had to tread a delicate path, and his speech warned the USA not only of the horrors of war but also the problems with neutrality. Roosevelt suggested a quarantine of the aggressors but was careful not to mention specific countries.

Source H Excerpt from Roosevelt's 'Quarantine Speech', 5 October 1937. From the Miller Center archive of US presidential speeches.

It seems to be unfortunately true that the epidemic of world lawlessness is spreading ... Innocent peoples, innocent nations are being cruelly sacrificed to a greed for power and supremacy which is devoid of all sense of justice and humane considerations. ... War is a contagion, whether it be declared or undeclared. It can engulf states and peoples remote from the original scene of hostilities. We are determined to keep out of war, yet we cannot insure ourselves against the disastrous effects of war and the dangers of involvement. We are adopting such measures as will minimize our risk of involvement, but we cannot have complete protection in a world of disorder in which confidence and security have broken down ... There must be positive endeavors to preserve peace.

Source I Excerpt from the *Boston Herald*'s editorial, 6 October 1937, the day after Roosevelt's 'Quarantine Speech'.

The mantle of Woodrow Wilson lay on the shoulders of Franklin Roosevelt when he spoke yesterday in Chicago. It may be true that 'the very foundations of civilization are seriously threatened'. But this time, Mr. President, Americans will not be stampeded into going 3,000 miles [5,000 km] across water to save them. Crusade, if you must, but for the sake of several millions of American mothers, confine your crusading to the continental limits of America!

The USA then made further amendments to the Neutrality Act in November 1939. The fifth Neutrality Act meant that the president could authorise the 'cash and carry' export of arms and munitions to countries at war, but they had to be transported in the countries' own ships. In addition, the president could specify which areas were theatres of war in time of war, through which US citizens and ships were forbidden to travel, and proclaimed the North Atlantic a combat zone. He did this because German U-boats were attacking British ships and bringing the war close to the USA. Roosevelt ordered the US Navy to patrol the western Atlantic and reveal the location of the German submarines to the British.

The US response to the European War, 1939–41

To what extent did the USA move away from neutrality in the years 1939–41?

Roosevelt began to express his strong support for the Western democratic states. After the **Munich Agreement** Hitler announced further rearmament and so did Roosevelt with a further $300 million granted to the defence budget. In October 1938, Roosevelt opened secret talks with the French on how to bypass US neutrality laws and allow the French to buy US aircraft. After tortuous negotiations in 1939, the French government placed large orders with the US aircraft industry.

The USA censured Germany in March 1939, and recalled its ambassador for breaking the Munich Agreement and seizing parts of Czechoslovakia. As tensions heightened in Europe, Roosevelt called on Germany and Italy to give assurances that they would not attack any European country over a period of ten years.

> **What differences are there between Sources H and I in their views of American foreign policy?**

> **KEY DATES: USA AND THE NEUTRALITY ACTS**
>
> **1936** First Neutrality Act.
>
> **1937** Second Neutrality Act.
>
> **1938** Third and Fourth Neutrality Acts.
>
> **1939** Fifth Neutrality Act.

> **NOTE-MAKING**
>
> Using a spider diagram (see page x) make notes on the following topics: the American response to the war in Europe and Lend-Lease and the Atlantic Charter.

> **Munich Agreement** – This was signed in September 1938 by Britain, France, Germany and Italy. It allowed Germany to annex part of Czechoslovakia.

Embargo – An official ban on trade or commercial activity

America First Campaign

This was set up by isolationists meanwhile to keep USA out of the conflict. Among its leaders was the aviator Charles Lindbergh. Much of the campaign's finance came from the German Embassy. An American Nazi Party, the *Volksbund*, upset many Americans by its paramilitary style and attacks on Jews. Increasingly, out-and-out isolationists were seen, fairly or otherwise, as supporters of Germany. This diminished their support.

To what extent do you think this speech (Source J) marks a turning point in US policy towards the war in Europe?

The changing situation in Europe

When Britain and France went to war with Germany in September 1939, Roosevelt summoned Congress into special session to repeal the arms embargo terms of the Neutrality Acts. Most Americans sympathised with the Allied cause and wanted to see Germany defeated. This was because they disliked the aggression of Nazi Germany. Many feared that if it conquered the European continent it would threaten the USA next.

In November 1939, in a vote on party lines, Congress agreed to sell arms on a strictly cash-and-carry basis. No American ships would carry weapons. However, it was felt the sales would benefit the Allies rather than Germany as British warships could protect their own vessels and destroy German carriers. Clearly Congress had not anticipated the threat to British shipping from German U-boats.

Most Americans wanted Britain and France to win, but as German successes mounted, this seemed decreasingly likely. The problem was compounded in the summer of 1940 when France was defeated and Britain stood alone against Germany. Britain had placed orders for 14,000 aircraft and 25,000 aero-engines, but was increasingly unable to pay. Roosevelt had overestimated Britain's wealth and began to realise that the USA would have to help more if Britain was to stay in the war.

In 1940, Roosevelt 'traded' Britain 50 destroyers for six Caribbean bases. British bases on Bermuda and Newfoundland were also leased to the USA. This was good business for Roosevelt. He had swapped some elderly destroyers for valuable bases. Nevertheless, it marked a shift to active support for Britain in the war that allowed her to continue to defend her merchant ships.

1940 Presidential election

Although the Republicans and their candidate, Wendell Willkie, were seen as the party of non-involvement, support for neutrality did cross party lines. Roosevelt decided to stand for a third term partly because there seemed no suitable successor within the Democratic Party. He repeated to audiences how much he hated war. Indeed, in Boston in September, Roosevelt made a famous speech in which he assured listeners that American 'boys were not going to be sent into any foreign wars'. However, Roosevelt was beginning to appeal more to businessmen who would do well out of war and less to his more traditional supporters whose boys would be fighting in one. Despite what he said, the USA was moving ever closer to war. Although his victory was smaller than in 1936, by 27 to 22 million votes, Roosevelt decided to act more boldly after winning.

In a fireside chat of 29 December 1940 he called the USA 'the arsenal of democracy', meaning the provider of arms to Britain (Source J).

Source J Excerpt from President Roosevelt's 'fireside chat' of 29 December 1940.

This is not a fireside chat on war. It is a talk on national security ... The people of Europe who are defending themselves do not ask us to do their fighting. They ask us for the implements of war, the planes, the tanks, the guns, the freighters which will enable them to fight for their liberty and for our security. Emphatically, we must get these weapons to them, get them to them in sufficient volume and quickly enough so that we and our children will be saved the agony and suffering of war which others have had to endure ... We must be the great arsenal of democracy.

Lend-Lease and the Atlantic Charter

Lend-Lease was introduced with Congressional approval in May 1941. Britain would be 'loaned' the means to keep fighting. Roosevelt likened it to lending a neighbour a garden hose to fight a fire that might otherwise have spread to his own property, but everyone knew you did not lend weapons. The USA was effectively giving Britain the means to remain in the war. This too showed a switch in policy. Roosevelt had been reluctant to give Britain weapons in 1940 in case she was defeated and Germany subsequently used America's own weapons against her.

In the meantime, in August, Roosevelt had met with the British Prime Minister, Winston Churchill, on the British battleship *Prince of Wales*, anchored off the Newfoundland coast of Canada. After three days of talks, they issued the Atlantic Charter. This was a powerful expression of a vision of what the world should be like after 'the final destruction of Nazi tyranny', with international peace, national self-determination and freedom of the seas. Roosevelt agreed to send aid to the USSR, which had been invaded by Germany in June 1941. In November 1941, Lend-Lease was extended to the USSR.

Roosevelt was clearly giving Britain 'all aid short of war' but he still was not prepared to formally go to war with Germany. He had no wish to be a president who took his country into war. He had made great play throughout his career of how much he hated war. He realised that, while the majority of Americans supported Britain, they still wished to keep out of the conflict, although a Gallup Poll in May 1941 showed only nineteen per cent of respondents thought he had gone too far in helping Britain.

> **KEY DATES: THE US RESPONSE TO THE EUROPEAN WAR, 1939–40**
>
> **1941** Presidential election. Roosevelt elected for third term.
> **1941 May** Lend-Lease.
> **1941 August** The Atlantic Charter.

The USA and Japan

Why did the USA go to war with Japan in 1941?

In the late 1930s, Japan edged closer to alliances with the fascist dictators in Europe. The US government became alarmed as it watched Japan's military encroachments into Indochina. Roosevelt showed his displeasure by pressuring Japan economically in the hope that such actions would end Japanese activities. The Japanese military held such power in government that it dictated foreign policy. Its key aim was to destroy any chance of the USA interfering with imperial and economic expansion.

Worsening relations

Japan and US relations had deteriorated since the Japanese invasion of China, which had begun in 1937. Japan declared the open door policy obsolete. Roosevelt retaliated by lending funds to China to buy weapons and by asking US manufacturers not to sell planes to Japan. Japan was dependent on supplies of industrial goods from the USA and if these dried up it realised it needed to find new suppliers, by force if necessary.

In July 1940, Congress limited supplies of oil and scrap iron to Japan. After the signing of the Rome–Berlin–Tokyo axis, Roosevelt banned the sale of machine tools to Japan. In spring 1941, Secretary of State Cordell Hull met with the Japanese Ambassador Kichisaburo Nomura to resolve differences between the two countries. Hull demanded Japan withdraw from China and promise not to attack Dutch and French colonies in South-east Asia. Japan did not respond because the USA offered them nothing in return.

> **NOTE-MAKING**
>
> Using a flow-chart show the key developments in relations between the USA and Japan 1937–41.

> **Indochina** – The region of South-east Asia, which was a colony of France.

Operation Magic

Roosevelt and his advisers felt some security because they were able to decipher Japanese radio traffic because of Operation Magic, established in the 1920s to break military and diplomatic codes. Operation Magic also gave information about Japanese ship movements, but did not allow them to find their destinations. US intelligence knew that the Japanese had set 25 November as a deadline for making diplomatic progress. When Hull addressed the US Cabinet on 7 November, he informed them that the USA should anticipate a military attack by Japan 'anywhere, anytime'.

KEY DATES: THE USA AND JAPAN

1937 Japanese invasion of China.

7 Dec 1941 Japanese attack on Pearl Harbor.

8 Dec 1941 The USA declares war on Japan.

ACTIVITY

1 To what extent do you agree with the interpretation in Source K of the outbreak of war between the USA and Japan?

2 Was it the attack on Pearl Harbor that led to war between the USA and Japan?

The European powers were involved in the war in their own continent and could not defend their Asian possessions, for example, in the Dutch East Indies. When France was defeated by Germany, the Japanese marched into the French colonies in Indochina. Japan subsequently announced the setting up of the Greater East-Asia Co-Prosperity Sphere. This was effectively a means by which Japan could economically exploit countries under its control.

In July 1941, the USA responded by freezing Japanese assets in the USA and an embargo on oil. Japan was almost wholly dependent on US oil.

As the military increasingly took over in Japan, the new Japanese Ambassador in Washington, Kichisaburo Nomura, told Hull that Japan would halt any further expansion if the USA and Britain cut off aid to China and lifted the economic blockade on Japan. Japan, indeed, promised to pull out of Indochina if a 'just peace' was made with China. Some historians believe today that Japan, bogged down in its Chinese war, was genuinely seeking a face-saving way out. However, few feel that Japan would actually have honoured any agreement it made with China.

Attack on Pearl Harbor

Few in the USA at the time trusted Japan. The USA did not respond to the Japanese offers and so the Japanese made preparations to attack the US naval base at Pearl Harbor, on the island of Oahu, Hawaii. The objective of this attack was to immobilise the US Navy so it could not stop Japan's expansion into East Asia, to areas such as the Dutch East Indies with their supplies of oil. Japan had not told its European allies of its intentions.

In the early morning of Sunday 7 December 1941, when most of the garrison were asleep, the Japanese launched a ferocious attack on Pearl Harbor. Catching the defenders by surprise, their fighter planes and bombers destroyed 180 American aircraft, and sank seven battleships and ten other vessels. Over 2,400 American servicemen were killed. However, the American aircraft carriers were out at sea and avoided being attacked. Further, the Japanese had missed the American fuel stores, which if hit would have meant the entire naval base would have had to return to the USA, thus leaving the region entirely undefended against further Japanese aggression.

On 8 December, the USA declared war on Japan. On 11 December, honouring his treaty obligations, Hitler declared war on the USA, as did his ally, Italy.

The stunning surprise of the attack on Pearl Harbor has raised questions about how it was possible. Right-wing historians have accused Roosevelt of deliberately withholding information about the Japanese attack from the commander of Pearl Harbor, knowing that the shock of the attack would justify war.

Others disagree, suggesting that, although there is evidence of the mishandling of information, there was no deliberate withholding of crucial warnings on 7 December. There is little evidence that Roosevelt would have deliberately put the Pacific Fleet at such a risk. He knew, by November 1941, that war was inevitable, but delay was favoured more than incitement. The disaster at Pearl Harbor was more likely due to confusion and incompetence at all levels.

Source K The diplomat John Paton Davies describing the USA/Japan/China triangle. Quoted in *The American Age: US Foreign Policy at Home and Abroad*, 2nd edn, by W. LaFeber, (W.W. Norton & Co.), 1994, p.105.

Japan was the actor; China the acted upon. And the US was the self-appointed referee who judged by subjective rules and called fouls without penalties, until just before the end of the contest. This provoked the actor into a suicidal attempt to kill the referee.

4 The USA and the Second World War

US forces were to play a significant role in the war in the Pacific and the war in the Far East and the war itself brought profound economic, political and social changes on the Home Front.

NOTE-MAKING

Using bullet points (see page x) summarise the political effects and economic effects of the war.

> **The role of US forces in the Second World War**
>
> American forces were involved both in the war in Europe and in the Far East. In the war in Europe, US forces played a key role in the successful D-Day landings of June 1944, with the Supreme Commander being an American, Dwight D. Eisenhower. After D-Day the Allies, with a strong US military presence, advanced quickly on Germany, culminating in March 1945 with the Allies pushing across the River Rhine. In April, Soviet forces captured Berlin. In the Pacific, the turning point was the Battle of Midway in which the US fleet defeated its Japanese counterpart. After its successes at sea, the USA focused on regaining some of its lost territory as a first step in the land war against Japan by a strategy of island-hopping with US forces moving from island to island, using each as a base for capturing the next. However, despite defeats on land, at sea and in the air, Japan repeatedly refused to the unconditional surrender the USA demanded. President Truman then made the decision to use atomic bombs, which were dropped on Hiroshima and Nagasaki in early August 1945. This brought an end to the war in the Pacific.

The impact of the Second World War on the USA

To what extent did the Second World War bring economic and social change to the USA?

The Second World War brought significant political, economic and social changes to the USA, further extending the role of the Federal Government.

Political effects

The Government took over more control of people's lives. In 1940, the Smith Act had been passed which made it illegal to threaten to overthrow the government of the USA. Originally aimed at supporters of fascism, it later became associated with the attack on Communists. The Selective Service Act of the same year had introduced conscription. As the war developed the Office of War Mobilization was created to control the supply of goods and prices; the National War Labor Board set wages. The War Management Commission, set up in 1942, had to recruit workers where they were needed most. Moreover, the Office of Scientific Research and Development mobilised thousands of scientists to develop new methods of death, from bazookas to the atomic bomb, as well as new methods of saving the lives of those who were wounded in battle.

The Office of Price Administration and Civilian Supply was set up in August 1941 to control inflation. In April 1942, it issued a General Maximum Price regulation which froze prices at March 1942 levels to prevent inflation. It had the power to control all prices (except agricultural commodities) and ration scarce items. Eventually such items as petrol, tyres, coffee, sugar and other foodstuffs were rationed. Almost 90 per cent of food items were subject to price controls.

Economic effects

Economically, the Second World War played a much greater role in economic recovery than the New Deal with nearly 9 million still out of work as late as 1941. Indeed, American involvement in war production made the New Deal irrelevant. Between 1941 and 1945, the USA produced 86,000 tanks, 296,000 aircraft and 15 million rifles. Farm income grew by 250 per cent. Unemployment effectively ceased by 1942; in 1944 it stood at 1.2 per cent, having fallen from 14.6 per cent in 1940. In 1944 alone, 6.5 million women entered the labour force; by the end of the war almost 60 per cent of women were employed. The number of African Americans working for the federal government rose from 50,000 in 1939 to 200,000 by 1944. In the years between 1940 and 1944, 5 million African Americans moved to the cities where a million found jobs in defence plants. Gross National Product (GNP) meanwhile rose from $91.3 billion in 1939 to $166.6 billion by 1945.

Year	Spending ($ billions)	Percentage of gross domestic product (GDP)
1941	6.1	5.1
1942	22.1	15.9
1943	46.6	32.2
1944	62.9	36.0
1945	64.5	37.2

▲ **Figure 5** American defence spending, 1941–45.

However, under the Office of War Mobilization, food prices and rents were strictly controlled. Some items such as meat, sugar and petrol were rationed, and the production of cars for ordinary motorists stopped entirely. While many consumer items such as clothes were made from far less material and became simpler in style and others disappeared from the shops, most Americans were comparatively well paid during the war and did not suffer the deprivations of those in other belligerent countries. Although prices rose by 28 per cent during the war years, average wages increased by 40 per cent; people may not have had much to spend these wages on but they could and did save. It was the spending power of these consumers that helped to fuel the post-war boom period (see pages 217–18).

As a result of the costs of the war, the National Debt which stood at $41 billion in 1941 had risen to $260 billion by 1945. The federal government spent twice as much between 1941 and 1945 as it had before in 150 years.

Roosevelt hoped to pay for much of the war production by increased taxes. The highest earners paid 94 per cent tax. This gave a sense of greater equality. The poor grew more wealthy during the war years and the rich received a smaller proportion of national income.

The Second World War brought enormous economic changes to the USA. Unemployment collapsed and the USA became an economic powerhouse. The government had direct control, unthinkable in previous periods.

Social effects

However, while the economy grew significantly during the war years, the most dramatic changes occurred in the lives of ordinary Americans.

Treatment of Japanese Americans

Towards the end of 1941, as US–Japanese relations worsened, 2,000 Japanese-labelled subversives had been rounded up (along with 14,000 Germans and Italians), although there was no official desire for internment. In fact, General John L. Dewitt, Chief of the Army West Coast Command, dismissed any such talk as 'damned nonsense'. However, increasing fears of a Japanese attack on the West Coast led to calls for internment even by respected journalists such as Walter Lippmann. Dewitt, responsible for West Coast security, gave in to this pressure, saying it was impossible to distinguish between loyal and traitorous Japanese and therefore all should be locked up.

Between February and March 1942, 15,000 Japanese Americans, many of whom had relations fighting in the American forces, voluntarily left Dewitt's area of command. However, other areas of the USA refused to accept them. The Attorney-General of Idaho, for example, said his state was for whites only. Dewitt decided on compulsory relocation; ten 'relocation centres' were set up throughout the West, where 100,000 Japanese Americans were forcibly sent. They had to leave their property unprotected. Much looting went on in their absence. One source estimated the community suffered losses worth $400 million.

The relocation centres, meanwhile, were akin to concentration camps with armed guards and barrack-type accommodation. Riots in the camp at Manzanar left two inmates dead. One of the guards said the only thing that stopped him machine gunning them was what the Japanese might do to the American POWs in retaliation.

By 1944, as fear of Japanese attack receded, the internees began to return home. In December 1944, the Supreme Court forbade the internment of loyal Japanese Americans. Nevertheless, neither their fellow Japanese-American citizens who lived outside Dewitt's command nor German or Italian Americans had been interned in this way, and so ill-feeling among many of those involved remained for some time.

Women

During the 1940s, the traditional role of a woman was still seen as a wife and mother. Nevertheless, at the beginning of the Second World War, there were about 13 million female workers and at the height of the war in 1944, this figure had increased to 19 million. Many did take on the jobs of men but many employers and male workers considered them inferior colleagues. Eleanor Roosevelt, the First Lady, was a powerful spokeswoman for female workers during the war.

Many new jobs during the war were in traditionally 'male' occupations such as the shipyards, aircraft factories and munitions. One in three aircraft workers and half of those working in electronics and munitions were women. Indeed, the pay in munitions work could be double that normally paid to women in 'female' occupations.

In 1942, a poll showed that 60 per cent of Americans were in favour of women helping with the war industries, yet there was a degree of ambivalence to the employment of women throughout the war.

NOTE-MAKING

Using the 1–2 method (see page x) make notes on the following section under these three headings: 'Treatment of Japanese Americans', 'Women' and 'African Americans'. Compare your notes with those of a partner and expand upon what each of you has written.

Some US states made equal pay between men and women (for the same role) compulsory, while others tried to protect women from workplace discrimination. However, racial discrimination continued, for instance African-American women were, by and large, almost always the last to be hired. There were also many 'hate strikes', such as the ones at the Packard car factory in Detroit as a result of the employment of African-American women.

At the end of the war, the majority of women gave up their wartime jobs and returned to their traditional pre-1941 'female' roles. In 1945, despite some progress in the position of women, there were still problems:

- They were generally excluded from the top, well-paid jobs.
- On average, women earned 50–60 per cent of the wage that men earned for doing the same job. In 1944, the average weekly wage for working women was $31.21 and for men it was $56.65.
- A woman could still be dismissed from her job when she married.

▲ A poster from wartime USA featuring 'Rosie the Riveter', 1942. 'Rosie the Riveter' was a fictional female worker used by the US government to encourage women to help with the war effort.

African Americans

When war broke out, there was increased optimism that things would change among African Americans. After all, if the USA was fighting fascism and racism, how could it continue to discriminate and deny civil rights to large sections of its own population?

In 1940, there were 12.9 million African Americans in the USA. The census of that year showed that there were almost 5.4 million employed, of whom 3.5 million were male. The vast majority of those employed had menial jobs, which were low paid. The average annual wage was $537 for men in 1939 and $331 for women. Both earned less than half that of their white counterparts. When the war broke out in Europe, unemployment among whites was fourteen per cent and as war-related industries began to seek workers, whites were taken on immediately. Unemployed African Americans did not benefit from this initial boom.

A survey conducted by the US Employment Office in 1940 among the defence industries indicated that more than half would not employ African Americans. In some cases, it was not simply the companies' owners who were propounding discrimination, it was their workers. The owners did not wish to fall foul of their employees.

The Double V Campaign

Despite the valuable contribution that African Americans made to the war effort, they continued to be treated poorly. An African-American newspaper, *Pittsburgh Courier*, created the Double V Campaign after readers began commenting on the second-class status of African-American workers during wartime. 'Double V' meant victory at home in terms of improved civil rights as well as victory abroad against fascism and dictatorship. The newspaper promoted the campaign by publishing numerous articles, letters and photographs. The effect was immediate and black newspapers across the USA began to support the campaign, thereby raising the profile of civil rights.

The March on Washington Movement

A. Philip Randolph, one of the most prominent leading African-American activists and trade unionists, was appalled at the discrimination not only in the war industries but also in the US armed forces. Randolph called for immediate action and sought to shame the government into action and bring an end to the inequality. He wanted direct action and organised the March on Washington Movement. It was expected that the march would include up to 100,000 demonstrators and, if this were publicised across the world, then it could do little to sustain the USA's image of the upholder of liberty and democracy.

Roosevelt was concerned that the march would discredit and embarrass not only the government, but the USA as a whole. Eventually they came to a compromise. Randolph called off the march and Roosevelt issued Executive Order 8802 and set up the Fair Employment Practices Commission (FEPC) to prevent discrimination at work. However, Randolph did not completely disband the March on Washington Movement. He continued to encourage African Americans to go on protest rallies to ensure that the issue of discrimination remained firmly in the public view. He also encouraged acts of civil disobedience to show opposition to laws that permitted unfair and unequal treatment.

Direct action – The use of acts, such as strikes, marches and demonstrations, to achieve a political or social end.

Civil disobedience – A non-violent way of protesting in order to achieve political goals.

Fair Employment Practices Commission (FEPC)

As a result of Executive Order 8802, the FEPC was set up in June 1941. Paragraph 3 of Order 8802 permitted the FEPC to investigate complaints and take action against alleged employment discrimination. As jobs in the defence industries increased, many African Americans migrated from the South in search of employment. They were joined by those in the North who sought better paid jobs. However, when African Americans were hired for jobs most were still given menial posts.

By 1943, the FEPC had become aware of widespread discrimination within a number of companies. Roosevelt then issued Executive Order 9346, which gave the Commission greater powers, and increased its budget to nearly half a million dollars. The FEPC investigated about 8,000 instances of discrimination and was successful with 66 per cent of its cases in the North-east, 62 per cent in the Mid-west and 55 per cent in the West.

African Americans and the armed forces

The war highlighted the racism and discrimination in the armed forces. Many African-Americans enlisted in what became known as the Jim Crow army. On occasions, African-American soldiers were given inferior training, had few recreational facilities, and endured racial slurs and even serious physical mistreatment. Moreover, many white officers thought that African-American soldiers were undisciplined, morally wanting, mentally deficient and even cowardly in battle.

African-Americans performed the menial non-combat tasks such as cooking, guarding prisoners, delivering supplies and building camps and roads. They found promotion difficult and the highest rank most reached was first lieutenant. As late as the spring of 1943, only 79,000 out of a total of 504,000 African American soldiers were overseas, simply because white army commanders did not want them.

African Americans had not been allowed to enlist in the developing air force. However, in 1940, President Roosevelt ordered the air corps to recruit an all-African-American flying unit. By the end of 1945, more than 600 pilots had been trained, although they were not allowed to fly in the same groups as whites. The all-African-American squadron was based in Tuskegee, Alabama. It became known as the Tuskegee Airmen (332nd Fighter Group) and won great acclaim acting as fighter escorts for US bombers.

There had been progress for African Americans during the Second World War in employment and the armed forces, and many African Americans had become more active in campaigning for civil rights. On the other hand, discrimination and segregation remained a way of life in the Southern states.

Jim Crow army – A reference to the African Americans serving in the segregated military in the Second World War. It is a reference to the segregation laws brought in by Southern states after the Civil War.

The Navy

Discrimination was worst in the Navy with African-American sailors given the most dangerous job of loading ammunition on ships bound for war zones. For example, in July 1944 a horrific accident occurred at Port Chicago in California when ammunition that was being loaded onto two vessels detonated, killing 323 people – most of them African-American sailors. Hundreds of African-American sailors went on strike the following month in protest at the dangerous working conditions. This was called the Port Chicago Mutiny and 50 sailors were arrested and imprisoned. The Navy examined its treatment of African Americans in the light of events at Port Chicago and began to effect changes that would help lead to desegregation in the force in 1946.

Source L This 'prayer' appeared in the *Baltimore Afro-American*, 16 January 1943, a weekly newspaper founded in 1842 and published in Baltimore, Maryland, USA.

Draftee's prayer

Dear Lord, today

I go to war:

To fight, to die

Tell me what for

Dear Lord, I'll fight,

I do not fear

Germans or Japs,

My fears are here.

America!

Source M Extract from *Freedom From Fear* by David M. Kennedy, (Nelson Thornes), 1999, p.130.

The young Americans who went off to war in 1941 came home to a different country. The war had shaken the American people loose and freed them from a decade of economic and social paralysis. The war had flung them around their country and into new forms of life. It was a war that so richly delivered on the promises of the wartime advertisers and politicians that it nearly banished the memories of the Great Depression. At the end of the depressed Thirties, nearly half of white families and almost 90 per cent of black families still lived in poverty. By the war's end unemployment was negligible. Small wonder that Americans chose to remember it as a Good War.

1 What can you learn about the USA in 1943 from Source L?
2 To what extent do you agree with the view of Source M of the impact of the Second World War on the USA?

WORKING TOGETHER

1 Working with a partner, make a copy of the following table and use your notes to complete it.

	Change	Continuity
Economy		
Japanese Americans		
Women		
Black Americans		

2 Having completed the table discuss to what extent the Second World War brought economic and social change.

KEY DATES: THE IMPACT OF THE SECOND WORLD WAR ON THE USA

1940 President Roosevelt ordered the air corps to recruit an all-African American flying unit.

1941 Fair Employment Practices Commission set up.

1941 The March on Washington.

1942 Beginning of the Double V Campaign.

Chapter summary

- Roosevelt aimed to bring about reform, relief and recovery through his first New Deal policies.
- During his first hundred days in office he introduced a series of 'alphabet agencies' such as the CCC, the NRA and the TVA as part of this New Deal.
- These aroused opposition from the right in politics, especially the Republicans who thought he was doing too much and the left who felt he was doing too little.
- His second New Deal also focused on social reform, including the National Labor Relations Act and the Social Security Act.
- This brought opposition from the Supreme Court, which was dominated by Republican judges.
- Roosevelt's attempts to reform the Supreme Court aroused much criticism and were unsuccessful.
- In foreign policy Roosevelt continued the 'Good Neighbor' policy of his predecessor and introduced a series of Neutrality Acts, which confirmed US isolation.
- Increasing rivalry with Japan in the Far East culminated in the attack on Pearl Harbor and the US declaration of war in 1941.
- The Second World War brought further expansion in the role of the Federal Government, which had been extended under Roosevelt and the New Deal.
- The Second World War also brought profound changes to the US economy and had important effects on women, Japanese Americans and African Americans.

▼ Summary diagram: The USA and the Second World War

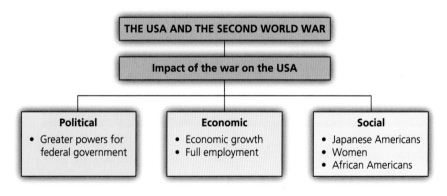

Working on essay technique

Remember the advice from Chapters 1–4 and the summary provided at the end of Chapter 5 (see page 171).

Consider this practice A-level question:

'The main reason for changes in US foreign policy in the years 1920–41 was rivalry with Japan.' Assess the validity of this view.   (25 marks)

This is a complex question, which you can approach in different ways. One way, for example, would be to:

- Identify 'changes in US foreign policy'. In what ways did the foreign policy of the USA change? Greater involvement in Latin America? 'Good Neighbor' policy? Relations with Europe and Japan?
- What were the causes?
  - Economic (expanding markets in Latin America)
  - Political (Japanese threat to US interests in the Far East)
  - Work of individuals (Roosevelt and his support for Britain 1939–41)

Therefore, follow the stages outlined on page 171 at the end of Chapter 5.

This essay title encompasses a wide area, both in breadth and chronologically, covering over 20 years of US foreign policy. There is absolutely no opportunity to describe anything. Events will need to be referred to – but with snippets of precise detail to avoid superficiality.

In particular, this essay allows for complexity, with arguments and counter-arguments, because the interpretation provided in the quotation:

- Gives you a reason for a change – and there are also others to be considered.
- Makes the assumption that there was change – the extent of which can be debated.

This complexity can be reflected in your introduction and/or your conclusion.

The subject also gives you the opportunity to show awareness of different historians not always agreeing. This might be because of:

- different opinions on which factors were most important
- a different emphasis on how the various factors inter-relate.

So, for example, in this question:

- Some historians have been keen to stress the role of Roosevelt himself in bringing about change, possibly exaggerating it.
- It is possible to inter-relate the issues in different ways, e.g., Did the increased Japanese threat in the Far East encourage greater US involvement in the European conflict, 1939–41?

Working on interpretation skills: extended reading

How successful was the New Deal?

Lecturer Dr David Sim provides an analysis of the New Deal in American society.

The New Deal did not restore the United States to full economic health. However, it had a significant impact on the lives of millions of Americans. Franklin Roosevelt's administration provided relief for those who needed it and developed government work schemes to employ millions who would otherwise have remained unemployed. It also introduced   5 measures to shelter the American people from future downturns *and* enacted reforms designed to make those downturns less frequent and less severe. The New Deal, then, was more than a package of policies to mitigate the effects of the Depression.

As economist John Kenneth Galbraith argued, one of the most important   10 features of the New Deal was the development of 'countervailing power' that would produce more stable and equitable economic growth in the future. In particular, New Deal programmes focused on developing the political and economic power of people, groups and regions in order to produce a more socially and geographically balanced recovery. For   15 instance, the 1935 Wagner Act facilitated the formation of trade unions in order to give workers greater bargaining power and, by extension, a greater share of the fruits of their labours. A number of major public works programmes, such as the Rural Electrification Administration, focused on the south and west of the country, which were underdeveloped   20 compared to the wealthier, more heavily industrialised north-east. And the government provided greater security to American citizens by more closely regulating the financial sector, establishing a minimum wage and a maximum workweek and, through the 1935 Social Security Act, providing benefits to the elderly; welfare payments for those with   25 dependent children; and unemployment insurance.

In addition to these longer-term goals, we shouldn't underestimate the New Deal's contribution to an improvement in the American economy during the 1930s. During Herbert Hoover's presidency, more than one-fifth of American banks failed. Roosevelt's early commitment to restructuring   30 and regulating the banks stabilised the sector and secured greater confidence in the country's financial institutions. Public work schemes like the Civilian Works Administration and the Works Progress Administration saw the government directly employ citizens on major public work schemes such as building bridges, airports, highways, and schools. Aside   35 from a second slump in 1937–38, itself produced by a reduction of New Deal expenditure, the economy grew at a remarkable average rate of around ten per cent per year between 1933 and the end of the decade.

Despite all this, we should be wary about thinking about the New Deal as a wholly coherent programme. In practice, Roosevelt's policies were often worked out in a pragmatic fashion and, occasionally, those policies conflicted with one another. Some were ineffectual – others were outright damaging. For example, the National Recovery Administration (NRA), which was the centre-piece of early efforts to combat the Depression, encouraged collusion amongst business owners under the guise of 'self-regulation'. Bureaucratic and unwieldy, it did little to stimulate the economy. Roosevelt himself came to recognise its shortcomings, describing the NRA as 'a mess' and 'pretty wrong'.

We should also be prepared to ask *for whom* the New Deal was a success. Just as different parts of the population felt the impact of the Great Depression in distinct ways, so people's experience of the New Deal was uneven. Roosevelt was a Democrat and in the early twentieth century Democratic candidates for the presidency were heavily dependent upon the Party's southern wing, which was firmly in favour of segregation. Additionally, Roosevelt shared a broader American aversion to expanding the power of the federal government. As such, the New Deal relied heavily on state and local agencies to put national programmes into practice, and so state and local prejudices structured the way that many ordinary citizens experienced New Deal projects. African Americans were often the first to be fired in the downturn, and faced significant discrimination in the labour market; women, too, found themselves losing work as employers prioritised the hiring of white males.

Did the New Deal always produce efficient and desirable outcomes? No. Was there a discriminatory bias in favour of providing welfare and work for white, male citizens? Undoubtedly. Still, the New Deal had a beneficial effect on the American economy in the 1930s. It didn't 'end' the Great Depression – unemployment remained near double-digits until 1940, and it was only with wartime mobilisation that the economy returned to its pre-Depression levels – but it had a demonstrably positive impact in halting the destructive cycle of the early Depression years and in promoting rapid recovery after the Depression bottomed-out in spring 1933.

Dr David Sim is Lecturer in US History at University College London.

ACTIVITY

Having read the essay, answer the following questions.

Comprehension

1 What does the author mean by the following phrases?
   a) 'provided relief for those who needed it' (para 1)
   b) 'in favour of segregation' (para 5)
   c) 'discrimination in the labour market' (para 5)

Evidence

2 Using paragraphs 2 and 3, list the ways in which the author suggests that the New Deal helped Americans and the economy.

Interpretation

3 Using your knowledge from your study of the New Deal, list evidence to challenge the view that the New Deal was to some extent a success.

Evaluation

4 How far do you agree with the author's analysis of the New Deal?
   • The author suggests that the National Recovery Administration was unsuccessful. Were any other New Deal measures a failure?
   • The author also suggests that the New Deal was a success because it brought improvement to the American economy. To what extent can you support and challenge this view?

Post-War America, 1945–60

This chapter covers developments in the USA during the presidencies of Truman and Eisenhower, including post-war affluence and the beginning of the Cold War. It deals with a number of areas:

● The USA and international relations – the Cold War and relations with the USSR and China.
● Economic change and developments: the rise of the consumer society and economic boom.
● The domestic policies of Truman and Eisenhower and post-war reconstruction.
● McCarthyism, civil rights and youth culture.

When you have worked through the chapter and the related activities and exercises, you should have detailed knowledge of all those areas, and you should be able to relate this to the key breadth issues defined as part of your study, in particular how did the role of the USA in world affairs change in the years 1945–60 and how important were ideas and ideology?

For the period covered in this chapter the main issues can be phrased as a question:

To what extent were USA policies at home and abroad influenced by the fear of Communism?

The focus of the issue is on the USA and international relations, especially with the USSR and China.

CHAPTER OVERVIEW

The USA emerged from the Second World War as the richest country on Earth with unparalleled growth and opportunities for expansion. Domestically, American prosperity led to a movement to the suburbs occasioned by affordable housing and a growth in car ownership.

There was, however, a real fear of the spread of Communism. This led to an anti-Communist witch-hunt in the USA led by the House of Un-American Activities Committee (HUAC) and Senator Joseph McCarthy. The period saw the growth of the media, especially television, and a slow improvement in the role and status of ethnic minorities, although few Native Americans gained from the policy of termination. There were significant milestones in African-American civil rights including the 1954 court case *Brown v. Topeka Board of Education*. Moreover, the USA greatly expanded its role abroad as it became involved in a Cold War in Europe and Asia with the USSR and China.

1 International relations, 1945–60

There was a great change in foreign policy in the years after the Second World War as the USA moved away from a policy of isolation to one of containment of Communism in Europe and Asia and became far more involved in world affairs.

The development of the Cold War, 1945–51

Why did the USA become involved in a Cold War in the years 1945–51?

In 1945, the USA had a monopoly on nuclear weapons. By the end of the decade this was to end. While after 1945 there was concern that the USSR was spreading its rule into Eastern Europe, by 1950 there was the realisation that Communism was a worldwide issue. If the USA was to prevent the spread of Communism, it was therefore making a global commitment. China fell to the Communists in 1949. In 1950, the USA became involved in a full-scale war in Korea.

Post-war relations

The USA had been an unlikely ally of the USSR during the Second World War. Once the common enemy of Nazi Germany was defeated, their differences began to emerge. The Soviet leader, Stalin, could argue that his country had suffered grievously during the war: possibly as many as 27 million dead, with 25 million homeless and 6 million buildings destroyed. Nazi Germany, with whom it had a treaty of non-aggression, had invaded the USSR without warning. Nine of its fifteen republics had been fought over during the war. The USSR wanted the security of knowing that it could not be attacked without warning again. The best way to ensure this was to control its neighbours, so that they might act as a buffer zone between the USSR and the rest of Europe. By invading Eastern European countries such as Poland in the latter stages of the war, it demonstrated that it would maintain a considerable influence on them in the future.

At a series of meetings with Allied leaders towards the end of the war, Stalin presented this as a done deal. At Yalta in February 1945, Roosevelt, visibly ill, seemed to sympathise with Stalin. It was agreed, for example, that Germany should be divided and forced to pay war reparations, half of which would go to the USSR. The USSR should gain land from Poland and in turn Poland should be compensated with land from Germany.

Truman

In April, Roosevelt died. His successor, Harry S. Truman, seemed more critical of Stalin. Unlike Roosevelt, and indeed Churchill, Truman had not had the experience of co-operating with Stalin to defeat a common enemy. The USA had not suffered during the War in any way commensurate with the USSR. It had endured less than two per cent of the human losses of the USSR. Roosevelt had considered this fact in his responses to Soviet demands; Truman did not. The next meeting at Potsdam in July, in which Britain also had a new leader, was less amicable although the Yalta agreements were confirmed. In an extensive poll, 50 per cent of Americans still felt that wartime co-operation between the two superpowers should continue.

By this time Stalin was imposing Communist regimes on many of the countries 'liberated' from Nazi influence or occupied by the Soviets. In Romania, for example, at a meeting with the Soviet deputy foreign minister, the King was given two hours to introduce a pro-Communist government.

NOTE-MAKING

Using the 1–2 method (see page x) make notes on the following topics:
- The development of the Cold War
- The Truman Doctrine and Marshall Plan
- The Berlin Airlift
- The Korean War

While Truman was clearly worried about this forcing of Communism on Eastern European countries, he could do little about what had already happened in areas where there were still Soviet armies of occupation. However, he was increasingly concerned that Communism should not spread to countries not currently under Soviet control.

To Truman it seemed that the USSR was seeking not just to protect its borders from any future invasion, but rather to control the whole of Europe. In 1946, Winston Churchill, visiting Fulton, Missouri, spoke of an Iron Curtain descending through the middle of Europe. This seemed even more pertinent when the Soviets forced Czechoslovakia to adopt Communism in 1948. Countries such as Romania, Poland, Hungary, Bulgaria and Yugoslavia were now governed by Communists. Only Greece, where a civil war was taking place between Communist and non-Communist forces, held out against Soviet dominance in Eastern Europe. People said a state of Cold War had developed between the USA and USSR.

> **Iron Curtain** – An imaginary border between Communist and non-Communist countries. It refers to the political, military and ideological barrier erected by the Soviet Union after the Second World War with the 'iron' a reference to the strength of this barrier.
>
> **Cold War** – Confrontation without actually directly fighting each other.

The Truman Doctrine

In 1947, Truman had offered the support of the USA to countries struggling against Communism. In a speech Truman said:

'I believe that it must be the policy of the United States to support peoples who resist being enslaved by armed minorities or by outside pressure. I believe that we must help free peoples to work out their own destiny in their own way'.

The policy was known as the Truman Doctrine or containment because it seemed to imply the USA would stem the spread of Communism. The doctrine was first applied in Greece to give aid to the non-Communist forces. Greece did not become Communist; hence the first intervention appeared successful.

Marshall Aid

In the following year the USA went further, offering a $13 billion package to help European countries to recover from the effects of the Second World War. This was Marshall Aid, named after the US Secretary of State General George Marshall. A conference of 22 nations was set up to assess the economic needs of the affected countries. The USSR did not attend and refused permission for countries under its sphere of influence to do so. Eventually sixteen Western European nations formed the Organisation of European Economic Cooperation (OEEC) to spend this money. The aid was in part intended to help countries to recover their prosperity so that Communism would lose any appeal. The aid did help Western European countries to recover economically and fears of Communism in countries such as Italy and France receded.

In the ensuing years, however, two crises emerged in which direct confrontation between the USA and USSR seemed likely.

Berlin Airlift 1948–49

Germany had been divided into four zones of occupation following the end of the war. The capital, Berlin, was also divided although it physically lay within the Soviet zone. The Western occupying powers, the USA, Britain and France, relied on Soviet goodwill to travel through its zone to their sectors in Berlin. By 1948, it was clear that the three Western sectors were co-operating and recovery was well on the way through Marshall Aid. In contrast, the Soviet zone remained poor. Increasingly, it was having Communism imposed upon it.

In June 1948, the Western zones introduced a new common currency, the Deutschmark. When their leaders tried to introduce it into their sectors of Berlin, Stalin ordered all transport links with the West cut. He believed he could blockade Berlin into accepting Communist rule and therefore make the capital part of the future Communist East German state.

In retaliation Britain and the USA organised an airlift of essential supplies to the city under siege. By March 1949, 8,000 tons of supplies per day were being delivered despite Soviet threats to the aircraft, which were of course flying through Communist-controlled airspace. On 9 May, Stalin called off the blockade and things returned to normal. It appeared that in the first great confrontation, the USA had won.

Source A From a speech by Truman in 1949.

We refused to be forced out of the city of Berlin. We demonstrated to the people of Europe that we would act and act resolutely, when their freedom was threatened. Politically it brought the people of western Europe closer to us. The Berlin blockade was a move to test our ability and our will to resist.

Source B The Soviet version of the crisis, written in 1977.

The crisis was planned in Washington behind a smokescreen of anti-Soviet propaganda. In 1948 there was danger of war. The conduct of the western powers risked bloody incidents. The self-blockade of the western powers hit the West Berlin population with harshness. The people were freezing and starving. In the Spring of 1949 the USA was forced to yield. Their war plans had come to nothing, because of the conduct of the Soviet Union.

1 What differences are there between Sources A and B in their views of the Berlin Crisis?

2 Why do you think they are so different?

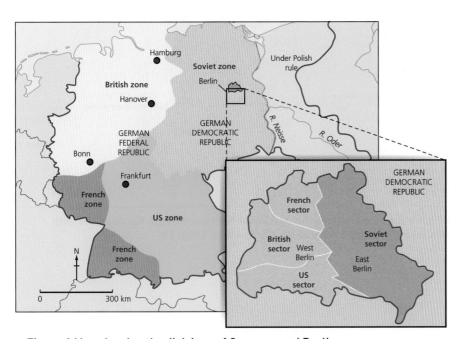

▲ **Figure 1** Map showing the divisions of Germany and Berlin.

NATO

The Berlin Crisis had confirmed Truman's commitment to containment in Europe and highlighted the Soviet threat to Western Europe. Western European states, even joined together, were no match for the Soviet Union and needed the formal support of the USA. In April 1949, the North Atlantic Treaty Organization (NATO) was signed. Although a defensive alliance, its main purpose was to prevent Soviet expansion.

The countries agreed that an armed attack against one or more of them in Europe or North America would be considered an attack against them all (see Warsaw Pact, page 221).

Korean War 1950–53

Korea is a country in Asia that shares a border with both the USSR and China. Following the Second World War it was divided into North and South with a border at the 38th parallel (a line of latitude). While the government of the South supported the USA, that of the North was Communist and hostile. In March 1950, North Korea invaded the South. The UN sent forces to stop this invasion; the vast majority were American under an American Commander, General Douglas MacArthur.

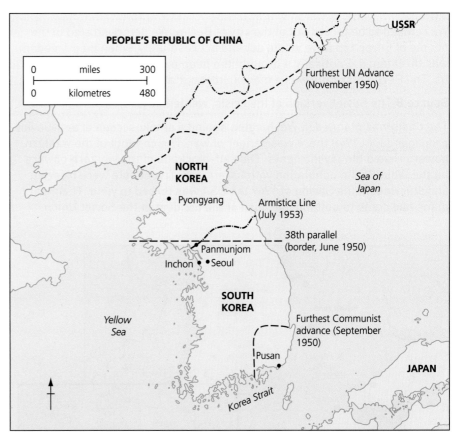

▲ **Figure 2** A map showing the division of North and South Korea by the 38th parallel and the key events of the Korean War, 1950–53.

UN forces succeeded in liberating South Korea. However, on MacArthur's urging, they then went on to invade the North, ignoring China's warnings of the consequences. President Truman faced tremendous hostility within the USA when he fired MacArthur for going beyond his instructions. To many it seemed he was soft on Communism. Some felt UN troops should have finished off North Korea and then invaded China itself to reverse the Communist threat.

In the meantime, China became involved in the war, sending thousands of troops to help the North Koreans. The war effectively became a stalemate for three years. The USA alone lost 27,000 troops and one million Korean civilians died. In 1953, a peace of sorts was agreed in which Korea remained divided into a Communist North and non-Communist South. It is known now that the Soviets secretly sent air forces to help the North Koreans. Had this been known at the time, the consequences could have been profound, with the confrontation between the USA and the USSR possibly spreading to Europe.

Results of war

The USA had learned that Communism was a global issue and if they were to prevent its spread then a global commitment was necessary. In the early 1950s, President Eisenhower spoke of the domino theory. While the policy may appear incredibly simplistic, it was nevertheless a deeply held view and was later used to justify full-scale US involvement in the Vietnam War.

In its second phase, the war had been in effect a Sino–American war. Sino–American hostility was greatly increased, and the United States gave increased support to Taiwan. Moreover, it helped to sustain McCarthyism and generally worsened the Cold War antagonism. However, the three leading powers showed that they were unwilling to risk World War III. The sacking of MacArthur signalled that America planned to stick to containment.

> **Domino theory** – The belief that if one state fell to Communism it would be quickly followed by neighbouring states.

> **WORKING TOGETHER**
>
> 1 Put together a flow chart showing how the Cold War developed in the years 1945–53.
> 2 To what extent do you agree that the main reason for US involvement in the Cold War was the attitude of Truman?

KEY DATES: THE DEVELOPMENT OF THE COLD WAR, 1945–51

1947 Truman Doctrine and Marshall Plan.

1948 Beginning of the Berlin Crisis.

1949 Setting up of NATO.

1950 Outbreak of Korean War.

Foreign policy under Eisenhower

To what extent was there a thaw in the Cold War during Eisenhower's presidency?

President Eisenhower and his Secretary of State, John Foster Dulles, appeared to be real 'Cold Warriors'. They had attacked Truman and the Democrats for being 'soft on Communists' in the presidential election campaign of 1952. America was very much in the grip of McCarthyism (see page 228) and Eisenhower and Dulles talked about a 'roll back' (of Communism) and 'massive retaliation' as they planned to base American defence on nuclear weaponry.

Eisenhower and Khrushchev

In 1955, Nikita Khrushchev succeeded Stalin as leader of the Soviet Union. His response to Eisenhower was a mixture of conciliation and provocation. He tried to stir up the West Europeans to halt German rearmament and to win friends in the Middle East. In order to tighten the Soviet bloc militarily, he created the Warsaw Pact.

> **NOTE-MAKING**
>
> Using bullet points (see page x) make notes on the key features of Eisenhower's foreign policy.

Warsaw Pact

Stalin saw NATO as an 'aggressive alliance' aimed against the Soviet Union. Within six years, in 1955, the Soviet Union had set up its own rival organisation known as the Warsaw Pact. It was a military alliance of eight nations headed by the Soviet Union and was designed to counter the threat of NATO. Members were to support each other if attacked. A joint command structure was set up under the Soviet Supreme Commander.

Espionage – Spying.

On the other hand, Khrushchev returned a naval base to Finland and decreased the Red Army by half a million men. He agreed to talks on agriculture and the peaceful use of atomic energy with the USA. In May 1955, he signed the Austrian peace treaty, under which the four occupying powers at last got out of Austria, which became an independent and neutral state. The Soviet Union had thus surrendered territory for the first time since the Second World War.

However, Eisenhower was not convinced by these policies, believing that this was simply a new style of leadership rather than a change in their basic aim of expansion. This seemed to be confirmed by events in Hungary.

Hungary

In 1956, Khrushchev began a policy of relaxing the controls Stalin had imposed on Eastern Europe. However, when moderate Communists in Hungary, led by Imre Nagy, threatened to leave the Warsaw Pact, Khrushchev sent in tanks to quell the rebellion. Nagy was removed and shot, and a more acceptable leader, Janos Kadar, took over. In spite of appeals by the rebels, the US government did not intervene. A more moderate government in Hungary might have helped the USA 'contain' the Soviet Union, but the risks of intervention were thought to be too high. Moreover, the USA was preoccupied with the Suez crisis (see below).

Berlin

Khrushchev faced problems over Germany. First, the West refused to recognise the legitimacy of the East German state. Secondly, America, Britain and France used West Berlin for espionage and sabotage. Khrushchev tried to force the West to recognise East Germany, by threatening to give East Germany control of the West's access routes to West Berlin. Then he gave the West an ultimatum that they must do something about West Berlin within six months, or face dire consequences (November 1958). However, when it became clear that the West would stand firm, Khrushchev backed down in March 1959.

Khrushchev and Eisenhower had their first ever summit meeting in September 1959. Although the atmosphere was surprisingly relaxed, they made no progress on Berlin. Khrushchev hoped for a Berlin agreement at the Paris summit in May 1960. However, this summit failed as, just before the meeting, the Soviet Union shot down a U-2 American spy-plane and captured the pilot, Gary Powers. Eisenhower was forced to admit the plane's intent and Khrushchev refused to attend the summit.

Suez

In July 1956, the Egyptian leader, Gamal Nasser, took control of the Suez Canal, the important trade waterway that gave a quicker route from the Mediterranean to the Indian Ocean. Britain and France were particularly angered and with Israel's help, invaded the Canal Zone. They were not supported by the USA who forced them to withdraw by the use of financial sanctions. Eisenhower wanted to keep in with the Arab nations, believing the Western world needed their oil and friendship against the Communist bloc. In addition, Eisenhower was furious that Britain, France and Israel had acted without keeping him informed.

Results of the Suez crisis

The crisis illustrated that Britain and France were no longer world powers and were heavily dependent on the USA. Moreover, it increased American involvement in the Middle East. In January 1957, Eisenhower asked Congress for military and economic aid for any Middle East country that was threatened by aggression or subversion. This became known as the Eisenhower Doctrine and was an extension of containment to the Middle East. However, Egypt and Syria turned increasingly to the USSR, as the Anglo–French actions had reminded them of the Western 'colonial' mentality. Both the USA and the USSR gave and/or sold increasing amounts of armaments to their allies in this area.

Source C From *A People and a Nation*, 6th edn, by M. B. Norton et al., (Houghton Mifflin), 2001, p.838.

Partisan Democrats promoted an image of Eisenhower as a bumbling, passive, aging hero. Eisenhower did not always stay abreast of issues because he chose to delegate authority to others, and he seemed stuck in tired views just when the international system was becoming more fluid. Without doubt, though, the president commanded the policy-making process and tamed the more hawkish proposals of Vice-President Richard Nixon and the Secretary of State, John Foster Dulles.

> What can you learn about Eisenhower from Source C?

China, 1949–60

The USA was involved in the Chinese Civil War in the years 1945–49. The USA gave aid to Chiang Kai-shek and the Chinese Nationalists in their struggle against Mao and the Chinese Communist Party (CCP). However, by 1949 the USA had abandoned Chiang, who fled with thousands of followers to the island of Taiwan. America was unhappy with Mao's success in late 1949, fearing that other Asian countries might follow China's lead.

The United States refused to formally recognise the People's Republic of China (PRC) and, instead, the USA maintained diplomatic relations with the Republic of China government in Taiwan, recognising it as the sole legitimate government of China. After the Civil War, the USA seemed to lose interest in China. However, the Korean War changed the US attitude. Truman sent the US Seventh Fleet to the Taiwan Straits and relations with China remained cool during the presidency of Eisenhower.

- The USA hated Communism and was convinced that Beijing was Moscow's puppet. Dulles, the US Secretary of State under Eisenhower, insisted that Chinese Communism was more threatening than Soviet Communism. China had more people and greater cultural influence and prestige in Asia. There were major Chinese minorities in most nations in Asia and other Asian nations were relatively weak.
- Mao hated capitalism, felt that America was imperialistic and resented American aid to Chiang during and after the Civil War.
- The USA interpreted the Korean War as a sign that Chinese-sponsored Communism was expansionist and threatened US security. It convinced America that China was determined to aid revolutions throughout the world.
- China interpreted the Korean War as a sign that the USA was aggressive, wanted to get a foothold on the Asian mainland and was likely to attack China itself.

Relations continued to deteriorate after the Korean War. The USA put a trade embargo on China and kept it out of the United Nations, as well as establishing military bases in Taiwan. Mao was infuriated by the US–Taiwan Defence Treaty, which was signed in 1954. In the following year, Communist China shelled the Chinese Nationalist islands of Quemoy and Matsu, which were very close to the Chinese mainland. Eisenhower hinted in public that he was considering the use of atomic weapons to protect Taiwan. Mao, furious and humiliated, backed down. There was a similar crisis in 1958 over the same two islands. Once again the USA threatened military action and Mao backed down.

> **WORKING TOGETHER**
>
> Working with a partner decide whether there was a thaw in the Cold War under Eisenhower.
> - One of you should find evidence of a thaw in relations.
> - The other should look for evidence of relations remaining 'cold'.
> - Share your findings.
>
> Overall, do you agree with the view that there was a thaw in the Cold War under Eisenhower?

KEY DATES: FOREIGN POLICY UNDER EISENHOWER

1956 The Soviet invasion of Hungary.

1956 The Suez crisis.

1960 U-2 incident and Paris summit.

NOTE-MAKING

Create two sets of notes, one headed 'atomic weapons' and the other 'defence spending'. Compare your notes with those of a partner and expand upon what each of you has written.

WORKING TOGETHER

During the years 1945–60 relations between the USA and the Soviet Union generally worsened. Working as a class, suggest reasons why relations worsened in these years. To help you, you could make use of the flow chart you made on the early Cold War (page 213).

Military–industrial complex – A network of individuals and institutions involved in the production of weapons and military technologies.

KEY DATES: THE ARMS RACE

1949 The Soviet Union tested its first atomic bomb.

1952 The USA tested its first hydrogen bomb.

1953 The Soviet Union tested its first hydrogen bomb.

The arms race

Why did the USA become involved in an arms race in the years 1945–60?

In the years following the Second World War the USA became involved in an arms race, particularly with the Soviet Union, to develop ever more powerful weapons, which worsened relations between the two superpowers during the Cold War.

Atomic weapons

Stalin had been shocked in 1945 by the news that the USA had tested its first atomic bomb. The Soviet atomic research programme was transformed over the next few years, partly due to the use of Soviet spies in the USA who were able to find out American atomic secrets. In 1949, the USSR exploded its first nuclear weapon. The USA had therefore lost its monopoly on atomic weapons. President Truman said the USA would seek to develop a hydrogen bomb, with as much as a thousand times the power of an atomic bomb. When this weapon was finally tested in Bikini Atoll in March 1954, both sides were entering into an arms race and developing weapons of mass destruction that could, if used, have led to the end of the world.

Eisenhower inherited the hydrogen bomb from Truman. Within a year (1953) the Soviets had caught up. Each superpower wanted more and better atomic weaponry than the other. The first American surface-to-surface ballistic missiles were tested in 1947. When the USSR's long-range Inter-Continental Ballistic Missile (ICBM) was operational a few weeks before the American ICBM, America was humiliated. In 1954, America's first nuclear-propelled submarine was operational and, in 1960, America tested a missile fired from a submerged submarine to hit any target on the globe. At this point, the Soviet navy was years behind the American navy.

Military spending

The prospect of other countries developing nuclear weapons meant the USA could be attacked. As a result the military–industrial complex was to develop, with defence spending between $40 to $50 billion per year in the 1950s and 90 per cent of foreign aid to US allies going on military spending.

Billions of dollars were spent on maintaining a military presence throughout Western Europe and South-east Asia, equipping the armed forces, and weapons research and development. Defence establishments were built in otherwise poor areas such as the Southern states; often they were to be found in the areas represented by politicians on the appropriate committees in Congress. Desert areas in Arizona and New Mexico became centres for weapons testing. Many firms followed the military to their new bases, being awarded lucrative contracts to provide weapons, research and equipment. Some historians have argued that this post-war boom in military spending helped to smooth out the former economic inequalities within the USA. California, in particular, benefited from military contracts. One of the knock-on effects was the development of an industry in high technology that was to see it become the centre of the computer industry; the first IBM computer was introduced in 1953.

2 The age of affluence

The USA emerged from the Second World War as the richest country on Earth with unparalleled growth and opportunities for expansion. The Federal Government gave grants to veterans through the GI Bill of Rights, and opportunities abounded. While some groups feared the prosperity might not last and saved their money, before long these concerns had diminished and a consumer boom developed. This was fuelled by the movement to the suburbs occasioned by affordable housing and the growth in car ownership.

The economy

Why did the USA experience prosperity in the years after the Second World War?

The economic problems that often follow wars were not repeated in the USA in 1945. As we saw in Chapter 6, the US economy grew significantly during the war. Gross National Product (GNP) had risen 35 per cent since 1941. The USA had seven per cent of the world's population but possessed 42 per cent of global income.

Post-war prosperity

Per capita income at $1,450 was almost twice as high as Great Britain. Urban Americans consumed about 3,000 calories per day, about 50 per cent more than most people in Western Europe. The federal government spent more – $36.5 billion in 1948, admittedly significantly less than the $92.2 billion expended in 1945 but considerably more than the $9.4 billion of 1939. This figure was to rise significantly in 1950 with the onset of the Korean War and a massive defence budget in the 1950s and beyond. States, meanwhile, spent more on roads and schools.

Economic expansion created greater employment opportunities in many industries, for example aircraft production, chemicals and electrical goods. As consumer tastes changed, processed food production made huge gains. Tobacco companies made vast profits and employed many people. As we will see, there was a huge migration to centres of plentiful employment.

Many Americans remembered the pre-war Depression, however, and, despite the prosperity, many on average earnings of about $3,000 per annum or below tended to live carefully and save where they could. While consumption rose it was not necessarily conspicuous or wasteful – at least not until, by the late 1940s, it became apparent that the prosperity was going to last. Then the consumer boom gathered apace.

One should note, too, that not all areas of the USA were equally prosperous. Some had a lot of catching up to do. These were mainly in the poorer areas of cities and the South. In 1947, 33 per cent of US homes lacked running water and 40 per cent flush toilets. Many families lived in rented accommodation and could hardly have imagined owning their own property. It was a measure of economic success that by 1960 so many were able to take these things for granted and home ownership had risen from 55 per cent in 1950 to 62 per cent ten years later.

Growing mobility

The spectacular growth of the car industry led to much greater mobility and the development of suburbs. This meant that many Americans no longer needed

NOTE-MAKING

Using bullet points (see page x) make notes on key developments in the economy in the years 1945–60. Your main side headings should be 'post-war prosperity' and 'the growth of the car industry'.

Per capita income – A measure of the amount of money that is being earned per person in a certain country.

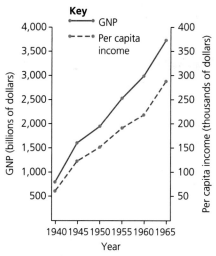

▲ **Figure 3** A graph showing GNP and per capita income, 1940–65.

GI Bill of Rights

The Government had passed the GI Bill of Rights (also known as the Selective Servicemen's Readjustment Act) in 1944 offering grants to veterans to improve their education, learn new skills or set up businesses. Eight million veterans took advantage of this measure. All former combatants were to receive $20 per week while looking for work. In fact, less than twenty per cent of the money set aside for this was actually distributed because so many jobs were available for returning veterans. Universities expanded considerably to accept former servicemen whose fees were paid by the Government. The University of Syracuse, for example, trebled its number of students. The GI Bill also offered low-interest home loans that allowed ex-servicemen and their families to move to new houses in the suburbs.

WORKING TOGETHER

Economic growth was also due to the 'baby boom', the term used to describe the rapid increase in the birth rate after 1945. Working in a group, carry out further online research on the reasons for and effects of this baby boom.

KEY DATES: THE ECONOMY

1944 The Government passed the GI Bill of Rights.

1952 The first Holiday Inn opened between Memphis and Nashville in Tennessee.

1955 Des Moines, Idaho, saw the opening of the first McDonald's.

1956 The Interstate Highway Act.

---

to live in crowded towns and cities. The home became very important in terms of privacy and offering a comfortable lifestyle. Even more significantly, it came to symbolise the prosperity of ordinary people because they were owner-occupiers. One day, when the mortgage was paid off, it would be theirs. They weren't spending their wages on rent but investing it in bricks and mortar. It was the lynchpin of the development of the 1950s middle-class family.

Growth of the car industry

Sales of new cars rose from 69,500 in 1945 to 6.7 million by 1950. The vast majority were US-made; in 1950 there were only 16,000 foreign cars on US roads. Clearly this led to a great expansion in the car industry, dominated by the 'Big Three' – Ford, General Motors and Chrysler. Cars seemed to symbolise the confidence of the age – they were sleek, 'gas-guzzling', big and colourful. In 1958, Ford produced a 5.79-metre-long Lincoln model. Choice was paramount, too. In 1961, there were 350 different models on sale. They weren't cheap – a new Chrysler cost $1,300 or about 40 per cent of the average family income – but most were bought on credit. The number of two-car families doubled between 1951 and 1958. As a result, there were more cars in Los Angeles than in the whole of Asia and General Motors was wealthier than Belgium in terms of GDP.

The growth of car ownership also helped develop the facilities associated with them such as roadside hotels, motels, gas stations and garages. The first Holiday Inn opened in 1952 between Memphis and Nashville in Tennessee. Des Moines, Idaho, saw the first McDonald's in April 1955; by 1960, 228 McDonald's restaurants enjoyed annual sales of $37 million.

Road building itself was given a major boost by the 1956 Interstate Highway Act, which boosted federal subsidies for road building and developed the infrastructure of US highways. It created a 41,000-mile system, mainly of dual carriageway, designed to eliminate unsafe roads, bottlenecks and other factors that impeded free traffic movement. Interestingly, the bill was intended to create 'a national system of interstate and defence highways' to facilitate speedy evacuation in the event of nuclear attack. However, road building developments also signified the demise of public transport in the USA. Passenger services on railroads lost an average $700 million per year by the mid-1950s (although this was partly due to the growth of long-distance air travel).

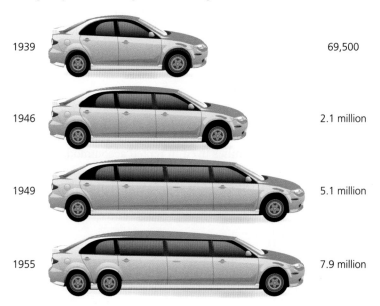

1939	69,500
1946	2.1 million
1949	5.1 million
1955	7.9 million

▲ Figure 4 Growth in car ownership in the USA from 1939 to 1955.

Social change

To what extent did the lifestyle of Americans change in the 1940s and 1950s?

This period saw the media, including the growing television network, applauding the nuclear family as the American ideal. It often depicted women simply as homemakers and excluded ethnic groups except as stereotypes. This was slow to change. There were lots of young people – 'baby boomers' – and a market reflecting their interests began to develop.

Growth of suburbs

House construction away from urban centres had begun during the war years but expanded rapidly in the years thereafter. In 1944, 114,000 new family homes were built, rising to 1.7 million in 1950. In the decade following 1945, 15 million houses were built mainly for private purchase. The percentage of Americans owning their own homes rose from 50 per cent in 1945 to 60 per cent by 1960. Many acquired mortgages through the government-sponsored Federal Housing Administration or Veterans' Administration. These offered mortgages of up to 90 per cent of the cost price and interest rates as low as four per cent.

The percentage of people living in suburbs grew from seventeen per cent in 1920 to 33 per cent by 1960. Critics complained that these suburbs all looked the same and lacked variety. Cinema and restaurant managers in urban centres complained of a lack of business as people stayed home. Too often conditions deteriorated in residential inner-city areas as they were left to the poor, often members of ethnic minorities, and they lost funding due to the 'flight of the middle classes' who would have paid taxes to live there. The suburbs, meanwhile, saw the development of new facilities such as the shopping mall. In 1946 there were eight, and over 4,000 by the late 1950s. Here everything could be purchased in one centre arrived at by car. These developments spelled disaster for many small shopkeepers. The development of the suburbs as a result of increased prosperity and car ownership effectively changed the lives of millions of ordinary Americans forever.

The consumer society

The growth of suburbs and increasing confidence that the prosperity was here to stay led to a huge consumer boom. Wages generally rose. By 1953, the average family's annual income had reached $4,011. This meant many people had money to spend – in fact their disposable income rose on average by seventeen per cent.

The consumer boom

There was a rapid expansion in consumer items fuelled by incessant advertising – itself a multi-billion dollar industry rising from $6 billion in 1950 to over $13 billion by 1963. By 1960, there were over 50 million televisions in the USA. Due to the boom in population, baby clothes and nappies were in particular demand. By 1957, nappies alone became a $50 million per year industry. In 1980, historian Landon Jones wrote, 'the cry of the baby was heard across the land' as their numbers grew. Four million babies were born each year between 1954 and 1964. In 1964 40 per cent of the population had been born before 1946.

NOTE-MAKING

Your notes should focus on the main aspects: consumer society, the growth of the suburbs, the position of women and cultural change. Make notes on each development and compare those of a partner, then expand upon what each of you has written.

Levitt houses

Levitt houses were among the most famous of suburban dwellings. William Levitt (1907–94) has variously been called the 'king' or the 'inventor of suburbia'. While this is going too far, he nevertheless was instrumental in the development of cheap, affordable housing. Levitt was born into a family building firm that operated in the New York area. During the war he served in the 'seabees' or engineers and, after leaving the forces, simply applied the techniques of building military installations he had learned during the war to commercial construction. His houses came in 27 separate parts to be constructed on site. The parts themselves were manufactured in factories using the techniques of mass production. Before the war the average builder had constructed five houses per year; in 1947, Levitt built 2,000 on a site in Long Island where the post-war housing shortage had been so intense that some people were living in coal sheds. By 1951, this original Levittown had grown to 17,000 homes in 24.283 square kilometres, housing 82,000 people.

This was possibly the golden age of the American nuclear family. The divorce rate fell from 17.9 per 1,000 marriages in 1946 to 9.6 by 1953. The average age of marriage for females fell from 21.5 years in 1940 to 20.1 by 1956 and within seven months of marriage most women were pregnant.

The amount of leisure time rose, too. One commentator reported that by 1956 many Americans were spending more time watching television than actually working for pay. They were filling their homes with labour-saving devices. By 1951, 90 per cent of American families had fridges and 75 per cent possessed washing machines and telephones – often paid for with credit. The amount of debt increased from $5.7 billion in 1945 to $56.1 billion by 1960. The first Diners' Club cards were introduced in 1950 – made of cardboard. They became plastic in 1955. American Express dates from 1958. Among the new products were frozen and convenience food and TV dinners, long-playing records, electric clothes dryers and Polaroid cameras. All saved time and effort. The introduction of plastics and artificial fibres meant it was easier to keep items clean.

Consumption rocketed. With six per cent of the world's population in the early 1950s, the USA consumed a staggering 33 per cent of all the goods in the world and controlled 66 per cent of the world's productive capacity. On a more basic level, just the consumption of hot dogs increased from 750 million in 1950 to 2 billion by 1960. A famous photograph showed a typical family with the two and a half tons of food they consumed yearly, including 300lb beef, 31 chickens and 8.5 gallons of ice cream. Their weekly budget for this amount was $25.

While at first many looked to the example of the 1920s and worried that the prosperity may not continue, as the 1950s developed there seemed no end to the post-war boom and so more and more Americans felt confident that this time it would last. With such confidence at home, the threat most people feared to their way of life was the influence of the USSR, the new foreign enemy.

Source D From *A Troubled Feast, American Society since 1945* by William E. Leuchtenberg, (Little Brown), 1973.

When the Paris Editor of the 'U.S. News and World Report' came home to the United States in 1960 after twelve years abroad, he was astonished at the changes. He had been living in France where only one family in ten had a bath tub with hot running water and was coming home to a country where, in some sections of California, at least one family in ten owned a swimming pool. With larger incomes than ever before, there were, for consumers, shopping precincts with piped music, supermarkets with row on row of brilliantly coloured cartons. A Swiss department store chain told its customers 'live like an American'.

Source E Part of a speech by Adlai Stevenson, a Democrat Senator, in 1952.

How can we talk about prosperity to the sick who cannot afford proper medical care? How can we talk about prosperity to the hundreds of thousands who can find no decent place to live at prices they can afford? And how can we talk about prosperity to a share-cropper living on worn-out land, or to city dwellers packed six to a room in a unit tenement with a garbage-strewn alley for their children's playground? To these people, national prosperity is a mockery – to the eleven million families in this nation with incomes of less than $2,000 a year.

Figure 5 A table comparing the percentage of American families owning consumer goods in 1950 and 1956.

	Cars	Televisions	Refrigerators	Washing machines
1950	60.0	26.4	86.4	71.9
1956	73.0	81.0	96.0	86.8

220

Study Sources D and E. What differences are there in their views of US society in the 1950s?

The position of women

The Second World War had mixed results for the position of women. They had shown they could do jobs that traditionally had been male-dominated. Four US states made equal pay for women compulsory, while other states tried to protect women from discrimination in their jobs. In 1940, women made up 19 per cent of the workforce. This had risen to 28.8 per cent ten years later. Nevertheless, at the end of the war the majority of women willingly gave up their wartime jobs and returned to their role as mothers and wives and their traditional 'female' jobs.

Stereotyping

The media appeared to both create and develop the stereotype of women as homemakers. Commentators cite the many periodicals aimed at women such as *Ladies' Home Journal* and *McCall's*, which were full of articles on cooking, fashion, homecare and how to keep your husband happy. Dr Spock, whose hugely influential books on childcare sold over a million copies every year throughout the 1950s, emphasised the need for a mother's presence and love. Adverts focused on the woman as housewife and mother. As with TV, the image the media portrayed was usually of white and middle-class women; working-class and ethnic minority women did not feature significantly. Many women's magazines featured articles that emphasised the domestic role of women, although not all would go so far as Mrs Dale Carnegie, who asserted in *McCall's* magazine in 1954 that there is 'simply no room for split-level thinking – or doing – when Mr and Mrs set their sights on a happy home, a host of friends and a bright future through success in HIS job'.

The reality behind the stereotype may be more complex. While periodicals may have promoted a particular message, we have little idea how effectively they informed actual relationships. Writing in 2000, historian Nancy Walker has shown that even the persuasive view of the periodicals is simplistic. *Ladies' Home Journal*, for example, ran a series of articles 'How America lives', which did show the wide ethnic and class mix. She argues that the periodicals reflected the complexities of life more than they reinforced stereotypes. The magazine *Redbook*, for example, ran a $500 prize competition in 1960 inviting readers to write on 'Why You Feel Trapped'. They received 24,000 entries. While many women may have accepted a largely domestic role, many others either did not or felt frustrated and unfulfilled by it; the seeds were being sown here for the women's liberation movement of the 1960s.

Women and work

Feminist Betty Friedan conducted research into the subsequent careers of former students of the exclusive all-female Smith College in 1957 and found that 89 per cent were homemakers. However, we should remember that her well-educated, wealthy respondents were hardly typical of women in the USA. Despite the stereotype of women staying in the home, the percentage of women in the labour force did increase in the 1950s from 33.8 per cent in 1950 to 37.8 per cent by the end of the decade. Opportunities for jobs with career advancement prospects had not noticeably increased. Unions did not generally favour women in the workforce – although they did support a campaign for better working conditions for waitresses.

The biggest increase of women in work was among those who were married – from 36 per cent in 1940 to 60 per cent by 1960. This may have been necessary to help make ends meet. Many commentators have shown that the consumer culture always left people wanting more – the latest model, the newest gadget – and advertising was so persuasive that luxury items became, in many people's

WORKING TOGETHER

1 Working with a partner make a copy of and complete the following table. One of you should complete the column on progress and the other should complete the column on continuity. Compare your findings.

Progress for women, 1945–60	Continuity for women, 1945–60

2 To what extent do you think that the position of women changed in these years?

view, necessities. Writing in 1996, historian James T. Patterson has concluded that many women in the 1950s sought jobs more than careers, in order to supplement the family income. Clearly, however, this does not negate the effort many were prepared to make to rise in the profession of their choice.

However, women who went out to work instead of getting married were treated with great suspicion by the rest of society. Indeed, one very influential book, *Modern Woman: the Lost Sex*, actually blamed many of the social problems of the 1950s, such as teenage drinking and delinquency, on career women.

In the 1950s, growing numbers of women, especially from middle-class backgrounds, began to challenge their traditional role as they became increasingly frustrated with life as a housewife. There was more to life than bringing up children and looking after their husbands. Many female teenagers were strongly influenced by the greater freedom of the 'swinging sixties' which, in turn, encouraged them to challenge traditional attitudes and roles.

Women were now much better educated so they could have a professional career. In 1950, there were 721,000 women at university. By 1960, this had reached 1.3 million. However, many of these had a very limited choice of career because, once they married, they were expected to devote their energies to their husband and children. Many became increasingly bored and frustrated with life as a suburban housewife.

Cultural change

Popular culture in the USA of the second half of the twentieth century was greatly influenced by the cinema and the increasing popularity of television.

The cinema

The cinema remained popular but less so than the inter-war years because of the influence of television. Average weekly cinema attendances fell from 90 million a week in 1946 to 47 million ten years later. However, the drive-in cinema, first opened in the 1930s, became very popular in the 1950s and early 1960s, particularly in rural areas, with some 4,000 drive-ins spreading across the United States. Among its advantages was the fact that a family with a baby could take care of their child while watching a movie, while teenagers with access to autos found drive-ins ideal for dates. In the 1950s, the greater privacy afforded to patrons gave drive-ins a reputation as immoral, and they were labelled 'passion pits' in the media.

In the period following the Second World War, young people wanted new and exciting symbols of rebellion. Hollywood responded to audience demands – the late 1940s and 1950s saw the rise of the anti-hero, with stars like newcomers James Dean, Paul Newman and Marlon Brando replacing more 'proper' actors like Tyrone Power, Van Johnson and Robert Taylor.

The growing power of television

In 1954, water officials in the city of Toledo, Ohio began to investigate why there seemed to be huge upsurges in demand during random three-minute periods each evening. They solved the mystery when they correlated the mass flushing of toilets with commercial breaks on TV. By this time television was a national phenomenon. The number of sets had risen from 60,000 in 1947 to 37 million by 1955; three million were sold in just the first six months of 1950. By 1956, Americans spent $15.6 billion on the sale and repair of TV sets. The TV was the lynchpin of the home. 1954 saw the arrival of TV dinners so the family need not waste precious viewing time eating around the table.

Popular programmes

Popular programmes were viewed by millions. By 1960, it is estimated that watching TV was the favourite leisure activity of half the population. It is estimated, too, that half the population saw Mary Martin take to the air as Peter Pan in a 1955 spectacular. A regular audience of 50 million watched *I Love Lucy*. Comedienne Lucille Ball broke the stereotypical mould of passive females, being both performer and producer. In 1953, she was awarded an $8 million contract. The irony was *I Love Lucy* itself was about a dizzy blonde who created comic mayhem wherever she went.

Many sitcoms celebrated the American family as the heart of the USA – *Leave it to Beaver*, for example, showed the boy Beaver learning that mum and dad were always right and life for those outside a family group was uncertain and unpleasant. In this sense, family values and the position of the sexes was always reinforced with mum as the homemaker and dad going out to work – such as the *Donna Reed Show* where housewife Donna always saved the day with her good sense and quiet manner.

Television became a huge factor in popular culture not only in the USA but throughout the world. Studios grew large and impressive, rivalling those of film, and major actors such as Loretta Young and Ray Milland were recruited to TV.

TV advertising

TV stations in the USA were, like radio, always commercial concerns and advertisers adapted to funding programming as readily as they had on radio, sponsoring programmes such as *The Colgate Comedy Hour* and broadcasting adverts in between programmes, often competing to make theirs the most memorable and entertaining. Some programmes could generate income themselves – when Walt Disney launched his Davy Crockett series in 1955 it was accompanied by sales of $300,000 in tie-in merchandising.

Youth culture

In 1950, 41.6 per cent of the population was under 24 and, in 1960, 44.5 per cent. Teenagers were increasingly seen as a discrete group with common interests and concerns. As a market developed to cater for their interests, they seemed to look and act differently to their parents.

These changes were due to several factors:

- Young people in the 1950s had far more money to spend than any previous generation of teenagers had had and companies responded with new products specifically targeted towards them. In 1957, it was estimated that the average teenager had between $10 and $15 a week to spend, compared with 1–2 dollars in the 1940s. Teenagers' annual spending power climbed from $10 billion in 1950 to $25 billion in 1959.

- Many teenagers were influenced by the youth films of the 1950s. *Rebel Without a Cause* was the first film to appeal specifically to a teenage audience. As such, it was also the first film to address the issue of a generation gap. The film made a cult hero of James Dean, the more so as he was killed in a car accident in 1955 aged only 24. Dean plays a character who rebels against his parents, even coming to blows with his father, and gets in trouble with the local police for drunkenness.

- The establishment of rock and roll music was a crucial development, for it gave teenagers music of their own to listen to, instead of having to listen to their parents' type of music. The more parents disliked the new music, the more popular it was with teenagers. In 1956, Elvis Presley erupted onto the pop music scene, singing songs that broke all sales records, such as *Heartbreak Hotel* and *Hound Dog*. He was a phenomenal success with teenagers, while their parents and teachers deplored his sensual style of performing, his tight jeans and his permanent sneer.

- The increasing popularity of television also opened teenagers up to a new world that they didn't know about. These new experiences that teenagers were having made them realise that they were their own person, and they could do their own thing if they wanted. They didn't have to follow the same path as their parents.

Teenage rebellion?

However, there were increasing concerns that young people were out of control. Evidence was presented of gang fights, teenage drunkenness and disrespectful behaviour toward adults. In 1956, the number of murders carried out by teenagers in New York rose by 26 per cent over the previous year. So-called experts from various academic disciplines, particularly psychology, argued that aberrant behaviour could be cured once the problem was recognised. They offered various explanations of delinquency.

In 1954, psychologist Frederic Wertham published *The Seduction of the Innocent*, which exposed the violence and brutality of comic books that sold in their millions. After this, in fact, the content of comics was moderated but not before thirteen states passed laws regulating their publication, distribution and sale.

Some experts offered the explanation of poor role models, particularly the depiction of rebellious behaviour in movies such as Lāszlō Benedek's *The Wild One* (1954) and Nicholas Ray's *Rebel Without a Cause* (1955). The former is about a motorcycle gang who terrorise a sleepy town. When asked what he is rebelling against, their leader, played by Marlon Brando, answers, 'What you got?' It was argued that there was a link between violence and rebellion on the screen and in real life.

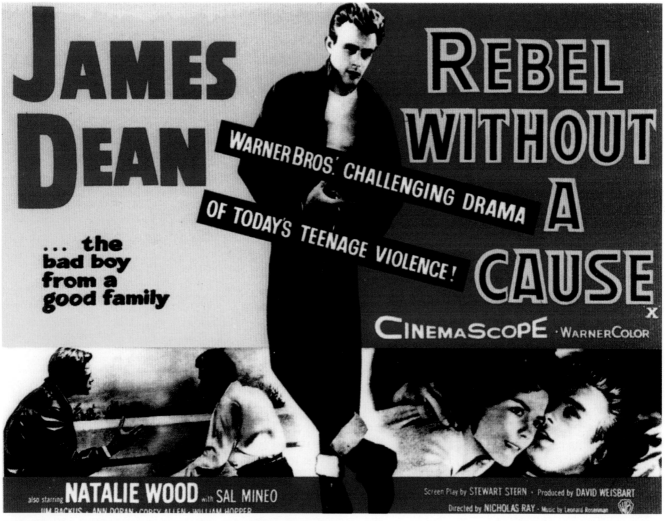

▲ A poster from 1955 advertising the film *Rebel Without a Cause.*

Others argued there were too many 'latch-key kids' whose parents were always out at work so exercised little control. The Senate was so concerned that it held hearings on delinquent behaviour throughout the decade.

Although teenagers in the first half of the 1950s may have had more money than their predecessors – the teenage market was reported to be worth $10 billion per year by 1955 – most were just as conservative and deferential. It should be remembered, too, that one-half of male teenagers during the course of the 1950s were drafted into the armed forces where discipline and traditional values were vigorously reinforced. Meanwhile the average age of marriage, young in itself in 1940 at 21.5 years, reduced even lower to 20.3 years; comparatively young women became housewives and mothers. While teenage rebellion was to become a much wider phenomenon as the decade progressed, there were in the early years of the 1950s few real signs of its stirrings – certainly not in middle-class white America.

ACTIVITY

1 Make a note of the evidence for and against teenage rebellion on a copy of the scales.

Evidence of teenage rebellion

Evidence against teenage rebellion

2 To what extent do you believe that there was teenage rebellion in these years?

3 Political developments

In the 1940s and 1950s the USA was gripped by the fear of Communism. Concern about Communist subversion affected all areas of public life and led to the emergence of Senator Joseph McCarthy.

Truman and Eisenhower

To what extent have the domestic achievements of Truman and Eisenhower been underestimated?

Between the death of Roosevelt in April 1945 and the election of John F. Kennedy as president in the 1960s, there were two presidents, Truman and Eisenhower.

Harry S. Truman

In April 1945, following the death of Franklin Roosevelt, Truman became president and was responsible for a series of policies at home and abroad which brought about post-war reconstruction. He had little experience and was not seen as FDR's obvious successor. However, he was convinced that the USA was the world's best hope for peace and prosperity and he believed that this hope could be best realised if the USA developed a political and social system that was an example to the rest of the world. Truman realised that not all Americans lived in prosperity and aimed to widen the scope of the New Deal, proposing, in 1945, wide-ranging reforms of housing and health care.

Full Employment Bill, 1945

However, his immediate concern was the matter of employment. In 1945, he introduced the Full Employment Bill to Congress. This Bill declared employment to be a right and required the government to ensure that jobs were available. The Bill also increased the dole, included a higher minimum wage, farm price supports and a public works programme. However, Congress was to water down many of Truman's proposals.

Labour relations

The Second World War had brought about inflation which, in turn, encouraged union leaders to call strikes demanding wage rises. Truman called a special labour-management conference in November 1945 in an attempt to prevent further strike action but the conference ended without agreement. In April 1945, the United Mine Workers came out on strike for a pay increase. In May, the railroads were hit by strikes. Truman now decided on firm action and announced that he would **conscript** the railroad workers and have the army run the railroads. He also wanted to introduce legislation that would restrict the right to strike against the government and would impose severe penalties on those that broke the law. This proved unnecessary, because the rail strike was called off. Truman had demonstrated the continued hostility of the Federal Government to labour and strike action.

As a result of the 1946 mid-term elections, Truman faced major political opposition as his political opponents, the Republicans, won control of both Houses of Congress. This was shown in the following year when Congress proposed the Taft–Hartley Bill, which made labour unions liable for violations of contracts, and prevented them from insisting that all workers must join a

---

Harry S. Truman (1884–1972)

Harry S. Truman was born in Missouri on 8 May 1884. He did not go to college but worked at a variety of jobs after high school including as a clerk and a bookkeeper at two separate banks in Kansas City. In 1917, with the First World War in full force, Truman joined the army. He served in France and left the army as a captain in May 1919. One month later, he married Elizabeth Wallace. After failing in the haberdashery business, Truman ran for county judge in Jackson County, Missouri. In 1926, he was again elected judge, a post he held until 1934 when he ran for the US Senate and won. During the Second World War, Senator Truman headed the Truman Commission, which investigated fraud in defence contracts. Truman was responsible for saving the Government several million dollars. He remained in the Senate until President Franklin Roosevelt chose him as his running mate for his fourth term in 1944. Truman became president in 1945 and served until March 1952 when he announced that he would not run for re-election. On 26 December 1972, Harry S. Truman died in Kansas City, Missouri at the age of 88.

Conscript – Someone compulsorily enrolled for service in the armed forces.

trade union as a condition of employment. Truman, however, unwilling to lose the support of labour, vetoed the bill but Congress passed it despite his objections. In 1948, Truman called Congress into special session and tried, unsuccessfully, to pass various New Deal-type measures.

1948 presidential election

Truman was expected to lose the presidential election of 1948. His party, the Democrats, was split. Henry Wallace, a former vice-president of FDR, set up the Progressive Party. Strom Thurmond, a southern conservative, disliked Truman's support for civil rights and also stood against Truman. Opinion polls suggested that the Republican candidate, Thomas E. Dewey, would win the election. However, Truman promised New-Deal type measures and went on a 30,000 mile whistle-stop tour of the USA, defending his achievements as president and criticising the Republican 'do-nothing' Congress. In one of the biggest electoral surprises in US history, Truman won a majority of over 2 million votes and the Democrats regained control of Congress.

The Fair Deal

In 1949, Truman declared that 'Every segment of our population and every individual has a right to expect from our government a fair deal'. He tried to introduce a whole range of welfare measures but Republican and Democratic conservatives blocked many of his reform proposals. He did, however, succeed in raising the minimum wage, extending the Social Security Act and passed an act to assist slum clearance and to provide housing for the poor.

Eisenhower

Eisenhower's presidency divided opinion both at the time and in later years. Critics at the time accused him of being far too conservative, a do-nothing president who spent his time playing golf. He has also been accused of representing big business, especially as his cabinet was composed mainly of millionaire businessmen, three of whom had worked in the car industry. He also seemed to show little sympathy for civil rights.

However, more recently historians such as Stephen Ambrose have become more sympathetic to his presidency, seeing him as a safe pair of hands who made things look deceptively easy. They suggest that he chose an able team, delegated well and had a good record as a mediator. Eisenhower insisted that leadership only works through 'persuasion and conciliation and education and patience'. Historians refer to Ike's 'hidden-handed' presidency. He knew where he wanted to go and steered the country in that direction. He worked well with a Congress which, for most of his presidency, was controlled by the Democrats and was popular with most Americans.

Domestic achievements

As a moderate Republican, Eisenhower was able to achieve numerous legislative victories despite a Democratic majority in Congress during six of his eight years in office. He called his programme 'dynamic conservatism'. This meant, he said, being 'conservative when it comes to money and liberal when it comes to human beings'. He was determined to, and succeeded in, decreasing the role of federal government. For example, he ended wage and price controls and reduced farm subsidies.

Even so, he accepted that federal government should have some responsibility for the welfare of its citizens and that it should promote economic growth. In addition to continuing most of the New Deal and Fair Deal programmes of his predecessors (Franklin Roosevelt and Truman, respectively), he strengthened

Dwight D. Eisenhower (1890–1969)

Dwight D. Eisenhower, later nicknamed 'Ike', was born on 14 October 1890 in Denison, Texas. He won an appointment to the US Military Academy at West Point, New York, and graduated in the middle of his class in 1915. In the 1930s, he worked under General Douglas MacArthur, US army chief of staff. Eisenhower played a prominent military role during the Second World War. He headed Operation Torch, the successful Allied invasion of North Africa, and the amphibious invasion of Sicily and the Italian mainland in 1943. Made a full general in early 1943, Eisenhower was appointed supreme commander of the Allied Expeditionary Force in December of that year and led the successful D-Day landings of June 1944 and the subsequent advance on Germany. In 1952, leading Republicans persuaded Eisenhower to run for president and he defeated Adlai Stevenson to become the 34th president of the United States. Four years later, Eisenhower beat Stevenson again in a landslide to win re-election. After leaving office in January 1961, he retired to his farm in Gettysburg, Pennsylvania. He worked largely on his memoirs, and would publish several books over the following years. He died on 28 March 1969 after a long illness.

the Social Security programme, increased the minimum wage and created the Department of Health, Education and Welfare. In 1956, Eisenhower created the Interstate Highway System, the single largest public works programme in US history, which would construct 41,000 miles of roads across the country. In addition, huge sums of money were spent completing the St Lawrence Seaway, linking the Great Lakes with the Atlantic.

KEY DATES: TRUMAN AND EISENHOWER

1945 Truman becomes president on death of Roosevelt.

1948 Truman re-elected as president.

1952 Eisenhower elected as president.

1956 Eisenhower re-elected as president.

WORKING TOGETHER

1 Working with a partner make a copy of and complete the following table. One of you complete the achievements of Truman and Eisenhower and the other the shortcomings.

	Achievements	Shortcomings
Truman		
Eisenhower		

2 To what extent do you believe the domestic achievements of Truman and Eisenhower have been underestimated?

NOTE-MAKING

Using a mind map, summarise the reasons for the development of the Red Scare. Begin with the most important at 12 o'clock and work your way clockwise to the least important.

McCarthyism and the Red Scare

Why was there a growing fear of Communism in the USA in the 1940s and 1950s?

In the years following the Second World War there was growing rivalry between the USA and the Soviet Union due partly to the American fear of the spread of Communism. The USA felt vulnerable against Communist influence at home too. The US Communist Party had never attracted more than 100,000 supporters and far fewer actual members. There was, however, a fear that if such supporters were in influential positions they could do untold damage within the USA.

The development of the 'Red Scare'

Various developments shocked Americans in the years following the Second World War and led to the development of the 'Red Scare'.

External developments

Developments outside the USA increased the fear of Communism. The fall of China to the Communists in 1949 was unexpected and some felt the State Department could have done more to prevent it. This led to the creation of a powerful 'China lobby', which campaigned for action against the new Communist regime and also a detailed investigation to discover how the USA had come to let it fall. Pat McCarran, a Democratic Senator from Nevada, was a key figure in the Senate Internal Security Subcommittee that tried to persuade people that China had fallen to Communism as a result of the work of secret Communist infiltrators within the State Department.

In addition, the development of the Cold War in Europe in the years after 1945 and increasing US involvement in Asia, particularly the Korean War, intensified the fear of the spread of Communism to the USA.

Developments in the USA

There was a series of spy scandals in Britain, Canada and the USA that scared the Americans. A British physicist, Klaus Fuchs, was convicted of giving nuclear secrets to the USSR. One of his associates, Harry Gold, was arrested on the same charge in the USA. It was felt the USSR had been able to develop its own nuclear weapons so quickly through the infiltration of Soviet agents into the Manhattan Project. Scientists Julius and Ethel Rosenberg were executed for giving away atomic secrets. One Soviet official wrote that they acquired the necessary information about how the atomic bombs were made in the USA and what they were made of in Britain. There was no doubt that Communists had infiltrated many branches of US government during the war; the Soviets later claimed that they had 221 operatives spying in the various branches of government.

Source F From Judge Irving Kaufman, when sentencing the Rosenbergs to death in April 1951.

Your crime is worse than murder, for you put into the hands of the Russians the A-bomb years before our best scientists predicted Russia would perfect the bomb. This has already caused, in my opinion, the Communist aggression in Korea, with the resultant casualties exceeding 50,000. Who knows but that millions more innocent people may pay the price of your treason. Indeed, by your betrayal, you undoubtedly have altered the course of history to the disadvantage of our country.

It was, however, the trial of Alger Hiss that really caught the public imagination. Hiss was President of the Carnegie Institute.

> ### Alger Hiss trial
>
> A former Communist, Whittaker Chambers was now editor of *Time* magazine, which was particularly anti-Communist. He accused Hiss of being a Communist during his time at the State Department, which he had joined in 1936. Hiss had been an important official who had been a key figure at the Yalta Conference. When Hiss sued Chambers, the latter was able to produce evidence that suggested Hiss had in fact handed over copies of secret documents to the Soviets in 1938. While Hiss's alleged treason had been too far in the past for him to be prosecuted for it, he was nevertheless found guilty of perjury for lying to the court and sentenced to five years' imprisonment.

The case led to widespread accusations of Communism in high places in the USA.

In 1947, President Truman appeared to fuel these charges by introducing the Loyalty Review Board to check up on government employees. Any found to be sympathetic to 'subversive organisations' could be fired. Within four years at least 1,200 had been dismissed and a further 6,000 resigned. Over 150 organisations were banned, of which 110 were accused of supporting Communism. Eleven leaders of the Communist Party were prosecuted under the 1940 Smith Act and sentenced to up to five years in prison. It was argued that their beliefs suggested they would try to overthrow the government in the USA; they had not actually done anything.

In 1949, the USSR exploded their first nuclear weapon. The USA had therefore lost its monopoly on atomic weapons. President Truman said the USA would seek to develop a hydrogen bomb, with as much as a thousand times the power of an atomic bomb. When this weapon was finally tested in 1954, both sides were entering into an arms race and developing weapons of mass destruction that could, if used, have led to the end of the world.

Manhattan Project – A research and development project that produced the first atomic bombs during the Second World War.

What can you learn about the growing fear of Communism from Source F?

The House Committee on Un-American Activities

The House Committee on Un-American Activities (HUAC) set up by Congress in 1938 relentlessly investigated those suspected of supporting Communism. There had already in the late 1940s been a campaign against members of the Hollywood film community who were accused of making films with Communist content aimed at brainwashing Americans. This saw, among others, the film-maker Charlie Chaplin, a British citizen, being forced to leave the USA. While many Hollywood actors such as Gary Cooper had supported the Committee's investigations, others had refused to answer questions. The 'Hollywood Ten', mainly a group of writers and directors, were fired from their jobs and eventually sent to prison for contempt of Congress for refusing to testify before the HUAC.

Never in the history of the world was one people as completely dominated, intellectually and morally, by another as the people of the United States by the people of Russia in the four years from 1946 to 1949 ... all this took place not in a time of national weakness or decay, but precisely at the moment when the United States, having engineered a tremendous triumph and fought its way to a brilliant victory in the greatest of all wars, had reached the highest point of world power ever achieved by a single state.

> To what extent do you agree with the view in Source G of the USA in these years?

McCarthyism

Joseph McCarthy was the hard-drinking and previously insignificant junior Senator for Wisconsin. On 9 February 1950, he made a speech in which he said the State Department was infested with spies. Although he hadn't a shred of evidence to back up his claims, many listened and believed him.

The speech saw the inauguration of a witch-hunt against members of the State Department, other public servants, and finally the army. In 1953, McCarthy was subsequently given control of the Senate Committee on Government Operations and its subcommittee on Investigations. His team included the future Senator, Bobby Kennedy.

At first McCarthy was highly successful. No one in the public eye seemed safe from his accusations and McCarthy became one of the most popular men in the USA. He gained support from such diverse groups as the American Legion and Christian fundamentalists. Much of his support was also derived from the less well-educated and less affluent members of society; those of whom, it is often alleged, would be more prepared to believe simplistic conspiracy theories. These were also the groups that had supported the attacks against the well-off members of the State Department.

Many argued that New Deal measures were Communist inspired and these now came under renewed attack. Those advocating civil rights measures, support for the United Nations and any redistribution of wealth could all be accused of having Communist sympathies. Indeed, the fear of Communism gripped the USA to almost ridiculous proportions. One school librarian in Indiana banned books about Robin Hood because she said in robbing the rich to give to the poor, his story promoted Communism. Many books including classics were re-examined for subversive content.

Joseph McCarthy (1908–57)

Joseph McCarthy was born on a farm in Appleton, Wisconsin, on 14 November 1908. He left school at fourteen and worked as a chicken farmer before managing a grocery store in the nearby town of Manawa. McCarthy returned to high school in 1928 and, after achieving the necessary qualifications, won a place at Marquette University. After graduating, McCarthy worked as a lawyer but was fairly unsuccessful and had to supplement his income by playing poker. McCarthy was originally a supporter of Franklin D. Roosevelt and the New Deal. However, after failing to become the Democratic Party candidate for district attorney, he switched parties and became the Republican Party candidate in an election to become a circuit court judge. When the United States entered the Second World War, McCarthy resigned as a circuit judge and joined the US marines. After the war, McCarthy ran against Robert La Follette to become Republican candidate for the Senate. McCarthy died in 1957 when he was discovered to have cirrhosis of the liver. As the newspapers reported, McCarthy had drunk himself to death.

McCarthy's downfall

However, it was McCarthy's manner and accusations that saw his downfall. Not only did he condemn such highly respected figures as General George Marshall, who had introduced Marshall Aid, but in 1954 he also began to investigate the army as hiding a possible nest of Communists. In so doing, he appeared to criticise an institution until recently embroiled in a full-scale war against Communism in Korea: the very thing he was accusing its members of supporting.

Millions saw the hearings on the new medium of television in December 1954 where they turned against the bullying tactics of McCarthy, who also appeared at times to be drunk. Children mocked his manner at school and in the streets; but generally his audiences saw he was completely bereft of any hard evidence to support his accusations. The army's attorney, Joseph Welch, stood up to McCarthy when he accused a junior member of Welch's team of having belonged to an organisation that he claimed had been pro-Communist, while at college. He accused McCarthy of attacking people without a shred of evidence in support. President Eisenhower, a former military commander, was critical of McCarthy's investigation of the army. However, the tables appeared to turn in particular when McCarthy himself was accused of seeking preferential treatment for one of his aides who had been drafted into the army. He was censured by the Senate and returned to obscurity until his death from alcoholism in 1957. The 'Red Scare', which he had done so much to exaggerate, gradually died away.

KEY DATES: MCCARTHYISM AND THE RED SCARE

1947 Truman set up the Loyalty Review Board.

1949 Fall of China to the Communists. The Soviet Union explodes its first atom bomb.

1950 McCarthy's speech accusing the State Department of being infested with spies.

1954 McCarthy's bullying tactics exposed when he investigates the army.

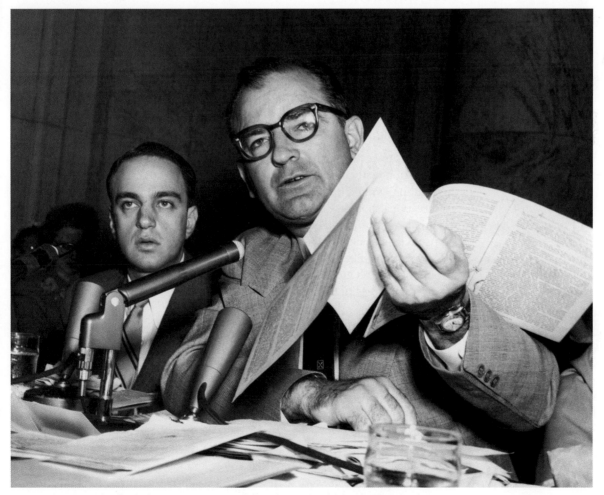

▲ Joseph McCarthy (right) at the McCarthy hearings, 1 November 1954.

4 The Divided Union?

There was a slow improvement in the role and status of ethnic minorities in the years 1945–60, although few Native Americans gained from the policy of termination. In addition, there were significant milestones in civil rights in the 1950s including the 1954 court case *Brown v. Topeka Board of Education* and the Montgomery bus boycott. However, white Southerners were to fight tenaciously to maintain segregation and by the 1950s much was still to be achieved on the path to civil rights.

Native Americans

To what extent did the lives of Native Americans change, 1945–60?

During the war, 25,000 Native Americans served in the armed forces and a further 40,000 worked in war production. This meant many left the reservations to live in the same way as other groups in the cities and production centres. Meanwhile, there were concerns that the reservations were no longer viable, that too many Native Americans were living in poverty, and this was no longer acceptable in a wealthy society. Indian Commissioner John Collier had suggested as early as 1941 that reservation life would not be able to accommodate returning servicemen and their families in adequate living standards. The following year he began to hint at a return to assimilation.

Termination

In 1944, the Indian Claims Commission was set up to offer financial compensation to Native Americans for claims for lost lands – but not to return the lands themselves. The idea was to compensate Native Americans for past exploitation as a prelude to their taking their place as American citizens. As President Truman said, 'With the final settlement of all outstanding claims which this measure ensures, Indians can take their place without special handicaps or special advantages in the economic life of our nation and share fully in its progress'.

However, it was under the administration of President Eisenhower that termination really developed apace. In August 1953, a House Concurrent Resolution, Number 108, announced the termination policy: that the reservations should be broken up and Native Americans encouraged to move to urban areas to live like other American citizens. Native Americans weren't consulted. The idea was effectively that federal government would absolve itself of any responsibility for Native Americans as a separate group. Their lands would be sold off and the profits distributed among tribal members who would go to urban areas to find work and live as normal US citizens.

Termination began with the sale of valuable lands belonging to the Menominee and Klamath tribes in Wisconsin and Oregon respectively. The whole policy of termination was a disaster from the start. It was a case of federal government ridding itself of its responsibilities in an attempt to save money, of cutting Native Americans loose without any real effort to acclimatise them to urban life. Many who left the reservations drifted into unemployment and alcoholism and gradually began to move back. By 1960, only 13,000 out of 400,000 Native Americans had moved permanently and only three per cent of reservation land had been lost. The policy was abandoned but it left a lasting ill-feeling that would develop in the 1960s into Red Power and more militant Native American action. Hispanics, too, were to develop more militant strategies to combat exploitation in the 1960s, but the 1950s saw a more passive stance.

NOTE-MAKING

Using the 1–2 method (see page x) make notes on the changes to the lives of Native Americans between 1945 and 1960.

KEY DATES: NATIVE AMERICANS

1944 The Indian Claims Commission set up.

1953 A House Concurrent Resolution, Number 108, announced the termination policy.

1960 Only 13,000 out of 400,000 Native Americans had moved permanently.

African Americans and civil rights

To what extent was there progress in civil rights for African Americans in the 1940s and 1950s?

By 1945, there had been some progress in employment and the armed forces, and many African Americans had become more active in campaigning for civil rights. On the other hand, discrimination and segregation remained a way of life in the Southern states, while the migration of many African Americans to the industrial cities of the North had created greater racial tension.

The legacy of the Second World War

The Second World War did provide a stimulus to the civil rights movement.

The membership of the National Association for the Advancement of Colored People (NAACP) rose from 50,000 in 1940 to 450,000 by 1945. Many of these were professionals, although there were also many new urban workers (whose wages now enabled them to afford subscriptions). The NAACP began to play an important part in the civil rights movement after the war because it raised the profile of issues not only within the African American community but also within the white community, and encouraged activism.

The Congress of Racial Equality (CORE) was founded by James Farmer, a civil rights activist, in 1942. Increasingly, Americans saw the incongruity of racial inequality in a country that promoted freedom and equality of opportunity. This was particularly apposite in the post-war period. The USA had fought against the most racist regime of modern times, and supported decolonisation throughout the world. Communist regimes, moreover, promoted racial equality and could easily criticise the USA for the lack of it. Racial inequality therefore made the USA vulnerable to criticism and lacking credibility in the wider world.

Truman's presidency

Harry S. Truman was the first president since Lincoln to make a significant contribution to the development of civil rights. In September 1946, Truman set up the Civil Rights Committee to investigate racial abuse. In 1947, it published a report 'To Secure These Rights', which stated bluntly that the USA couldn't claim to lead the free world while African Americans were treated so unequally. It called for laws to prevent lynching, the abolition of the poll tax, and the FEPC to be made a permanent fixture.

Unfortunately, a coalition of 20 Southern Democrats and 15 Republicans blocked every civil rights measure that was introduced into the Senate, for example anti-lynching bills. Often these conservatives justified their opposition by either saying that they were upholding states' rights and the issue of race was actually irrelevant, or equating civil rights with Communism. Most historians agree that their opposition was fundamentally a result of racism.

Eisenhower's presidency

President Eisenhower was less committed to desegregation, although, as we shall see, it became a more significant issue during his administration. Eisenhower maintained that legislation couldn't change people's hearts so passing laws to stop desegregation wouldn't work. However, having said this, he was no racist.

NOTE-MAKING

Using a spider diagram (see page x), make notes on the following topics on African Americans: the impact of the Second World War, the *Brown v. Topeka* case, Little Rock, and the Montgomery bus boycott.

Desegregation of the armed forces

One measure that was successfully enacted was Executive Order 9981, passed by Truman in July 1948 to desegregate the armed forces entirely and guarantee fair employment opportunities in the civil service. A Fair Employment Board was set up to replace FEPC, but its impact suffered from underfunding.

While senior military personnel feared the impact of desegregation, it went extremely well. Indeed by 1950, the Navy and Air Force were completely integrated. The Army followed during the Korean War, initially where necessity demanded it through the amount of casualties. Even the military training camps in the South were integrated without significant issues. The successful desegregation of the armed forces gave hope for the future.

Look back to Chapter 3, page 88. What were the origins, aims and early achievements of the NAACP?

NAACP and schools

The NAACP realised early on that the quality of schools was crucial to the promotion of equality of opportunity. The 1896 *Plessy v. Ferguson* case had allowed segregation and emphasised that facilities must be separate but equal. However, educational facilities in the South were glaringly unequal. In 1930, the NAACP commissioned the Margold Report to investigate the ruling. It reported in 1933. It argued that *Plessy v. Ferguson* had been imprecise, poorly thought out and vaguely written. The NAACP sent out researchers to investigate how schools in the South were unequal. Their evidence was stark. For example, the state of South Carolina spent three times more on white schools than African-American schools and one hundred times more on school transport. African-American schools were often tumbledown shack-like buildings without facilities. School materials were often dog-eared books that had already served their useful life in white schools. African-American teachers were usually paid considerably less than their white counterparts. No wonder then that in 1946 one-quarter of African-Americans in the South were functionally illiterate. The NAACP was determined, once again, to challenge the separate but equal ruling in education.

Eisenhower's major achievement in terms of civil rights was to facilitate desegregation in Washington DC. Geographically it was a Southern city governed during the 1950s by Congress but with largely segregated facilities. Eisenhower passed Executive Orders desegregating government-run shipyards and veterans' hospitals and tried to encourage integration of schools in the capital, particularly after the landmark *Brown v. Topeka* case ruled that schools should not be segregated. The city itself was desegregated as the 1950s progressed.

Brown v. the Board of Education of Topeka

The NAACP sought people who were prepared to bring cases against inequalities in education. While the NAACP amassed its evidence, would-be plaintiffs were attacked, dismissed from their jobs, had their houses burned and were forced out of their state.

The NAACP decided of all their cases to lead with *Brown v. the Board of Education of Topeka*. Topeka was a town in Kansas. Brown was Reverend Oliver Brown, an African American, whose seven-year-old daughter Linda had to cross railroad tracks and wait for a bus to get to school on the other side of town while a good white school nearby had plenty of spaces.

The Supreme Court had a new chief justice, Earl Warren, who was sympathetic to issues of civil rights. On Monday 17 May 1954 the Court ruled that in the question of education, the notion of separate but equal had no place. This was a monumental decision. Some called it a second American Revolution. Others referred to it as 'Black Monday'. Warren said that for students 'segregation' generates a feeling of inferiority 'as to their status in the community that may affect their hearts and minds in a way unlikely ever to be undone'.

Impact of the ruling

While most historians agree on the importance of this ruling, they emphasise its significance in different ways. Writing in the 1950s and 1960s, C. Vann Woodward argued that the initial response in the South was to 'wait and see'. Panic set in when local courts began to enforce segregation as a result of cases brought by the NAACP. Forty years later, Cottrol, Diamond and Ware tended to agree in that the courts involved themselves in more aspects of life following the Supreme Court's lead. After *Brown v. Topeka*, courts were more willing to become involved in political disputes and controversial issues. James T. Patterson focused somewhat on opposition to the decision and criticised Eisenhower for not giving more overt support. Patterson felt that had he done so, there would have been less opposition. Journalist Adam Cohen has argued that the impact was not on school desegregation as such but on the wider area of civil rights.

Many commentators were wildly optimistic about the ruling, believing it would quickly end segregation in schools. The NAACP chief counsel, Thurgood Marshall, said all schools would be desegregated within five years. Other critics took solace from the vagueness of the ruling. It did not, for example, address what schools should teach or do. It did not set a deadline. Even when it turned to implementation in May 1955, having given the states a year to prepare, the Supreme Court forbore to implement any deadlines, recognising the difficulties involved. It merely placed the responsibility for implementation on local education authorities within a reasonable time. There were no sanctions for non-implementation.

By the school year 1956–57, 723 school districts were desegregated, involving 300,000 African-American schoolchildren, but 240,000 remained in entirely segregated schools – mainly in the eight states of Alabama, Florida, Georgia, Mississippi, Louisiana, North and South Carolina and Virginia. Most of these states had penalties for any district that did begin desegregation procedures. All followed the lead of Alabama whose legislators declared the *Brown v. Topeka* ruling 'null, void and of no effect'. Attitudes were hardening, moreover, and moderate Southern politicians were either having to become more conservative or give way to more extreme colleagues in elections. In the meantime, white Southerners became more anxious to promote their own views on race relations in their region.

Source H From a lecture *Brown v. Board of Education and the Civil Rights Movement*, 2005 by the historian James T. Patterson.

I still believe *Brown* was pivotal in a number of ways, especially as a constitutional precedent against state-mandated segregation. This was a precedent that the Supreme Court, later in the 1950s, used as the basis for a series of decisions declaring that other publicly mandated forms of segregation, such as at municipal golf courses, in bus transportation, and at public beaches, were also unconstitutional. *Brown* also stimulated many other movements for rights, which in turn drove a nationwide surge of rights consciousness that has been vitally important in the United States since the 1960s.

> To what extent do you agree with the interpretation in Source H of the *Brown v. Topeka* case?

Progress in education in the later 1950s

While the prevailing mood in the South may have been 'wait and see' after the 1954 *Brown v. Topeka* ruling, attitudes were hardening. This may have been because local courts, respecting the Supreme Court ruling, were increasingly finding in favour of desegregation – even though judges were putting themselves at risk by doing so. By January 1956, they upheld the ruling in nineteen cases, demanding a prompt start to desegregation or overturning existing laws on segregation. The NAACP had upwards of 170 cases pending.

Southern school boards were finding various ingenious methods to oppose desegregation beyond the penalties already referred to. The most common was to give grants to private schools, which could continue to be segregated. Georgia and North Carolina gave grants to white students to attend private schools. As late as 1959, Prince Edward County, Virginia, did in fact close all its public schools enabling its white children to attend private segregated ones.

Some authorities passed 'public placement' laws, which enabled officials to give racially biased tests to ensure white children went to the best schools. Some states delegated all educational powers to the local boards so every one of them would have to be sued individually for desegregation to take place. The state of Mississippi actually passed a law to make desegregation illegal. Most didn't need to take so drastic a step. By 1964, only two per cent of African Americans in the eleven Southern states went to fully integrated schools, and where schools were integrated, few African-American teachers were allowed to work in them.

In March 1956, 22 Southern Senators and 82 of the 106 Southern representatives came up with the Southern Manifesto, which accused the Supreme Court of abusing its powers. It insisted the question of segregation was one of states' rights. Moreover, it promised to fight the decision.

Little Rock High School, 1957

Eisenhower was moved to take action after a clear example of Southern resistance to integrated education occurred at Little Rock, Arkansas. In 1957, Governor Orval Faubus used National Guard troops to bar the entry of nine black children to the Central High School after a federal district court had ruled that the school must be desegregated. Eisenhower used his authority as Commander-in-Chief to send federal troops and announced that the 10,000

The murder of Emmett Till, 1955

The year 1955 saw a deterioration in race relations and violence grew. Of the eleven lynchings in the 1950s, eight took place in 1955. Some of the most horrific murders, including that of schoolboy Emmett Till, took place that year. Fourteen-year-old Emmett Till was visiting relatives in Money, Mississippi, on 24 August 1955, when he reportedly flirted with a white cashier at a grocery store. Four days later, two white men kidnapped Till, beat him and shot him in the head. The men were tried for murder, but an all-white male jury acquitted them. Till's murder and open casket funeral galvanised the emerging civil rights movement.

▲ Elizabeth Eckford attempting to enter Little Rock High School, 4 September 1957.

troopers of the Arkansas National Guard were to be kept under federal control. The soldiers, who had barred the way, now kept white protestors back and escorted the children into school.

Little Rock was significant because it was the only occasion when President Eisenhower used his federal authority to intervene and enforce the Brown ruling and it demonstrated that states could be overruled by the federal government when necessary. The demonstrations were seen on television and in newspapers across the world. It did the USA no good to be seen as an oppressive nation when it was criticising Communist countries for not allowing their citizens basic human rights. Moreover, African American activists were beginning to realise that reliance on the federal courts was not enough to secure change.

The Montgomery bus boycott

In the South, separation on public transport was always the most resented form of segregation. African Americans were frequently made to stand, given the poorer seats, thrown off buses for little reason and generally spoken down to or humiliated by white drivers and passengers. The majority of African Americans lived in their own out-of-town areas and needed to travel frequently to employment in town centres.

On 1 December 1955, Rosa Parks was thrown off a bus in Montgomery for refusing to give up her seat for a white person. The driver called the police and she was removed from the bus and arrested. This seemingly small incident gave birth to a new and important phase in the civil rights movement, a bus boycott. Over the following weekend, officials organised a massive boycott of the bus system by 50,000 black supporters in the city. The boycott, which lasted 381 days, gained the near unanimous support of ordinary African Americans and was an impressive display of unity with African Americans walking to work instead of using the local bus company.

It put financial pressure on the authorities which initially unwisely refused the slightest concessions. But in November 1956, after an initiative by the NAACP, the Supreme Court in *Browder v. Gayle* gave another favourable verdict. It ruled segregation on buses to be unconstitutional with similar reason to the *Brown v. Topeka* case. At the end of that long year the buses were totally desegregated.

The role of Martin Luther King

Martin Luther King had been a minister at the Dexter Avenue Baptist Church, Montgomery, for less than a year when the boycott began. He was chosen as leader of the bus boycott because he was seen as cautious and a very good speaker. King proved to be an effective organiser, a brilliant speaker and motivator. He organised frequent night-time rallies in his and other local churches as well as carpools to transport African Americans to work. By articulating the feelings and frustrations of the black community in a clear, intelligent and persuasive way, he created a vital close link between the black civil rights leadership and the less educated African Americans that the NAACP had often failed to achieve. His belief in non-violence was powerfully argued – the idea that true progress could only be made when the cycle of hate and violence was broken. Within a year, King had set up a new civil rights organisation, the Southern Christian Leadership Conference (SCLC).

Source I From a speech made by Martin Luther King, 5 December 1955.

We are here, we are here this evening because we're tired now. Now let us say that we are not here advocating violence. We have overcome that. I want it to be known throughout Montgomery and throughout this nation that we are Christian people. We believe in the Christian religion. We believe in the teachings of Jesus. The only weapon that we have in our hands this evening is the weapon of protest. And secondly, this is the glory of America, with all of its faults. This is the glory of our democracy. If we were incarcerated behind the iron curtains of a Communistic nation we couldn't do this. If we were trapped in the dungeon of a totalitarian regime we couldn't do this. But the great glory of American democracy is the right to protest for right.

The boycott had shown that unity and solidarity could win and victory offered hope to those who were fighting for improved civil rights. Moreover, the boycott demonstrated the benefits of a peaceful approach and showed that African Americans were able to organise themselves. It brought King's philosophy to the fore and gave the movement a clear moral framework. Success also encouraged King to consider further action that would confront inequality and bring about more change.

KEY DATES: AFRICAN AMERICANS

1954 *Brown v. Topeka* case.
1955–56 Montgomery bus boycott.
1957 Little Rock High School.

Rosa Parks (1914–2005)

Rosa Parks was a Methodist and a member of the NAACP, who was highly regarded in the local community. Others had been arrested for similar reasons, but campaigners wanted to pick a person of impeccable character and morals, to whom breaking the law would normally be unthinkable, and therefore Rosa Parks, a respectable middle-aged African American, was ideal. After the boycott, harassment by angry white Americans in Montgomery forced the Parks family to move to Detroit in 1957. She later set up the Rosa and Raymond Parks Institute for Self-Development, giving career training to black youths. She was awarded the Presidential Medal of Freedom in 1996 and the Congressional Gold Award in 1999.

What can you learn from Source I about the methods used by King?

WORKING TOGETHER

This is often seen as a period when there was real progress in civil rights for African Americans. Set up a class debate to assess their progress in this period, with one group arguing 'for' progress, and another 'against'. You could use the motion: 'This class believes that African Americans made real progress in civil rights in these years'.

Chapter summary

- The USA economy had greatly benefited from the Second World War and experienced further growth in the years that followed.
- Prosperity among many Americans led to the move to the suburbs and further growth in car ownership.
- Television played an increasingly important role in the lives of many Americans.
- Women made little progress and continued to be stereotyped by the media as mothers and housewives.
- The 1950s saw the emergence of a youth culture with increasing concern about the behaviour of many teenagers.
- The USA was gripped by a wave of anti-Communism in the years after the Second World War, which was partly fuelled by developments in the Cold War in Europe and Asia.
- Senator Joe McCarthy took advantage of the anti-Communist hysteria to lead a witch-hunt against officials in the State Department.
- African Americans made some progress in civil rights due to landmark developments such as *Brown v. Topeka,* Little Rock High School and the Montgomery bus boycott.
- The USA became involved in a Cold War in Europe and Asia with the USSR and China and adopted a policy of containment.
- The USA also became involved in an arms race with the Soviet Union, which led to the development of weapons of mass destruction.

▼ Summary diagram: Crises and the Rise to World Power, 1920–75

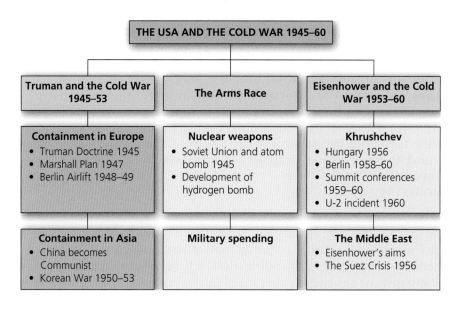

Working on essay technique

So far in the advice given, the skills being developed could help a student to write a good essay.

To write an outstanding essay though, all the same skills are needed. In addition:

- All those skills are shown at a high level.
- There will be a good understanding shown of issues and concepts (which might on this breadth paper include showing awareness of longer-term perspectives).
- The conclusion will contain a well-substantiated judgement.

Try to demonstrate these top-level skills in answering the following A-level practice question:

To what extent was the Second World War the main reason for the changes in US foreign policy in the years 1933–60? (25 marks)

Working on interpretation skills

At the ends of Chapters 2, 4 and 5, there have been sections on interpretations. In the A-level examination Section A you are given three sources and asked to evaluate their views.

First, have a look back at this advice on pages 69–70, and 129–30. Remind yourself of the skills that are being tested. Then study the three extracts below on the theme of US foreign policy and answer the A-level practice question.

Using your understanding of the historical context, assess how convincing the arguments in these three extracts are in relation to the change in US foreign policy from isolationism to involvement in the Cold War in the years 1920–50. (30 marks)

Extract A

The origins of US involvement in the Cold War lies in the deteriorating relations which followed Lenin's take-over of Russia as Lenin took Russia out of the war against Germany and the United States joined with other Western powers in a policy of intervention in Russia. That the aim, at least nominally, was to protect Western interests in Russia rather than unseat the Bolsheviks did not erase the Soviets' conviction that the United States was out to strangle the Revolution in its cradle. Throughout the 1930s relations between the United States and the Soviet Union themselves were cool, despite American diplomatic recognition of the Soviet Union on Franklin Roosevelt's assumption of the presidency. Relations were also distant. There were neither major areas of agreement nor pressing conflicts of interest. The Cold War was in important respects an outgrowth of the Second World War. The latent ideological antagonism stemming from 1917 was, so to speak, energized by the demands placed upon the United States and the Soviet Union for cooperation during the war and its aftermath.

Adapted from 'The United States and the Cold War 1941–53' by Richard Crockatt, BAAS Pamphlet No. 18, 2010.

Extract B

The Cold War grew out of a complicated interaction of external and internal developments inside both the United States and the Soviet Union. The external situation – circumstances beyond the control of either power – left Americans and Russians facing one another across prostrated Europe at the end of World War Two. Internal influences in the Soviet Union – the search for security, the role of ideology, massive post-war reconstruction needs, the personality of Stalin – together with those in the United States – the need for self-determination, fear of Communism, the illusion of omnipotence fostered by American economic strength and the atomic bomb – made the resulting confrontation a hostile one. Leaders of both superpowers sought peace, but in doing so yielded to considerations, which, while they did not precipitate war, made resolution of differences impossible.

Adapted from *The United States and the Origins of the Cold War 1941–47* by John Lewis Gaddis, (Columbia University Press), 1972.

Extract C

In a short time the United States had moved from isolation to leadership. Inclined to parochialism [focus on its own interests], she had been thrust into the center of internationalism. The only great nation to emerge from the war materially unscathed, she elected to assume responsibility for relief and reconstruction. The only democratic power able to resist the advance of Communism, she committed herself to that perilous task throughout the world. But, as the United States advanced in strength, so too did Russia. As America poured financial aid into Western Europe, the Soviet Union revolutionized the economies of Eastern Europe. As the USA built up systems of alliances, the USSR created its own blocs. And as the United States made atom bombs, so too did the Russians.

Adapted from *The Growth of the American Republic,* 6th edn, by S. Morison, H. Commager and W. Leuchtenburg. (OUP), 1969.

Conflict at home and abroad, 1960–75

This chapter covers developments in the USA from the election of Kennedy as president in 1960, to 1975, the year after the resignation of Nixon. It deals with a number of areas:

- The domestic policies of Kennedy, Johnson and Nixon.
- US involvement in the Cold War and Vietnam.
- Ideological, social, regional and ethnic divisions: protest and the mass media.
- The USA by 1975: superpower status.

When you have worked through the chapter and the related activities and exercises, you should have detailed knowledge of all those areas, and you should be able to relate this to the key breadth issues defined as part of your study, in particular how united was the United States during this period, and how important was the role of key individuals? For the period covered in this chapter the main issues can be phrased as a breadth question:

Was the Vietnam War the main reason for divisions in American society in the 1960s?

The focus of the issue is on social and political developments and of causal factors that contributed to these divisions, as set out briefly below.

CHAPTER OVERVIEW

There were three presidents during these years: John F. Kennedy, who introduced a policy known as the New Frontier; Lyndon B. Johnson, who continued the work of Kennedy with his own programme known as the Great Society; and Richard Nixon, whose second term in office was dominated by the Watergate scandal. However, each president faced increasing social divisions which manifested in a series of different protest groups including the civil rights movement, dominated by Martin Luther King, the student movement, greatly influenced by US involvement in the conflict in Vietnam, and the women's movement. Moreover, the USA was still greatly involved in the Cold War, including the Cuban Missile Crisis of 1962, and *détente* under Nixon, as well as the conflict in Vietnam, which dominated the latter years of the period.

1 Domestic policies under Kennedy, Johnson and Nixon

The domestic policies of Kennedy and Johnson were dominated by economic, social and civil rights reforms. Nixon's administration was overshadowed by the Watergate affair.

Kennedy and the New Frontier

To what extent was Kennedy's New Frontier a success?

Few presidents in the twentieth century ruled for a shorter time than John F. Kennedy (JFK), yet few are so well known or have such a high reputation. Kennedy's personal life and period as president continue to fascinate and divide historians. To some he was a breath of fresh air, who greatly changed US society and politics. Others believe he was all image and his achievements have been greatly exaggerated. Kennedy is one of the great 'what ifs' in history. People asked what might have been. What would he have achieved had he not been assassinated in 1963?

The 1960 election

The 1960 election was between Kennedy and the Republican candidate, Richard Nixon, who had served as vice-president under Eisenhower. The election, which was the closest since 1888, gave JFK a majority of just 118,574 votes. Kennedy's victory was due to several factors:

- Kennedy was Catholic and, although this probably lost him some Protestant votes in the South, he retained and even won back some Catholic support.
- He was the son of one of the richest men in the USA – Joseph Kennedy.
- Kennedy's image also helped. He appeared youthful – at 43 he was four years younger than Nixon and had good looks and a glamorous wife.
- There was a desire for change after the apparent complacency of the Eisenhower administration (see pages 233–4). JFK promised a 'New Frontier', although he was vague about what that actually meant.
- Communism seemed a greater threat than ever, especially when the USSR launched the first space satellite, *Sputnik,* in 1957. Kennedy promised that he would beat Communism.
- Kennedy also took advantage of the popularity of Martin Luther King. In October 1960, King was arrested for trying to desegregate a restaurant in Atlanta. JFK phoned King's wife, stating his support and his brother, Robert Kennedy, used his influence to obtain King's release. This was well publicised and ensured African-American support.
- Television also played an important role – 70 million viewers watched the four televised debates and were more impressed with JFK than with Nixon. Paradoxically, those who listened to the debates on the radio believed Nixon had won.

The New Frontier

At first the New Frontier was simply a slogan JFK used to try to inspire and unite young Americans behind him. However, it soon became a programme of reform and change in which Kennedy hoped to make the USA a fairer society by giving equal rights to all African Americans, and by helping them to better themselves. He called it the 'New Frontier' to excite voters. Above all else, he

NOTE-MAKING

Using the 1–2 method (see page x) make notes on Kennedy's domestic policies. For example write 'Reasons for his election victory' in the left-hand section and a bulleted point list of the reasons in the right-hand section.

John F. Kennedy (JFK) (1917–63)

John Fitzgerald Kennedy was born in 1917 into a wealthy Massachusetts family and was educated at Harvard University. During the Second World War, he served in the US Navy and was badly wounded but also decorated for his bravery. After the war he entered politics, being elected a Democratic Congressman in 1947 and, five years later, was elected to the US Senate. In the 1950s, he wrote two best-selling books, including *Profiles in Courage,* which was published in 1953. In 1960, the Democrats chose him to run for president. Kennedy had an image that suited American politics of the early 1960s, especially his good looks and apparently happy marriage to his glamorous wife, Jackie. The public were unaware at the time of his numerous extra-marital affairs.

wanted to make the USA a fairer and better place and he asked Americans to join him as 'New Frontiersmen'.

Kennedy also made major changes to central government to ensure that the 'New Frontier' was carried out. For example, he gathered a team of the brightest young experts from American universities, most of whom had never worked for the government before. These were known as the Brains Trust. Kennedy hoped that because they were young and fresh, they would come up with new ideas for tackling the problems of the USA.

Civil rights

JFK has a mixed record on civil rights. Before 1963, he was somewhat hesitant, largely because he did not wish to alienate conservative Southerners whose votes he needed to pass other measures. He appointed five federal judges, including Thurgood Marshall. Marshall was a leading civil rights activist. JFK also threatened legal action against the state of Louisiana for refusing to fund schools that were not segregated.

In October 1962, he sent 23,000 government troops to ensure that one black student, James Meredith, could study at the University of Mississippi. He introduced a Civil Rights Bill to Congress in February 1963. This aimed to give African Americans equality in housing and education, but was defeated in Congress.

The economy

The New Frontier included economic changes. Kennedy introduced a general tax cut as more spending would mean more goods sold. There were also public works that cost $900,000,000. The Federal Government would begin a series of projects, such as new roads and public buildings. Grants were also given to high-tech companies to invest in high-tech equipment to train workers. JFK increased spending on defence and space technology, all of which secured or created jobs, and also promised that the USA would put a man on the Moon by the end of the decade. He also limited prices and wages to ensure inflation did not spiral out of control.

However, there was still unemployment in traditional industries such as coal, iron and steel, with unemployment twice as high among African Americans. Moreover, the boom was heavily dependent on government spending.

Social reform

JFK was also active in social reform.

- He increased the minimum wage from $1.00 to $1.25 an hour.
- The Manpower and Training Act was passed, providing retraining for the long-term unemployed.
- The Area Redevelopment Act allowed the Federal Government to give loans and grants to states with long-term unemployment.
- The Housing Act provided cheap loans for the redevelopment of inner cities.
- The Social Security Act gave greater financial help to the elderly and unemployed.
- Social security benefits were extended to each child whose father was unemployed.

Again, however, there were limitations. Kennedy planned to start Medicare, which was a cheap system of state health insurance, but this was thrown out by Congress. Slum clearance created housing shortages in inner-city areas. Moreover, the minimum wage only helped those who already had a job and the poorest people could not afford to pay back the housing loans.

WORKING TOGETHER

- Firstly, compare with a partner the notes that you have made on this section. Add anything that you have missed and check anything that you have disagreed on.
- Next, divide your paper into two. One of you should identify the achievements of the New Frontier. The other should note the shortcomings.
- After you have finished, combine your findings.

Overall, to what extent do you agree that Kennedy's New Frontier was a success?

Lyndon B. Johnson (1908–73)

Lyndon Baines Johnson was born in Texas in 1908. He became a teacher and saw, first hand, much of the poverty in the area, which made him a supporter of social reform. In 1937, he was elected to Congress as a Democrat and became a strong supporter of Roosevelt's New Deal. In 1948, he became a senator and, within five years, he was appointed leader of the Democrats in the Senate. In 1960, he was chosen as Kennedy's vice-presidential candidate due to his skilful handling of Congress. He became president in 1963 after Kennedy's assassination. He did not seek re-election as president in 1968 and, five years later, died of a heart attack. Johnson was an experienced politician who knew how to get things done and how to make deals with Congress. He was far more successful than nearly any other president in getting measures passed through Congress. Also, because he was a Southerner, he knew how to deal with the Southern Democrats and overcome their opposition – especially to civil rights. Some believe his six-foot five-inch frame helped him to dominate others.

Opposition to the New Frontier

Kennedy seemed to be in a powerful position as president as his party had a majority in both houses of Congress. However, little was achieved during his 1,000 days in office. This was partly due to his own failings as a politician as well as powerful opposition to the New Frontier. He seemed preoccupied with foreign policy and lacked a clear and coherent programme, with his piecemeal proposals being blocked by conservatives.

The greatest opposition came from Southern Congressmen, even Democrats, members of his own party, who disliked his commitment to civil rights. They felt that equal rights for African Americans would cost them the votes of whites in the South. Some opposed the further extension of the power of federal government and greater central government spending. Many still believed in the values of 'rugged individualism' (see page 143).

Johnson and the Great Society

To what extent have Johnson's domestic achievements been underestimated?

Lyndon B. Johnson (LBJ) was president from 1963 to 1968. His achievements have often been underestimated and overlooked due to the reputation of Kennedy and the US involvement in the war in Vietnam.

The Great Society

The Great Society included important economic and social reforms as well as civil rights legislation.

Civil rights

LBJ achieved far more in civil rights than his predecessor, JFK. The Civil Rights Act of 1964 banned discrimination in public places, in federally assisted programmes and in employment. In the following year, the Voting Rights Act of 1965 appointed agents to ensure that voting procedures were carried out properly. In 1967, the Supreme Court declared all laws banning mixed race marriages were to be removed.

Economic reform

The Great Society also tackled economic reform. Johnson cut taxes to give consumers more money to spend and, in turn, to help businesses grow and to create more jobs. The Appalachian Recovery Programme provided federal funds for the development of the Appalachians, a mountainous area in the Eastern states. Moreover, the Office of Economic Opportunity set up schemes to help poor people in inner cities. It funded new education and community projects and provided loans for local schemes. These schemes were the basis of Johnson's Programme for Poverty.

Manufacturers and shops had to label goods fairly and clearly. Consumers had the right to return faulty goods and exchange them. The Johnson administration spent $1.5 billion on the Head Start Programme, so that teachers could provide additional education for very young, poor children.

Social reform

Social reform was another significant area.

- The Medical Care Act provided Medicare (for the old) and Medicaid (for the poor). This was an attempt to try to ensure that all Americans had equal access to health care.

- The Elementary and Secondary Education Act provided the first major federal support for state education ever. Federal money was provided to try to ensure that standards of education in all states were equal.
- The Model Cities Act continued Kennedy's policy of urban renewal. It was in the centres of the big cities that living conditions were at their worst and where crime was highest. The Act provided federal funds for slum clearance and the provision of better services.
- The minimum wage was increased from $1.25 to $1.40 an hour.

Opposition to the Great Society

Just like Kennedy, with his policies, Johnson faced powerful opposition to his Great Society measures. This opposition, however, was distorted due to attitudes to US involvement in the war in Vietnam. Republicans accused him of wasting money on welfare programmes and undermining 'rugged individualism'. He was accused of overspending on welfare programmes with rapid increases in health spending in particular.

The greatest problem for Johnson was the escalation of the US involvement in the war in Vietnam. This was not only costly, meaning spending was diverted from the Great Society to paying for the war, but it also led to increasing criticism of Johnson himself (see page 266). His great election victory of 1964 seemed in the distant past, and many Americans celebrated his decision not to run for re-election as president in 1968.

The outbreak of violence in US cities in the late 1960s (see page 264) has often been regarded as evidence that the Great Society was a failure. The programme had aroused expectations that it was then unable to deliver. However, for all the criticisms made of the Great Society, millions benefited from its education and health care programmes. Johnson had done much for the poorer sections of American society, with 25 million given access to decent health care for the first time. The number of African Americans living below the poverty line fell by over 50 per cent. Above all, like Roosevelt in the 1930s, he had greatly extended the role of federal government in intervening to make a difference, especially in the reduction of poverty.

Source A From an online article 'How Do Historians Evaluate the Administration of Lyndon Johnson?' written in 2002 by Robert Dallek. Accessed at George Mason History News Network HNN http://hnn.us/article/439. Dallek is the author of *Flawed Giant: Lyndon Johnson and His Times, 1961–1973*.

Johnson was not content to simply embrace JFK's proposals. He successfully took up the cudgels [came to the defence] for the voting rights, open housing, immigration reform, environmental protections, consumer safety bills, cabinet departments of transportation and housing and urban development, cultural reforms like the National Endowments for the Arts and Humanities and the Freedom of Information Act. Although a number of Johnson's initiatives fell short of what he hoped they might accomplish, his domestic reforms added up to a record of liberal alterations that rivalled FDR's New Deal …

Moreover, Johnson's civil rights actions permanently transformed the South. They destroyed the long standing *de jure* [by law] and *de facto* [in practice] traditions of racial segregation and opened the way to equal treatment of African Americans in every region of the country. Johnson himself believed that this was his greatest achievement.

LOOK AGAIN

Look back to pages 187–8 in Chapter 6.

To what extent did Roosevelt extend the role of federal government in his New Deal measures of the 1930s?

Poverty line – The income level at which a family is unable to meet its basic needs.

To what extent does the article in Source A prove that Johnson's domestic achievements have been underestimated?

KEY DATES: JOHNSON AND THE GREAT SOCIETY

1963 Johnson becomes president after the assassination of JFK.

1964 Johnson launches the Great Society.

1968 Johnson decides not to seek re-election as president.

NOTE-MAKING

Using bullet points (see page x) make notes on Nixon's domestic policies, in particular the Watergate scandal.

Richard M. Nixon (1913–94)

Nixon was born in California in 1913 and became a brilliant scholar and lawyer. He was elected to Congress and, in 1950, won a seat in the Senate. Nixon began to make a name for himself in the McCarthy anti-Communist witch-hunts (see pages 238–40). In 1952, he was Eisenhower's running mate for the presidency and became his vice-president from 1953–61. He was narrowly defeated by Kennedy in the 1960 presidential election but was successful in 1968 and 1972. Nixon was something of a loner who tended to see conspiracy at work against himself and the USA, and liked to conspire in turn. His main interest was foreign policy. Nixon died in 1994.

Middle America – The traditional or conservative people of the middle class in the US.

Devalued the dollar – The value of the dollar was reduced against the other major currencies to encourage exports and improve the country's trade deficit.

Nixon and Watergate

To what extent was Nixon's presidency a failure in domestic affairs because of the Watergate scandal?

Nixon's presidency is overshadowed by the Watergate scandal. However, he did have other social and economic achievements as well as successes in foreign policy. In 1968, Nixon promised to 'bring Americans together again'. He faced major problems including inflation caused by over-spending on the conflict in Vietnam as well as the Great Society. There was a growing trade gap and unemployment. He was the first president since 1849 to face a Congress in which both chambers were controlled by the opposition. In addition, US society seemed very divided, with many young Americans questioning traditional values and institutions as well as the USA's involvement in the war in Vietnam.

The 1968 election

The 1968 election was fought between Nixon and the Democrat candidate, Herbert Humphrey, who had served as vice-president under Johnson. Nixon defeated Humphrey by 500,000 votes, winning 302 of the electoral college votes to Humphrey's 191.

- Nixon appealed to 'Middle America' by championing those people worried by the Great Society, as well as the black inner-city riots. In addition, he promised 'peace with honour' in Vietnam.
- Humphrey, on the other hand, campaigned to continue the war in Vietnam as well as the Great Society. Moreover, the Democrat Convention in Chicago highlighted the divisions in the party with clashes between the police and left-wing protestors outside the convention hall.

Domestic achievements

Nixon's achievements were limited partly because he was far more interested in foreign policy and the Democrats controlled Congress, which would make it very difficult to pass domestic legislation. In addition, he was conservative by nature and wanted to win the support of Middle America: those who were opposed to feminism, the student movement and the radical changes brought in by the Great Society.

Nixon showed little interest in civil rights, although there was some progress. By 1971, there were thirteen black congressmen and 81 black mayors. He introduced the Family Assistance Plan (FAP), which attempted to replace the range of different benefits brought in by the Great Society with a direct grant of $1,600 to poorer families. However, this was rejected by Congress. Nevertheless, there was increased spending on the social programmes introduced by the Great Society.

Economic achievements

Nixon faced difficult economic problems, especially a rise in prices, and tried to reduce this by strict control of borrowing by the US people and business. This did not work so, in 1971, he introduced a 90-day wages and prices freeze, and a reduction in income tax. He hoped to encourage the purchase of consumer goods. This was followed by the introduction of a Pay Board, which kept wage increases down to 5.5 per cent, as well as a Price Commission, which limited price increases to 2.5 per cent and devalued the dollar. This led to a temporary boom in the economy.

The 1972 election

Nixon won this election convincingly with the greatest electoral triumph achieved by a Republican candidate, winning 47 million votes to the 29 million of his opponent, the Democrat candidate, George McGovern. Nixon was relatively popular at this time. There was a temporary boom in the economy and the Vietnam War seemed to be coming to an end. Moreover, he had other achievements in foreign policy, notably visits to China and the USSR.

The Watergate scandal

This scandal had huge repercussions for Nixon himself and the status of the US presidency.

The events of the scandal

In 1972 Nixon, concerned that he might not be re-elected, set up CREEP – Committee to Re-Elect the President. It was encouraged to use whatever methods necessary to ensure his re-election, with $350,000 set aside for 'dirty tricks'. On 17 June 1972, five members of CREEP were arrested for breaking into the Watergate offices of the Democrat Party. It soon became obvious that they were not ordinary burglars, but were there to plant bugging devices. Two reporters from the *Washington Post,* Carl Bernstein and Bob Woodward, discovered that all five burglars were employed by CREEP and that the CREEP fund was controlled by the White House. Nixon strongly denied all involvement by himself and his advisers, and went on to win a landslide victory in the 1972 presidential election.

In January 1973, the Watergate burglars went on trial and were all convicted. In March, James McCord, one of the convicted, claimed in court that there had been a White House cover-up. Again Nixon denied all knowledge of the break-in or cover-up. However, he did admit that two of his top advisers, Bob Haldeman and John Ehrlichman, had been involved. They resigned. The investigation of a Senate Committee set up to investigate the scandal was televised between May and November 1973. It became increasingly obvious that White House officials had been involved. One of them, John Dean, claimed there had been a cover-up directed by Nixon.

One White House aide told the Senate Committee that in 1971 Nixon had installed a tape-recording system in the White House and that all the President's conversations had been taped. After at first refusing to produce the tapes, Nixon handed over seven of the nine tapes but they had been heavily edited. One of them had eighteen minutes missing. Finally, Nixon was made to hand over all the tapes, unedited. They showed that he had been involved in the dirty tricks campaign and had repeatedly lied throughout the investigation. The tapes also shocked the nation because of the foul language used. Any foul language was indicated by 'expletive deleted', which occurred at regular intervals.

Effects of the scandal

In July 1974, Congress decided to impeach Nixon. This meant that he would be put on trial with the Senate acting as the jury. On 8 August 1974, Nixon resigned, giving his reason in a televised broadcast, to avoid impeachment. His successor, Gerald Ford, issued a decree pardoning Nixon for any criminal acts that he had taken part in. Nixon may well have been unlucky to be caught out. Previous presidents had almost certainly used similar tactics. However, he had abused power more than his predecessors, with some 31 of Nixon's advisers going on to serve prison terms for Watergate-related offences. It utterly

WORKING TOGETHER

Working in pairs:
- One of you make a note of any successes in domestic affairs in Nixon's presidency.
- One of you make notes on any failures.

To what extent do you agree that, because of the Watergate scandal, Nixon's presidency was a failure in domestic affairs?

destroyed Nixon's reputation. He was seen as untrustworthy and was given the nickname of 'Tricky Dicky'. For many years afterwards the Watergate scandal overshadowed all his other achievements.

As a result of the scandal, the powers of the Executive were reduced by a series of measures including:

- The Election Campaign Act of 1974, which set limits on election contributions to prevent corruption.
- The War Powers Act of 1973, which required the president to consult Congress before sending American troops into combat.
- The Privacy Act of 1974, which allowed citizens to have access to any files that the government may have had on them.
- The Congressional Budget Act, 1974, which meant that the president could not use government money for his/her own purposes.

The scandal greatly undermined people's confidence in politics and politicians. In 1976, Americans voted for the presidential election candidate they believed they could trust, Jimmy Carter, who promised never to lie.

KEY DATES: NIXON AND WATERGATE

1968 Nixon elected president for the first time.

1972 Nixon elected president for the second time.

1972 Five men associated with CREEP break into the Watergate Hotel in Washington.

1974 Nixon resigns as president to avoid impeachment.

▲ The day after resigning from the presidency, Richard Nixon gives a farewell speech to his staff. His wife Pat, daughter Tricia and son-in-law Edward F. Cox stand close to him.

2 The USA and international relations, 1960–75

The role played by the USA in world affairs continued to grow in the years 1960–75, as the Cold War intensified, especially during the Cuban Missile Crisis of 1962. In addition, America extended its policy of containment to Asia with direct military involvement in the conflict in Vietnam but, under Nixon, achieved improved relations with China.

The USA and the Cold War, 1960–75

To what extent did US relations with the Soviet Union worsen in this period?

The rivalry between the USA and the Soviet Union had intensified in the second half of the 1950s with the Soviet invasion of Hungary as well as the space and arms race.

The Berlin Wall Crisis, 1961

Khrushchev remained determined to force the West out of Berlin (see page 211). In June 1961, he met Kennedy at Vienna and gave the US President an ultimatum: something had to be done about Berlin by December 1961 or Khrushchev would hand over the Berlin access routes to East Germany.

This ultimatum greatly increased Cold War tension. Then, in August 1961, Khrushchev ordered the construction of a wall to separate East Berlin from West Berlin. He believed he could bully the new, inexperienced president of the USA, Kennedy, especially after the Bay of Pigs fiasco (see page 250). There was tension after the construction of the Wall. From 5 p.m. on 27 October to 11 a.m. on 28 October, US and Soviet tanks, fully armed, faced each other in a tense stand-off. Then, after eighteen hours, the US tanks pulled back. Kennedy had been forced to back down but was furious with the USSR.

The Berlin Wall crisis was significant for several reasons:

- In some ways it could be said to have brought some stability to Germany and Berlin, in that it finally sealed off the two Berlins.
- It increased Cold War tension as both the USA and the USSR resumed nuclear testing.
- Soviet propaganda claimed that the Wall was a success for Russia as the USA had been unable to prevent its construction. On the other hand, Western writers claimed that the Wall was a triumph because it showed that East Germany had to wall its people in.
- Some historians believe Khrushchev saw it as a success and it encouraged him to place missiles in Cuba, leading to the Cuban Missile Crisis.

NOTE-MAKING

For each of the events listed below, create a table to show how they either improved or worsened relations between the USA and USSR.
- Berlin Wall Crisis
- Cuban Missile Crisis
- SALT 1
- Helsinki Agreements.

The Cuban Missile Crisis, 1962

The Cuban Missile Crisis, which took place over a few days in October 1962, brought the superpowers to the brink of nuclear war. The crisis showed how the Cold War had spread outside the confines of Europe to the wider world.

Causes

Cuba had been a thorn in the side of the USA since 1959, when a revolution had brought Fidel Castro to power. Castro had ejected all US businesses and investment. In retaliation, the USA refused to buy Cuba's biggest export – sugar. The Soviet Union offered to buy Cuban sugar. The Soviet leader, Khrushchev, was keen to extend Soviet influence in the Caribbean and wanted to out-manoeuvre John F. Kennedy, the inexperienced American president.

In April 1961, Kennedy sanctioned an invasion of Cuba by exiles who had left Cuba in 1959, which was to land in the Bay of Pigs, create a national uprising and overthrow Castro. The Bay of Pigs invasion was a disastrous failure due to poor planning and lack of support in Cuba, where Castro was popular. It was a humiliation for the USA, further strengthened Castro's position in Cuba and drew Cuba even closer to the Soviet Union. At the end of 1961, Castro announced his conversion to Communism.

Khrushchev now saw the opportunity to further extend Soviet influence in Cuba. He was concerned by US missile bases in Italy and Turkey and wanted to establish Soviet bases in Cuba to redress the balance. In September 1962, Soviet technicians began to install ballistic missiles. On 14 October, an American U2 spy plane took photographs of Cuba which revealed that Soviet intermediate range missiles were being constructed. These were in range of almost all US cities and posed a serious threat to the country's security.

Ballistic missiles – Missiles (rockets) that follow a ballistic flightpath moving under the force of gravity with the objective of delivering one or more warheads to a predetermined target.

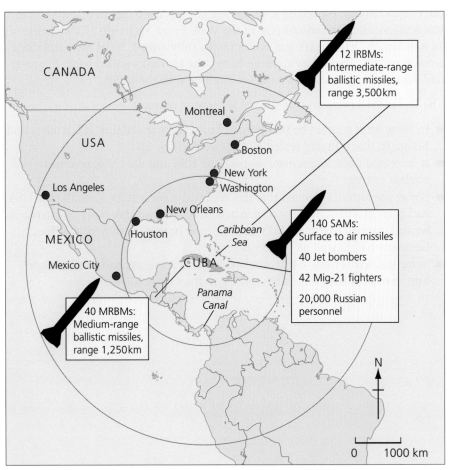

▶ **Figure 1** A map showing the build-up of Soviet missiles in Cuba.

The October crisis

The crisis lasted over thirteen days in October 1962.

16 October
Kennedy was told that Khrushchev intended to build missile sites on Cuba.

18–19 October
Kennedy held talks with his closest advisers. The 'Hawks' wanted an aggressive policy, while the 'Doves' favoured a peaceful solution.

20 October
Kennedy decided to impose a naval blockade around Cuba to prevent Soviet missiles reaching Cuba. They searched any ship suspected of carrying arms or missiles.

21 October
Kennedy made a broadcast to the American people, informing them of the potential threat and what he intended to do.

23 October
Khrushchev sent a letter to Kennedy insisting that Soviet ships would force their way through the blockade.

24 October
Soviet ships approached the blockade line and then retreated. Khrushchev issued a statement insisting that the Soviet Union would use nuclear weapons in the event of a war.

25 October
Kennedy wrote to Khrushchev asking him to withdraw missiles from Cuba.

26 October
Khrushchev replied to Kennedy's letter. He said he would withdraw the missiles if the USA promised not to invade Cuba and withdrew missiles from Turkey.

27 October
A US spy plane was shot down over Cuba. Robert Kennedy (brother of the President) agreed a deal with the Soviet Union. The USA would withdraw missiles from Turkey as long as it was kept secret.

28 October
Khrushchev accepted the deal and broadcast his answer on Radio Moscow. The Voice of America radio station in Europe broadcast US acceptance.

▲ **Figure 2** The escalating crisis.

Results of the crisis

The crisis had several important results. On the one hand, Kennedy seemed to have won the war of words and the perception was that Khrushchev had backed down, especially as the deal over Turkey was not disclosed at the time. The Americans felt that they had won some kind of victory. This led to over-confidence, especially in Vietnam. The Soviets were determined that they would never have to back down again. They worked hard and successfully to achieve nuclear parity by the end of the decade.

The superpowers had almost gone to war – a war that would have destroyed much of the world. There was a relief that the crisis was over and there was a great reduction in tension. To ensure that the two leaders did not have to communicate by letter in the case of a crisis, a hotline telephone link was established between the White House in Washington DC and the Kremlin in Moscow. Further improvements came when the Partial Test Ban Treaty was signed in August 1963, whereby both the USA and the USSR agreed to stop testing nuclear weapons in the atmosphere.

The USA and China

One of Nixon's greatest achievements in foreign policy was to improve US relations with China, which had deteriorated since the Chinese Civil War of 1945–49 when the USA had provided aid to Mao's opponent, Chiang (see page 215). They worsened even more during the Korean War (see pages 212–13) which the US interpreted as a sign that Chinese-sponsored Communism was expansionist. After the Korean War, the US put a trade embargo on China and kept it out of the UN. The US then established bases on Taiwan, which infuriated Mao.

Expansionist – Following a policy of territorial expansion.

Détente – An easing of strained relations.

Sino–US relations – Relations between America and China.

Reasons for improved relations

In April 1971, the USA lifted its 21-year old trade embargo with China. There were several reasons for improved relations between the USA and China.

- Relations between China and the USSR had worsened in the later 1960s, especially after the Chinese denounced the Soviet invasion of Czechoslovakia in 1968. Nixon saw an opportunity to exploit this split between the two leading Communist nations. Nixon and Kissinger wanted to use China to counter Soviet power and force the USSR into *détente*.
- Nixon also hoped that closer relations with China might help to end the war in Vietnam, as the Chinese were close allies of the North Vietnamese. This was another example of his policy of linkage (see page 253).
- Mao believed that China needed *détente*, especially the potential stimulus to Chinese trade and industry. He was also convinced that Nixon would withdraw US troops from Asia, especially Vietnam, which made America less of a threat than the Soviet Union.

'Ping-pong' diplomacy

The new period of diplomacy began at the World Table Tennis Championship held in Japan on 6 April 1971, when the Chinese ping pong team formally invited the US team to play in their country on an all-expenses paid trip. When American player Glenn Cowan missed his team's bus after practice, he was offered a ride by Chinese player, Zhuang Zedong. This friendly display of good will was well publicised and, later that day, the American team was formally invited to China. They were among the first group of US citizens permitted to visit China since 1949.

On 14 April 1971, the US Government lifted a trade embargo with China that had lasted over 20 years. Talks began to facilitate a meeting between top government officials and, eventually, a meeting between Mao Zedong and President Richard Nixon.

The 'ping-pong diplomacy' was important because it led to the restoration of Sino–US relations, which had been cut for more than two decades. This triggered a series of other events, including the restoration of China's legitimate rights in the United Nations by an overwhelming majority vote in October 1971, and the establishment of diplomatic relations between China and other countries.

Source B From *The Memoirs of Richard Nixon,* published in 1978, quoted in *America 1870–1975* by J. O'Keeffe, (Longman), 1984.

The arrival

Our plane landed smoothly. Chou En-lai stood at the foot of the ramp, hatless in the cold. Even a heavy overcoat did not hide the thinness of his frail body. When we were about halfway down the steps, he began to clap. I paused for a moment and then returned the gesture, according to the Chinese custom. I knew that Chou had been deeply insulted by Foster Dulles's refusal to shake hands with him at the Geneva Conference in 1954. When I reached the bottom step, therefore, I made a point of extending my hand as I walked towards him. When our hands met, one era ended and another began …

Using evidence from Source B, to what extent does this source show how determined Nixon was to improve relations with China?

Détente

The improvement in relations between the USA and the USSR in the years after the Cuban Missile Crisis became known as *détente* – a French word that refers to a reduction in tension, in this case, between the superpowers.

Reasons for *détente*

This relaxation in relations was due to several reasons. The threat of a nuclear war during the Cuban Missile Crisis had had a sobering effect on all concerned. The hotline between the White House and the Kremlin improved the speed of communications and the Test Ban Treaty showed a willingness to look at the issue of developing nuclear missiles.

Both the USA and the USSR were keen on arms limitation talks as a means of reducing their ever-increasing defence spending. Nixon and his foreign policy adviser, Henry Kissinger, were fearful of the growing military strength of the USSR. They also knew that the American public and economy made it impossible to counter increased Soviet power with a massive arms race. Containment had to be achieved by a different method – *détente*.

The USA's involvement in Vietnam had not gone well and, by 1968, the USA was seeking to end the war. After Nixon became president, it was hoped that if the USA improved trade and technology links and made an offer of arms reduction, then Brezhnev might persuade his North Vietnamese ally to negotiate an end to the war. The idea of offering concessions was called 'linkage' by Nixon's advisers. Nixon visited Moscow in 1972 and made it clear that he did not see Vietnam as an obstacle to *détente*.

Nixon had visited China three months earlier and the Soviet leader, Brezhnev, did not want to see a Chinese–US alliance develop. The Soviet leader was keen to gain access to US technology and further grain sales.

SALT 1

SALT stands for Strategic Arms Limitation Treaty and the first of these, SALT 1, was signed in 1972. Early in Nixon's presidency, a decision was made to talk about nuclear weapons. Talks held in Helsinki and Vienna over a period of almost three years produced SALT 1, the first Strategic Arms Limitation Treaty, which imposed limits on the nuclear capability of the USSR and the USA. SALT 1 was significant because it was the first agreement between the superpowers that successfully limited the number of nuclear weapons they held.

The Helsinki Agreements, 1975

In the Helsinki Agreements the USA and the USSR, along with 33 other nations, made declarations about three distinct international issues (called 'baskets' by the signatories).

- The West recognised the current national boundaries in Eastern Europe and the Soviet Union accepted the existence of West Germany. West Germany renounced its claim to be the sole legitimate German state.
- Each signatory agreed to respect human rights and basic freedoms such as thought, speech, religion and freedom from unfair arrest.
- There was a call for closer economic, scientific and cultural links, which would lead to even closer political agreement.

> **KEY DATES: USA AND THE COLD WAR**
>
> **1961** The Berlin Wall Crisis.
> **1962** The Cuban Missile Crisis.
> **1972** Nixon's visit to China.
> **1975** The Helsinki Agreements.

The conflict in Vietnam

Why was the USA unable to win in Vietnam?

Under President Johnson the USA became directly involved in the war in Vietnam. This involvement was to have major effects on US foreign and domestic policy.

Reasons for US involvement

During the 1950s the USA became far more involved in Vietnam as part of its policy of containment to stop the spread of Communism. The fundamental reason was the domino theory. The USA was convinced that if Vietnam fell to Communism it would be followed by its neighbouring states, especially Laos and Cambodia. American involvement increased in the years 1954–64.

> ### Vietnam during and after the Second World War
>
> In 1939, Vietnam was part of an area known as French Indo-China. This included contemporary Vietnam, Laos and Cambodia. Japan invaded and occupied Indo-China in 1940. In 1941, two leading Vietnamese Communists, Ho Chi Minh and Nguyen Vo Giap, a history teacher, set up the League for the Independence of Vietnam (or **Vietminh**) in southern Vietnam with the aim of establishing an independent Vietnam free from French and Japanese rule through **guerrilla** activities against the Japanese. In August 1945, the Japanese were defeated in the Second World War and Ho Chi Minh quickly announced that Vietnam was an independent and democratic republic. However, within weeks the French quickly restored control over Vietnam. The Vietminh, led by Ho Chi Minh, continued their guerrilla campaign against the French. The decisive battle for control of Vietnam took place at the French garrison of Dien Bien Phu in 1954. The Geneva Agreement of 1954 that followed divided Vietnam temporarily along the 17th parallel into North and South Vietnam. North Vietnam would be led by Ho Chi Minh and the South would be led by Ngo Dinh Diem.

NOTE-MAKING

1 Using a spider diagram, summarise the main reasons why the USA was unable to win in Vietnam. Begin with the most important reason at 12 o'clock. Moving clockwise, put the rest in rank order of importance.
2 Swap your spider diagram with a partner and compare which each of you thinks is the most important reason.

Vietminh – The League for the Independence of Vietnam, a nationalist and Communist dominated organisation, later known as the Vietcong.

Guerrilla – A member of an irregular armed force that fights a stronger force by sabotage and harassment.

During the elections of 1956 the USA was determined to prop up the government of South Vietnam and prevent any reunification with the Communist-controlled north. Indeed, the USA prevented the elections taking place realising that the Communists would win. South Vietnam was ruled by Diem. He was a corrupt and unpopular ruler whose government was propped up the USA which sent military advisers to train the South Vietnamese army. In 1959, Ho Chi Minh issued orders to the Vietminh (which became known as the Vietcong) to begin a terror campaign against the South.

In November 1963, Diem was overthrown and replaced by a series of short-lived and weak governments. The Vietcong became more popular in the South. Under Kennedy, the USA tried to reduce Communist influence through the Strategic Hamlet policy. This involved moving peasants into fortified villages, guarded by troops. It did not stop the Communists and was very unpopular with the peasants.

By 1964, President Johnson wanted more direct military involvement in Vietnam but needed an excuse. On 2 August 1964, the US destroyer *Maddox* was fired at by North Vietnamese patrol boats in the Gulf of Tonkin. Two days later there was a second alleged attack. Evidence later showed that this second attack did not happen. Johnson was able to use these attacks to persuade Congress to support greater US involvement. Congress passed the Gulf of Tonkin Resolution that gave Johnson the power to take any military measures he thought necessary to defend South Vietnam. Some people suggest that the administration engineered the Gulf of Tonkin Crisis as an excuse for much greater military involvement in Vietnam. At the time, 85 per cent of people supported this policy and no one in the House of Representatives and only two members of the Senate opposed the Resolution.

The Ho Chi Minh Trail

This was a supply line from the North of Vietnam to the Vietcong in the South. It ran through Laos and Cambodia in an attempt to avoid US bombing raids. The journey lasted two months and was very dangerous due to the possibility of disease and attack. Nevertheless, it was the key to the success of the Vietcong as it ensured the replacement of troops and supplies.

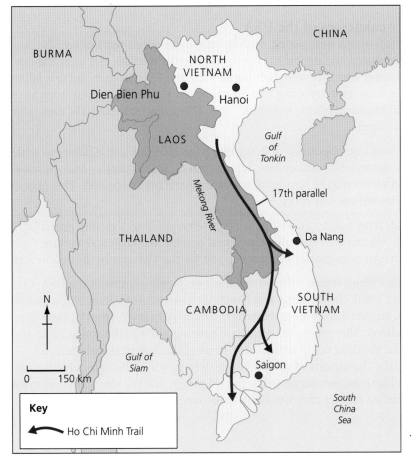

◀ **Figure 3** A map showing Vietnam, including the Gulf of Tonkin.

The My Lai massacre

The worst offence committed by US troops took place on 16 March 1968. A US patrol was carrying out a 'Search and Destroy' mission just south of Khe Sanh during the Tet Offensive. Lieutenant Calley and his platoon wiped out the village of My Lai, killing at least 347 men, women, children and babies. Some of the women had been raped first. The US military tried to keep news of the massacre quiet. In November 1969, the US press got hold of the story from a soldier who had heard about the massacre. *Life* magazine published details of the massacre and this sparked off an official investigation. Calley and ten other officers were formally charged with murdering 109 people. Calley was the only one found guilty and was given 20 years of hard labour in 1971. He was released in 1974. My Lai shocked US public opinion. It was the clearest evidence that the war was going wrong. However, a large number of Americans either refused to believe the massacre had happened or felt it was justified because the villagers were helping the Vietcong.

Napalm – An inflammable sticky jelly used in bombs in order to set fire to people, trees and buildings

Reasons for US defeat

The USA was eventually defeated due to the strengths of the Communists and their own weaknesses.

The strengths of the Communists

One of the greatest strengths of the North Vietnamese and the Vietcong was that they were fighting for a cause – Communism and the reunification of Vietnam. They would not surrender, refused to give in to US bombing, and were prepared to accept very heavy casualties. In addition, there was an army in North Vietnam that played a significant role in the Tet Offensive of 1968.

The Vietcong fought a 'low-tech' war using very successful guerrilla tactics which, for the most part, avoided pitched battles and reduced the effectiveness of the 'high-tech' methods and superior weaponry of the USA. These methods were ideally suited to the jungle terrain of South Vietnam.

The Vietcong feared US bombing raids. The Communist forces dug deep tunnels and used them as air-raid shelters. For example, the tunnels around Saigon ran for 320 km. These were self-contained and booby-trapped and provided not only refuge from the bombing, and a safe haven for the guerrilla fighters, but were also a death trap for the US forces and the Army of the Republic of South Vietnam (the AVRN).

In addition, many people living in the South supported the North and the Vietcong. Some believed in Communism and reunification and others were alienated by US tactics and brutality. Their support, in turn, made the Vietcong guerrilla tactics far more effective. Moreover, both the Soviet Union and China supported the reunification of Vietnam under the Communist North. They supplied the North and Vietcong with rockets, tanks and fighter planes.

The weaknesses of the USA

Many US troops were young, with some only nineteen years of age, inexperienced and unable to cope with guerrilla warfare, and most did not understand why they were fighting in Vietnam. This, in turn, led to a fall in morale with some resorting to drug-taking and brutal behaviour, such as the My Lai massacre where, in March 1968, US troops murdered 347 men, women and children.

There was also opposition at home (see page 266) due to the failure to achieve a quick victory, the casualty rate, with a total of 58,000 deaths, and the televised pictures showing the horrors of war such as the use of napalm. This opposition undermined the war effort.

The US army failed to develop an effective response to Vietcong guerrilla tactics. US tactics, especially search and destroy and chemical warfare, encouraged even greater peasant support for the Vietcong in the countryside.

The Tet Offensive had a disastrous effect on public opinion in the USA. On 31 January 1968, the Vietcong and North Vietnamese Army launched a massive attack on over 100 cities and towns in South Vietnam during the New Year, or Tet holiday. This proved an important turning-point in the conflict as it showed that the Vietcong could strike at the heart of the American-held territory, especially the capture of the US Embassy in Saigon. It brought a further loss of US military morale, suggested to the US public that the war was unwinnable, and fuelled further criticism of US involvement.

US methods of warfare in Vietnam

There were several methods used by the USA during the course of the 1960s to try to defeat the Vietcong.

- 'Operation Rolling Thunder' – the US bombing campaign of North Vietnam that lasted three and a half years, from 1965 to 1968, in the hope of destroying Vietcong supply routes to the South. The USA also used chemical warfare, such as napalm, and defoliants to destroy the jungle cover for the Vietcong, such as 'Agent Orange', a highly toxic weed killer used to destroy the jungle.
- In addition 'Search and Destroy' was introduced by the US commander, Westmoreland. This method used helicopters to descend on a village suspected of assisting the Vietcong forces and then to destroy it. The troops called these attacks 'Zippo' raids after the name of the lighters they used to set fire to the thatched houses of the villages.

> **Defoliants** – Chemicals sprayed on plants to remove their leaves.

Impact of the mass media on the war in Vietnam

Vietnam was the first television war. By the mid-1960s television was the most important source of news for the American public. During the Korean War of the early 1950s, only about ten per cent of US homes had television. Most of the newsreel film was taken by official military cameramen. However, by 1966, 93 per cent of homes had televisions and there was an estimated daily television audience of 50 million. Most Americans got their news from television, partly because the visual element of television made viewers feel that they were part of the action. Television reporters soon became household names. By 1967, 90 per cent of the evening news was devoted to the war.

In Vietnam, the news film was produced by the American TV networks, who were allowed to move freely and operate as they wished. There was no military censorship. Using lightweight cameras, they had easy access to events and could send their pictures back to the USA with great speed. American viewers could witness every mistake and defeat. They could see Americans bombing and shelling Vietnamese homes in Saigon after the Tet Offensive. Moreover, in the mid and later 1960s, colour television became more readily available, which worsened the bloody nature of what was shown.

The Tet Offensive and after

From 1965 to 1967, television coverage was generally supportive of the war in Vietnam. However, this was to change during the Tet Offensive of 1968. New film of the offensive had a dramatic effect. Especially stunning was film of the Vietcong fighting in the grounds of the American embassy in Saigon. Television, however, portrayed the attack as a brutal defeat for the US; the media, not the military, confirmed the growing perception that the US was unable to win the war.

This was followed by other incidents in the war that shocked Americans, some of which appeared to be war crimes, particularly the My Lai massacre as well as the execution on a street in Saigon, live on television in 1968, of a Vietcong suspect by the Saigon Chief of Police.

The significance of television coverage

There has been much debate about the significance of television coverage on attitudes to the war in Vietnam. Both Professor Hallin, in his book *The Uncensored War: The Media and Vietnam,* published in 1968, and the American historian Stanley Karnow in *Vietnam, A History,* published in 1997, have questioned the importance of this coverage. Karnow suggests that public opinion surveys at the time made it plain that the Tet Offensive hardly altered attitudes to the war and that public support for the war had been slipping for two years before the war because of increased casualties. Hallin concludes that television was probably more a follower than a leader in the nation's change of course in Vietnam.

▲ A photograph taken in 1972 showing a naked nine-year-old girl, Kim Phuc, centre left, running down a road nude near Trang Bang in Vietnam after a napalm attack.

However, there can be little doubt that dramatic film showing the effects of chemical weapons, such as the naked girl running away from a napalm attack (shown above), had a dramatic impact on public opinion in America and attitudes to the war.

US withdrawal

As early as 1969, the USA were moving towards a policy of withdrawal from Vietnam, which was finally achieved four years later.

Reasons for withdrawal

- It seemed obvious, especially after the Tet Offensive, that the USA could not win in Vietnam. Indeed, in 1968 the 'Wise Men', a group of senior advisers, advocated a retreat.
- Nixon was elected president on the promise of US withdrawal from Vietnam and was very aware of the strong protests against the war. Indeed, without these protests, which increased after the US extended the war to the bombing of Cambodia in 1970, Nixon may have conceivably continued the war.
- By the end of the 1960s, the war was very unpopular. The media, including television, radio and the majority of newspapers, turned against the war after the Tet Offensive, in 1968, by which time more than 36,000 members of the US military had been killed, and protests were being held in every major city.
- US involvement in Vietnam was very expensive. In 1964, it had cost the US taxpayer less than half a billion dollars. By 1968, this cost had spiralled to $26.5 billion. The war was a main cause of the government's budget deficit of $25 billion and rising inflation in 1968.

▲ Dead and wounded US soldiers after a Vietcong attack of 1967. This image was shown on television in the USA.

In May 1969, President Nixon, who had been elected the previous year on a promise of withdrawing US troops from Vietnam, unveiled his plan to end US involvement, known as Vietnamisation. The idea was that the South Vietnamese soldiers would be trained and equipped to take the place of US troops as they were gradually withdrawn. The strategy did not work because the South Vietnamese troops were no match for the Communist forces.

Peace talks to end the war had begun as early as 1968 but made no real progress until Nixon's visit to China in 1972, after which the Chinese encouraged more co-operation from the government of North Vietnam. On 23 January 1973, a ceasefire was signed in Paris followed four days later by a formal peace treaty in which the USA promised to fully withdraw all its troops, and the Vietcong was allowed to hold on to all captured areas of South Vietnam. Within two years, the Communists had defeated the South Vietnamese armed forces and re-united Vietnam.

The effects of the war

- The USA spent around $30 billion each year on the war. This did much to undermine Johnson's spending on the Great Society. The war also made Johnson very unpopular and heavily influenced his decision not to seek re-election as president in 1968.
- The inability to win the war pushed Nixon into considering different diplomatic strategies that affected the Cold War. His decision to visit China to establish closer relations, and also to develop *détente* with the Soviet Union, were attempts to drive a wedge between the two main supporters of North Vietnam.
- From the war emerged the Nixon Doctrine, which stated that the USA expected its allies to take care of their own military defence. The Vietnam War was the first war that the USA had lost and there was an unwillingness to become involved in future conflicts.
- There was also a terrible human cost for the USA with 50,000 American deaths in Vietnam and a further 300,000 wounded.

KEY DATES: CONFLICT IN VIETNAM

1964 The Gulf of Tonkin incident.

1968 The Tet Offensive.

1969 Nixon introduces his policy of Vietnamisation.

1973 The Paris peace treaty.

3 Ideological, social, regional and ethnic divisions

The campaign for civil rights for African Americans dominated the 1960s, although the peaceful methods advocated by Martin Luther King were challenged by Malcolm X and the Black Power Movement.

Progress in civil rights under Martin Luther King

To what extent has the role of Martin Luther King in achieving civil rights for African Americans in the years 1960–68 been exaggerated?

The 1960s saw tremendous gains for African Americans. Martin Luther King worked hard and effectively to end segregation and gain civil rights for African Americans in the South. His profile was raised by a number of marches that gained worldwide publicity. However, some historians have questioned the importance of the role of King in bringing about civil rights legislation in the 1960s.

Progress in the early 1960s

The profile of the civil rights movement had been raised by events such as Montgomery and Little Rock (see pages 234–6) and was raised even further by sit-ins and the freedom riders.

In 1960, some students in Greensboro, North Carolina, used a sit-in to protest against an all-white café. King supported them. By August 1961, the sit-ins had attracted over 70,000 participants and resulted in over 3,000 arrests.

This direct action led activists to challenge the deep-rooted racism in the South even further in what became known as the 'freedom rides'. The Supreme Court decided in December 1960 that all bus stations and terminals that served interstate travellers should be integrated. The Congress of Racial Equality (CORE) wanted to test the decision by employing the tactic of the freedom ride. The freedom riders were civil rights activists who rode interstate buses into the Southern states where segregation laws were still in operation. These freedom rides began in Washington DC in May 1961 and continued throughout the summer of 1961, with over 300 of the riders being imprisoned. On 22 September, the Interstate Commerce Commission issued a regulation that ended racial segregation in bus terminals.

King's leadership

By 1963, King had become the leading figure in the civil rights movement (see page 237). He aimed to end segregation and to gain political equality for African Americans in the South. His methods were not particularly original, being very similar to Gandhi's in India and those advocated by previous black leaders such as Booker T. Washington (see page 88). King wanted African Americans to help themselves through peaceful methods such as marches and boycotts, to avoid the unnecessary alienation of white Americans.

Peace marches

When the Student Non-Violent Co-ordinating Committee (SNCC) mobilised students in Albany, Georgia, to protest against segregation, King went along to lead the march and was arrested. He used marches to draw attention to segregation but also to get himself arrested. Arrests such as this put a spotlight on the civil rights cause, providing national and international publicity.

WORKING TOGETHER

Working together, collect evidence on the key developments in the civil rights movement of the 1960s including civil rights legislation.

- One of you should collect evidence on the achievements of King.
- The other should collect evidence on the shortcomings of King's work.

Overall to what extent do you agree that the role of Martin Luther King in achieving civil rights for African Americans in the years 1960–68 has been exaggerated?

Such methods were again employed in Birmingham, Alabama, in May 1963 where King led a march knowing that the racist police chief, Bull O'Connor, would act violently. O'Connor allowed his men to set dogs on the protestors and he then called in the fire department to use powerful hoses. Connor arrested 2,000 demonstrators as well as almost 1,300 children. Television witnessed the events, which were seen not only across the USA but also all over the world. This gave King all the publicity he wanted as it showed the violence of the authorities in the face of peaceful demonstrations. At this stage, President Kennedy became involved and it was agreed that desegregation would take place within 90 days.

After Birmingham, the civil rights groups wanted to maintain their high profile by organising a march on Washington. The march, which took place on 28 August 1963, began as a call for jobs and freedom, but it broadened to cover the aims of the whole of the civil rights movement. People came from all over America with as many as 250,000 taking part. King was the final speaker of the day and made his famous 'I have a dream speech'. The march was televised across the USA and did much for the civil rights movement. After the march, King and other leaders met to discuss civil rights legislation with President Kennedy, who confirmed his commitment to the cause.

President Johnson pushed Kennedy's Civil Rights Bill through Congress and it became law in 1964 (see page 244). However, it did not guarantee African Americans the vote. King decided, in 1965, to hold another march from Selma, Alabama, to Birmingham, to present a petition demanding voting rights. However, the marchers were attacked by police and state troopers on what became known as 'Bloody Sunday'. This encouraged President Johnson to introduce the Voting Rights Act of 1965 (see page 244).

The Southern Christian Leadership Conference (SCLC)

This was set up in 1957, just after the Montgomery bus boycott had ended. Its main aim was to advance the cause of civil rights but by non-violent methods. Martin Luther King helped to establish the SCLC and was its president from when it was set up until his assassination in 1968. The SCLC played a major role in the freedom marches of 1963 and the Voting Rights campaign, as well as the Selma marches.

▼ A photograph taken during the Birmingham civil rights march of 1963. It shows the fire department using powerful fire hoses against the marchers.

SNCC

The Student Non-violent Co-ordinating Committee was founded at Shaw University in Raleigh, North Carolina, in April 1960. Its first chairman was Nashville college student and political activist Martin Berry. In 1961, the group expanded its focus to support local efforts in voter registration as well as desegregation of public facilities. It played a major role in events in the early 1960s – sit-ins, freedom rides, the March on Washington and the Voter Registration campaign.

KEY DATES: MARTIN LUTHER KING

1960 First sit-in in Greensboro.

1963 Birmingham and Washington marches.

1965 Selma march.

1968 The assassination of Martin Luther King.

To what extent is Source C a valid interpretation of the achievements of King?

Achievements

On 4 April 1968, the day after giving a speech in Memphis in support of black refuse workers who were striking for equal treatment with their white co-workers, King was assassinated by a white racist, James Earl Ray.

The methods used by King were often very successful. However, has his role been exaggerated? Historians such as Kevern Verney have questioned the 'King-centric' approach – the overemphasis on the role of King to the civil rights movement of the 1960s – believing that it has underestimated the role of other individuals such as Philip Randolph and presidents Kennedy and Johnson, as well as the work of activists in organisations such as the National Association for the Advancement of Colored People (NAACP), see page 234, the Congress of Racial Equality (CORE), see page 260, the Southern Christian Leadership Conference (SCLC) and the Student Non-violent Coordinating Committee (SNCC).

- King was not directly involved in the sit-ins and freedom rides of the early 1960s. Indeed, it was the SNCC that mobilised the sit-ins. CORE, the SNCC and the NAACP worked together on the freedom rides. The Albany campaign of 1961–62 did not achieve anything for African Americans in Albany in the short term.

- Other activists played a key role, for example, female campaigners such as Gloria Richardson who, in 1962, set up the Cambridge Non-violent Action Committee in Cambridge, Maryland. This was the first adult-led affiliate of SNCC, and Richardson became its official spokesperson. It began with black Cambridge residents sitting in at segregated movie theatres, bowling alleys and restaurants, but the movement evolved into a struggle for the economic rights of Cambridge citizens, many of whom were burdened with low wages and unemployment. In addition, Fannie Lou Hamer was an American voting rights activist and civil rights leader. She was instrumental in organising Mississippi Freedom Summer for the Student Non-violent Coordinating Committee.

- The civil rights marches of 1963 helped to bring about important civil rights legislation. The Birmingham march of 1963 did not lead to desegregation. However, it did much to persuade Kennedy to introduce civil rights legislation in Congress. The Washington march of the same year was an important reason for the Civil Rights Act of 1964.

- The Voting Rights campaign and Selma marches were also important in encouraging the Voting Rights Act of 1965, after which there was a great rise in the number of African Americans voting in the South.

- During the years 1965–68 King remained in the forefront of the civil rights movement, focusing his attention on economic and social improvements for African Americans. In 1966, he focused his efforts on helping African Americans in the North by means of a major campaign in Chicago and, in 1968, he became involved in the Poor People's Campaign. However, in his 1967 book *Where Do We Go From Here?*, he admitted that this campaign 'just isn't working. People aren't responding'.

Source C An extract from *Access to History: Civil Rights in the USA 1945–68* by Vivienne Sanders, (Hodder Education), 2008, p.106.

The extent of King's contribution has always been controversial: Ella Barker insisted, 'the movement made Martin rather than Martin making the movement'. Although we have seen that King was frequently led rather than leading, his actions and involvement always gained national attention and sometimes provided the vital impetus for reform. His organisational skills were limited, but his ability to inspire others was peerless. Although his tactics and strategy were sometimes unsuccessful (and unappealing), the problems blacks faced were long-standing and enormous. He was a relatively moderate leader who made a massive contribution to the black cause.

Malcolm X and Black Power

Why was there growing support for the Black Power movement in the later 1960s?

The mid-1960s saw the emergence of black power and support for more militant black leaders such as Malcolm X, Stokely Carmichael, Bobby Seale and Huey Newton. For some in the civil rights movement, progress had been painfully slow. Moreover, there was a growing feeling that King's methods would never bring equality in politics or opportunities in life.

A group that had never accepted King's ideas was the Nation of Islam (or Black Muslims). Its supporters openly sought separatism. Members rejected their slave surnames and called themselves 'X'. The Nation of Islam had been set up in 1930 by Wallace Fard but, by the early 1960s, was led by Elijah Muhammad, a Baptist preacher from Georgia.

The Nation of Islam

Elijah Muhammad claimed that Allah originally created people black and other races were created by an evil scientist, Yakub. Whites would rule the world for several thousand years, but then Allah would return and end their supremacy. The Nation of Islam aimed to provide African Americans with an alternative to the white man's Christian religion, to persuade members to live a religious life, to increase black self-esteem, to keep black and white Americans separate and to encourage African Americans to improve their economic situation.

Malcolm X

The most famous member of the Nation of Islam was Malcolm X, whose brilliant oratorical skills had increased membership of the group to about 100,000 in the years 1952–64. He was a superb organiser and, during his membership of the Nation of Islam, he travelled across the USA winning converts. Malcolm X helped set up educational and social programmes aimed at black youths in ghettos. By 1960, 75 per cent of members of the Nation of Islam were aged 17–35. He did much to connect young African Americans to their African heritage.

Malcolm X was very critical of King and other leaders of the civil rights movement and their methods. He criticised the 1963 March on Washington, which he called 'the farce on Washington', because he could not understand how so many black people were impressed by a march that was organised by whites. He felt that violence could be justified not only for self-defence but also as a means to secure a separate black nation.

In March 1964, Malcolm left the Nation of Islam after a falling out with Elijah Muhammad. The latter was increasingly jealous of Malcolm's greater fame and influence. Malcolm wanted to make political speeches, to which the Nation of Islam was opposed. A 1964 visit to Mecca, however, changed Malcolm. He saw Muslims of different races interacting as equals and came to believe that Islam could be a means by which racial problems could be overcome. He still urged African Americans to defend themselves if necessary, so that he remained hated by whites. He was also unacceptable to the Nation of Islam, which he increasingly attacked in his speeches. He was assassinated in 1965, probably by the Nation of Islam.

His achievements

Malcolm X is often seen as a failure in comparison to the apparent successes achieved by King. His support for violence led to many enemies and critics. Moreover, his advocacy of separatism was unrealistic and unattainable.

NOTE-MAKING

1 Using a spider diagram (see page x), summarise the reasons for increasing support for more extreme groups such as Black Power and the Black Panthers.
2 To what extent was this support due to frustration with the methods used by Martin Luther King?

Separatism – Keeping races apart. Two separate countries for black and white Americans.

Malcolm X

Malcolm X was born Malcolm Little in Omaha in 1925 and six years later his father was murdered by white supremacists. By 1942, Malcolm was living in New York and was involved in pimping and drug dealing. In 1946, he was found guilty of burglary and imprisoned. By the time of his release from jail, in 1952, he had become a follower of the Nation of Islam and had changed his surname to 'X'. In 1964, he left the Nation of Islam and formed Muslim Mosque, Inc. and the black nationalist Organisation of Afro-American Unity. In February 1965, he was shot by assassins who were probably members of the Nation of Islam.

However, Malcolm was a realistic role model for ghetto African Americans who could relate to him, much more than King. He had changed himself from pimp, cocaine addict, armed robber and convict, into a national African-American leader. He helped raise the self-esteem of African-Americans more than any other individual in the civil rights movement. His views and ideas became the foundation of the more radical movements such as Black Power and the Black Panthers.

Black riots

From 1964 to 1966, the black city ghettos of the North, Midwest and West witnessed around 300 riots. Many young African Americans were frustrated and felt anger at the high rates of unemployment, continuing discrimination and poverty. On 11 August 1965, this frustration exploded into a major riot involving 30,000 people in the Watts district of Los Angeles. The riot left 34 dead and caused about $40 million of damage. There were riots across the USA's major cities in the following two summers, peaking in the summer of 1967, when there were riots in 125 cities. It took 21,000 federal troops and 34,000 National Guardsmen to restore order during the riots of 1965–67, with a total of $145 million of damage. Black ghettos in cities such as Chicago and Newark became no-go areas for whites.

Black Power

The frustration and anger that led to the inner-city riots also encouraged the emergence of the Black Power movement. By 1966, SNCC had moved away from King and began to support Black Power. Black Power was originally a political slogan but it came to cover a wide range of activities in the late 1960s that aimed to increase the power of blacks in American life. One of the leading figures in this movement was Stokely Carmichael. Carmichael and other leading figures in the SNCC wanted his followers to take pride in their heritage and they adopted the slogan 'Black is beautiful'. They wanted African Americans to develop a feeling of black pride as well as promoting African forms of dress and appearance. Carmichael was criticised because of his aggressive attitude and his denouncement of US involvement in the war in Vietnam. Black Power gained tremendous publicity at the 1968 Mexico City Olympics.

The Black Panthers

At the same time as the urban riots and the development of Black Power, the Black Panthers emerged. This party was founded by Huey Newton and Bobby Seale in October 1966 in Oakland, California. They were both heavily influenced by Malcolm X. The Black Panthers had a ten-point programme, which included an end to police brutality as well as decent housing, education and full employment for African Americans. They were prepared to use revolutionary means to achieve them.

The Panthers set up practical community action programmes, which won them support among ghetto African Americans. They served breakfasts to poor African American children, established healthcare clinics and provided childcare for working mothers. Moreover, they helped to leave a legacy of greater awareness of black culture and history, which culminated in more African American studies in educational institutions.

The Panthers wore uniforms and were prepared to use weapons, training members in their use. Their rally call was 'Power to the People'. They rejected the dominant white culture and sported 'Afro' haircuts. By the end of 1968, they had 5,000 members. However, internal divisions and the events of 1969, which saw 27 Panthers killed and 700 injured in confrontations with the police, saw support diminish. They were constantly targeted by the FBI and, by 1982, the party was disbanded.

Stokely Carmichael

Carmichael was born in Port of Spain, Trinidad and Tobago, in 1941 but moved to New York in 1943. He attended Howard University where he gained a degree in Philosophy. He became actively involved in the civil rights movement, taking part in the freedom rides in 1961 when he was jailed for seven weeks, and becoming chairman of the SNCC in 1966. He wanted blacks to take responsibility for their own lives and to reject white help.

The Mexico Olympics

The Black Power movement gained worldwide publicity at the 1968 Mexico Olympics, at the winners' ceremony for the men's 200m relay. The American black athletes Tommie Smith and John Carlos wore part of the movement's uniform – a single black glove and a black beret – and also gave the clenched-fist salute. During the ceremony, when the US national anthem was being played, Smith gave the salute with his right hand to indicate Black Power and Carlos with his left to show black unity.

KEY DATES: MALCOLM X AND BLACK POWER

1965 Assassination of Malcolm X. Riots in Watts district of Los Angeles.

1966 Black Panthers set up by Bobby Seale and Huey Newton.

1968 Black power salute by Tommie Smith and John Carlos at Mexico Olympics.

The student movement

How far did the student movement bring about change in the 1960s and early 1970s?

The student movement was one example of the deep divisions in American society in the 1960s. It began in the early 1960s with a demand for a greater say in how courses and universities were run, but gathered increasing support and momentum due to opposition to the war in Vietnam.

Reasons for student protest

There were several reasons for the emergence of the student protest movement of the 1960s.

- Many students wanted a greater say in their own education. They wanted to take part in running the universities and in bringing an end to college rules and restrictions imposed upon them. In addition, student societies tried to expose racism in their own colleges.
- For many young Americans, white and black, their first experience of protest was in civil rights. Martin Luther King's methods proved inspirational and many white students supported the freedom marches, freedom rides and the sit-ins of the early and mid-1960s.
- The 1960s were also a time of student protest across the world. For example, in the later 1960s there were student protests in Northern Ireland for civil rights for Catholics and in 1968 student demonstrations in Paris were so serious they almost overthrew the government.
- Under presidents Kennedy and Johnson, the USA became more and more involved in the conflict in Vietnam (see page 255). US involvement in the war in Vietnam divided US society, especially as the casualty list mounted and the media highlighted US atrocities against Vietnamese civilians. In contrast, opposition to the war united the student movement. Half a million young Americans were fighting in the war and many others would be called up by the draft or conscription system.
- The 1960s also saw an explosion in pop music which, in turn, was an expression of this emerging youth culture, and an expression of protest against important issues of the day. Bob Dylan's protest songs such as 'Blowin' in the Wind' and 'A Hard Rain's Gonna Fall' covered the themes of the changing times, nuclear war, racism and the hypocrisy of waging war.

Activities of the student movement

The movement was heavily involved in civil rights, protest against the war in Vietnam as well as a greater say in university life.

Civil rights

Students were heavily involved in the civil rights movement, in organisations such as the SNCC and CORE and, by the mid-1960s, were ready to use this experience to campaign for greater rights for themselves. In 1964, student societies organised rallies and marches to support the civil rights campaign. Many were appalled at the racism in American society and were determined to expose racists in their own colleges.

NOTE-MAKING

How important was the student movement of the 1960s and early 1970s?
- Create your own spider diagram summarising the achievements of the student movement.
- Rank order its achievements clockwise from the most to the least important.

The SDS

One of the first student protest groups to emerge in the USA was Students for a Democratic Society (SDS). It was set up in 1959 by Tom Hayden to give students a greater say in how courses and universities were run. Hayden was a student at the University of Michigan. The SDS denounced the Cold War and adopted a position of 'anti anti-Communism', demanding controlled disarmament to avoid the possibility of a nuclear war. The SDS also wanted to help the poor and disadvantaged. It eventually formed groups in 150 colleges and universities and had 100,000 members by the end of the 1960s. Its support increased after President Johnson announced bombing raids on North Vietnam in 1965.

The SDS first achieved national prominence when, in 1964, it organised a sit-in against a ban on political activities at the University of California at Berkeley. This was followed by a series of similar sit-ins across the USA. Membership greatly increased when, in 1966, President Johnson abolished student draft deferments, which had allowed some men to delay their call up for the armed forces. The SDS set up 300 new branches. The SDS organised a variety of activities against the war in Vietnam including staging draft card burnings, harassing campus recruiters for the CIA, occupying buildings in universities and destroying draft card records.

At the 1968 Democratic Convention in Chicago, SDS protestors, organised by Tom Hayden, created a riot in order to destroy the election chances of the pro-war candidate, Hubert Humphrey. Hayden and six others were arrested and convicted of crossing state lines to incite a riot. They became known as the Chicago Seven.

In the later 1960s, the student movement became more radical in its views. Some of its members called themselves 'Weathermen' and began to support violence to achieve their aims. They took their name from the Bob Dylan song 'You Don't Need a Weatherman to Know Which Way the Wind Blows'. They bombed army recruitment centres and government buildings. Tom Hayden disapproved of this extremism and left the movement in 1970. This radicalism slowed down when three of the Weathermen accidentally blew themselves up. Nixon, who exaggerated the threat posed by student radicalism, used the FBI and CBI to subvert these extreme student organisations.

Opposition to the war in Vietnam

Opposition to the Vietnam War united the student movement. Opposition grew due to the increasing US death toll and the tactics employed by the US (see page 257). Moreover, a disproportionate number of African American students were called up to fight in Vietnam. Influential black figures such as Martin Luther King spoke out against the war.

The anti-war protests reached their peak during 1968–70. In the first half of 1968, there were over 100 demonstrations against the war, involving 400,000 students. In 1969, 700,000 marched in Washington DC against the war. Students at these demonstrations often burned draft cards or, more seriously, the US flag, which was a criminal offence. This, in turn, led to angry clashes with police.

The worst incident occurred at Kent State University, Ohio in 1970. Students were holding a peaceful protest against President Nixon's decision to bomb Cambodia as part of the Vietnam War. National Guardsmen, called to disperse the students, used tear gas to try to move them. When they refused to move, shots were fired. Four people were killed and eleven injured. The press in the USA and abroad were horrified and some 400 colleges were closed as 2 million students went on strike in protest against this action.

The 'hippie' movement

Other young people protested in a totally different way. They decided to 'drop out' of society and become hippies. This meant they grew their hair long, wore distinctive clothes and developed an 'alternative lifestyle'. Often they travelled around the country in buses and vans and wore flowers in their hair as a symbol of peace rather than war. Indeed, their slogan was 'Make love, not war'.

Because they often wore flowers and handed them out to police, they were called 'flower children', and often settled in communes. San Francisco became the hippy capital of America. Their behaviour, especially their use of drugs, frequently led to clashes with the police who they nicknamed 'pigs'. They were influenced by groups such as The Grateful Dead and The Doors.

Achievements

The student movement did bring about social, political and cultural change. One of its more long-lasting achievements was on youth culture itself. By the end of the 1960s, there were profound changes in the whole lifestyle of the young. This was partly reflected in fashion, with the young becoming far more fashion-conscious and determined to move away from the 'norm' of the older generation.

Although the SDS and student protests did not bring an end to the war in Vietnam, there is no doubt that they helped to force a shift in government policy and make the withdrawal from Vietnam much more likely. They certainly influenced President Johnson's decision not to seek re-election in 1968.

In addition, they provided greater publicity for the racism still prevalent in US society. The support of many white students for black civil rights strengthened the whole movement and showed that most American youths would no longer tolerate discrimination and segregation.

Source D Extract from *Put Your Bodies Upon the Wheels, Student Revolt in the 1960s* by Kenneth J. Heineman, part of The American Way series, (Ivan R. Dee, Chicago), 2001, p.3.

Student protest in the 1960s, which began as a rejection of parental authority and the Vietnam War, rapidly evolved into a social movement. The Students for a Democratic Society (SDS), the chief organization of the campus-based New Left, gained strength as Democratic politicians lost control of the war in Vietnam and the unrest in America's inner cities. SDS, which began in the 1960s with just a few members, ended the decade 100,000 strong. By then it had committed itself to violent confrontation with university and government officials. More than 300 of the nation's 2,000 campuses experienced sit-ins, building takeovers, riots and strikes in the 1960s.

WORKING TOGETHER

Music, art, literature and the theatre played an important role in the growth of the student protest movement and the anti-Vietnam War protests. Carry out research on key cultural developments in the USA in the 1960s. Divide into pairs or small groups and allocate one factor per group; research and develop your factor and feed back to the rest of the group. Your research should include the following sub-headings: 'Context', 'Main strands' and 'Impact' and be limited to one side of A4.
- Music, including protest singers such as Bob Dylan
- Literature
- Theatre
- Art

The Woodstock Festival

The highlight of the hippie movement came at the Woodstock Festival of August 1969, attended by over 400,000. This movement was of particular concern to the older generation because these youths refused to work and experimented in drugs such as marijuana and LSD. Many were from the middle classes rather than underprivileged backgrounds. They rejected all the values that their parents believed in.

Youth culture – The beliefs, attitudes and interests of teenagers.

According to Source D, how did the student movement change?

KEY DATES: THE STUDENT MOVEMENT

1959 Setting up of the Students for a Democratic Society.

1964 Berkeley Free Speech Movement.

1969 Woodstock festival.

1970 Kent State University shootings.

The women's movement

How successful was the women's movement of the 1960s and early 1970s?

A strong feminist movement, inspired by Betty Friedan's best-selling book *The Feminine Mystique,* emerged in the USA in the 1960s and achieved some progress in the position of women. However, the women's movement was not totally successful because of divisions in the movement, especially with the emergence of the more extreme Women's Liberation Movement.

Emergence

The movement was inspired by two women, Eleanor Roosevelt and Betty Friedan.

Eleanor Roosevelt

Eleanor Roosevelt made an important contribution to the cause when, in 1960, she set up a commission to investigate the status of women at work. President Kennedy appointed Roosevelt to chair the commission but she died just before the commission issued its final report. (See page 188 for more on her life.) The results were reported in 1963 and highlighted women's second-class status in employment. For example, 95 per cent of company managers were men, as were 85 per cent of technical workers. Only seven per cent of doctors were women and even less, four per cent, lawyers. Women only earned 50 to 60 per cent of the wages of men who did the same job and they generally had low-paid jobs.

Betty Friedan

Betty Friedan was even more influential in the emergence of the woman's movement. In 1963 she wrote *The Feminine Mystique.* Her book expressed the thoughts of many women – there was more to life than being a mother and housewife. Indeed the expression 'The Feminine Mystique' was her term for the idea that a woman's happiness was all tied up with her domestic role.

Friedan was important because she called for women to reject this 'mystique' and for progress in female employment opportunities. She insisted that bringing up a family should be a shared role that would enable the wife to pursue her career, if she wanted. Disillusioned with the lack of progress in employment opportunities despite government legislation in 1963 and 1964, she set up the National Organization for Women (NOW) in 1966.

National Organization for Women (NOW)

This organisation was set up by mainly white middle-class women in order to attack obvious examples of discrimination. By the early 1970s, it had 40,000 members and had organised demonstrations in a number of American cities. They challenged discrimination in the courts and, in a series of cases between 1966 and 1971, secured $30 million in back pay owed to women who had not been paid wages equal to men.

Women's Liberation Movement

The Women's Liberation Movement was the name given to women who had far more radical aims than NOW. They were also known as feminists and were much more active in challenging discrimination. Indeed, the really extreme feminists wanted nothing to do with men. All signs of male supremacy were to be removed. These included male control of employment, politics and the media.

Feminist – Supporter of women's rights who believes that men and women are equal in all areas.

Feminists believed that even not wearing make-up was an act of protest against male supremacy and were determined to get as much publicity for their cause as possible. For example, they burned their bras as these were also seen as a symbol of male domination. In 1968, others picketed the Miss America beauty contest in Atlantic City and even crowned a sheep 'Miss America'. The whole contest, they argued, degraded the position of women.

However, the activities of the Women's Liberation Movement did more harm than good. Their extreme actions and protests brought the wrong sort of publicity. Burning their bras in public brought ridicule to the movement and made it increasingly difficult for men and other women to take the whole issue of women's rights seriously. They were a distraction from the key issues of equal pay and better job opportunities.

Campaign to legalise abortion

Abortion was illegal in the USA. Feminists challenged this, arguing it was wrong to force women to have a child they did not want, and began to challenge it through the courts of law. The most important case was *Roe v. Wade*, which lasted from 1970 to 1973. A feminist lawyer, Sarah Weddington, defended the right of one of her clients, Norma McCorvey (named Jane Roe to protect her anonymity), to have an abortion. She already had three children, who had all been taken into care, and did not want any more. She won the right to have an abortion. The victory led to abortions becoming more readily available.

Achievements

The women's movement also made some progress in other areas.

- The 1963 Equal Pay Act required employers to pay women the same as men for the same job. However, it did not address the issue of discrimination against women seeking jobs in the first place.
- The 1972 Educational Amendment Act outlawed sex discrimination in education, so that girls could follow exactly the same curriculum as boys. This, in turn, would give them greater career opportunities. It took a long time for schools to change their traditional curriculum and for the benefits to filter through to the education of girls.
- In the same year the Supreme Court ruled that the US Constitution did give men and women equal rights. However, many opponents of equal rights for women did not accept this.
- An increasing number of women entered professions that had once been perceived as male preserves, such as law and medicine. The two-career family began to replace the traditional pattern of male breadwinner and female housekeeper.
- The Equal Rights Amendment Act was passed by Congress but was not ratified by the states.
- The women's movement did attract many middle-class women. However, few working-class women took an interest and the movement became divided between moderate and more extreme feminists.

LOOK AGAIN

Look back at pages 149–51 in Chapter 5.

To what extent did women make progress in the USA in the 1920s?

Occupational group	1950	1960	1970
All workers	8	33	38
White collar	40	43	48
Professional	40	38	40
Managerial	14	14	17
Clerical	62	68	74
Sales	34	37	39
Blue collar	24	26	30
Crafts	3	3	5
Operatives	27	28	32
Labourers	4	4	8
Private households	95	96	96
Other services	45	52	55
Farm workers	9	10	10

▲ **Figure 4** The percentage of women working in various occupations in the years 1950–70.

KEY DATES: THE WOMEN'S MOVEMENT

1963 Publication of Betty Friedan's *The Feminine Mystique.*

1964 Setting up of Equal Opportunities Commission.

1966 Setting up of NOW.

1972 The Educational Amendment Act.

ACTIVITY

1 To what extent does Figure 4 suggest that there had been progress in in women's job opportunities?
2 Make a copy of the scales below and list the achievements and shortcomings of the women's movement.

4 The USA by 1975

A superpower is a country that holds a dominant position in international affairs and has the ability to exert a very strong influence on world affairs through military, economic and diplomatic strength. It requires a strong economy in order to sustain its military power. The term was first applied to Britain in the first half of the twentieth century. However, the Second World War brought a significant decline in Britain's economic and military position and the United States and the Soviet Union came to be regarded as the two remaining superpowers.

The making of a superpower

To what extent was the USA a divided nation by 1975?

The USA had by 1975 become the most powerful nation in the world. However, it was still very much a divided nation, particularly because of the treatment of Native Americans, African Americans and women.

The impact of Watergate

For more than 40 years the power and authority of the president had grown. This meant that other branches of government, both the Supreme Court and Congress, found it impossible to limit what the president did. However, after Watergate there was a new determination to enforce limits on what a president could do.

The Watergate affair left the position of the presidency much weakened by 1975. Many Americans were disillusioned with their system of government and felt that the president had too much power. They no longer had confidence in or respect for their own politicians and government.

The economy

After the Second World War, the USA had experienced a prolonged economic boom and in the 1970s was still the most advanced economy in the world. However, the boom was clearly over by the 1970s. When Gerald Ford succeeded Nixon as president in 1974, he inherited high inflation, which had reached nine per cent in 1976, and a high rate of unemployment of 5.4 per cent. This was known as 'stagflation', which meant slow economic growth with high unemployment and rising prices.

Ford also inherited an energy crisis. In 1973, the Arab oil-producing countries had imposed an oil embargo in retaliation to US support for their great enemy, Israel, especially during the Yom Kippur War. As oil prices rocketed, the New York stock exchange prices plummeted. The USA, like other countries, suffered even further when the Organization of Petroleum Exporting Countries (OPEC) quadrupled the price of oil in December 1973.

Position in world affairs

By the mid-1970s the USA was not only one of the two superpowers, but had assumed a global role as the so-called champion of democracy against the spread of Communism. The more direct confrontation symbolised by the Cuban Missile Crisis of 1962 (page 250) had given way to a new approach – *détente* – with both China and the Soviet Union, culminating in the Helsinki Agreements of 1975 (page 254). The conflict in Vietnam ensured that the American public and Congress were far more inclined to monitor any future crisis that looked likely to lead to 'another Vietnam'. For example, when the USSR intervened in Angola in 1974, Nixon and Kissinger failed to persuade Congress to vote for US military intervention.

The USA was also increasingly involved in events in the Middle East, especially the conflict between Israel and her Arab neighbours, providing material and diplomatic support for the Israelis. During the War of Yom Kippur of 1973, Nixon and Kissinger were able to restrain the Israelis and, at the same time, prevent Soviet intervention on the side of the defeated Arab states. However, US support for Israel had serious economic repercussions. In 1973, the Arab nations imposed an oil embargo in retaliation for the Americans supplying arms to Israel.

Social cohesion

By 1975, there were still problems and divisions in US society.

African Americans

Although African Americans had made great gains in the 1960s with the Civil Rights and Voting Rights Acts, there was still a long way to go. Politically, there was progress by the mid-1970s with increased representation for African Americans. For example, while there were no black mayors in 1960, in the 1970s a black mayor was elected in Los Angeles, Detroit, Cleveland, Birmingham, Oakland and Atlanta. The number of African Americans in Congress had increased from eleven in 1970 to eighteen by the end of the decade.

Socially, however, there were some improvements. For example, the proportion of black families earning over $10,000 a year was three per cent in 1960 but had increased to 31 per cent by the beginning of the 1970s. However, black male teenage unemployment was 50 per cent and half of black teenagers dropped out of high school before graduation. An African American child was twice as likely to die before the age of one as a white child, and twice as likely to drop out of school.

Native American Indians

Of all the minority groups, the Native Americans were still by far the worst off. Many lived on reservations. Unemployment among Native American Indians was ten times higher than other Americans; on average they lived twenty years less than everyone else and the suicide rate was one hundred times higher than for whites. Their plight was highlighted by events at Wounded Knee, Dakota, which was occupied by several hundred Native Americans in March 1973. This was the site of the brutal massacre of nearly 200 Indians by the US Army in 1890. The protestors presented the Government with a list of grievances that included broken treaties. Two hundred FBI agents and other police surrounded Wounded Knee and the siege achieved national and international publicity and encouraged much public support for the plight of the Native American Indians. The Government did agree to look into their grievances.

Women

Women's rights had changed dramatically since the early 1960s. These changes had been stimulated by new attitudes to work, sex, family and personal freedom. Over two-thirds of female college students rejected the idea that a woman's place was in the home. Most women now expected to work for most of their lives, even if they had young families. More and more women were entering what had been seen as traditionally masculine occupations, such as medicine and law.

However, there was still much to be done. Women only received 73 per cent of the salaries paid to professional men and still dominated low-paid jobs. Moreover, 66 per cent of adults who were classified as poor were female. There were still relatively few women in positions of power, whether at local, state or national level.

By 1975, the great optimism of the 1960s inspired by the presidency of Kennedy and the achievements of civil rights leaders such as Martin Luther King had given way to the cynicism of Nixon and the Watergate scandal. The USA was indeed a superpower but with a divided society.

Source E From *Years of Discord, American Politics and Society, 1961–74* by J. M. Blum, (W. W. Norton), 1991.

Presidential power, swollen by the responsibilities of the White House for foreign policy in the nuclear age, had become corrupt. And constant public stress had exhausted the country. The resolution of the Watergate scandal terminated fifteen years of social and political discord – racial conflict over civil rights, nuclear confrontation with the Soviet Union, war in Vietnam, angry protest against that war, three devastating assassinations, riots in cities and violence on the campuses. With the resignation of Richard Nixon, most Americans felt a sense of weary relief. The confidence of the New Frontier and the bright promise of the Great Society had faded; the liberal spirit was spent.

Source F From *The Unfinished Journey – A History of Our Time* by W. Chafe and H. Stikoff, (Oxford University Press), 1999.

For thirty years from 1945 American politics had functioned on the premise that nothing was impossible if America wished to achieve it. Americans would be guardians of freedom, send a man to the moon, conquer social injustice, eliminate poverty, develop impressive technology – in short, control the universe. That sense of confidence, and of power, had been the hallmark of all political factions in the country, even young radicals who thought that by their own endeavours they could change the world. In the 1970s, a new sense of limits struck home. The American tendency to what the Greeks called *hubris* – the arrogant confidence that one can do anything – had come face to face with the realities of human frailty: mortality and interdependency.

1 What view does the author of Source E express about the USA by 1975?
2 To what extent is this supported by Source F?
3 To what extent do you agree with these views of the USA by 1975?

Date	Key development	Change or continuity
1961–63	Kennedy and New Frontier	Great changes with economic and social reforms. Continuity with failure to pass civil rights reform.
1963–68	Johnson and Great Society	Social and economic change. Significant changes in civil rights with Civil Rights Act and Voters Registration Act.
1968–74	Nixon and Watergate	Significant changes in attitudes towards president and politics as result of Watergate scandal.
1960–70	Civil Rights movement	Continuity with 1950s with peaceful methods used by Martin Luther King. Change to more extreme groups such as Black Power and Black Panthers.
1960–70	Student movement	Change to more extreme movement in the later 1960s and much greater protest against conflict in Vietnam.
1960–75	Women's movement	Much more active in 1960s with setting up of NOW. Change to more extreme Women's Liberation Movement.
1960–75	USA and Cold War	Continuity with rivalry with USSR with Cuban Missile Crisis. Change to *détente* under Nixon with USSR and China.
1963–73	USA and Vietnam	Change to direct US involvement under Johnson and then gradual withdrawal under Nixon.

▲ **Figure 5** Key developments, 1961–73.

Chapter summary

- Kennedy and the New Frontier – great changes with economic and social reforms. Continuity with failure to pass civil rights reform.
- Johnson and the Great Society – social and economic change. Significant changes in civil rights with the Civil Rights Act and Voters Registration Act.
- Nixon and Watergate – significant changes in attitudes towards the president and politics as a result of the Watergate scandal.
- The Cold War in the 1960s with the U-2 incident, the building of the Berlin Wall and the Cuban Missile Crisis.
- *Détente* under Nixon in the 1970s, including improved relations with China and the Soviet Union.
- Civil rights movement – peaceful methods under Martin Luther King including peace marches at Washington and Birmingham.
- Civil rights movement – more extreme methods advocated by Malcolm X, Black Power and the Black Panthers.
- Student movement – emerged in the early 1960s demanding greater say in universities and played an important part in the protest against the conflict in Vietnam.
- Women's movement emerged due to the influence of Betty Friedan and Eleanor Roosevelt and the work of NOW.
- USA by 1975 was a world superpower due to its military and economic power.

▼ Summary diagram: Conflict at home and abroad, 1960–75

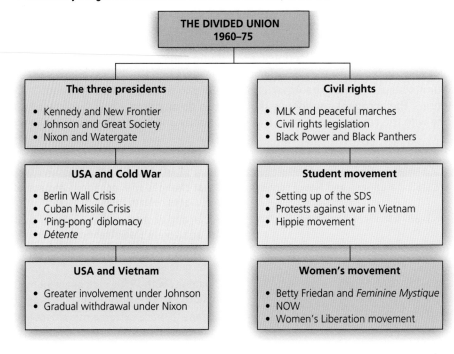

Working on essay technique

In previous chapters, you have built up skills in planning and writing essays. In particular, in the second part of this book you should have become more confident in producing answers at a higher level.

Here is another practice question:

'The main reason for divisions in US society in the years 1945–75 was the fear of Communism.' Assess the validity of this view. (25 marks)

As in previous chapters, you could plan an answer by looking at divisions in US society during this period, episode by episode. It is perhaps easiest to look at divisions caused by McCarthyism, the war in Vietnam, African Americans and civil rights, the student and women's movements. Then examine the reasons for these divisions. Was it due to the fear of Communism or were there other reasons?

Then, before you start writing, think how you can write an effective plan that:

● balances the fear of Communism with other reasons
● has precise dates and events
● ranges across the period without becoming a chronological description
● reaches a substantiated judgement.

After writing the essay, look at the mark scheme for essays (see page 100). Start at Level 4 and consider whether you have shown those skills. Then look at Level 5 to see if you think you deserve this top level.

Working on interpretation skills: extended reading

To what extent did the Civil Rights Movement achieve its aims in the years 1960–68?

This is an essay by Dr Joe Street on the achievements of the civil rights movement in the 1960s.

Between 1960 and 1968 the civil rights movement played a pivotal role in the reshaping of American democracy. It pushed two Democratic Presidents towards supporting legislation which destroyed the legal foundations of racial segregation. These Acts, the 1964 Civil Rights Act and the 1965 Voting Rights Act, fundamentally transformed the United States. The first outlawed discrimination based on race, colour, religion, sex, or national origin; the second prohibited racially discriminatory voting practices and withdrew federal funds from school boards that had not desegregated schooling in compliance with the 1954 *Brown vs Board of Education* Supreme Court decision. It is no overestimation to state that this comprised a major turning point in American history.

Although it is difficult to prove direct causality, the great campaigns of the movement in Birmingham, Alabama (1963), St. Augustine, Florida (1964), and Selma, Alabama (1965), and the 1963 March on Washington, undoubtedly contributed to the sense in Washington that the time was right to end legal and political support for racial segregation. These campaigns attracted national and international media attention which was crucial in solidifying popular support for the movement. The campaigns were also characterised by the leadership of Rev. Dr. Martin Luther King, Jr., a Baptist preacher and president of the Southern Christian Leadership Conference. One of the great public speakers in American history, Dr King achieved international renown for uniting the Gandhian practice of nonviolence with the spirit and motivation of Christian teachings. Historians such as Taylor Branch and David Garrow place him at the movement's core and the FBI considered him such a dangerous threat that it monitored his every activity between October 1963 and his death in April 1968, having observed him from a distance since his emergence as a national figure in 1956.

The impact of the civil rights movement should not be limited to its legislative successes or by a focus on Dr King, however. In mobilising millions of Americans of all races, the movement proved that segregation was not as popular as its defenders liked to suggest. It convinced many thousands of people who had been excluded from American political life that they could take part in the democratic process, and through its campaigns demonstrated that ordinary people could influence the political process. Yet it also went further. As historians such as William Chafe, John Dittmer, and Charles Payne argue, the movement was transformative when it engaged with local communities. Activists from the Student Nonviolent Coordinating Committee led a series of projects which endeavored to develop new generations of local leaders who would not be reliant on individual, media-friendly figures such as Dr King. Although small in scale,

5

10

15

20

25

30

35

40

these local projects left behind a legacy of politically-aware communities and networks throughout the southern states. The movement also spurred many women to become politically active. As historians such as Belinda Robnett have suggested, women like Gloria Richardson and Fannie Lou Hamer became vital to grassroots civil rights activism. Moreover, the civil rights movement left behind an often forgotten cultural legacy. From the freedom songs that were sung during civil rights marches, through popular songs such as Sam Cooke's 'A Change is Gonna Come' to politically-engaged literature, theatre and art, the movement inspired and popularised numerous cultural products that enriched the lives of its participants and touched the lives of many more.

Despite its monumental legislative achievements, the civil rights movement failed in a number of its other aims. Although the legal basis of segregation was smashed, the United States remained racially divided long after the movement faded. King himself understood that the quest to transform the nation's morals was a much tougher proposition than the legal and legislative campaign. The rise of Black Power sentiment among a younger generation of African Americans in the mid-1960s reveals that many supporters of the movement became frustrated at its progress. Urban rebellions in Los Angeles, Chicago, and Newark, New Jersey during the late 1960s suggested that racial tension had not been quashed by the movement; countless instances of white-on-black violence in the decades since indicate that racism remains a salient feature of American life. Similarly, if the movement's goal was for a more equal nation, it failed. African American employment, educational achievement, income, and property ownership levels remain lower than those for whites, while the proportion of African Americans in prison and on Death Row has been consistently higher. This indicates that the promise of the movement's anthem, 'We Shall Overcome,' has yet to be fulfilled.

Dr Joe Street is Senior Lecturer in History; Programme Leader in American Studies at the University of Northumbria.

ACTIVITY

Having read the essay, answer the following questions.

Comprehension

1 What does the author mean by the following phrases?
   a) 'the Gandhian practice' (line 22)
   b) 'legal basis of segregation' (line 53)
   c) 'the rise of Black Power' (line 57)

Evidence

2 Using paragraph 3, list the ways in which the author evidences the impact of the civil rights movement apart from the achievements of Martin Luther King.

Interpretation

3 Using your knowledge from your study of civil rights in the 1960s, list evidence to support the author's view that 'between 1960 and 1968 the civil rights movement played a pivotal role in the reshaping of American democracy'.

Evaluation

4 How far do you agree with the author's view that the civil rights movement failed in a number of its aims?
   • To what extent did the civil rights movement achieve its aims? You need to analyse the work of MLK and the significance of civil rights legislation in the 1960s.
   • To what extent did it fail to achieve other aims? What were these other aims? What changes, if any, had taken place in the political, economic and social position of African Americans by 1968?

Key Questions: The making of a superpower: USA 1865–1975

The specification you have been studying on the USA highlighted six key questions. We reviewed these at the end of Part One (pp. 132–5), providing opportunities for you to think about themes that run through your study of the period. Now there is the opportunity for you to review this on the whole period.

In the examination the essays will be focused on broad areas of the content and will reflect one or more of the six key questions. Therefore, this section should be of great help to you in your revision, both looking at themes and also revisiting the detailed content you have studied.

KEY QUESTION 1:
How did government, political authority and political parties change and develop?

Questions to consider

- To what extent did US involvement in war, especially the Civil War and First and Second World Wars, affect the powers of government and the political parties?
- To what extent did the two main parties change throughout this period?
- To what extent did the presidencies of the years 1920–75 bring about changes to the Democrats and Republicans, particularly the Republican presidencies of the 1920s, and the Democratic presidencies of F. D. Roosevelt, Kennedy and Johnson?

Working in groups

1 Discuss the ways in which the powers of the presidency changed, especially under Theodore and F. D. Roosevelt and the latter's successors.
2 Discuss any changes in the two leading parties – the Democrats and Republicans – and how different they had become by the end of the period, 1975.
3 Discuss the impact of events such as the assassination of Kennedy, the war in Vietnam and Nixon and the Watergate scandal, on attitudes to and the powers of the presidency.
4 Discuss how historians have, over time, assessed and re-assessed the achievements of US presidents during this period in American history.

KEY QUESTION 2:
In what ways did the economy and society of the USA change and develop?

Questions to consider

- Why did the growth and development of the US economy in the years after the Civil War, and the First and Second World Wars, take place?
- Why did periods of slump and recession, for example the depressions of 1873, 1893 and the 1930s, take place and what effects did they have? How far do you agree with the 'boom and bust' description of the US economy?
- To what extent did workers benefit from periods of prosperity such as the 1920s and the years following the Second World War? How badly affected were they by periods of depression?
- F. D. Roosevelt, Kennedy and Johnson brought in economic changes. To what extent did the changes brought in by F. D. Roosevelt, Kennedy and Johnson stimulate economic revival and growth?

Working in groups

1 Discuss to what extent the economy changed bearing in mind the depressions of the 1870s and 1890s and the Great Depression of the 1930s.
2 Discuss how working and living conditions changed throughout the period. How affluent was US society in periods of prosperity such as the 1920s and the 1950s?
3 Discuss the impact of immigration on the US economy and society before and after the First World War. To what extent did opposition to immigrants increase during this period?
4 How far did US governments encourage economic growth during this period?

KEY QUESTION 3:
How did the role of the USA in world affairs change?

Questions to consider

- Why did changes in US foreign policy take place in the years between the two world wars?
- Why did the USA become involved in major conflicts in the twentieth century?
- Why did the role of the USA in world affairs change in the years after the Second World War?
- To what extent did US foreign policy become more expansionist throughout the period?

Working in groups

1 Discuss the extent to which the USA was isolationist throughout the period.
2 Discuss how the USA became more involved in Latin America, the Pacific and the Far East throughout the period.
3 Discuss the similarities and differences in reasons that led to USA involvement in four wars – the Spanish–American War, the First and Second World Wars and conflict in Vietnam.
4 How different was the US role in world affairs at the end of the period (1975) to what it had been at the beginning (1865)?

KEY QUESTION 4:
How important were ideas and ideology?

Questions to consider

- What ideas influenced the USA in the years after the Second World War?
- Did the ideas of Manifest Destiny and the Monroe Doctrine continue to influence policies in the twentieth century?
- How far did ideas about the role of government – especially the contrast between the *laissez-faire* attitude of the nineteenth and earlier twentieth centuries and the greater federal state involvement in the two world wars and the New Deal – encourage economic and social change or continuity?

Working in groups

1 Discuss to what extent there were differences about the role of government throughout the period 1865–1975, and how these differences influenced change.
2 Discuss the influence of ideals such as the Manifest Destiny and the Monroe Doctrine on Westward expansion in US foreign policy throughout the period 1865–1975.
3 Discuss the impact of the fear of Communism on US political and external policies in the years 1918–75, particularly McCarthyism, the Red Scare and the Cold War.

KEY QUESTION 5:
How united were the states during this period?

Questions to consider

- Did the divisions between North and South during and after the Civil War continue between 1920 and 1975?
- How far were the divisions in US society in the years after the Second World War accentuated by the fear of Communism and the war in Vietnam?
- Did the civil rights movement accentuate the divisions between African Americans and white Americans?
- How did Westward expansion affect unity between Native Americans and white Americans? How were the Native Americans treated in the later nineteenth century? Was there any improvement in their situation in the twentieth century?
- To what extent did immigration accentuate divisions in US society especially in the 1920s?

Working in groups

1 Discuss how far the differences between North and South changed throughout the period 1865–1975.
2 Discuss the position of African Americans. To what extent did their position improve during this period, 1865–1975? Were they still second-class citizens by the end of the period?
3 Discuss the extent to which the USA was more or less divided by the end of the period.

KEY QUESTION 6:
How important was the role of key individuals and groups and how were they affected by developments?

Questions to consider

- What were the most significant changes made to the USA by Presidents Theodore and F. D. Roosevelt, Truman, Kennedy and Nixon?
- What contribution was made to African American civil rights by individuals such as William Du Bois, Booker T. Washington, Martin Luther King and Malcolm X?
- How effective was the contribution of Eleanor Roosevelt and Betty Friedan to female civil rights?
- How was the student movement affected by developments such as the US involvement in the war in Vietnam?
- How did key political, economic or social developments in the USA influence individuals or groups during the years 1865–1975?

Working in groups

1 Discuss which presidents made the most significant contribution to the development of the USA during the years 1865–1975.
2 Discuss the significance of any other key individuals to the development of the USA at home and abroad. Has their contribution been underestimated or exaggerated?
3 Discuss the different interpretations of the contribution of individuals such as Martin Luther King and John F. Kennedy.
4 Discuss the overall significance of groups in bringing about change in the period, 1865–1975. Which group brought about the most change?
5 Discuss which development in the USA had the most effect on individuals or groups in the USA, 1865–1975.

Glossary

Accommodation Acceptance of economic, political and social circumstances not of your own making or liking.

Agribusiness The business of agricultural production. It includes breeding, crop production, distribution, farm machinery, processing, supply, marketing and retail sales.

Allies The countries fighting against Germany including Britain, France, Belgium and Russia.

Alsace-Lorraine Area of France taken by Germany after the 1871 Franco–Prussian War.

Anarchism Belief in no government, no private ownership and the sharing out of wealth.

Annex To incorporate a territory into an existing political unit such as a country, state, county, or city.

Anti-Semitic Hostility towards or discrimination against Jews as a religious group or race.

Arbitration Where two opposing sides go to a neutral body for a judgement in their dispute.

Associated power Power not formally allied to other countries fighting against a common enemy, therefore having independence as to military strategy and the subsequent peace settlement.

Ballistic missiles Missiles (rockets) that follow a ballistic flightpath moving under the force of gravity with the objective of delivering one or more warheads to a predetermined target.

Belligerents Countries engaged in warfare.

Bible belt Area of Southern USA where Christian belief is strong.

Bimetallists Those who wanted both silver and gold used in the coinage.

Bipartisan Supported by members of two parties.

Black press A term used to describe newspapers, magazines and periodicals aimed at a largely black audience.

Blackleg labour Strike-breakers.

Blockade The surrounding or blocking of a place.

The Blue Eagle A symbol used in the United States by companies to show compliance with the National Industrial Recovery Act.

Boll weevil An insect which attacked the cotton crop, eating its buds and flowers.

'Bonanza' farms Very large farms in the United States performing large-scale operations, mostly growing and harvesting wheat.

Boom When the economy of a country is rapidly developing.

British blockade of Germany British naval blockade to prevent goods leaving and entering German ports.

Bull market A time when share prices are rising.

Bureau of Indian Affairs The Bureau of Indian Affairs (BIA), also known as the Office of Indian Affairs, was set up in 1824 to centralise the work with Native Americans within the War Department.

Cartel A group of companies agreeing to fix output and prices in order to reduce competition and increase profits.

Central Powers Germany and its allies such as Austria-Hungary and Turkey.

Civil disobedience A non-violent way of protesting in order to achieve political goals.

Civil rights Having the vote in free elections; equal treatment under the law; equal opportunities, e.g. in education and work; freedom of speech, religion and movement.

Cold War Confrontation without actually directly fighting each other.

Colonisation The forming of a settlement or colony by a group of people who seek to take control of territories or countries. It usually involves large-scale immigration of people to a 'new' location and the expansion of their civilisation and culture into this area.

Concessions Favourable trading rights.

Conscript Someone compulsorily enrolled for service in the armed forces.

Constitution A document containing the rules by which a country is to be governed. The American Constitution originally had seven articles, the first of which described the role of Congress and the second that of president.

Consumerism An increase in the production of consumer goods on the grounds that high spending is the basis of a sound economy.

Corollary A statement that follows on from another statement.

Declaration of Independence This is the name of the statement made on 4 July 1776 which announced that the original thirteen American colonies, then at war with Britain, regarded themselves as thirteen newly independent colonies, no longer a part of the British Empire.

Deflation A fall in prices and goods.

Defoliants Chemicals sprayed on plants to remove their leaves.

Détente An easing of strained relations.

Devalued the dollar The value of the dollar was reduced against the other major currencies to encourage exports and improve the country's trade deficit.

Direct action The use of acts, such as strikes, marches and demonstrations, to achieve a political or social end.

Dominion A self-governing nation within the British Empire.

Domino theory The belief that if one state fell to Communism it would be quickly followed by neighbouring states.

Embargo An official ban on trade or commercial activity.

Entrepreneur A person who sets up a business or businesses, taking on financial risks in the hope of making profits.

Espionage Spying.

Expansionist Following a policy of territorial expansion.

Federal Reserve Board A centralised system that allowed banks to run their own affairs with only limited government interference.

Federal system of government There is a central system of government and also state governments. Each state has its own powers that are not subject to interference from central government.

Feminist Supporter of women's rights who believes that men and women are equal in all areas.

Fenians An Irish republican organisation set up in the USA in 1858, fighting for Irish independence from Britain.

Free trade International trade that is left to run its course according to market forces and is not subject to duties or taxes.

Ghetto A densely populated area of a city inhabited by a socially and economically deprived minority.

GNP Gross National Product (GNP) is the market value of all the products and services produced in one year by labour and property supplied by the citizens of a country.

Gold Standard Where the value of money is based on the amount of the nation's gold reserves.

Good Neighbor Foreign policy adopted by Roosevelt to mend and improve relations with Latin America.

Great Powers The most powerful countries such as Russia, Britain and Germany.

Gross National Product (GNP) The total value of all final goods and services produced within a nation in a particular year.

Guerrilla A member of an irregular armed force that fights a stronger force by sabotage and harassment.

Hemispheric Relating to the western or eastern or northern or southern part of the world. In this case, it refers to North and South America.

Hire purchase A system of credit whereby a person may purchase an item by making regular payments while already having the use of said item.

Holding company Where one very large company obtains a controlling interest in smaller companies in order to control the market.

Hun Derogatory term for Germans, derived from Huns, a warlike tribe renowned for their cruelty and barbarism in the fifth century.

Impeachment This is a formal process in which an official is accused of unlawful activity.

Inauguration The ceremony that begins the president's term of office.

Indochina The region of South-east Asia that was a colony of France.

Inflation Rise in prices due to more money being in circulation.

Iron Curtain An imaginary border between Communist and non-Communist countries.

Isolationism A policy by which the USA detached itself from foreign affairs. A policy of non-involvement and non-intervention in other government's internal affairs and wars.

Jim Crow army A reference to the African Americans serving in the segregated military in the Second World War.

Labour battalions Troops who worked in construction or loading or transportation of equipment rather than serving in combat.

Labour intensive crops Cotton and tobacco required more workers than other crops because machinery could not always be used.

Labour unions US term for a trade union formed to look after the interests of its members.

Laissez-faire A policy of no direct government interference in the economy.

Legalistic Following the letter of the law.

Manhattan Project A research and development project that produced the first atomic bombs during the Second World War.

Mechanisation The use of machines.

Middle America The traditional or conservative people of the middle class in the US.

Military–industrial complex A network of individuals and institutions involved in the production of weapons and military technologies.

Mobilisation Gearing the country for war, including recruiting, equipping and transporting the military.

Munich Agreement This was signed in September 1938 by Britain, France, Germany and Italy. It allowed Germany to annex part of Czechoslovakia.

Munitions Weapons and ammunition.

Napalm An inflammable sticky jelly used in bombs in order to set fire to people, trees and buildings.

Native plutocracy Wealthy, white Americans who controlled the government of the USA.

Nativism The policy of protecting the interests of native-born or established inhabitants against those of immigrants.

NATO (North Atlantic Treaty Organization) Members included the United States, Britain, France, Luxembourg, Holland, Belgium, Canada, Portugal, Italy, Norway, Denmark and Iceland.

Nomadic The Native Indians did not live in any one place permanently. They followed the buffalo herds, living in tepee villages that could be quickly assembled or demolished in response to the movement of the buffalo.

Nordic This relates to a group or physical type of the Caucasian race characterised by their tall stature, long head, light skin and hair, and blue eyes originating in Scandinavia.

Normalcy Harding meant by this a return to the situation before the First World War which he believed to be the norm, of as little government intervention as possible at home and in foreign affairs.

'Open Door' This was a term first used to guarantee the protection of equal privileges among countries trading with China. The policy proposed to keep China open to trade with all countries on an equal basis; thus, no international power would have total control of the country.

Pan-American Relating to all countries on the American continent.

Peace societies Various groups set up in the USA in the 1920s to encourage support for peace. One example was the World Peace Association.

Per capita income A measure of the amount of money that is being earned per person in a certain country.

Philanthropy Showing a concern for human welfare and advancement, usually manifested by donations of money, property, or work to needy persons.

Poverty line The income level at which a family is unable to meet its basic needs.

Primary election An early stage of voting in which the whole electorate can choose a political party's candidates for election, rather than having the candidates chosen for them by the party.

Prohibition The prevention by law of the manufacture and sale of alcohol.

Protectorate A state that is controlled and protected by another. For example, after the United States Navy took possession of eastern Samoa on behalf of the United States, the existing coaling station at Pago Pago Bay was expanded into a full naval station. In 1911, the US Naval Station Tutuila, which was composed of Tutuila, Aunu'u and Manu'a, was officially renamed American Samoa.

Pump priming The activity of helping a business, programme, economy, etc. to develop by giving it money.

Puppet emperor A ruler controlled by others.

Rediscount rates The interest rate at which banks borrow money from the Federal Reserve Banks.

Reparations War damages to be paid by a defeated country.

Secede To withdraw from an organisation.

Secretary of State US official responsible for the administration of foreign policy.

Sectional Political, economic and social differences between the North and South.

Separatism Keeping races apart. Two separate countries for black and white Americans.

Sharecroppers These were tenant farmers. A landlord allows a tenant to use an area of land in return for a portion of the crop produced on the land.

Sino–US Relations between America and China.

Speakeasy An illegal drinking shop.

Speculators Speculators are risk-taking investors with expertise in the market(s) in which they are trading.

Spoils system The practice whereby a political party, after winning an election, gives government jobs to its voters as a reward for working toward victory, and as an incentive to keep working for the party – as opposed to a system of awarding offices on the basis of some measure of merit independent of political activity.

State of the Union Address The US President's message to the country at the start of a new session of Congress.

Stocks and shares Certificates of ownership in a company.

Syncopation This refers to the off-beat rhythms that characterise jazz music.

Tariffs Taxes on imported goods from other countries.

Totalitarianism When political regimes suppress political opposition and control all aspects of people's lives.

Trench warfare The defensive network on the Western Front in which millions died.

Unconditional surrender Surrender without conditions, in which no guarantees are given to the country that is surrendering.

Unrestricted submarine warfare Attacking any ship en route to an enemy port.

Vertical integration When a company expands its business into areas that are at different points on the same production path, such as when a manufacturer owns its supplier and/or distributor.

Vietminh The League for the Independence of Vietnam, a nationalist and Communist dominated organisation, later known as the Vietcong.

War bonds Debt securities issued by a government to finance military operations and other expenditure in times of war.

War indemnity Compensation from a defeated nation to the victors following a war.

War profiteering Making excess profits during war time, for example by charging artificially high prices.

'Yellow Press' The term used to describe the sensationalist journalism of the 1890s. Journalists such as William Randolph and Joseph Pulitzer competed with each other to print stories about apparent Spanish atrocities in Cuba including the ill-treatment of female prisoners. It became known as the Yellow Press after a cartoon character called the Yellow Kid, from Pulitzer's *New York World*.

Youth culture The beliefs, attitudes and interests of teenagers.

Further research

General recommendations

There are many excellent books on the USA 1865–1975, some more detailed than others. Some are written specifically with A-level students in mind. Other academic books are written for more specialist audiences, but many are very accessible to students who already possess the necessary background knowledge.

Also listed in this Further research are a number of novels and films which are recommendations to extend your overall sense of the period.

Prosperity, Depression and the New Deal: The USA 1890–1954 by P. Clements, Access to History series, (Hodder Education), 2005.

Sound survey of key developments in the USA in this period. Useful introduction to American history.

Emergence of the Americas in Global Affairs 1880–1929 by P. Clements, (Hodder Education), 2013.

Thorough analysis of key features of US foreign policy in this period.

The USA, 1920–55: Boom, Bust and Recovery by P. Clements, (Hodder Education), 2014.

Very comprehensive coverage of this period. Especially strong on the New Deal.

Modern America, The USA, 1865 to the Present by Joanne de Pennington, (Hodder Education), 2005.

Comprehensive coverage of the period with interesting and useful written and visual sources.

The American Century by H. Evans, (Jonathan Cape), 1998.

Introductory thematic analyses, then examines events and personalities separately.

American History 1860–1990 by A. Farmer and V. Sanders, Access to History series, (Hodder Education), 2002.

Provides very useful framework for key developments at home and abroad throughout this period.

Colossus by N. Ferguson, (Penguin), 2003.

Study of the nature of US imperialism with especially useful earlier chapters on the historical background.

From Colony to Superpower: US Foreign Relations since 1776 by G. C. Herring, (Oxford University Press), 2008.

A comprehensive and up-to-date analysis.

A History of the American People by P. Johnson, (Phoenix), 2000.

Right-wing and celebratory in style, but still a good read.

A Concise History of US Foreign Policy, 2nd edition by J. P. Kaufman, (Rowman and Littlefield Publishers), 2010.

Useful brief history of foreign policy.

Freedom from Fear by D. M. Kennedy, (Oxford University Press), 1999.

A thorough, specialist interpretation.

Civil Rights in the USA 1863–90, D. Paterson, D. Willoughby and S. Willoughby, (Heinemann), 2001. (Chapters 4 and 5)

Provides sound coverage of key developments in race relations throughout the period.

American Diplomacy in the Twentieth Century by R. D. Schulzinger, (OUP), 1990.

Comprehensive coverage of the key developments in foreign policy in this period.

Race Relations in the USA Since 1900 by V. Sanders, (Hodder Education), 2000.

Very useful introduction to twentieth-century race relations.

Books on particular chapters

Chapter 1

There are several excellent books published on this period in recent years. Some of these are:

Bury My Heart at Wounded Knee: An Indian History of the American West by D. Brown (Vintage), 1991.

Fairly recent analysis of the impact of expansion West on Native Americans.

The Gilded Age: Perspectives on the Origins of Modern America C. W. Calhoun, ed., (Rowman and Littlefield), 2007.

A series of essays on different aspects of the years 1870–1900 including industrialisation, immigration, political life, African Americans and foreign and imperial policies.

America in the Gilded Age by S. Cashman, (New York University Press), 1993.

Useful analysis of US history after the Civil War. Divided into chapters on industrial America and Politics and Discontent.

Coming to America: A History of Immigration and Ethnicity in American Life 2nd edition by R. Daniels, (Perennial), 2002.

Detailed analysis of reasons for and impact of immigration on the USA.

The American Civil War: Causes, Course and Consequences, 1803–77 by A. Farmer, Access to History series (Hodder Education), 2008.

Gives a very good introduction to the period as well as comprehensive analysis of Reconstruction.

Reconstruction: America's Unfinished Revolution, 1863–77 by E. Foner, (Harper and Row), 1988.

A revisionist view of Reconstruction.

Chapter 2

This has often been a neglected period in the history of the USA. Nevertheless there are several useful works.

Bury My Heart at Wounded Knee: An Indian History of the American West by D. Brown, (Vintage), 1991.

The Gilded Age: Perspectives on the Origins of Modern America C. W. Calhoun, ed., (Rowman and Littlefield), 2007.

America in the Gilded Age by S. Cashman, (New York University Press), 1993.

Coming to America: A History of Immigration and Ethnicity in American Life 2nd edition by R. Daniels, (Perennial), 2002.

The New Commonwealth 1877–1890 by J. Garraty, (Harper & Row, New York), 1968.

Scholarly and detailed analysis of the period.

The Transformation of the American Economy, 1865–1914, An Essay in Interpretation by R. Higgs, (Wiley, New York), 1971.

Interesting view of the impact of economic change.

Andrew Carnegie and the Rise of Big Business by H. C. Livesay, (Longman), 1999.

Useful analysis of his career and impact.

The Rise of Big Business 1860–1920 by G. Porter, (Harlan Davidson), 2006.

Very detailed analysis.

Chapter 3

There are a limited number of texts which focus solely on these years. These include:

The Gilded Age: Perspectives on the Origins of Modern America C. W. Calhoun, ed., (Rowman and Littlefield), 2007.

America in the Gilded Age by S. Cashman, (New York University Press), 1993.

Not Like Us: Immigration and Minorities in America 1890–1924 by R. Daniels, (Ivan Dee), 1992.

Comprehensive analysis of immigration and its effects.

Theodore Roosevelt and World Order by J. Holmes, (Palgrave), 2007.

Sound analysis of his foreign and imperial policies.

The War with Spain in 1898 by D. Trask, (Bison), 1996.

Very detailed analysis of causes, events and results of the war with Spain.

Chapter 4

There is no one text which focuses only on this brief period. However, there are several useful biographies of Wilson.

Woodrow Wilson: A Biography by J. M. Cooper, (First Vintage Books), 2009.

Recent assessment of his career and achievements.

Woodrow Wilson and World War One, 1917–21 by R. Ferrell, (Harper Row), 1993.

Thorough analysis of Wilson's policies during and after the war.

Woodrow Wilson by W. Heckscher, (Scribner), 1991.

This is the first biography that covers his public and private life.

Chapter 5

There are many excellent books on the 1920s, as the decade has been the subject of much detailed research in the last 60 or so years.

The Twenties in America by P. A. Carter, (Routledge and Paul), 1968.

An evaluative account with useful historiographical discussions.

Only Yesterday: An Informal History of the 1920s in America by F. L. Allen, (Penguin), 1938.

An entertaining journalistic account from the 1920s in the USA – still in print and readily available.

One Summer: America, 1927 by B. Bryson, (Transworld Publishers), 2010.

Engaging account of all the events of the summer of 1927.

The Perils of Prosperity by W. E. Leuchtenburg, (University of Chicago Press), 1957, especially Chapters 4, 8, 9 and 10.

Thorough examination of the 1920s.

Anything Goes: A Biography of the Roaring Twenties by L. Moore, (Atlantic Books), 2008

Entertaining account of the Roaring Twenties with the focus on social history.

The Twenties in America by N. Palmer, (Edinburgh University Press), 2007.

A concise but useful history of the period.

America in Prosperity and Depression, 1920–1941 by M. Parrish, (Norton), 1992.

Detailed analysis of the period.

America in the Era of the Two World Wars, 1910–1945 by P. Renshaw, (Longman), 1997.

Useful survey of key developments in this period.

The USA 1917–45 by D. Willoughby and S. Willoughby, (Heinemann), 2000.

Sound introduction to boom and bust in the 1920s.

Chapter 6

There are various books available, some aimed at Advanced level work, and some at university studies.

The New Deal: The Depression Years 1933–40 by A. J. Badger, (Palgrave Macmillan), 1989.

This is a standard account of the New Deal, thorough and accessible.

Franklin D. Roosevelt and American Foreign Policy, 1932–45 by R. Dallek, (Oxford University Press), 1979.

Detailed analysis of foreign policy in these years.

New Deal or Raw Deal: How FDR's Economic Legacy Has Damaged America by B. Folsom, (Simon and Schuster), 2009.

A highly regarded example of 'New Right' thinking that the New Deal harmed the USA.

Anxious Decades by M. Parrish, (W. W. Norton), 1992, especially Part Two.

Comprehensive and readable with lots of examples in support of the ideas.

The Forgotten Man by A. Shaels, (Pimlico), 2009, especially Introduction, Chapters 6, 7, 8, 11 and 13.

Accessible and well-written argument that the New Deal harmed the USA, with focus on selected individuals.

The US Economy in World War II by H. G. Vatter, (Columbia University Press), 1985.

These texts give excellent accounts of the transition to a wartime economy and also of the impact of the war on industry.

The USA 1917–45 by D. Willoughby and S. Willoughby, (Heinemann), 2000.

Sound introduction to the New Deal and the USA during the Second World War.

The Second World War and the Americas 1933–45 by J. Wright, (Hodder Education), 2013.

Very useful analysis of changes in US foreign policy before and during the Second World War.

Chapter 7

There are many excellent books on the 1940s and 1950s, as this period has been the subject of much detailed research in the last 60 or so years.

V Was For Victory: Politics and Culture During the Second World War by J. M. Blum, (Harcourt Brace Jovanovich), 1976.

Accessible account with focus on the relationship between politics and culture.

The Life and Times of the Thunderbolt Kid by B. Bryson, (Transworld Publishers), 2007.

Funny and moving memoir about growing up in the 1950s.

Alistair Cooke's American Journey by A. Cooke, (Allen Lane), 2006.

Evocative contemporary account from a leading British journalist of a journey through the USA as it geared up to war production in 1942; published after the author's death.

America in the Forties by R. A. Goldberg, (Syracuse University Press), 2012, especially Chapter 2.

Chapter 2 deals comprehensively with the home front.

The Crucial Decade and After: America 1945–1960 by E. F. Goldman, (Vintage), 1960.

Thorough almost contemporary account of the period.

Grand Expectations: The United States 1945–1974 by J. T. Patterson, (Oxford University Press), 1996, especially Chapters 1–6, 9–13.

Well-written and engaging text, accessible and thorough.

Civil Rights in the USA by V. Sanders, Access to History series, (Hodder Education), 2008.

Useful coverage of the civil rights movement in the 1940s and 1950s.

Double Victory: A Multicultural History of America in the Second World War by R. Takaki, (Little, Brown and Company), 2000.

Very useful for the study of ethnic groups during the war.

The Strange Career of Jim Crow, 3rd revised edition by C. Vann Woodward, (Oxford University Press), 1974, especially sections iv and v.

The classic account of ethnic relations between African and white Americans in the South, still useful and relevant.

Chapter 8

There are several excellent books published on this period in recent years. Some of these are:

Years of Discord: American Politics and Society, 1961–1974 by J. Blum, (W. W. Norton and Co), 1991.

Very useful analysis of the presidencies of Kennedy and Johnson.

The Unfinished Journey: America Since World War Two 4th edition by W. Chafe, (Oxford University Press), 1999.

Analyses the significant cultural and political themes, including issues of race, class, gender, foreign policy, and economic and social reform.

Flawed Giant: Lyndon B. Johnson and His Times by R. Dallek, (Oxford University Press), 1988.

A very thorough account of Johnson's years in office, drawing on hours of newly released White House tapes and dozens of interviews with people close to the President.

The Cold War: A Very Short Introduction by R. McMahon, (Oxford University Press), 2003.

Useful starting point.

In Retrospect: The Tragedy and Lessons of Vietnam by R. McNamara, (Times Books, New York), 1996.

Very useful assessment of US involvement in Vietnam.

Politics, Presidency and Society in the USA, 1968–2001 by V. Sanders, Access to History series, (Hodder Education), 2008.

Useful coverage of the presidency of Nixon.

Novels

The Great Gatsby by Scott Fitzgerald, (Wordsworth Classics), 1925.

This novel follows a cast of characters living in the fictional town of West Egg on prosperous Long Island in the summer of 1922.

The Grapes of Wrath by J. Steinbeck, (Penguin), 1939.

This is an American realist novel. It is set during the Great Depression and focuses on the Joads, a poor family of tenant farmers driven from their Oklahoma home by drought, economic hardship and agricultural industry changes.

All the King's Men by R. P. Warren, (Fontana), 1946.

This novel portrays the dramatic political rise and governorship of Willie Stark, a cynical Populist in the American South during the 1930s.

Films
The USA 1890–1920
There Will be Blood P. T. Anderson (dir), 2007, (15).

This film tells the story of a silver miner-turned-oilman on a ruthless quest for wealth during Southern California's oil boom of the late nineteenth and early twentieth centuries.

Meet Me in St Louis V. Minnelli (dir), 1944.

This is a musical film from Metro-Goldwyn-Mayer which tells the story of an American family living in St. Louis in 1904.

The USA 1920–41
The Grapes of Wrath J. Ford (dir), 1940.

This film was based on John Steinbeck's Pulitzer Prize-winning novel of the same name, see above.

People's Century: Great Escape BBC, 1996.

The influence of cinema on people's lives.

Vietnam War
Two Vietnam films by director Oliver Stone:

Platoon, 1986, (12). Stone wrote the story based upon his experiences as a US infantryman in Vietnam to counter the vision of the war portrayed in John Wayne's *The Green Berets*. It was the first Hollywood film to be written and directed by a veteran of the Vietnam War.

Heaven and Earth, 1993, (15). This follows the true story of a Vietnamese village girl who survives a life of suffering and hardship during and after the Vietnam War.

Full Metal Jacket S. Kubrick (dir), 1987, (15).

A US Marine observes the dehumanising effects the Vietnam War has on his fellow recruits from their brutal boot camp training to the bloody street fighting in Hue.

Apocalypse Now Francis Ford Coppola (dir.), 1979, (15).

One of the classic Vietnam films. During the Vietnam War, Captain Willard is sent on a dangerous mission into Cambodia to assassinate a renegade colonel who has set himself up as a god among a local tribe.

Watergate
All the President's Men A. Pakula (dir), 1976, (15).

This film tells the story of how reporters Woodward and Bernstein uncover the details of the Watergate scandal that leads to President Nixon's resignation.

Websites

The Library of Congress and the National Archives have a wealth of material to explore:

www.loc.gov

www.archives.gov

Universities have a wide range of electronic records, for example

www.fordham.edu

www.stanford.edu

For presidents there are a variety of useful websites

www.ipl.org./ref./POTUS

www.fdrlibrary.marxist.edu

www.jfklibrary.org

www.lbjlib.utexas.edu

Other useful sites:

For the USA in the 1950s www.fiftiesweb.com

For Civil Rights www.webcorp.com/civilrights

For Watergate www.washingtonpost.com

The Spanish Civil War www.sanamwar.com

US imperialism http://shprs.clas.asu.edu/history-education/history_resources

Index